INDIVIDUALS IN INTERNATIONAL HUMANITARIAN LAW

This book offers a new, more critical perspective on the regulation and protection of individuals under international humanitarian law.

Providing a historical account of the changing conceptualisation of individuals since 1864, the study draws on social constructivism. This approach casts light on the struggle of making sense of, and agreeing on, the position of individuals in armed conflicts during the law-making process, often hidden by international humanitarian law's conventional narratives. This intriguing study grapples with a difficult and disputed area of the law of armed conflict, making a singular and significant contribution, which will be welcomed by all scholars in the field.

Volume 97 in the series Studies in International Law

Studies in International Law

Recent titles in this series

Private Actors as Participants in International Law: A Critical Analysis of Membership under the Law of the Sea
Armando Rocha

Truth and Transitional Justice: Localising the International Legal Framework in Muslim Majority Legal Systems
Alice Panepinto

State Responsibility for Non-State Actors: Past, Present and Prospects for the Future
Richard Mackenzie-Gray Scott

International Agreements between Non-State Actors as a Source of International Law
Melissa Loja

Judicial Decisions in International Law Argumentation: Between Entrapment and Creativity
Letizia Lo Giacco

South-South Migrations and the Law from Below: Case Studies on China and Nigeria
Oreva Olakpe

Territorial Status in International Law
Jure Vidmar

Marine Bioprospecting, Biodiversity and Novel Uses of Ocean Resources: New Approaches in International Law
Edited by Niels Krabbe and David Langlet

The Standard of Review Before the International Court of Justice: Between Principle and Pragmatism
Felix Fouchard

Global Lawmaking and Social Change: The Varieties of Customary International Law
Gregor Novak

The Effectiveness of the Inter-American Court of Human Rights: The Case of Indigenous Territorial Rights
Gabriela CB Navarro

Individuals in International Humanitarian Law: A Historical Analysis
Sarina Landefeld

For a complete list of titles in this series see www.bloomsbury.com/uk/series/studies-in-international-law/

Individuals in International Humanitarian Law

A Historical Analysis

Sarina Landefeld

• HART •
OXFORD • LONDON • NEW YORK • NEW DELHI • SYDNEY

HART PUBLISHING

Bloomsbury Publishing Plc

Kemp House, Chawley Park, Cumnor Hill, Oxford, OX2 9PH, UK

1385 Broadway, New York, NY 10018, USA

29 Earlsfort Terrace, Dublin 2, Ireland

First published in Great Britain 2024

A catalogue record for this book is available from the British Library.

A catalogue record for this book is available from the Library of Congress.

ISBN: HB: 978-1-50996-822-0
ePDF: 978-1-50996-824-4
ePub: 978-1-50996-823-7

Typeset by Compuscript Ltd, Shannon

For my parents

Acknowledgements

THIS BOOK WOULD not have been possible without the studentship and additional funding by the Arts and Humanities Research Council/ Midlands3Cities Doctoral Training Partnership.

I would like to thank my PhD supervisors, Dino Kritsiotis and Neville Wylie, for their guidance and help throughout my doctoral research and the years since then. In particular, I am grateful for Dino's promotion of unconventional approaches to international law and his thought-provoking ideas, and Neville's interdisciplinary insights and advice, as well as the supply of archival material. I would also like to thank Eyal Benvenisti and Nigel White, who examined the doctoral thesis and provided me with valuable comments. Several colleagues offered helpful advice along the process of bringing the manuscript to publication including Richard Mackenzie-Gray Scott, Stefan Mandelbaum, Julia Shaw, Christy Shucksmith-Wesley and Katja Ziegler. Lastly, my warmest thanks are due to my family; my parents for their unconditional support even in difficult times, and my sister for her enthusiasm and encouragement. I owe a lot to my husband for his patience and support throughout the many years of writing my PhD and this book, even though he would not read it because he thinks it is not interesting enough.

Contents

Abbreviations

1864 Geneva Convention	Convention for the Amelioration of the Condition of the Wounded in Armies in the Field
1868 Additional Articles	Additional Articles Relating to the Condition of the Wounded in War
1899 Hague Regulations	Annex to Convention (II): Regulations Respecting the Laws and Customs of War on Land
1906 Geneva Convention	Convention for the Amelioration of the Condition of the Wounded and Sick in Armies in the Field
1907 Hague Regulations	Annex to Convention (IV): Regulations Respecting the Laws and Customs of War on Land
1938 ILA Draft Convention	Draft Convention for the Protection of Civilian Populations against New Engines of War
1956 Draft Rules	Draft Rules for the Limitation of the Dangers Incurred by the Civilian Population in Time of War
1965 ICRC Resolution	Resolution XXVIII on the Protection of Civilian Populations Against the Dangers of Indiscriminate Warfare
1969 IDI Resolution	Resolution on the Distinction Between Military Objectives and Non-military Objectives in General and Particularly the Problems Associated with Weapons of Mass Destruction
1971 Conference	Conference of Government Experts on the Reaffirmation and Development of International Humanitarian Law Applicable in Armed Conflicts (24 May – 12 June 1971)
1972 Conference	Conference of Government Experts on the Reaffirmation and Development of International Humanitarian Law Applicable in Armed Conflicts (3 May – 3 June 1972)

Additional Protocols Commentary	Yves Sandoz, Christophe Swinarski and Bruno Zimmermann (eds), *Commentary on the Additional Protocols of 8 June 1977 to the Geneva Conventions of 12 August 1949*
AICRC	Archives du Comité International de la Croix-Rouge
AP I	Protocol Additional to the Geneva Conventions of 12 August 1949, and Relating to the Protection of Victims of International Armed Conflicts (1977)
AP II	Protocol Additional to the Geneva Conventions of 12 August 1949, and Relating to the Protection of Victims of Non-International Armed Conflicts (1977)
Brussels Declaration	Project of an International Declaration Concerning the Laws and Customs of War (1874)
CA3	Article 3 common to the 1949 Geneva Conventions
CDDH	*Official Records of the Diplomatic Conference on the Reaffirmation and Development of International Humanitarian Law Applicable in Armed Conflicts: Geneva (1974–1977)*
CIL	customary international law
CIHL	customary international humanitarian law
DPH	direct participation in hostilities
GC III	Geneva Convention Relative to the Treatment of Prisoners of War (1949)
GC III Commentary	Jean S Pictet (ed), *The Geneva Conventions of 12 August 1949, Commentary III: Geneva Convention Relative to the Treatment of Prisoners of War*
GC IV	Geneva Convention Relative to the Protection of Civilian Persons in Time of War (1949)
GC IV Commentary	Jean S Pictet (ed), *The Geneva Conventions of 12 August 1949, Commentary IV: Geneva Convention Relative to the Protection of Civilian Persons in Time of War*

Hague Draft Rules	Hague Rules concerning the Control of Wireless Telegraphy in Times of War and Air Warfare (1923)
IAC	international armed conflict
ICJ	International Court of Justice
ICMMP	International Committee of Military Medicine and Pharmacy
ICRC	International Committee of the Red Cross
ICRC Study	Jean-Marie Henckaerts and Louise Doswald-Beck, *Customary International Humanitarian Law, Rules and Practice*
ICTY	International Criminal Tribunal for the Former Yugoslavia
IDI	Institut de Droit International
IHL	international humanitarian law
IHRL	international human rights law
IIHL	International Institute of Humanitarian Law
ILA	International Law Association
Interpretive Guidance	*Interpretive Guidance on the Notion of Direct Participation in Hostilities under International Humanitarian Law*
Lieber Code	General Orders No 100: Instructions for the Government of Armies of the United States in the Field (1863)
Monaco Draft	First Draft Convention adopted in Monaco (Sanitary cities and localities) (1934)
NIAC	non-international armed conflict
NLM	national liberation movement
NLW	national liberation war
Oxford Manual	The Laws of War on Land – Manual published by the Institute of International Law (1880)
PMSC	private military and security company
POW	prisoner of war

San Remo Manual	*The Manual on the Law of Non-International Armed Conflict*
St Petersburg Declaration	Declaration Renouncing the Use, in Time of War, of Explosive Projectiles under 400 Grammes Weight (1868)
Tallinn Manual	*Tallinn Manual on the International Law Applicable to Cyber Warfare*
Teheran Conference	International Conference on Human Rights (1968)
Tokyo Draft	Draft International Convention on the Condition and Protection of Civilians of Enemy Nationality Who Are on Territory Belonging to or Occupied by a Belligerent (1934)
UDHR	Universal Declaration of Human Rights
UNGA	United Nations General Assembly
UNSG	United Nations Secretary-General

Table of Cases

1

Introduction

INTERNATIONAL HUMANITARIAN LAW (IHL) applies to situations of war and international armed conflicts (IACs) between states, and non-international armed conflicts (NIACs) where at least one of the parties to the armed conflict is a non-state actor. Within these forms of organised violence between collective entities, the individual human being should not be forgotten. Individuals actively participate in hostilities; individuals, however, are also the victims of armed conflicts as they may lose their property, well-being, liberty and life; moreover, individuals provide care and treatment as independent persons, or as members of organised medical, religious and humanitarian assistance. It is the objective of this book to examine how individuals have been perceived and discussed in the law-making processes and, as a result, how they are recognised as subjects of obligations, or beneficiaries of protections under the law.

IHL provides for the legal status of persons which enables and constrains their conduct, or determines their targetability and treatment in the hands of a party to the armed conflict.[1] Specific regulations currently exist, for instance, for wounded, sick and shipwrecked persons; women and children; medical and religious personnel; mercenaries and spies; journalists; and humanitarian actors.[2] Most notably, however, the prevalent understanding of the law classifies all individuals as belonging to one of two mutually exclusive, diametrically opposed primary categories: combatants and civilians.[3] Combatants have the right to participate directly in hostilities.[4] They may not be prosecuted for their conduct in warfare, so long as they comply with IHL, and they are entitled to prisoner of war status if captured. While they enjoy this 'combatant privilege', they are also legitimate targets of attack. Civilians are all those individuals who are not combatants,[5] and thus the other side of the coin. They are generally protected from the effects of military operations and enjoy 'civilian immunity',

[1] See, eg, GD Solis, *The Law of Armed Conflict: International Humanitarian Law in War*, 3rd edn (Cambridge, Cambridge University Press, 2022) ch 6.

[2] L Hill-Cawthorne, 'Persons Covered by International Humanitarian Law: Main Categories' in B Saul and D Akande (eds), *The Oxford Guide to International Humanitarian Law* (Oxford, Oxford University Press, 2020).

[3] R Kolb, *Advanced Introduction to International Humanitarian Law* (Cheltenham, Elgar, 2014) 126.

[4] Protocol Additional to the Geneva Conventions of 12 August 1949, and relating to the Protection of Victims of International Armed Conflicts (Geneva, 8 June 1977) (AP I), art 43(2).

[5] ibid art 50.

which means they may not be directly attacked unless and for such time as they take a direct part in hostilities.[6] Yet they may be prosecuted under domestic law for their direct participation in hostilities.

The so-called 'principle of distinction' requires all belligerent parties to distinguish between combatants and civilians.[7] The belief in the significance of this principle is ubiquitous in scholarship and jurisprudence. It has been hailed as a 'fundamental' or 'cardinal' principle of IHL,[8] as the principle at the 'core'[9] or the 'very heart' of the law,[10] and as the 'cornerstone',[11] 'keystone',[12] 'bedrock'[13] or 'the pith of humanitarian law'.[14] To emphasise its centrality for the legal framework, it has also been portrayed as the 'fulcrum' around which IHL essentially revolves,[15] and as one of 'the red-threads weaving through the whole tissue' of IHL.[16] While the principle primarily relates to the notion of civilian immunity and thus the so-called 'Hague Law', regulating the conduct of hostilities, it has been argued that it also underlies the so-called 'Geneva Law', protecting persons in the power of a party to the conflict. It has been said that the distinction between combatants and civilians remains essential in this area of law since 'the protective regimes of the two categories of persons are different'.[17] Similarly, although the combatant status only exists in the law of IACs, the principle of distinction is still believed to apply in NIACs.[18] Notwithstanding

[6] ibid art 51.

[7] ibid art 48.

[8] See, eg, *Legality of the Threat or Use of Nuclear Weapons* (Advisory Opinion) [1996] ICJ Rep 226, para 78; *Prosecutor v Kordić and Čerkez*, Judgment (17 December 2004) IT-95-14/2-A, para 54; J Crowe and K Weston-Scheuber, *Principles of International Humanitarian Law* (Cheltenham, Elgar, 2013) 44; N Melzer, 'The Principle of Distinction between Civilians and Combatants' in A Clapham and P Gaeta (eds), *The Oxford Handbook of International Law in Armed Conflict* (Oxford, Oxford University Press, 2014) 297; Kolb (n 3) 80; Y Dinstein, *The Conduct of Hostilities under the Law of International Armed Conflict*, 3rd edn (Cambridge, Cambridge University Press, 2016) paras 112 and 189; R Heinsch, 'Distinction' in D Djukić and N Pons (eds), *The Companion to International Humanitarian Law* (Leiden, Brill, 2018) 307.

[9] K Ipsen, 'Combatants and Non-Combatants' in D Fleck (ed), *The Handbook of International Humanitarian Law*, 4th edn (Oxford, Oxford University Press, 2021) 93; Solis (n 1) 210.

[10] S Darcy, *Judges, Law and War: The Judicial Development of International Humanitarian Law* (Cambridge, Cambridge University Press, 2014) 141.

[11] J Gardam, *Non-Combatant Immunity as a Norm of International Humanitarian Law* (London, Martinus Nijhoff, 1993) 2; A van Engeland, *Civilian or Combatant? A Challenge for the 21st Century* (Oxford, Oxford University Press 2015) ch 1; N Melzer, *International Humanitarian Law: A Comprehensive Introduction* (Geneva, ICRC, 2019) 18.

[12] E-C Gillard, 'Protection of Civilians in the Conduct of Hostilities' in R Liivoja and T McCormack (eds), *Routledge Handbook of the Law of Armed Conflict* (London, Routledge, 2016) 159.

[13] MD Maxwell, 'The Law of War and Civilians on the Battlefield: Are We Undermining Civilian Protection?' (2004) 84(5) *Military Review* 17, 19.

[14] MN Schmitt, 'The Principle of Discrimination in 21st Century Warfare' (1999) 2 *Yale Human Rights & Development Law Journal* 143, 147.

[15] E Crawford, *Identifying the Enemy: Civilian Participation in Armed Conflict* (Oxford, Oxford University Press, 2015) 1.

[16] Dinstein (n 8) para 35.

[17] Kolb (n 3) 124.

[18] J-M Henckaerts and L Doswald-Beck, *Customary International Humanitarian Law, Volume I: Rules* (Cambridge, Cambridge University Press, 2009) Rule 1; Melzer, 'Principle of Distinction'

the frequent affirmation of the fundamental role of the principle of distinction in IHL, it has been questioned in relation to contemporary armed conflicts in which the distinction between combatants and civilians 'is increasingly difficult to apply'.[19] It has even been suggested that the principle of distinction 'has lost some of its importance'.[20]

The perceived centrality of the principle of distinction is linked to the prevalent understanding of its history which regards it as 'the foundation on which the codification of the laws and customs of war rests'.[21] It is often read into the first conventions in the field, including the 1868 St Petersburg Declaration Renouncing the Use, in Time of War, of Explosive Projectiles Under 400 Grammes Weight[22] and the 1899 and 1907 Hague Regulations with respect to the Laws and Customs of War on Land,[23] despite the occasional admission that no explicit reference to the principle is made in these instruments. Even when recognising the limited forms of protection for 'civilians', for example, in the Hague Regulations, scholars tend to emphasise that under customary international law '[t]he general principle was that the civilian was to be immune from the hostilities'.[24] Indeed, the absence of an explicit provision to this effect in early conventional IHL has been accorded to the apparent belief at the time that the inclusion of this 'generally accepted' rule would not be necessary in a written code.[25] It has been argued that, unlike today, '[i]n the nineteenth century, when most of the concepts and principles underlying modern IHL were conceived and formulated, the dividing line between civilians and combatants was still comparatively clear'.[26] At the same time, it has been suggested that '[t]he dividing line between the two categories has developed over time'.[27]

(n 8) 307; Crawford (n 15) 15; M Sassòli, *International Humanitarian Law: Rules, Controversies, and Solutions to Problems Arising in Warfare* (Cheltenham, Elgar, 2019) 226.

[19] Sassòli (n 18) 20.

[20] ibid 24.

[21] Y Sandoz, C Swinarski and B Zimmermann (eds), *Commentary on the Additional Protocols of 8 June 1977 to the Geneva Conventions of 12 August 1949* (Geneva, Martinus Nijhoff, 1987) (hereafter *Additional Protocols Commentary*) para 1863.

[22] ibid; APV Rogers, *Law on the Battlefield*, 3rd edn (Manchester, Manchester University Press, 2012) 11–12; Crowe and Weston-Scheuber (n 8) 71; E Salmón, 'Who Is a Protected Civilian?' in A Clapham, P Gaeta and M Sassòli (eds), *The 1949 Geneva Conventions: A Commentary* (Oxford, Oxford University Press, 2015) para 3; Solis (n 1) 210.

[23] *Additional Protocols Commentary* (n 21) para 1826; K Nabulsi, 'Evolving Conceptions of Civilians and Belligerents: One Hundred Years After the Hague Peace Conferences' in S Chesterman (ed), *Civilians in War* (London, Lynne Rienner, 2001) 10; MN Hayashi, 'The Principle of Civilian Protection and Contemporary Armed Conflict' in HM Hensel (ed), *The Law of Armed Conflict: Constraints on the Contemporary Use of Military Force* (Aldershot, Ashgate, 2006) 106–07.

[24] GIAD Draper, 'The "Protected Person" in Occupied Territory' (1965) 114 *Collected Courses of the Hague Academy of International Law* 119, 119; see also Gardam (n 11) 18 and 27.

[25] *Additional Protocols Commentary* (n 21) para 1864; see also Gardam (n 11) 18.

[26] Melzer, 'Principle of Distinction' (n 8) 297.

[27] M Sassòli, AA Bouvier and A Quintin, *How Does Law Protect in War? Cases, Documents and Teaching Materials on Contemporary Practice in International Humanitarian Law, Volume I*, 3rd edn (Geneva, ICRC, 2011) ch 5, 1.

Together with the principle of distinction, the concern for civilians in armed conflicts has been portrayed as a timeless principle of modern IHL.[28] Yoram Dinstein even declares that the history of the law 'to date can be described as a sustained effort to ensure that civilians (not directly participating in hostilities) are protected from the havocs of war'.[29] On the other hand, the historian Geoffrey Best notes that 'civilians were a minor consideration for the men at the centre of the business of making the law of land warfare through most of its formative centuries'.[30] The 1949 Geneva Convention Relative to the Protection of Civilian Persons in Time of War (GC IV) is generally understood as having introduced a distinct category of civilians into conventional IHL.[31] However, 'civilians' were not defined in international legal instruments until the adoption of the Additional Protocol to the Geneva Conventions relating to the Protection of Victims of International Armed Conflicts (AP I) in 1977.[32] As Amanda Alexander observes, '[t]he civilian has achieved such ascendancy in international law that it is hard to imagine a code of warfare or a world without civilians'.[33]

The prima facie simplicity of the principle of distinction appears desirable since it implies certainty regarding the privileges, obligations and protections of individuals who are either combatants or civilians.[34] The emphasis on the essential role of the principle may also seem appealing for narrating the history of the law as a tale of humanitarian imperatives and progress. The analysis of this book challenges this conventional narrative by dispelling common myths about the formation of the law. It overturns the dominant understanding that the principle of distinction has been foundational for the regulation and protection of individuals under IHL treaties. It argues that the established narrative obscures the intricacy, ambiguity, bias and incompleteness of the law, and oversimplifies its rich history. By providing a critical historical account of the evolving conceptualisations of individuals in IHL since 1864, it offers a more nuanced and deeper understanding of the regulation and protection of individuals in armed conflicts today. It thus contributes to the increasing critical legal and interdisciplinary scholarship which challenges the principle of distinction and established understanding of civilians.[35]

[28] LC Green, *The Contemporary Law of Armed Conflict*, 3rd edn (Manchester, Manchester University Press, 2008) 256.

[29] Dinstein (n 8) para 189; see also van Engeland (n 11) 25, despite noting earlier that in the Hague Regulations, 'Protection of Civilians was not yet at the core of the law', 15.

[30] G Best, *War and Law Since 1945* (Oxford, Clarendon Press, 1994) 264.

[31] Nabulsi (n 23) 19; H Kinsella, *The Image Before the Weapon: A Critical History of the Distinction Between Combatant and Civilian* (Ithaca, Cornell University Press, 2011) 104; van Engeland (n 11) 15.

[32] AP I, art 50.

[33] A Alexander, 'The Genesis of the Civilian' (2007) 20 *LJIL* 359, 360.

[34] See further R Sutton, *The Humanitarian Civilian: How the Idea of Distinction Circulates Within and Beyond International Humanitarian Law* (Oxford, Oxford University Press, 2021) 5–7.

[35] See, eg, C Carpenter, *Innocent Women and Children: Gender, Norms and the Protection of Civilians* (Aldershot, Ashgate, 2006); Alexander, 'Genesis' (n 33); Kinsella (n 31); C Garbett,

I. APPROACH AND ARGUMENTS

Critical scholars emphasise that the law itself is constitutive of the meaning of war,[36] and the concepts of combatants and civilians.[37] Claire Garbett specifies further that IHL 'determines how persons are "present" in situations of conflict as particular kinds of legal subjects'.[38] IHL provides for the scope *ratione personae* of the combatant and civilian status, as well as the respective privileges, obligations and protections. However, the legal status covers the concepts of combatants and civilians with a veil of apparent neutrality and objectivity. It conceals the bundle of meanings and dimensions they entail which are not inevitable, but which determine who is protected or regulated, how, when, where and why. As Garbett notes, by considering the development of IHL, 'it is possible to move beyond an analysis of the terms of its regulatory and protective framework to consider how it conceives of the persons it is seeking to protect'.[39] This is the central aim of this book.

The question at the heart of the analysis is how individuals who participate in or are affected by armed conflicts have been perceived, portrayed and discussed in the creation and development of IHL. It starts from the premise that the law itself does not emerge in a legal vacuum, but is grafted upon certain understandings of the actors involved in creating and shaping the rules and regulations. It emphasises that the concepts of combatants and civilians are not an objective reality; they are the result of negotiations and the production of meaning in social processes that are situated in distinct historical, political and social contexts. They are social constructs before they become incorporated into the law. Although they may emerge in the wider extra-legal environment, this study focuses on conscious attempts at developing IHL. It explores how the evolution of the law is related to emerging, persisting and changing understandings of individuals in armed conflicts in particular periods of time. The resultant findings may partly account for why certain rules and regulations may seem obsolete, revealing their basis in sometimes significantly diverging conceptualisations of individuals from a different period. At the same time, they refute

The Concept of the Civilian: Legal Recognition, Adjudication and the Trials of International Criminal Justice (Abingdon, Routledge, 2015); S Scheipers, *Unlawful Combatants: A Genealogy of the Irregular Fighter* (Oxford, Oxford University Press, 2015); OM Stern, *Gender, Conflict and International Humanitarian Law: A Critique of the 'Principle of Distinction'* (London, Routledge, 2018); Sutton (n 34).

[36] F Mégret, 'Theorizing the Laws of War' in A Orford and F Hoffmann (eds), *The Oxford Handbook of the Theory of International Law* (Oxford, Oxford University Press, 2016) 774; see also N Berman, 'Privileging Combat? Contemporary Conflict and the Legal Construction of War' (2004) 43 *Columbia Journal of Transnational Law* 1.

[37] F Mégret, 'From "Savages" to "Unlawful Combatants": A Postcolonial Look at International Humanitarian Law's "Other"' in A Orford (ed), *International Law and Its Others* (Cambridge, Cambridge University Press, 2006) 304.

[38] Garbett (n 35) 148.

[39] ibid 55.

certain common claims about the long-standing nature of some notions and the belief in past distinctions. Consequently, this study contributes to a more nuanced understanding of the contemporary state of the law, including its uncertainties and limits.

While this book examines when and how certain conceptualisations have emerged and evolved in the law-making processes, it understands these more widely than just the formal procedures of diplomatic conferences which adopt treaties. By also considering other deliberate attempts at developing the law, successfully or unsuccessfully, both in inter-state and non-state settings, it shows how the meaning of individuals which has become embedded in the law is not always shaped in the immediate negotiations of the treaty text. It explores which ideas and norms have influenced the development of the law, and, in particular, whether and how the principle of distinction has informed the understanding and regulation of individuals in this respect. Moreover, it analyses the role of different actors in the social processes of shaping the law. It is most closely related to Alexander's 'broader research project into the influences of external discourses and disciplinary histories, conventions and theories on the development of international law' especially regarding the protection of civilians.[40] Similar to her work, it shows that various actors besides states have played a role in the development of IHL. It also follows in her footsteps in 'pointing out historicity of current concepts, and illuminating more broadly the process, and the limits, of legal change'.[41]

Historicising the law is important since '[t]he histories of a legal regime help determine the pedigree, the identity, and the content of its norms'.[42] The dominant narrative regarding the history of IHL, outlined above, has influenced and arguably distorted the reading of the rules and regulations of earlier times. This anachronistic approach to the law is particularly serious in IHL since the legal framework has not been built on successive treaties which amended and replaced earlier ones. Instead, it consists of a fragmented system of conventional law from different periods, such as the 1907 Hague Regulations and the 1949 Geneva Conventions which are still in force today, and which vary in terms of the state parties to the treaties. Only the 1949 Geneva Conventions have achieved universal participation.[43] The prevailing perception of the history within the discipline

[40] A Alexander, 'The "Good War": Preparations for a War against Civilians' (2019) 15 *Law, Culture and the Humanities* 227, 229; see also Alexander, 'Genesis' (n 33); A Alexander, 'International Humanitarian Law, Postcolonialism and the 1977 *Geneva Protocol I*' (2016) 17 *Melbourne Journal of International Law* 15.

[41] Alexander, '"Good War"' (n 40) 230.

[42] P Wrange, 'Introduction: Historicizing International Humanitarian Law' in M Deland, M Klamberg and P Wrange (eds), *International Humanitarian Law and Justice: Historical and Sociological Perspectives* (Abingdon, Routledge, 2019) 10.

[43] N Tannenwald, 'Assessing the Effects and Effectiveness of the Geneva Conventions' in M Evangelista and N Tannenwald (eds), *Do the Geneva Conventions Matter?* (Oxford, Oxford University Press, 2017) 1.

may have rendered the principle of distinction, and with it the concepts of combatants and civilians, seemingly 'venerable'.[44] Nonetheless, their meaning and scope remain the subject of debate in the context of contemporary armed conflicts.

The conventional narrative, which places the principle of distinction at the heart of IHL treaties adopted over the past approximately 160 years, glosses over the struggle of the actors who were involved in the law-making processes in making sense of, and agreeing on, the position of individuals in armed conflicts. Moreover, it ignores the failure to achieve shared understandings at some events. This book, therefore, does not consider the history of IHL in terms of different configurations of the supposedly interdependent legal concepts of combatants and civilians over time. It rather tries to unravel different conceptual developments in the understanding of individuals leading to the adoption of IHL conventions. As Helen Kinsella advises in her genealogy of the principle of distinction, 'the comfort of preconceived categories must be relinquished and the familiarity of this venerable norm must be made strange'[45] for this purpose. As an empirical study of the law-making processes, this book examines which individuals were considered in need of being mentioned in the enabling, constraining and protecting written codes which regulate specific situations of organised violence. It thus highlights the diversity of understandings of individuals throughout the evolution of the law since the second half of the nineteenth century. Ultimately, it denaturalises and problematises the contemporary conventional understanding of the concepts of combatants and civilians by challenging their objectivity and inevitability.

II. OUTLINE OF THE BOOK

The analysis of the changing conceptualisation of individuals in IHL is loosely inspired by social constructivism, a theoretical approach in the discipline of International Relations. Chapter two explains these theoretical underpinnings. It identifies the concepts of combatants and civilians as social constructs which entail different layers of meaning. It elaborates the premise of the book, that the law is crafted upon shared understandings (and the absence thereof) among states and other actors in the law-making processes. This includes an outline of how certain ideas and values become embedded in international legal rules and regulations.

The substantive chapters then trace developments in the law and the underlying changes in the conceptualisation of individuals in chronological order over

[44] M Bothe, 'Customary International Humanitarian Law: Some Reflections on the ICRC Study' (2005) 8 *YIHL* 143, 166.

[45] Kinsella (n 31) 7.

four periods. The study relies on 'periods' as 'concepts helpful for organizing our knowledge, based on a choice of facts which are considered as "relevant" by an author in the light of the necessity to envelop historical time by some structure'.[46] The periods identified in this book are demarcated by the adoption of the 1899 and 1907 Hague Regulations, the 1949 Geneva Conventions, and the 1977 Additional Protocols, which are often perceived as milestones in the history of IHL. They are considered here as formalisations of the legal understanding of individuals in armed conflicts at the time as the law progresses into the next period. These moments of conventional law-making are contextualised in relation to preceding efforts within and outside of the inter-state level which crystalised understandings and assumptions about categories and principles in IHL. The chapters thus consider various attempts at shaping and creating IHL throughout the respective periods, and their influence on the adopted treaties. While international legal scholarship has dismissed some of these events as failures, or has largely forgotten other efforts by non-state actors, this book argues that they elucidate how armed conflicts were perceived and negotiated at the time, and thus how individuals were conceptualised.

The chronological approach may be subject to criticism. The periodisation risks conveying the idea of clearly defined and fixed stages of development; yet certain dynamics in the processes transgress these imaginary boundaries. Indeed, the conceptualisations of individuals themselves sometimes changed over the course of a period. Overlaps across and developments within the periods are, therefore, emphasised in the analysis. The culmination of each period in the adoption of binding legal instruments, with the exception of the last one, may imply a linear progress. However, the substantive analysis also considers failed attempts at creating IHL, and it reveals breaks and regressive movements in the adopted conventional law. It demonstrates how stability and changes in the law are the result of distinct forms of interaction between a variety of actors. The chronologic structure thus enables the tracing of continuities and differences regarding the understanding of individuals in armed conflicts over time and within the respective historical context.

Chapter three examines what is often perceived as the founding period of modern IHL due to the first attempts at drafting and negotiating multilateral conventions in the field. According to the received narrative, certain instruments adopted in this period, such as the 1863 Lieber Code, the 1868 St Petersburg Declaration, and the 1899 and 1907 Hague Regulations on the Laws and Customs of War on Land, laid the foundation for the principle of distinction and the contemporary concepts of combatants and civilians. In contrast, this chapter argues that many of the uncertainties and disputes regarding the understanding

[46] O Diggelmann, 'The Periodization of the History of International Law' in B Fassbender and A Peters (eds), *The Oxford Handbook of the History of International Law* (Oxford, Oxford University Press, 2012) 999.

of individuals in wars were not resolved by the end of this period. Additionally, it highlights that the concept of civilians, as it exists today, was indeed absent. The analysis emphasises the importance of the 1874 Brussels Conference for the development of the law, and scrutinises the varying influence of military officials, diplomats and lawyers on the law-making process. Overall, the chapter challenges prevailing assumptions about when, where and how key elements of contemporary IHL were formed and introduced into conventional law.

Chapter four argues that, although the 1949 Geneva Conventions were adopted in response to the Second World War, the foundations for the conceptualisation of individuals therein had been generally laid before. After addressing small modifications to the concept of combatants in this period, the analysis challenges the common belief of the emergence of the 'civilian' in GC IV. It demonstrates how the treaty's disparate protection regimes for 'protected persons' and the population as a whole evolved from two separate strands of developments in the inter-war years without establishing a unified concept of civilians. Lastly, the chapter explores the emerging rudimentary regulation of NIACs. It argues that the exclusionary understanding of 'protected persons' under the 1949 Geneva Conventions precluded their extension to internal armed conflicts. Overall, the chapter shows that the protection of individuals under the 1949 treaties was not only influenced by the Second World War, but more importantly informed and constrained by the ideational and normative frameworks of the inter-war years and the early written laws of war.

The first 1977 Additional Protocol to the 1949 Geneva Conventions established the principle of distinction and the concept of civilians alongside the concept of combatants for the first time in conventional IHL. However, chapter five argues that the concepts did not evolve in unison, despite being framed as interrelated in the treaty text. It highlights discrepancies in the understanding of civilians and the limited engagement with the notion during the diplomatic conference even though the legal concept was consolidated and institutionalised in the adopted treaties. On the other hand, the prolonged negotiation of the concept of combatants during the official law-making process did not lead to a shared agreement. Although 1977 also saw the dawn of a treaty dedicated to NIACs, the chapter argues that individuals were not meaningfully constructed in the context of such conflict situations. Lastly, it suggests that a third approach to conceptualising individuals, besides combatants and civilians, emerged in form of guarantees for all human beings. It critically scrutinises the common narrative regarding the influence of international human rights law on the development of IHL at the time.

Chapter six considers developments in IHL, or the absence thereof, since the adoption of the 1977 Additional Protocols. It contrasts the prevailing language implying new dimensions of warfare since the end of the Cold War with the abstention of states from addressing them through the adoption or modification of treaties. The chapter, therefore, examines efforts to develop the law by other means, including customary international law, international criminal jurisprudence and soft law instruments. In particular, it focuses on certain ambiguities and *lacunae* in the legal framework that have become the subject of debate in the last three decades. These include the exclusionary nature of the civilian 'protected person' status under the fourth 1949 Geneva Convention, so-called 'unlawful combatants', the 'civilianisation' of warfare due to civilian direct participation in hostilities, and the status of individuals in non-international armed conflicts. The chapter argues that the concepts of combatants and civilians are repeatedly reaffirmed, although their meaning and scope remain contested. The concepts have seemingly been naturalised, while the construction of individuals who are participating in or are affected by armed conflicts continues.

The concluding chapter briefly summarises the separate histories of the concepts of combatants and civilians drawing on overarching developments that have emerged throughout the analysis in this book. Furthermore, it emphasises the importance of a critical historical approach for understanding the long and continuing struggle of attaching meaning to individuals in the context of IHL.

2

Constructing Individuals for International Humanitarian Law

THIS CHAPTER OUTLINES how individuals in armed conflicts are conceptualised in law-making processes, and how layers of meaning are embedded in the concepts of combatants and civilians that form part of international humanitarian law (IHL) today.[1] Drawing on social constructivism[2] from the discipline of International Relations, it explains how different ways of understanding individuals in armed conflicts have emerged and evolved, and ultimately influenced the rules and regulations adopted in the conventional legal framework. It argues that the law is grafted upon certain intersubjective meanings promoted, sustained and reinforced by actors who are involved in the processes of shaping and creating the law. This exposition elaborates the theoretical premise for the historical account in the following chapters.

To begin with, however, a brief caveat may be in order. It needs to be emphasised that the main objective of this book is not theoretical, but historical and critical: it seeks an understanding of international legal developments in the past, and it denaturalises and problematises the regulation and protection of individuals under IHL today. It, therefore, does not aspire to propose a theoretical model of international legal norm change, or to develop constructivism more generally through theory building or theory testing.[3] Instead, this chapter's overt engagement with the ideas which underpin the central enquiry of this book is informed by the observation that even historians have 'theoretical preconceptions [which] affect the questions one asks, the data one selects to study, and the explanations that one constructs'.[4] Ultimately, the book aims to provide insights

[1] Parts of this chapter draw on S Landefeld, 'The Evolution of Norms and Concepts in International Law: A Social Constructivist Approach' in R Deplano (ed), *Pluralising International Legal Scholarship: The Promise and Perils of Non-Doctrinal Research Methods* (Cheltenham, Elgar, 2019).

[2] 'Social constructivism' and 'constructivism' are commonly used interchangeably in the literature and in this book.

[3] cf Giovanni Mantilla's theorisation of social pressure in the international law-making process in his study on the origins and development of the regulation of internal armed conflicts under IHL, G Mantilla, *Lawmaking under Pressure: International Humanitarian Law and Internal Armed Conflict* (Ithaca, Cornell University Press, 2020).

[4] JS Levy, 'Explaining Events and Developing Theories: History, Political Science, and the Analysis of International Relations' in C Elman and MF Elman (eds), *Bridges and Boundaries: Historians, Political Scientists, and the Study of International Relations* (Cambridge, MIT Press, 2001) 51.

into how particular international legal concepts have been created and changed over time, without overly theorising the complex events and processes.

I. CONCEPTUALISING INDIVIDUALS IN ARMED CONFLICTS

According to the prevalent narrative, individuals fall under one of two categories of persons in the context of armed conflicts. This fundamental distinction between combatants and civilians is commonly attributed to the doctrine proclaimed by Jean-Jacques Rousseau, who stated that war is a relationship between states, and that 'individuals are enemies only accidentally, not as men, nor even as citizens, but as soldiers'.[5] Wars are thus believed to be fought by members of regular armed forces, whereas civilians are placed outside the scope of hostilities. It is this distinction which is seen to underpin the modern laws of war, today also often referred to as IHL.

Individuals who are members of the regular armed forces of a state involved in an international armed conflict (IAC), or who are members of militias or volunteer corps which belong to a party to such a conflict and fulfil certain criteria, are combatants. Their belligerent privilege, also known as combatant immunity, permits them to participate in the hostilities without prosecution for their mere involvement. They may still be prosecuted for violations of IHL. They have a right to prisoner of war (POW) status when they find themselves in the hands of the opposing belligerent party, and they benefit from certain safeguards and care when wounded, sick or shipwrecked. Their combatant status makes them a lawful target of attack, but they remain protected under the general principle of humanity and the prohibition of unnecessary suffering. Combatant status is limited to IACs although the principle of distinction is commonly said to apply to non-international armed conflicts (NIACs) also. While fighters who are part of governmental armed forces or organised armed groups are distinguished from civilians in such conflict situations, they do not benefit from the privileged position of combatants.

Civilians, on the other hand, are not protected from prosecution when resorting to force. Their direct participation in hostilities suspends their civilian immunity which otherwise shields them from becoming the subject of targeted attacks. Even without such active involvement, they may suffer the effects of hostilities as the unintentional victims of attacks on military objectives subject to the principle of proportionality and precaution. As 'protected persons' they enjoy certain safeguards when in the hands of a party to an IAC or during belligerent occupation if they fulfil the nationality requirement under the Fourth Geneva Convention Relative to the Protection of Civilian Persons in Time of War.

[5] Cited in ME O'Connell, 'Historical Developments and Legal Basis' in D Fleck (ed), *The Handbook of International Humanitarian Law*, 4th edn (Oxford, Oxford University Press, 2021) 28.

Any other civilians are guaranteed minimum humanitarian safeguards. Civilians exist in both international and non-international armed conflicts. In relation to the former, they are defined as anyone who does not qualify as a combatant, and, in case of doubt, a person is presumed to be a civilian.

These brief, simplified summaries of the law form part of the concepts of combatants and civilians. The scope *ratione personae* which delineates who qualifies as a combatant or civilian, as well as their respective protection and regulation under the law, are some of the concepts' layers of meaning. However, conceptualisations of individuals in armed conflicts go beyond the legal rules, and may even obscure or distort the meaning of the law. As social constructs the concepts are imbued with certain ideas, assumptions, values and norms which may not be stipulated in the text of conventions or be apparent in the understanding of customary international law. They comprise not only legally required but also desired forms of protection, and not only lawful but also legitimate participation in hostilities. They imply presumptions or expectations about the individual's position in relation to the fighting, including their active involvement or peaceful conduct and even passivity. They are linked to notions such as innocence, vulnerability and victimhood.

A growing body of critical scholarship has revealed some of these additional meanings through non-doctrinal research and thus challenged the ostensibly neutral, objective and universal nature of the law. For example, Helen Kinsella argues that the principle of distinction is indeterminate and constantly produced in international law and politics through discourses of gender, innocence and civilization.[6] The combatant status has been shown to be rooted in an ideal of states' monopoly of force, and a preference for organised, disciplined and law-abiding warfare in which the combatant is visually distinguishable from civilians.[7] According to Frédéric Mégret, this reflects a Western idea of legitimate warfare which, in its colonial beginning, excluded the 'uncivilized' other.[8] The historical studies by Karma Nabulsi and Sybille Scheipers explore how ideologically-driven,[9] deliberate attempts to distinguish regular from irregular fighters have informed the making of conventional IHL, limiting the combatant status to the former.[10]

[6] H Kinsella, *The Image Before the Weapon: A Critical History of the Distinction Between Combatant and Civilian* (Ithaca, Cornell University Press, 2011).

[7] See, eg, A Alexander, 'Filling the Gaps: the Expansion of International Humanitarian Law and the Juridification of the Free-Fighter' (2023) 14 *Journal of International Humanitarian Legal Studies* 274.

[8] F Mégret, 'From "Savages" to "Unlawful Combatants": A Postcolonial Look at International Humanitarian Law's "Other"' in A Orford (ed), *International Law and Its Others* (Cambridge, Cambridge University Press, 2006) 304–08.

[9] K Nabulsi, *Traditions of War: Occupation, Resistance and the Law* (Oxford, Oxford University Press, 1999).

[10] S Scheipers, *Unlawful Combatants: A Genealogy of the Irregular Fighter* (Oxford, Oxford University Press, 2015).

In relation to civilians, Charli Carpenter uses empirical evidence from conflict situations to demonstrate that gendered beliefs affect how civilian immunity is promoted and implemented by the international society. The notion of civilians becomes conflated with women and children.[11] Claire Garbett, on the other hand, examines how the processes of international criminal justice conceptually shape civilian identities which are constituted on the basis of 'particular notions of gender, age, nationality and ethnicity'.[12] In a socio-legal study of the practices of distinction, Rebecca Sutton argues that the notion of 'civilianness' is associated with harmlessness, innocence and being outside the fight, whereas 'combatantness' suggests being 'complicit, dangerous, and participating in the conflict'.[13] Yet she also observes the complexity and fluidity of the civilian appearing as the 'civilian plus', 'mere civilian' and 'civilian minus'. Focusing on different aspects and processes, these studies expose how the concept of civilians is imbued with social understandings, ideas and bias in the interpretation and application of the law. In contrast, this book is concerned with the development of the law itself. It examines how such ideational factors informed the negotiation and drafting of the law and became embedded in varying legal concepts and norms at specific points in time.

II. CONSTRUCTING INDIVIDUALS IN THE LAW-MAKING PROCESSES

The main concern of this study is how the actors involved in law-making processes perceived, portrayed and discussed individuals in armed conflict, and how some of these conceptualisations are reflected in the conventional legal framework. The theoretical underpinnings of this approach are based on social constructivism which, as the name suggests, emphasises that meaning is socially constructed. Intersubjective or shared understandings are produced and reproduced in the interaction of actors between themselves and with their social environment. As a result, a 'social reality is somehow generated by the way we *think* or *talk* about it, by our consensus about its nature, by the way we *explain* it to each other, and by the *concepts* we use to grasp it'.[14] The 'shape and form' of these social constructs are 'imbued with social values, norms, and assumptions rather than being the product of purely individual thought or meaning'.[15]

[11] C Carpenter, *Innocent Women and Children: Gender, Norms and the Protection of Civilians* (Aldershot, Ashgate, 2006).

[12] C Garbett, *The Concept of the Civilian: Legal Recognition, Adjudication and the Trials of International Criminal Justice* (Abingdon, Routledge, 2015) 153.

[13] R Sutton, *The Humanitarian Civilian: How the Idea of Distinction Circulates Within and Beyond International Humanitarian Law* (Oxford, Oxford University Press, 2021) 2.

[14] F Collin, *Social Reality* (London, Routledge, 1997) 2–3.

[15] KM Fierke, 'Constructivism' in T Dunne, M Kurki and S Smith (eds), *International Relations Theories: Discipline and Diversity*, 4th edn (Oxford, Oxford University Press, 2016) 163; Norms in this context do not entail legal norms, but 'collective expectations for the proper behavior of actors with a given identity', PJ Katzenstein, 'Introduction: Alternative Perspectives on National Security'

Legal concepts, such as those of combatants and civilians, are not self-evident, objective facts that await to be discovered, but are based on meanings that actors ascribe explicitly or implicitly to a phenomenon, in this case to individuals who are involved in or affected by hostilities. The focus here lies not on specific human beings in a concrete conflict situation, but on categories of persons with perceived similarities and differences. Understandings of who may participate in warfare, as well as who should be protected from its consequences, change from one historical context to another. They are embedded in political, social and cultural ideas and norms of the period. This includes the historically contingent perception of the nature and purpose of IHL itself. For example, the changing understanding of the type and scope of situations to be governed, including the geographical reach of the rules beyond the battlefield, feeds into the assessment of which individuals should be formally regulated and protected under the law. Similarly, the professed objective of the legal regime as either regulating inter-state relations or alleviating human suffering has had differing effects on the conceptualisation of individuals in armed conflicts. Legal concepts and norms are crafted on such interpretations of reality which are formed prior to and during the negotiations, and thus precede the law. Meanings are attached to situations, acts and individuals before they can become legal terms of art or, more generally, part of a legal rule.

This book is interested in how the actors involved in the law-making processes engage with the material reality, ideas and norms in trying to make sense of a phenomenon or set of practices which is to be regulated or protected under IHL. It analyses which issues attract attention, and which sources are drawn upon in making sense of individuals in armed conflicts for this purpose. As part of this enquiry, it considers whether the principle of distinction has informed the conceptualisation of individuals. Furthermore, it examines whether the production of meaning is shaped by, for example, the experience and memory of war; cultural values and ideas including humanitarian concerns; scientific knowledge; or an interaction with the (especially animate) subjects of norms themselves. This is not to discard the importance of the material reality such as technological advances in warfare; yet it is social forces, within and outside of the institutionalised international legal system, which significantly shape the understanding of the participating actors, not least by informing and constraining their language, ideas and interests. The experience of recent warfare, the knowledge of ongoing hostilities, and the expectation of impending armed conflicts may form part of the actors' background knowledge. However, it is in their reflection on and discussion of armed conflicts rather than in the interaction of armed forces on the ground that shared understandings of individuals for the purpose of creating and shaping IHL are (re)produced. The deliberation of the conduct of hostilities and treatment of war victims is pursued at an abstract, and arguably sanitised, level removed from the practice of war and armed conflicts. In general, the construction of meaning for the purpose of developing international law lies at the intersection between prior experience and expectations about the future.

When it comes to the construction of intersubjective meaning, language and discourse are a particularly important medium.[16] A 'discourse' is here understood as 'a cohesive ensemble of ideas, concepts, and categorizations about a specific object that frame that object in a certain way and, therefore, delimit the possibilities for action in relation to it'.[17] Charlotte Epstein argues that discourses are simultaneously '*enabling*, in that they allow the actors to act in the social world' and '*constraining*' since, '[i]n order to make sense to others, the social actor has to both speak and behave according to shared social conventions'.[18] Discourses may become 'naturalised' and thus considered as 'obvious' and 'true', while their historical context-contingency and other possible meanings become 'evacuated'.[19] As a result, ideas also become 'taken for granted', leading to the delegitimisation of competing notions.[20] Critical constructivists, in particular, are interested in the operation of power in and through discourse. They emphasise, for example, the importance of hegemonic discourses, argumentation structures and legitimacy perceptions in imposing meaning on the material world.[21] Indeed, some believe that 'constructions of reality reflect, enact, and reify relations of power'.[22]

Deliberation in the law-making process has been recognised as 'an essential lubricant ... because it facilitates discussion, negotiation, compromise, persuasion, influence and participation'.[23] The analysis in this book applies a close reading to the deliberations of the participating actors to discover signs of their perception of individuals in armed conflicts. It identifies which conceptualisations are invoked, accepted or objected to and why, how and by whom. It sheds light on moments where different meanings crystalise or coalesce, and become part of the multi-layered concepts of combatants and civilians which exist today. This is achieved by searching for regularities and patterns in the discourses which indicate common understandings, and possibly even dominant discourses. Attention is also drawn to 'outliers', when individual or minority arguments stand out from the common discourses. It assesses whether such alternative understandings are influential.

in PJ Katzenstein (ed), *The Culture of National Security: Norms and Identity in World Politics* (New York, Columbia University Press, 1996) 5.

[16] E Adler, 'Constructivism and International Relations' in W Carlsnaes, T Risse and BA Simmons (eds), *A Handbook of International Relations*, 2nd edn (London, SAGE, 2013) 125.

[17] C Epstein, *The Power of Words in International Relations: Birth of an Anti-Whaling Discourse* (Cambridge, MIT Press, 2008) 2.

[18] ibid 13.

[19] ibid 10.

[20] E Adler, 'Seizing the Middle Ground: Constructivism in World Politics' (1997) 3 *European Journal of International Relations* 319, 340.

[21] See, eg, Epstein (n 17) 2–4 and 8–14; Adler, 'Constructivism and International Relations' (n 16) 125.

[22] M Finnemore and K Sikkink, 'Taking Stock: The Constructivist Research Program in International Relations and Comparative Politics' (2001) 4 *Annual Review of Political Science* 391, 398.

[23] A Boyle and C Chinkin, *The Making of International Law* (Oxford, Oxford University Press, 2007) 100.

The construction of individuals may be shaped by diverse discourses in existence in the same period under analysis. The actors involved in the process of shaping IHL may speak, metaphorically, different languages rooted in dissimilar understandings of situations of armed conflicts. Consequently, discourses may intersect but not align. Since discourses are historically, socially and politically context-contingent, dissimilar discourses can be traced over the different periods, and this book examines how they have influenced the development of IHL. Notice is taken of linguistic dissimilarities and varying argumentation styles since these may provide insights into changing conceptualisations over time.

The study explores what allows meaningful conversation and argumentation in negotiating the development of IHL to occur. Various (competing) interpretations of individuals in armed conflicts may exist with differing degrees of perceived legitimacy and acceptance among the actors participating in the process. Actors involved in promoting new norms or providing existing ones with new meaning 'usually try to associate their prescriptions with values that are already accepted as normative within the relevant speech community'.[24] Accordingly, it is believed that 'ideas are more likely to be influential if they fit well with existing discourses in a particular historical setting'.[25] Yet, as Mark Laffey and Jutta Weldes observe, '"fit" does not just happen; rather it is *made*' since it 'is actively *constructed* rather than simply "there" in the ideas themselves'.[26] Richard Price refers to the process of strategically and consciously building upon existing norms and understandings, in order for ideas to 'resonate' with existing frames, as 'grafting'.[27] For this purpose, this study contextualises the law-making process by analysing how ideational and normative constraints delineate the cognitive and effective possibilities of constructing violent situations discursively.

Framing is an important persuasion technique in this respect since actors thus 'provide a singular interpretation of a particular situation and then indicate appropriate behavior for that context';[28] or, in other words, 'situate issues within a broader social and historical setting'.[29] Labels can be employed as part of the framing to 'reinforce cognitive associations between an object, person, or a concept, and its attributes'.[30] This may involve the framing of long-standing

[24] C Reus-Smit, 'Human Rights and the Social Construction of Sovereignty' (2001) 27 *Review of International Studies* 519, 526.

[25] R Price, 'Reversing the Gun Sights: Transnational Civil Society Targets Land Mines' (1998) 52 *International Organization* 613, 630.

[26] M Laffey and J Weldes, 'Beyond Belief: Ideas and Symbolic Technologies in the Study of International Relations' (1997) 3 *European Journal of International Relations* 193, 203.

[27] Price, 'Gun Sights' (n 25) 630.

[28] RA Payne, 'Persuasion, Frames and Norm Construction' (2001) 7 *European Journal of International Relations* 37, 39.

[29] ibid 43.

[30] M Melillo, 'Labels as the *Visible* Part of International Law's *Invisible* Frames' in A Bianchi and M Hirsch (eds), *International Law's Invisible Frames* (Oxford, Oxford University Press, 2021) 142.

issues in new, innovative ways, which may lead to changes in actors' understandings, identities and interests.[31] Yet framing may not only generate change but also reinforce the *status quo*.[32] Certain interpretations of individuals in armed conflict may be invoked and instrumentalised in treaty-making not only to adopt desired rules, but also to maintain *lacunae* in the law. A variety of frames may be employed which are 'overlapping and layered, with varying degrees of consistency or coherence',[33] or, indeed, which are in competition and thus function as counterframes.[34] The analysis of the content and impact of frames can be enhanced by their historical contextualisation, comparison and contrasting with alternative frames, and the identification of their interrelatedness, tension and complexity.

Especially in later periods of the development of the law, efforts at treaty-making could be expected to build upon existing conventions which have become part of the actors' background knowledge.[35] However, actors may also reinterpret earlier recognitions of individuals in law, or be informed by a shared belief in the existence of a legal norm despite its absence in the established written (and customary) legal framework. As a result, the process may be framed as codifying and reaffirming the law even when the underlying understandings of individuals and, indeed, rules and regulations differ. Taking a long historical view reveals 'how normative material from one period is picked up later, adapted and used'.[36] Shifting social norms outside of the legal framework may also be transferred into IHL by their adoption in treaties. This book analyses when such social norms and concepts seem to have attained a dominant status in the wider legal discourse and, when in comparison, they are inscribed into treaty texts. Moreover, concepts and rules from one regime in IHL may be transferred into another, often based on arguments of analogy yet occasionally without a sustained engagement in social construction. This may lead to norm transplants, for example, from the law on IACs to NIACs, without attention being paid to the particularities of the situations and individuals which are thus regulated. Similarly, other fields of international law may also influence the development of IHL by informing the interests of actors and their interpretations of the world. Understandings of individuals in one field, such as international human rights law, may thus inspire the rules and regulations of another.

[31] ME Keck and K Sikkink, 'Transnational Advocacy Networks in International and Regional Politics' (1999) 51 *International Social Science Journal* 89, 95.

[32] A Klotz and C Lynch, *Strategies for Research in Constructivist International Relations* (London, Routledge, 2015) 56.

[33] ibid 54.

[34] Payne (n 28) 44.

[35] See W Alschner, 'Locked in Language: Historical Sociology and the Path Dependency of Investment Treaty Design' in M Hirsch and A Lang (eds), *Research Handbook on the Sociology of International Law* (Cheltenham, Elgar, 2020).

[36] W Sandholtz, *Prohibiting Plunder: How Norms Change* (Oxford, Oxford University Press, 2007) 265.

A complex interplay between different ideational and normative structures is thus at play which can be, for example, partly discerned from normative reasoning in the law-making process. The justification employed by actors may reveal certain shared values and expectations since 'it speaks directly to … normative context and shared social purpose'.[37] It may also change over time and thus indicate an evolution in the normative environment. Beliefs about what is good, desirable or legitimate may inform the emergence and development of international legal rules and concepts in accordance with what the actors deem to be appropriate. This may explain the directedness of attempts at adopting new regulations or changing existing ones. However, it may also elucidate the constraining effect of normative structures which hinders the development of new or amendment of existing law in accordance with the historical context and changing nature of warfare. The relationship is not pre-determined. As this book shows, the process of constructing individuals in armed conflicts has been informed by continuations as well as breaks from the existing legal framework. The analysis, therefore, seeks to highlight the dynamics of change in the regulation and protection of individuals under IHL. Some developments may be of a more incremental nature, characterised by only slow progress and long-term stability, whereas other norms may experience a leap, or possibly evolve in a less linear process occasionally moving backwards.

Silences also play an important role in a more nuanced appreciation of when and how the concepts of combatants and civilians have been shaped. Discourses at diplomatic conferences may reveal taken-for-granted understandings. The absence of a detailed, extensive and sustained engagement with the meaning of certain concepts may suggest common-sense assumptions among the participants who rely, instead, on seemingly unspoken intersubjective knowledge already in existence by the time of the event. On the other hand, certain discourses may be pre-empted from entering the discursive realm of diplomatic conferences. Consequently, it needs to be analysed how and why some understandings of individuals in armed conflicts, and not others, prevail in a particular historical context. This requires the uncovering of discourses which circulate in other settings, and which may be hidden from the formal law-making process. Comparisons are also made to the contemporary legal framework – not to interpret the construction of individuals at the time through a modern-day lens, but rather to emphasise what was *not* deliberated and regulated in earlier periods. For example, a detailed examination of whether, and if so how, individuals who would be considered civilians today were discussed at a particular diplomatic conference may illuminate the absence of the concept of civilians at that moment in time.

[37] M Finnemore, *The Purpose of Intervention: Changing Beliefs About the Use of Force* (Ithaca, Cornell University Press, 2003) 15.

The enquiry in this book focuses on how individuals have been conceptualised in the development of primarily conventional IHL. The purposeful nature of creating and shaping law through the deliberation and adoption of treaties provides a rich basis for an appraisal of the perceptions, actors and dynamics involved in the process. The law-making processes leading to conventional IHL are, however, conceived here more widely than just official diplomatic conferences convened for treaty-making. The discursive construction of the social reality precedes and transcends these formal, situated events of law-making. Other related deliberations intended to inform the creation and development of IHL are analysed as well. Specific events and sites of interaction where relevant discourses circulate and actors (re)produce meanings which influence IHL are, therefore, identified and examined in the substantive chapters. These include, for example, conferences, meetings and reports by non-state actors where existing conventional and customary IHL was discussed, and where necessary or desirable changes to the legal framework were proposed. These crucial moments may be described as 'bursts of rich debate',[38] where the social realities underlying the proposed rules and regulations are implicitly or explicitly constructed. The analysis not only considers these events in isolation but brings them into relation within and across the identified periods.

Additionally, the study draws on contemporaneous scholarship to contextualise and compare different discourses of a particular period and thus to identify divergences and similarities in the construction of individuals in armed conflicts. On the other hand, it refrains from tracing changing understandings of individuals in the actual conduct of warfare around the world throughout more than 160 years, and analysing the implementation of conventional law in practice. It also does not examine the prevailing public opinion, or the contributions of philosophers and novelists, or culture more generally.[39] While these wider practices and discourses may have shaped understandings outside the law-making processes and influenced perceptions at the events under analysis, a comprehensive study of the myriad of possible or actual conceptualisations of individuals in armed conflicts prior to and following the adoption of law exceeds the scope of this project. The construction of meaning through the interpretation and application of the law is only considered in relation to the last period under examination, namely the post-1977 era until today, albeit still not in relation to particular armed conflicts.

Once adopted treaties constitute a stabilisation of meaning, at least to some extent, because of its formalisation in written rules and regulations. This may include the entrenchment of certain assumptions, ideas and biases in the law. At the same time, as a result of synthesising interpretations of a complex world into

[38] R Price, *The Chemical Weapons Taboo* (Ithaca, Cornell University Press, 1997) 10.

[39] cf A Alexander, 'The Genesis of the Civilian' (2007) 20 *LJIL* 359; A Alexander, 'International Humanitarian Law, Postcolonialism and the 1977 *Geneva Protocol I*' (2016) 17 *Melbourne Journal of International Law* 15; A Alexander, 'The "Good War": Preparations for a War against Civilians' (2019) 15 *Law, Culture and the Humanities* 227.

abstract legal rules, certain nuances may be lost. The prevalence of compromise in treaty-making provides a fertile ground for uncertainties and new debates. However, the distinctive disciplinary understandings of international law and legal practice somewhat constrain the ongoing social production and reproduction of meaning. The interpretation of reality becomes bound by the nature of the international legal system, including its actors and processes, resulting in the exclusion of alternative meanings. While individuals may be constructed both in the development of conventional law, as well as through subsequent interpretation and application, different ideational and procedural factors enable and constrain the respective process, as will be further discussed in chapter six.

A final word on compromise in the law-making process appears to be opportune. Treaties have been famously described as 'a disagreement reduced to writing'.[40] Indeed, treaty-making may be dependent on 'being imprecise', with vague clauses deliberately inserted to achieve agreement between the participating parties; 'norms may be adopted precisely because they mean different things to different actors'.[41] The difficulties of socially constructing the meaning of individuals in armed conflicts in the process of developing IHL are highlighted throughout this book. While this may explain some of the failed attempts at treaty-making, conventional law has been repeatedly adopted without there being a clear shared understanding of individuals between the participating actors. The enquiry examines in more detail how their views vary, and which conceptualisations are embedded in the law to the exclusion of others.

The question arises whether the social construction of intersubjective meaning is indeed possible in the negotiation of treaties. It may be rare that meaning is generated or produced for the first time at a diplomatic conference. Instead, they are forums in which various ways of seeing individuals are discussed and contested, and where they may become strengthened and institutionalised. The value of the approach adopted in this book stems from the identification of different understandings, shedding light on alternative conceptualisations, and reflecting on the implications of the absence of shared understandings for the interpretation of the law both in subsequent law-making processes as well as in practice. Some disagreements and compromises, including formulations of the combatant and POW status, are commonly acknowledged in the literature. Yet other understandings, such as the vulnerability of civilians and the foundational role of the principle of distinction, are often perceived as constant and uncontested. The close reading of the law-making processes provided by this study challenges these assumptions by highlighting the difficulty of coming to a generally agreed conceptualisation, and enquiring whether any shared understandings indeed underpin the adopted treaty texts.

[40] P Allott, 'The Concept of International Law' (1999) 10 *EJIL* 31, 43.

[41] ML Krook and J True, 'Rethinking the Life Cycles of International Norms: The United Nations and the Global Promotion of Gender Equality' (2012) 18 *European Journal of International Relations* 103, 109–10.

III. ACTORS INVOLVED IN THE CONSTRUCTION OF INDIVIDUALS

This book highlights the importance of agency in shaping international legal concepts. Agency of actors is restrained 'by the webs of understanding of the practices, identities, and interests of other actors that prevail in particular historical contexts';[42] yet it may also function as a driver of change.[43] For example, it is the role of agents to translate intersubjective understandings into ideational and normative structures[44] including the law. Actors with the ability to influence intersubjective meaning and consequently identities, interests and practices of actors are considered as being in a position of power.[45] Silences, on the other hand, may not only derive from the actors' choice not to speak about certain situations, acts and individuals, but also from their lack of agency to participate in the discourse in the first place. The non-participation of certain actors may thus reveal power relations at play in interpreting armed conflicts for the purpose of shaping IHL. A constructivist approach not only provides an understanding of the actors which are involved in the process, but also their speaking position as well as the roles which they adopt or are imposed on them by others. As Mona Lena Krook and Jacqui True argue in their study of international norm dynamics, examining '"voice" – the ability of different kinds of agents to define and implement norms – matters in understanding how certain meanings of norms get constructed, reproduced and/or altered'.[46] With the marginalisation and silencing of certain voices, alternative visions of armed conflicts and individuals involved in or affected by them may be obscured and excluded.

According to the prevailing understanding in the discipline, conventional international law is made by states. The constitutive norms of the international legal system are exclusionary since they confer an unparalleled dominant status on states. However, the diversity among states also needs to be recognised. The absence of some states from the law-making processes is a sign of a power imbalance in the agency of states. While the historical account in this book endeavours to highlight the limited nature of participants in the law-making processes, it is, admittedly, characterised by a Western bias and is at times Eurocentric. In particular, it ignores the influence of non-Western traditions and approaches, apart from the participation of newly independent states during and after the de-colonisation process. As Scheipers observes, 'until the second half of the twentieth century, voices from the periphery did not feature largely

[42] T Hopf, 'The Promise of Constructivism in International Relations Theory' (1998) 23 *International Security* 171, 177.

[43] FV Kratochwil, *Rules, Norms and Decisions: On the Conditions of Practical and Legal Reasoning in International Relations and Domestic Affairs* (Cambridge, Cambridge University Press, 1989) 61.

[44] Payne (n 28) 38.

[45] Adler, 'Middle Ground' (n 20) 336.

[46] Krook and True (n 41) 112–13.

as agents in the process of the legal codification of the exclusion of the irregular [fighter]'[47] or the laws of war generally.

Furthermore, since actors are informed by a range of historical, political and social conditions, various understandings of individuals in armed conflicts may exist not only between different states, but also within one state throughout the years. Numerous states have been involved in the drafting of conventional IHL over an extended period of time, some for more than a century. As a result, a state's own reference framework, in the form of background knowledge and conceptualisations of individuals in armed conflicts, may have also changed. Yet the examination of intersubjective understandings at the heart of the analysis draws attention away from the actors' subjective beliefs and motivations. The perception and arguments of individual states are only considered in relation to their contribution to the overall discourse and their reception by other actors. The analysis does also not study these conceptualisations as a product of rational, self-interested actors engaged in cost-benefit calculations. Nor does it engage in depth with political conditions, material power relations or strategic interests of states at the international and domestic level which may have influenced these understandings. This is not to deny their importance in international affairs; yet other theories and theoretical approaches, not least from the discipline of International Relations, may be better suited to provide an explanation in this regard. The objective of this book is to identify and understand different conceptualisations of individuals under IHL rather than to provide causal explanations of change in the law.

The enquiry does, however, consider that states, as abstract entities, interact at diplomatic conferences through human beings. Accordingly, variations also exist at the individual level of state representatives even though the states themselves may *prima facie* remain the same actors. It needs emphasising that state delegations do not consist of homogenous or mechanical actors, unaffected by their social and epistemological environments. While state delegates participate in the formal, institutionalised law-making processes as representatives of their respective governments, their background knowledge, understanding and argumentation is likely to be informed by their professional and possibly even personal perspective. The shift from military-dominated diplomatic conferences towards an increase in lawyers and representatives of non-governmental organisations as participants, observed by Tanisha Fazal,[48] will be shown to be important in the analysis. Fazal herself suggests that 'not only were military delegates fewer in number over time, they also became less powerful within their delegations, increasingly relegated to the role of "technical advisor"'.[49] Martha Finnemore also argues that the professionalisation of law and increasing

[47] Scheipers (n 10) 24.

[48] TM Fazal, *Wars of Law: Unintended Consequences in the Regulation of Armed Conflict* (Ithaca, Cornell University Press, 2018) 23–30.

[49] ibid 26.

constitution of diplomatic staff of individuals with legal training changed the procedure and nature of deliberating international politics. These developments in the late nineteenth and early twentieth century led to a 'legalization' of diplomacy.[50] This book highlights how the language and practice of individual delegates may not only reflect the interests of the states that they represent but also their professional role and knowledge, for example, as military officials, diplomats, lawyers or medical personnel. In this respect, it needs to be examined which persons states have considered as their appropriate representatives in the formation of the rules and regulations of IHL.

Nevertheless, these simplistic classifications based on profession need to be seen with some reservation. Differences between types of lawyers, for example, have been observed in scholarship. David Luban notes a common cultural division between what he calls 'humanitarian lawyers' and 'military lawyers' who differ in their approach to the laws of war, including their perception of the law's purpose.[51] Robert Cryer adapts Martti Koskenniemi's distinction between the judge, adviser, activist and academic to the context of IHL.[52] He stresses, however, that individuals in these roles also vary in their beliefs, approaches and backgrounds, and that a person may 'have more than one role, both consecutively or sequentially'.[53] Indeed, some of the more prominent participants in the law-making processes, especially in the later periods under analysis in this book, were military lawyers who were also active in international professional legal associations and as academics.[54]

The book highlights some of these noteworthy personalities in the law-making processes who were influential in shaping the understanding of individuals or promoted relevant alternative understandings. It traces their reappearance at a variety of events and thus their role as agents in the development of the law. Yet with the increase in the number of delegations and their respective sizes at later diplomatic conferences, individual actors appear to become less influential. Moreover, a detailed examination of the interactions and relations between individual participants, as well as their personal biographies is beyond the scope of the enquiry. The work of historians may provide a more fine-grained analysis which better captures the complexity of the historical, political and social context in this regard.[55]

Focusing on agency in the law-making also draws attention to the involvement and influence of non-state actors in the multidimensional processes leading to

[50] Finnemore (n 37) 49–50.

[51] D Luban, 'Military Necessity and the Cultures of Military Law' (2013) 26 *LJIL* 315.

[52] R Cryer, 'The Impact of Human Rights Advocacy: Between (Mis)stating the Law and Pursuing Humanitarian Policies?' in H Krieger and J Püschmann (eds), *Law-Making and Legitimacy in International Humanitarian Law* (Cheltenham, Elgar, 2021).

[53] ibid 392.

[54] eg General JCC den Beer Poortugael, GIAD Draper and Richard Baxter.

[55] See, eg, G Ben-Nun, *The Fourth Geneva Convention for Civilians: The History of International Humanitarian Law* (London, IB Tauris, 2020); B van Dijk, *Preparing for War: The Making of the Geneva Conventions* (Oxford, Oxford University Press, 2022).

the adoption of international law. Constructivists have emphasised the influence of non-state actors in the process of norm change, commonly differentiating them in accordance with their roles as, for instance, norm entrepreneurs and epistemic communities.[56] Norm entrepreneurs 'draw on social resources – expertise and/or moral authority – to persuade the community at large to accept new norms',[57] a role commonly pursued by the International Committee of the Red Cross. They may be 'visionary leaders in policy communities, or powerful states in the world system';[58] but they could also be 'committed individuals who happen to be in the right place at the right time to instill their beliefs in larger global social structures',[59] such as Henri Dunant rallying for humanitarian protection for wounded soldiers in the field after the Battle of Solferino. Epistemic communities, on the other hand, consist of '[g]roups with specialized knowledge [who] often have a common set of norms and world views'.[60] With their recognised expertise, epistemic communities frame problems and propose solutions which may inform the understanding of decision-makers and persuade them to take certain action,[61] as can be seen especially in the context of international environmental law. Contrary to the narrow understanding of the concept by some social scientists, Andrea Bianchi argues that international lawyers generally and within their specific subject areas can also be considered as epistemic communities.[62]

As this book shows, certain non-state actors have presented written submissions to diplomatic conferences, or have themselves taken part as experts and observers in the preliminary and official stages of negotiating and drafting treaties in recent periods. More importantly, since the beginnings of the written laws of war, non-state actors such as the Institut de Droit International and the International Law Association have been engaged in processes of their own leading to the adoption of draft regulations. Their deliberations of the development of the law are related, albeit external, to the formal law-making procedures. Their efforts have been especially important during periods in which states themselves have abstained from (re)considering the law. Some non-state actors have evolved in terms of their participation from a sometimes even self-restrained, limited

[56] See, eg, PM Haas, 'Introduction: Epistemic Communities and International Policy Coordination' (1992) 46 *International Organization* 1; M Finnemore and K Sikkink, 'International Norm Dynamics and Political Change' (1998) 52 *International Organization* 887; Klotz and Lynch (n 32) 46–48; J Brunnée and SJ Toope, *Legitimacy and Legality in International Law: An Interactional Account* (Cambridge, Cambridge University Press, 2010) 59.

[57] D Armstrong, T Farrell and H Lambert, *International Law and International Relations* (Cambridge, Cambridge University Press, 2007) 99–100.

[58] ibid 99.

[59] JT Checkel, 'The Constructivist Turn in International Relations Theory' (1998) 50 *World Politics* 324, 332.

[60] Finnemore and Sikkink, 'Taking Stock' (n 22) 401.

[61] Haas (n 56) 2–3.

[62] A Bianchi, 'Epistemic Communities' in J d'Aspremont and S Singh (eds), *Concepts for International Law: Contributions to Disciplinary Thought* (Cheltenham, Elgar, 2019) 255–60.

role to more assertive and authoritative involvement. This enquiry, therefore, emphasises the changing nature of the participating actors in the international legal system, and where the law is meaningfully discussed by them outside of statist forums.

Similar to states, these non-state actors are represented at diplomatic conferences by human beings, and their own proceedings comprise reports and debates by individual members. Yet the nature, identity and interests of the non-state actor as a whole also need to be considered. Their self-understanding and role in relation to armed conflicts may inform how they perceive individuals and the protective scope of the law. This may lead to the reframing of an issue and the offering of an alternative approach to regulating situations and individuals. It also influences their agenda setting which may induce the development of the law in a new direction or (re-)introduce an issue in need of change.

IV. CONCLUSION

In summary, the approach adopted in this book provides insights into how understandings which underpin the law are constructed and reconstructed in the social process of developing IHL. It considers which actors are involved in shaping the meaning that permeates the substance of the law, even if they are not directly participating in the formal law-making process. It thus shows when and how certain ideas, beliefs and values enter the process of developing the law and inform the adopted legal rules and concepts. Moreover, it examines how certain constructions of individuals in armed conflicts emerge, evolve and become formalised in the law while others disappear, for example, because they are not contemplated in the institutionalised set-up of treaty-making, or because they lack persuasiveness and legitimacy among the relevant audience. Analysing the evolution of the law through the changing conceptualisation of individuals who participate in or are affected by armed conflicts may thus reveal the nuances of the meaning embedded in legal concepts and norms.

3

The Early Written Laws of War

THE YEARS BETWEEN 1863 and 1907 have often been described as the formational period for the modern laws of war. In his acclaimed study *Humanity in Warfare – The Modern History of the International Law of Armed Conflicts*, the historian Geoffrey Best argues that '[w]ithin the second half of the nineteenth century, the conventional … foundations of all subsequent law of war were laid'.[1] The established narrative begins with the 1863 General Orders No 100: Instructions for the Government of Armies of the United States in the Field,[2] also known as the Lieber Code. Despite its character as a national instrument and its creation in the context of a civil war, the Lieber Code is commonly regarded as an attempt to codify the laws and customs of warfare and as having been influential for the development of the international laws of war. One year later, the first 1864 Geneva Convention for the Amelioration of the Condition of the Wounded in Armies in the Field[3] was adopted following the norm entrepreneurship of Henri Dunant and his book *A Memory of Solferino*, which records his impressions of the suffering of soldiers in the Battle of Solferino. In 1868, states turned to limiting warfare itself and adopted the Declaration Renouncing the Use, in Time of War, of Explosive Projectiles Under 400 Grammes Weight[4] (St Petersburg Declaration). Shortly after the Franco-Prussian War, delegations from 14 European states and Turkey assembled in the capital of neutral Belgium to deliberate the laws and customs of war upon invitation by the Russian Tsar Alexander II. The resultant 1874 Brussels Declaration[5] was never ratified as a treaty, yet it sparked further developments in the field. In 1880, the Institut de Droit International (IDI) adopted the so-called 'Oxford Manual',[6] 'a private codification of the laws of

[1] G Best, *Humanity in Warfare – The Modern History of the International Law of Armed Conflicts* (London, Methuen, 1983) 128–29.

[2] (24 April 1863) (Lieber Code).

[3] (Geneva, 22 August 1864) (1864 Geneva Convention).

[4] (St Petersburg, 29 November/11 December 1868).

[5] Project of an International Declaration Concerning the Laws and Customs of War (Brussels, 27 August 1874) (Brussels Declaration), reprinted in D Schindler and J Toman (eds), *Laws of Armed Conflict: A Collection of Conventions, Resolutions, and Other Documents*, 4th edn (Leiden, Martinus Nijhoff, 2004).

[6] The Laws of War on Land – Manual published by the Institute of International Law (Oxford, 9 September 1880) (Oxford Manual) reprinted in Schindler and Toman (n 5).

land warfare',[7] in the hope that governments would incorporate its rules in their national legislations. This 'formational' period culminated in the two Hague Peace Conferences in 1899 and 1907 and the adoption of the first general treaties regulating land, maritime and, to a lesser degree, aerial warfare.

The 1899 and 1907 Hague Regulations on the Laws and Customs of War on Land,[8] for the first time, in a multilateral binding agreement, defined combatants and provided rudimentary safeguards for individuals who do not belong to the armed forces. They have been said to form 'the historical cornerstone in international conventional law for the distinction between persons who are legitimate targets and those entitled to protection during international armed conflicts'.[9] Consequently, they are seen as forming the basis for the contemporary concepts of combatants and civilians, often interchangeably referred to as 'non-combatants'. This chapter challenges the conventional narrative that the qualification of combatants and protection of civilians emerged as 'two sides of the same coin' in the early written laws of war.[10]

The first part of this chapter focuses on the status of combatants in the Brussels Declaration and the Hague Regulations. It shows that the concept of regular combatants evolved in a close relationship with the understanding of irregular fighters, as argued by Sybille Scheipers,[11] rather than with civilians. It also reveals that the main struggle over conceptualising legitimate and lawful participation in hostilities took place at the 1874 Brussels Conference and not at the First Hague Peace Conference. Ultimately, many uncertainties and disagreements regarding the combatant status were not resolved in the deliberations at Brussels or even with the adoption of the Hague Regulations.

The second part of the chapter analyses the marginal consideration of individuals who do not belong to the armed forces, who are today known as 'civilians'. Although 'the word civilian, in the sense of a non-military person' emerged in the mid-nineteenth century,[12] it did not yet feature in the international instruments on the laws and customs of war during this period. Instead, these individuals were commonly referred to as 'citizens', 'private persons', 'inhabitants' and collectively as 'population'. They were further characterised by

[7] SC Neff, *War and the Law of Nations: A General History* (Cambridge, Cambridge University Press, 2005) 187.

[8] Annex to Convention (II): Regulations Respecting the Laws and Customs of War on Land (The Hague, 29 July 1899) (1899 Hague Regulations); Annex to Convention (IV): Regulations Respecting the Laws and Customs of War on Land (The Hague, 18 October 1907) (1907 Hague Regulations).

[9] JK Kleffner, 'From "Belligerents" to "Fighters" and Civilians Directly Participating in Hostilities – On the Principle of Distinction in Non-International Armed Conflicts One Hundred Years After the Second Hague Peace Conference' (2007) 54 *Netherlands International Law Review* 315, 318–19.

[10] cf TL Dowdeswell, 'The Brussels Peace Conference of 1874 and the Modern Laws of Belligerent Qualification' (2017) 54 *Osgoode Hall Law Journal* 805, 821.

[11] S Scheipers, *Unlawful Combatants: A Genealogy of the Irregular Fighter* (Oxford, Oxford University Press, 2015).

[12] A Alexander, 'The Genesis of the Civilian' (2007) 20 *LJIL* 359, 360.

different qualifications such as 'peaceful' or 'peaceable', 'inoffensive', 'innocent' and, less often, 'civil' or 'civilian'. Amanda Alexander detects a similar diversity of vocabulary in contemporaneous scholarship and concludes that it 'indicates the difference in the category and the type of protection it attracted'.[13] She notes that '[a]t this time the word civilian was used sporadically to designate non-military persons, but without the associated connotations of protected or victimized non-combatants'.[14] The English translation of the Hague Regulations itself only referred to 'civilians' in relation to the treatment of spies.[15] The juxtaposition of the term with soldiers, and more importantly the fact that the authoritative French text refers to 'les militaires' and 'les non-militaires', suggest that the term was simply intended to denote the undefined, vague mass of individuals who are not members of the armed forces, without providing them with a distinct status. Consequently, the range of terminology can arguably not be understood as a mere inconsistency in the employment of language. While some overlaps existed and the implications of different words should not be exaggerated, this chapter argues that the various discrete rules relating to individuals who do not belong to the armed forces, taken together, do not infer a concept of civilians. They are based on diverse understandings of such individuals. This chapter deliberately abstains from referring to these individuals as 'civilians' to reflect the absence of this language as well as this concept during this period.

The analysis in this chapter, both in relation to combatants and individuals who do not belong to the armed forces, begins with the 1864 Geneva Convention and the 1868 St Petersburg Declaration. The examination of their drafting histories sets the scene for two approaches prevalent in the law-making processes of the early written laws of war. First, they expose a naturalised understanding of the state-centric nature of warfare. Second, the negotiation of the 1864 Geneva Convention and related subsequent instruments show the peripheral yet contested role of individuals who do not belong to the armed forces, who states intended to exclude from the battlefield. The main focus of the chapter, however, lies on the 1874 Brussels Conference and the 1899 and 1907 Hague Peace Conferences, where states failed to achieve an agreement at first only to adopt virtually the same rules in legal form at a later stage.

I. COMBATANTS – THE INTRODUCTION AND NEGOTIATION OF A CONCEPT

The 1864 Geneva Convention and the 1868 St Petersburg Declaration, as the first multilateral treaties on the laws of war on land, do not demarcate the concept of

[13] ibid 361; regarding the Hague Regulations see E Salmón, 'Who Is a Protected Civilian?' in A Clapham, P Gaeta and M Sassòli (eds), *The 1949 Geneva Conventions: A Commentary* (Oxford, Oxford University Press, 2015) para 9.

[14] Alexander, 'Genesis' (n 12) 360–61.

[15] 1899 and 1907 Hague Regulations, art 29.

combatants. They each provide specific regulations for the conduct of war and fulfil a narrow purpose. Namely, the former protects wounded and sick soldiers and regulates the neutrality of medical personnel and medical establishments, and the latter prohibits a particular type of explosive bullets. Yet the silences in these treaties and their drafting histories reveal certain assumptions about the nature of warfare and the purpose of the laws of war at the time.

According to its official title, the 1864 Diplomatic Conference in Geneva was convened for the neutralisation of military medical services in the field;[16] yet this reference was omitted from the title of the Convention. Similarly, although the intention of the Geneva Convention was formally professed as comprising generally to alleviate 'les maux inséparables de la guerre, de supprimer les rigueurs inutiles et d'améliorer le sort des militaires blessés sur les champs de bataille',[17] the treaty is concerned with the suffering of combatants alone. It establishes the neutrality of medical personnel, ambulances and military hospitals[18] as no more than a means for achieving the amelioration of the condition of wounded soldiers.[19] The functional contingency of the privilege of neutrality can also be seen in relation to civil hospitals. They are only designated as 'military', and consequently protected, if they are engaged in the treatment of wounded military personnel.[20] The Convention does not define the 'combatants' who fall under its scope by becoming *hors de combat*.[21] The reference to 'les militaires' in the authoritative French text suggests its limitation to the regular armed forces. The drafters appear to have believed it unnecessary to identify who would be recognised as such and thus benefit from the protection.

The St Petersburg Declaration proclaims 'that the only legitimate object which States should endeavour to accomplish during war is to weaken the military forces of the enemy' and 'that for this purpose it is sufficient to disable the greatest possible number of men'.[22] As will be discussed below,[23] the principle of distinction has often been read into this statement, implying that the Declaration refers to combatants. However, similar to the negotiation of the 1864 Geneva Convention, the meaning of combatants and the armed forces was not deliberated, but instead taken for granted.[24] The Declaration's inferred limited application to 'civilized States'[25] gives reason to believe that the drafters

[16] 'Protocoles des Conférences Internationales tenues à Genève, au mois d'août 1864' (1875) 20 *Nouveau recueil général de traités* 375.

[17] ibid 391; 'the evils inseparable from war, to eliminate unnecessary suffering and to ameliorate the condition of the wounded and sick in armies in the field' (author's translation).

[18] 1864 Geneva Convention, arts 1–2.

[19] 'Protocoles 1864' (n 16) 391–93.

[20] ibid 382.

[21] 1864 Geneva Convention, art 6.

[22] St Petersburg Declaration, preamble.

[23] See section II.A.

[24] 'Protocoles des Conférences militaires tenues à Saint-Pétersbourg, en 1868' (1873) 18 *Nouveau recueil général de traités* 450.

[25] R Kolb and M Milanov, 'The 1868 St Petersburg Declaration on Explosive Projectiles: A Reappraisal' (2018) 20 *Journal of the History of International Law* 515, 525.

had traditional regular armed forces of European states in mind. Yet it was for the states to decide who belonged to their armed forces.

The absence of a perceived need to discuss the lawful participants in hostilities may have been due to the character of the event at which the St Petersburg Declaration was drafted. It was conducted by an international military commission rather than a diplomatic conference. These military delegates were conceivably not concerned with the broader construction of conflict situations and individuals implicated therein, but only with the regulation of specific weapon technology pursuing narrow military interests. Indeed, the Declaration states that the Commission had 'by common agreement fixed the *technical limits* at which the necessities of war ought to yield to the requirements of humanity'.[26] As a result, the nineteenth-century understanding of war 'as a rule-governed, even ritualistic contest between professional armed forces',[27] which had been bestowed an 'institutional character',[28] appears to have been indirectly reaffirmed and naturalised, rather than problematised.

While the negotiations of the 1864 Geneva Convention and the 1868 St Petersburg Declaration suggest a common-sense idea of combatants and the armed forces, the 1874 Brussels Conference and the 1899 Hague Peace Conference were characterised by a more extensive engagement with the participants and victims in war. The Brussels Declaration has been said to imply three categories of persons, namely combatants, peaceful inhabitants in need of protection for their person and their property, and, finally, irregular fighters who 'méconnaissant les lois de la guerre, ne méritent point d'être traités comme des ennemis loyaux'.[29] However, as will be shown, the discourse at the Brussels Conference reveals the state delegates' primary concern with the legitimate and lawful participation in hostilities not only by soldiers, but also by individuals who do not belong to the armed forces. The Brussels Declaration served as a working draft for the deliberations 25 years later,[30] and the 1899 Hague Regulations indeed differ from the 1874 instrument primarily in their form rather than in substance. They reproduce its provisions on the privileges, obligations and protections of individuals almost verbatim. In 1907, the Second Hague Peace Conference revisited the matter and adopted an amended version of the 1899 Hague Regulations with only small modifications.

[26] St Petersburg Declaration (emphasis added).

[27] Neff (n 7) 163.

[28] ibid 186.

[29] IDI, 'Réglementation des lois et coutumes de la guerre – Examen par l'Institut de la Déclaration de Bruxelles de 1874 (Conclusions adoptées à La Haye)' (1877) 1 *AIDI* 133, 135; 'ignoring the laws of war, do not merit to be treated as loyal enemies' (author's translation).

[30] JB Scott (ed), *The Proceedings of the Hague Peace Conferences: The Conference of 1899 – Translation of the Official Texts* (Oxford, Oxford University Press, 1920) (hereafter *1899 Proceedings*) 564–78.

A. Combatants and the Lawful Participation in Hostilities

The Brussels Declaration and the Hague Regulations lay down the concept of combatants as it is known today. Combatants are recognised as lawful participants in the hostilities being part of a belligerent party to the conflict.[31] They have both rights and obligations under the laws of war.[32] If they fall into the hands of the enemy, they are protected as prisoners of war (POWs) and enjoy the rights that come with this status.[33] These implications of the combatant status were undisputed in the drafting of the international instruments. In contrast, the question of which persons may qualify for combatant status was a central point of debate both at the Brussels Conference and the First Hague Peace Conference.

The original *projet d'une convention internationale concernant les lois et coutumes de la guerre* (*projet*), which had been submitted by the Russian government as a draft and which formed the basis for the deliberations at the Brussels Conference, declared the commonly accepted doctrine at the time that international wars were fought between states and their organised armed forces.[34] While this principle, as well as the observation that armed groups who do not qualify as belligerents could be prosecuted for their participation[35] were ultimately removed from the Brussels Declaration, the state-centric understanding of combatants still prevailed during the deliberations. The recognition of members of the regular armed forces as combatants seems to have been self-evident and was not discussed by the drafters. Instead, the prolonged negotiations focused on irregular fighters and the conditions under which they may qualify as combatants.[36] Ultimately, Article 9 of the Brussels Declaration was adopted, stipulating that:

> The laws, rights, and duties of war apply not only to armies, but also to militia and volunteer corps fulfilling the following conditions:
>
> 1. That they be commanded by a person responsible for his subordinates;
> 2. That they have a fixed distinctive emblem recognizable at a distance;
> 3. That they carry arms openly; and
> 4. That they conduct their operations in accordance with the laws and customs of war.[37]

The Brussels Declaration thus first enshrined in an international instrument the criteria for combatant status which were then repeatedly reaffirmed in treaty negotiations over the next century, as will be seen in the next chapters.

[31] Brussels Declaration, pt 2; 1899 and 1907 Hague Regulations, s I ch 1.

[32] Brussels Declaration, art 9; 1899 and 1907 Hague Regulations, art 1.

[33] Brussels Declaration, art 11; 1899 and 1907 Hague Regulations, art 3.

[34] *Actes de la Conférence de Bruxelles de 1874 sur le projet d'une convention internationale concernant la guerre: protocoles des séances plénières, protocoles de la Commission déléguée par la Conférence, annexes* (Ministère des Affaires Étrangères 1874) (hereafter *Actes*) 4.

[35] ibid 5.

[36] See especially ibid 28–30 and 32–34.

[37] See also 1899 and 1907 Hague Regulations, art 1.

Additionally, under Article 10 of the Declaration, members of a so-called *levée en masse*,[38] and thus a part of or the entire population, may also qualify as combatants subject to narrowly defined conditions:

> The population of a territory which has not been occupied, who, on the approach of the enemy, spontaneously take up arms to resist the invading troops without having had time to organize themselves in accordance with Article 9, shall be regarded as belligerents if they respect the laws and customs of war.[39]

By the nineteenth century, it was commonly believed that the lawful conduct of war was reserved for states, and for individuals who were authorised by a state and bound to it by loyalty. In the 1863 Lieber Code, for example, the legitimating status of the 'belligerent' is linked to state sovereignty: '[s]o soon as a man is armed by a sovereign government and takes the soldier's oath of fidelity, he is a belligerent',[40] and even the *levée en masse* requires some form of prior state authorisation.[41] Before the Brussels Conference, 'there were few restrictions on what kind of fighters a sovereign power could authorize to wage war, or on the participation of the general civilian population'.[42] On the other hand, the *levée en masse* itself could have divergent meanings. Gerry Simpson argues that it 'can be understood of in two, potentially contrasting ways', namely 'a form of mass recruitment; or, instead, as the ongoing possibility of unplanned, impulsive revolt against invasion, occupation or domination'.[43] As part of the negotiation of inter-state conflicts, the Brussels Conference referred to spontaneous resistance against a foreign state rather than a turn against the population's own government. However, the question arose whether national defence by the population should be subject to organisation and regulation.

Although Article 10 of the Brussels Declaration does not require state authorisation, the *levée en masse* still derives its legitimacy and lawfulness as an agent of the state. The perceived right of the population to defend the nation was an indirect consequence of the sovereign right of the state itself to which it belonged.[44] Agreement seemed to exist at the Brussels Conference that the population would be motivated by patriotism, which was described as 'non-seulement un droit imprescriptible, mais encore un devoir sacré'.[45] Indeed,

[38] On the historical development of the *levée en masse* see also E Crawford, 'Tracing the Historical and Legal Development of the *Levée en Masse* in the Law of Armed Conflict' (2017) 19 *Journal of the History of International Law* 329.

[39] Brussels Declaration, art 10; see also 1899 and 1907 Hague Regulations, art 2.

[40] Lieber Code, art 57.

[41] ibid art 51.

[42] Dowdeswell (n 10) 812.

[43] G Simpson, 'Paris 1793 and 1871: *Levée en masse* As Event' in F Johns, RJ Joyce and S Pahuja (eds), *Events: The Force of International Law* (Abingdon, Routledge, 2011) 81; see also K Nabulsi, *Traditions of War: Occupation, Resistance and the Law* (Oxford, Oxford University Press, 1999) 53–55; Scheipers (n 11) 52.

[44] Dowdeswell (n 10) 844.

[45] *Actes* (n 34) 30; 'not only an imprescriptible right, but also a sacred duty' (author's translation).

the original *projet* as well as an amendment proposed during the negotiations included in the definition of the *levée en masse* that the population would 'prend les armes *pour la défense de la patrie*'.[46] The Spanish delegate Duke of Tetuan even declared that, 'tous les habitants qui, excités par le patriotisme, se lèvent en armes contre l'ennemi, sont belligérants'.[47] The French delegate Baron Baude promoted a similar proposal, only specifying the need for their conformity with the laws of war.[48] At the 1899 Hague Peace Conference, the patriotic defence of the country was again presented as a virtue of citizenship.[49] Even the states advocating a strict regulation of lawful participation in warfare did not question or deny the 'sacred rights' of national defence rooted in patriotism.[50] The individual members of the *levée en masse* were portrayed as loyal citizens with an obligation towards their country.[51]

While the ideal of patriotism was unchallenged, its desirability as a driving force in warfare was not undisputed. Karma Nabulsi remarks that suspicion towards nationalism and patriotism were informed by a fear of their potential 'fatal effect on the project of the laws of war', moving from professional warfare to 'war between peoples'.[52] The debate at the Brussels Conference thus turned on whether the *levée en masse* would expose the regular combatant to an irregular and potentially uncontrollable combatant in unorganised and cruel warfare. The Russian delegation emphasised the distinction between regulated and unregulated patriotism, voicing a strong preference for the former.[53] This desire for organised and regulated participation in warfare is reflected in the adopted stringent conditions for the *levée en masse*. Emily Crawford suggests that the time limitation in Article 10 ensures that the population's resistance 'beyond the initial stages of invasion' would be channelled through the regular armed forces or other authorised militia and voluntary corps.[54] Additionally, the requirement that the members of a *levée en masse* 'respect the laws and customs of war' was intended to compel its participants to abide by the same standards as regular combatants.[55] The 1907 Hague Regulations later modified the Brussels provision to also include an explicit obligation to carry arms openly.[56]

[46] ibid 6 and 57 (emphasis added); 'take up arms *for the defence of their country*' (author's translation).

[47] ibid 29; 'all the inhabitants who, excited by patriotism, rise in arms against the enemy are belligerents' (author's translation).

[48] ibid 33.

[49] *1899 Proceedings* (n 30) 504, see also the proposed amendment by the British delegation at 550; A Alexander, 'Filling the Gaps: the Expansion of International Humanitarian Law and the Juridification of the Free-Fighter' (2023) 14 *Journal of International Humanitarian Legal Studies* 274, 279–80.

[50] *1899 Proceedings* (n 30) 552.

[51] See, eg, *Actes* (n 34) 8 and 30.

[52] Nabulsi, *Traditions* (n 43) 63, see also 173.

[53] *Actes* (n 34) 7 and 29.

[54] Crawford, '*Levée en Masse*' (n 38) 342–43.

[55] ibid 343.

[56] 1907 Hague Regulations, art 2.

The attempt to impose on the population's patriotic action requirements which would force them to assume the characteristics of regular armed forces reflects what Frédéric Mégret calls a 'fantasy about sameness' based on the Western stereotype of armed forces and soldiering.[57] It also shows that, while the *levée en masse* was understood by some as a necessary extension of the state for the defence of the nation, others regarded it as a threat to the regular and organised conflict between standing armies.

The exceptional permission for individuals who do not belong to the armed forces to lawfully participate in hostilities was notably granted to the population of a *non-occupied* territory acting *collectively*. The *projet* stated explicitly, in 'chilling words' according to Nabulsi,[58] that resisting inhabitants of occupied territory 'peuvent être déférés à la justice et ne sont pas considérés comme prisonniers de guerre'.[59] The inhabitants of occupied territory were expected to submit to the new authority, despite the occupying power's lack of title of sovereignty. At one point, it was suggested that the resisting population could be recognised as combatants if they were fulfilling the conditions under Article 9, and if they were fighting in an organised manner for national defence, under the order of the government, and in accordance with the law.[60] Ultimately, in the absence of an agreement, the question of the legitimacy and lawfulness of a *levée en masse* in already occupied territory was deliberately left to 'le droit des gens non écrit'.[61] States which promoted the participation of the population in national defence, in particular, seemed to prefer the uncertainty and vagueness of the unwritten laws of war.[62] Similarly, individuals who acted in isolation, or who alternated between peaceful existence and participation in hostilities without fulfilling the conditions of regular combatants or the *levée en masse* were also removed from the Declaration to be left to *lex non scripta*.[63] The original *projet* had still declared the latter liable to be delivered to military justice.[64] In the adopted written laws of war, these irregular fighters were neither defined nor protected.[65]

The importance of the unwritten laws of war in this context should not be underestimated. The Italian delegation submitted a statement of interpretation at the Brussels Conference that the explicit definition of combatants in Article 9

[57] F Mégret, 'From "Savages" to "Unlawful Combatants": A Postcolonial Look at International Humanitarian Law's "Other"' in A Orford (ed), *International Law and Its Others* (Cambridge, Cambridge University Press, 2006) 307.

[58] Nabulsi, *Traditions* (n 43) 16.

[59] *Actes* (n 34) 6; 'may be delivered to justice and are not considered as prisoners of war' (author's translation).

[60] ibid 57.

[61] ibid 45 and 34.

[62] ibid 33.

[63] ibid 6, 34 and 45.

[64] ibid 6.

[65] Scheipers (n 11) 103.

of the Declaration was not exhaustive.[66] It found support among the participating small states and also France. The negotiations at the Conference indicate that it was considered neither advantageous nor feasible to provide every individual with a status under the written laws of war. Indeed, the delegates not only acknowledged the possibility that certain categories of individuals fall outside of its scope, but also that this may have both beneficial as well as detrimental consequences.[67] The written laws of war neither enabled nor constrained the participation of these individuals in hostilities; yet they also did not impose restrictions on the enemy state's response. Individuals who did not qualify as combatants could be subjected to military force, often with even less restraint than employed against lawful belligerents, if military necessity so required. This is because the combatant status in the written laws of war did not serve to identify the sole legitimate targets of attack. While states recognised the need for clarity and certainty that an international convention on the laws of war could provide, an understanding of the desirability of only regulating a limited field of situations under the instrument was widespread at the Conference. Consequently, certain *lacunae* were intentional in the creation of the rules.

A similar approach was adopted at the First Hague Peace Conference. The Belgian delegate Auguste Beernaert justified it by saying that 'there are certain points which cannot be the subject of a convention and which it would be better to leave, as at present, under the governance of that tacit and common law which arises from the principles of the law of nations'.[68] Although a renewed attempt to broaden the scope of the law to the population in already occupied territory was made,[69] the matter was again left to the unwritten laws of war. The general response to the proposed additional article[70] suggests that the right to resistance of the population in an invaded country continued to exist outside of the Hague Regulations. The incompleteness of the conventional law became entrenched in the so-called 'Martens Clause',[71] which declares:

> Until a more complete code of the laws of war is issued, the High Contracting Parties think it right to declare that in cases not included in the Regulations adopted by them, populations and belligerents remain under the protection and empire of the principles of international law, as they result from the usages established between civilized nations, from the laws of humanity, and the requirements of the public conscience.[72]

[66] *Actes* (n 34) 50.

[67] See, eg, ibid 31 and 39.

[68] *1899 Proceedings* (n 30) 502; see also 503 and 519.

[69] ibid 550.

[70] With the exception of the forceful rejection by the German delegate Colonel Gross von Schwarzhoff, see ibid 550 and 554.

[71] R Giladi, 'The Enactment of Irony: Reflections on the Origins of the Martens Clause' (2014) 25 *EJIL* 847, 862.

[72] Convention (II) with Respect to the Laws and Customs of War on Land and its Annex (The Hague, 29 July 1899), Preamble; Convention (IV) Respecting to the Laws and Customs of War on Land and its Annex (The Hague, 18 October 1907), Preamble.

While the Martens Clause 'has come to represent war's subordination to law' generally,[73] it was adopted in the particular context of the disagreement, or even stalemate, over the participation of inhabitants in a *levée en masse* in occupied territory.[74] Leaving this controversial issue deliberately to the silence of the unwritten laws of war seems to have enabled the adoption of an international written code. The Hague Peace Conferences succeeded in establishing a definition of combatants under conventional law. However, the treaty provisions on combatant status were again not regarded as an exhaustive statement of the law.[75] An agreement on the scope of legitimate and lawful participation in hostilities had still not been achieved by the end of the period.

B. The Brussels Conference

The purpose of the Brussels Conference was commonly perceived at the time as no more than an enquiry into the states' understandings of the law and an appraisal of a potential common ground. The Russian delegate and president of the Conference, Baron Jomini, repeatedly emphasised that the Conference did not seek the codification of the law in an instrument binding upon the governments of the participating delegations.[76] Yet it has been suggested that the inability to agree on the recognition of irregular fighters, including the *levée en masse*, as combatants was the principal reason for the failure of the Brussels Conference.[77] According to this interpretation, the absence of a shared understanding of the personal scope of the combatant status proved an obstacle for the creation of a treaty. This disagreement between the participating states was already anticipated at the beginning of the Brussels Conference, and it was decided to commence with the negotiation of less controversial sections. Some representatives voiced their disapproval or regret over this procedure given the importance of the recognition of combatancy for other articles.[78] Indeed, the provisions on the qualification of combatants were considered as 'les points cardinaux de tout le *Projet de convention*'.[79]

[73] Giladi, 'Enactment of Irony' (n 71) 863.

[74] Crawford, '*Levée en Masse*' (n 38) 346; on the controversial drafting history of the Martens Clause see further Nabulsi, *Traditions* (n 43) 161; Giladi, 'Enactment of Irony' (n 71).

[75] *1899 Proceedings* (n 30) 549 and 553–54; JM Spaight, *War Rights on Land* (London, Macmillan and Co, 1911) 54–56; ME O'Connell, 'Historical Development and Legal Basis' in D Fleck (ed), *The Handbook of International Humanitarian Law*, 4th edn (Oxford, Oxford University Press, 2021) 42.

[76] *Actes* (n 34) 4, 27 and 30.

[77] Spaight (n 75) 40; Nabulsi, *Traditions* (n 43) 8; E Crawford, *Non-Binding Norms in International Humanitarian Law: Efficacy, Legitimacy, and Legality* (Oxford, Oxford University Press, 2021) 45–46.

[78] *Actes* (n 34) 11, 16 and 23.

[79] ibid 32.

The Brussels Conference has often been described as an encounter between the different understandings of small and major military states.[80] The negotiations were characterised by mainly two dissimilar discourses of 'small states',[81] comprising Belgium, Switzerland, the Netherlands, Spain, Portugal and Turkey, on the one hand, and the representatives of Germany and Russia, on the other. The two prominent legal scholars who participated in the Brussels Conference, Johann Caspar Bluntschli and Fyodor Martens, later attributed the division between the militarily powerful and small states to their respective roles in history as occupying and occupied powers.[82] The states' corresponding interests significantly influenced their understanding of which individuals legitimately participate in warfare, as well as which individuals should be entitled to lawful participation as recognised combatants. All the small states, which commonly pursued defensive wars, submitted a declaration regarding the non-acceptance of any provision that may compromise their national defence.[83] They framed the *levée en masse* as a normative necessity of their sovereign identity, which conferred on them a right of national self-defence. Consequently, they regarded the population's participation in hostilities for this purpose as legitimate and pleaded for its lawfulness. By appealing to patriotism, 'a civic virtue based on identification with a distinct system of political values',[84] they were relying on a shared system of beliefs which was rooted in the ideational context of the nineteenth century. The ideas and values of nationalism, patriotism and self-defence seemingly legitimated the arguments and form of warfare of these states and their subjects.

The issue of the population's patriotic defence of the nation was of a particular magnitude, and arguably emotionality, for the representatives of small states. This is implied in a long speech by the Belgian delegate Baron Lambermont during the first session of the working commission at the Brussels Conference,[85] with which he defied the agreed order of the agenda which had left the negotiation of the definition of combatants to last. The small states emphasised that the involvement of the population was part of their history, and thus their respective national identity.[86] This argumentation is particularly emphatic in an address by the Spanish delegate Duke of Tetuan who emphasised that '[l]es traditions locales, les conditions géographiques, le caractère des habitants et jusqu'à son histoire' required the involvement of the entire nation in the country's defence.[87]

[80] See, eg, Neff (n 7) 208.

[81] Describing themselves as 'Etats secondaires' and 'petit[s] Etat[s]' in opposition to the 'grands Etats', *Actes* (n 34) 8, 27, 29 and 32.

[82] 'Communications de MM. Bluntschli et Martens sur la Conférence et la Déclaration de Bruxelles' (1874) 6 *Revue de Droit International et de Législation Comparée* 609, 609.

[83] *Actes* (n 34) 8, 11, 21, 24–25 and 41.

[84] Nabulsi, *Traditions* (n 43) 60.

[85] *Actes* (n 34) 8.

[86] ibid 29–30.

[87] ibid 29; 'the local traditions, geographical conditions, the character of the inhabitants and even its history' (author's translation).

The Spanish position may have been informed by the country's recent experience of wars which involved spontaneous patriotic armed resistance by solitary individuals as well as the population in military juntas and *guérillas*.[88] Indeed, the widespread practice in the nineteenth century of 'national wars of invasion and liberation had legitimized a far wider participation in the political sphere through the role played by the common people in resisting foreign occupations'.[89] States had 'both instigated and encouraged' the *levée en masse* as a form of national defence in practice.[90] It has been asserted that a *levée en masse* as described at the Brussels Conference and defined in the Declaration had not occurred in wars preceding the event.[91] Yet, regardless of actual past experience, the construction of the states' histories during the negotiations through narratives and self-portrayals informed their self-perception and interests. The identity of these small states was shaped in their interaction with larger military powers both in confrontation in wars in the past and in the debate at the Conference. This construction reinforced the perception of difference which posed them in opposition to the perceived 'other', the great military states.

On the other side, Germany and Russia 'both possessed large regular armies, [and] intended to keep the definition of lawful belligerency highly restrictive, hence not allowing for a defensive *levée en masse* or even militia forces'.[92] Rotem Giladi argues that they 'preferred law that granted broad licence and sanctified order legitimized by force over the challenges of patriotism, resistance, and revolution'.[93] The Russian delegates, including the president of the Brussels Conference, repeatedly tried to assure the delegations of the small states that the right and duty of states to defend themselves was not denied.[94] However, the main condition advocated by the great military states for the participation of the population was its organisation under military command and regulation under international law.[95]

Although the Franco-Prussian War was deliberately not discussed at the Brussels Conference,[96] the German opposition towards irregular fighters reflected its approach of immediate execution and relentless counter-measures in that war. The argumentation of the Russian delegation, on the other hand, was framed in terms of a collective identity spanning both great military states

[88] Nabulsi, *Traditions* (n 43) 47–49.

[89] ibid 44, see also 46–47.

[90] ibid 52; on 'nations in arms' in the nineteenth century see also Best, *Humanity* (n 1) 112–21.

[91] FF de Martens, *La paix et la guerre: la Conférence de Bruxelles 1874, droits et devoirs des belligérants (leur application pendant la guerre d'Orient 1874–1878), la Conférence de La Haye 1899* (Paris, A Rousseau, 1901) 377; Nabulsi discards Martens' assertion disputing the truthfulness of the work from which he draws, Nabulsi, *Traditions* (n 43) 168.

[92] Scheipers (n 11) 99.

[93] Giladi, 'Enactment of Irony' (n 71) 853.

[94] *Actes* (n 34) 9, 11, 27, 30 and 50.

[95] Nabulsi, *Traditions* (n 43) 16–17.

[96] E Benvenisti and D Lustig, 'Monopolizing War: Codifying the Laws of War to Reassert Governmental Authority, 1856–1874' (2020) 31 *EJIL* 127, 158.

and small states as 'civilised' states engaged in rule-governed warfare,[97] rather than historical state practice. In the opening address, Baron Jomini drew attention to the common challenges of modern warfare for states and their armed forces. Moreover, he appealed to ostensibly shared ideas and values, portraying the Conference as an endeavour based on 'un esprit de bon vouloir sérieux et pratique basé sur les sentiments d'humanité, les devoirs de la civilisation et la solidarité des intérêts généraux'.[98] He reminded the state representatives of the laws of nations already binding upon them, including the laws of war, but which were uncertain and vague and thus in need of clarification and regulation by a written instrument.[99] Nevertheless, the approach was not fully consistent since the Russian delegates also relied on instrumental self-interests in their attempt to persuade small states to adopt the *projet*.[100] For instance, Baron Jomini emphasised that inconveniences may arise from the lack of organisation of the *levée en masse*, endangering the public security of the state itself.[101] Neither of these persuasion techniques proved effective in achieving an agreement between the disparate groups of states. Indeed, invoking a collective identity of 'civilised' states, in particular, seems to have been no more than strategic rhetoric. Although the Russian delegate implied the existence of a community of states bound together in a common endeavour towards a new ideal of warfare, the *projet* was not perceived as a codification of shared values. Instead, '[t]he legal norms proposed so obviously favoured occupying forces that this text became known in European ministries as "The Code of Conquest"'.[102] Moreover, 'state interests' and an 'atomistic outlook' seemed to prevail at the time, where 'each set of state interests was independent of every other' and 'there was no such thing as a general community interest'.[103]

The two groups of states were thus speaking different languages. The discourses of small state identities and the great powers' insistence on the need for organised and regulated warfare intersected in the debate on the *levée en masse*, but they parted again without reaching an agreement. While the legitimacy of small state concerns was (rhetorically) accepted, the construction of diverging identities inhibited the emergence of a common ground and interests which would have facilitated the adoption of rules. The disagreement thus prevented the achievement of a shared understanding of lawful combatancy and possibly the creation of an international binding code at the Brussels Conference.

Indeed, a common normative framework that may have allied the two groups seems to have been absent. Different understandings were expressed whether

[97] See, eg, *Actes* (n 34) 4 and 32.

[98] ibid 4; 'a spirit of serious and practical good will founded on the sentiments of humanity, the duties of civilization, and the solidarity of general interests' (author's translation).

[99] ibid.

[100] ibid 29–30 and 34.

[101] ibid 30.

[102] Nabulsi, *Traditions* (n 43) 6.

[103] Neff (n 7) 171 and 162.

the *projet* was intended as a clarification of general and vague principles in the law of nations,[104] a codification of existing rules and norms,[105] or a progressive development of the law.[106] In its examination of the Brussels Declaration, the IDI described the instrument as containing 'des prescriptions nouvelles, conçues dans un esprit à la fois pratique, humain et progressif'.[107] It is noteworthy that the deliberations at the Conference scarcely drew on existing normative structures, even in the Russian delegation's appeal to a collective identity of rule-governed states. The normative argumentation of small states was framed in terms of legitimacy, rooted in identity, and not in relation to existing (customary) legal rules. Generally, the delegates portrayed 'practices' of warfare as idiosyncratic behaviour of individual states rather than as part of a system of norms.

One particularly remarkable absence in the (acknowledged) ideas and norms informing the negotiation of the combatant status at the Brussels Conference is the Lieber Code. This stands in contrast to the prominence of the 1863 instructions for the United States' armed forces in the conventional narrative on the history of the laws of war. A brief reference to the Lieber Code at the Brussels Conference has been interpreted as meaning that it 'provided the basis for a draft text presented to the various delegations which gathered at Brussels in the summer of 1874'.[108] However, the Code was alluded to only in passing, and without mentioning the author, in an introductory speech at the beginning of the Conference.[109] It is not clear from the original statement whether the national instrument constituted nothing more than an element in the general context of events and developments which inspired the endeavour of the Russian Tsar. Bluntschli and Martens, who had participated in the Brussels Conference, noted later that the Russian Tsar wanted to achieve in Europe what President Lincoln had done in America.[110] The Lieber Code may have thus been an impetus similar to the wars in Europe in the nineteenth century.

Richard Baxter, nonetheless, believes it is 'possible to trace a direct line of personal influence from Dr. Lieber's Code to the Hague Regulations' because of the role of Bluntschli as 'counsellor of the German delegation at the Brussels Conference of 1874, the work of which constituted the basis of the conventions prepared at the Hague Peace Conferences of 1899 and 1907'.[111] The relationship between Bluntschli's endeavour to document the laws of nations, including the

[104] *Actes* (n 34) 4.
[105] ibid 9.
[106] ibid 39.
[107] IDI, 'Examen' (n 29) 134; 'novel recommendations, designed in a spirit that is at once practical, humane and progressive' (author's translation).
[108] Nabulsi, *Traditions* (n 43) 5; see also J Crossland, *War, Law and Humanity: The Campaign to Control Warfare, 1853–1914* (London, Bloomsbury, 2018) 127.
[109] *Actes* (n 34) 7.
[110] 'Bluntschli et Martens' (n 82) 609; *1899 Proceedings* (n 30) 505–06.
[111] R Baxter, 'The First Modern Codification of the Law of War: Francis Lieber and General Orders No. 100 (II)' (1963) 3:26 *IRRC* 234, 249.

laws of war, and the Lieber Code is well-known. Bluntschli himself had declared the influence of his friend Lieber.[112] Commentators at the time remarked upon the resemblance between Bluntschli's work and the draft convention submitted to the Brussels Conference.[113] However, the authorship of the *projet* has been debated both 'in legal doctrine and the general press'.[114] While George Davis and Tracey Leigh Dowdeswell credit it to Bluntschli and Martens respectively, both emphasise the influence of the Lieber Code on these European scholars.[115] Martens proclaimed himself to be behind the Russian draft,[116] whereas Bluntschli's memoirs do not suggest his direct involvement. Instead, he notes in a letter to his wife that an unnamed Russian told him that the *projet* was drafted on the basis of his work.[117] In his study of the Russian Empire's role in the codification of international law, and in particular the laws of war, Peter Holquist makes a case for Martens' authorship of the *projet*.[118] Drawing on Russian archival material and unpublished papers, he observes that Martens' initial draft 'explicitly indicates which articles from the Lieber code serve as the basis for his own articles'.[119] The similarity between the Brussels Declaration and the Lieber Code was also noted by the IDI in its examination of the international instrument.[120] Nevertheless, important differences between the two documents also exist.[121]

More importantly, the Lieber Code, or Bluntschli's work were at no point invoked during the negotiations of the rules at the Brussels Conference. The discourse behind closed doors may have differed from the official recordings. Yet at least the communications of British officials at the time, including letters by the British delegate at the Conference to the Foreign Minister, suggest no more influence of the Lieber Code than the *travaux préparatoires*.[122] Although the

[112] JC Bluntschli, *Das Moderne Kriegsrecht der Civilisirten Staten: Als Rechtsbuch Dargestellt* (Nördlingen, Beck, 1866) III.

[113] Nabulsi, *Traditions* (n 43) 7.

[114] VV Pustogarov, *Our Martens: F.F. Martens, International Lawyer and Architect of Peace* (WE Butler ed and tr, The Hague, Kluwer Law International, 2000) 109.

[115] GB Davis, 'Doctor Francis Lieber's Instructions for the Government of Armies in the Field' (1907) 1 *AJIL* 13, 22; Dowdeswell (n 10) 823–24; Theodor Meron also accredits it to Bluntschli, seemingly on the basis of Davis, T Meron, 'Francis Lieber's Code and Principles of Humanity' (1997) 36 *Columbia Journal of Transnational Law* 269, 279.

[116] de Martens, *La paix* (n 91) VIII.

[117] JC Bluntschli, *Denkwürdiges aus meinem Leben, III. Band* (R Seyerlen ed, Nördlingen 1884) 354.

[118] P Holquist, 'Russian Empire as a "Civilized State": International Law as Principle and Practice in Imperial Russia, 1874–1878' (2004) The National Council for Eurasian and East European Research, Title VIII Program, www.ucis.pitt.edu/nceeer/2004_818-06g_Holquist.pdf, 11–12; see also V Ivanenko, 'The Origins, Causes and Enduring Significance of the Martens Clause: A View from Russia' (2022) 104:920–921 *IRRC* 1708, 1716–17.

[119] Holquist (n 118) 32.

[120] IDI, 'Examen' (n 29) 133–34.

[121] A Roberts, 'Foundational Myths in the Laws of War: The 1863 Lieber Code, and the 1864 Geneva Convention' (2019) 20 *Melbourne Journal of International Law* 158, 180–81.

[122] *Brussels Conference vol 1: Rules of War and Miscellaneous* (11 April 1874–14 July 1874) FO83/481, The National Archive (TNA); *Brussels Conference vol 2: Rules of War and Miscellaneous*

debate at the Brussels Conference focused on irregular combatants, the negotiations bear no sign that the detailed categorisation and differentiated treatment of individuals in the Lieber Code,[123] nor Lieber's work on guerrilla warfare[124] were considered by the state representatives. John Fabian Witt still believes that the Lieber Code influenced the Brussels Declaration's provisions on belligerents and guerrilla fighters. Attributing the authorship of the *projet* to Martens, he argues that the conditions for combatant status are derived from 'Lieber's functional redefinition of legitimate combatants'.[125] However, the criteria listed in Article 9 of the *projet* and the Brussels Declaration as such appear neither in the Lieber Code nor in Bluntschli's elaboration of *Das Moderne Kriegsrecht.* Eyal Benvenisti and Doreen Lustig observe Bluntschli's evolving understanding of irregular fighters throughout his successive publications in the 1860s and 1870s, culminating in the portrayal of 'the conditions stipulated in Brussels' Article 9 as reflecting the law' in his 1877 edition of *Das Moderne Völkerrecht der Civilisirten Staten.*[126] The criteria in Article 9 had been notably proposed prior to the Diplomatic Conference by a legal practitioner in Great Britain, Henry Richmond Droop.[127] Dowdeswell argues that Droop's paper submitted to the Juridical Society in 1870 contains an 'early formulation' of the criteria for the qualification as combatants.[128] Although it precedes the Brussels Conference, no recognition of Droop's work can be found in the deliberations at the Conference either. It is, therefore, uncertain whether the similarity is due to a correlation or to causation. Yet if Martens authored the *projet* underlying the Brussels Conference, it is noteworthy that he is known to have read Droop's paper and believed that '[c]et auteur examine en détail la question contestée des francs-tireurs ou des volontaires'.[129]

(15 July 1874–18 September 1874) FO83/482, TNA; *Brussels Conference vol 3: Rules of War, Sir A. Horsford and Miscellaneous* (25 July 1874–21 September 1874) FO83/483, TNA; *Brussels Conference vol 4: Rules of War, Sir A. Horsford and Miscellaneous* (27 July 1874–4 September 1874) FO83/484, TNA; *Brussels Conference vol 5: Rules of War and Miscellaneous* (28 September 1874–31 August 1874) FO83/485, TNA.

[123] Lieber Code, arts 81–85.

[124] F Lieber, *Guerrilla Parties: Considered with Reference to the Laws and Usages of War* (New York, D Van Nostrand, 1862).

[125] JF Witt, *Lincoln's Code – The Laws of War in American History* (New York, Free Press, 2012) 344–45.

[126] Benvenisti and Lustig, 'Monopolizing War' (n 96) 160.

[127] HR Droop, 'On the Relations between an Invading Army and the Inhabitants, and the Conditions under which Irregular Troops are Entitled to the Same Treatment as Regular Soldiers' in *Papers Read Before the Juridical Society: 1863–1870*, vol 3 (London, Wildy & Sons, 1871).

[128] Dowdeswell (n 10) 828; Droop himself stated that his proposed criteria for combatant status 'are probably in some respects rather beyond what is expressly required by Professors Lieber and Bluntschli, the most recent authorities who have treated the subject at any length, but I do not think there is much substantial difference between us', Droop (n 127) 720–21.

[129] de Martens, *La paix* (n 91) 96–97 and 374–75, 'this author examines in detail the contested question of *francs-tireurs* and volunteers' (author's translation); see also Dowdeswell (n 10) 831–32; Bluntschli also already referred to Droop's paper prior to the Brussels Conference, JC Bluntschli, *Das Moderne Völkerrecht der Civilisirten Staten: Als Rechtsbuch Dargestellt* (Nördlingen, Beck, 1872) 321.

Arguably, the initial motivation behind the invitation of states to Brussels and the line of descent of the *projet* may be less important for the understanding of individuals under the Brussels Declaration than the negotiations at the Diplomatic Conference themselves. While the drafter(s) of the *projet* may have relied on existing rules such as the Lieber Code, the state delegations seemingly still considered it necessary to deliberate the meaning and status of individuals participating in warfare in depth at the Brussels Conference. They discussed the issue in light of their respective histories and within their identity discourses, as mentioned above, rather than in relation to definitions and rules in written texts. Their deliberations were informed by individual and common experiences in the past, and their expectations of wars in the future in the European context.

The non-mentioning of the Lieber Code in the discourse may have been partly due to the Eurocentric nature of the Brussels Conference. Different explanations have been offered for the non-participation of the United States of America,[130] which Baron Jomini described as the most natural participant given that it was the first to codify the laws of war.[131] An invitation was deliberately not extended to South American states since the participating delegations believed it more practical to limit the general inquiry into the matter, without the adoption of a treaty, to European states.[132] The Conference was thus at first confined to European states with representatives of Turkey arriving late.[133] In this continental context, some delegates drew comparisons between the rules under deliberation and military codes of their own governments and European states more generally.[134] It is likely that as an American domestic instrument, the Lieber Code may not have been perceived as part of the normative environment within which the participating states attempted to make sense of situations of warfare for the purpose of international rules binding upon them. It remains open to speculation whether the United States' involvement in the negotiations would have changed the dynamics of the discourses.

The nature of the negotiations and arguments at the Brussels Conference, including the absence of a normative discourse rooted in the Lieber Code and international legal scholarship, may have also been the result of the dominance of military officials and diplomats. State representation had evolved since the military commission which negotiated the 1868 St Petersburg Declaration

[130] See, eg, G Rolin-Jaequemyns, 'Chronique du droit international. 1871–1874' (1875) 7 *Revue de Droit International et de Législation Comparée* 70, 88; P Bordwell, *The Law of War between Belligerents: A History and Commentary* (Chicago, Callaghan & Co, 1908) 102; Pustogarov, *Our Martens* (n 114) 112.

[131] *Actes* (n 34) 15.

[132] ibid 15, see also 29.

[133] ibid 32.

[134] ibid 9, 13 and 43.

given that Bluntschli and Martens formed part of the 1874 delegations as jurisconsults.[135] Yet not only have these two lawyers been described as having had 'progovernmental leanings',[136] but also their influence on the negotiation of the regulation and protection of individuals was arguably minor. During the debate over the constitution of commissions, Bluntschli submitted that in addition to military and diplomatic perspectives, the viewpoint of lawyers would also be important.[137] In his centennial study of the Brussels Declaration, Jean de Breucker derives from a letter by Baron Lambermont, the head of the Belgian delegation, that a commission of jurists had been indeed considered, but was opposed by Italy, England and France.[138] Although Bluntschli's proposal that states could draw on their military, diplomatic or legal delegates as their respective representative in the working commission was accepted,[139] no jurist was selected. Only Bluntschli himself was present from the beginning, while Martens joined two weeks late. The *travaux préparatoires* offer no indication of their role behind the scenes, but their involvement in the plenary meetings was limited to commenting on drafts prepared by the working commission. An asymmetric power relationship between diplomatic actors and especially military officials, on the one hand, and lawyers, on the other, persisted.[140] The laws of war were seemingly still perceived as the domain of the military, and not the lawyers.

Indeed, the expert knowledge of lawyers was only referred to with reservations and when it aligned with the state's preconceived perspective. Baron Lambermont emphasised the difference between 'un publiciste déposant ses idées dans une revue et un gouvernement responsable de ses actes et de ses paroles'; namely, '[l]'écrivain parle du service obligatoire et universel et il en proclame l'excellence' whereas 'le représentant du pays s'exprime avec prudence'.[141] Baron Jomini invoked an extract of the work of the eminent Belgian lawyer Gustave Rolin-Jaequemyns in support of the Russian position requiring the regulation of the population's involvement in national defence.[142] However, it was emphasised

[135] Rolin-Jaecquemyns, 'Chronique' (n 130) 90. The Belgian delegate Charles Faider, a jurist and the chief prosecutor at the Court of Cassation in Belgium, has also been described as a representative of the science of international law, É de Laveleye, *Les actes de la Conférence de Bruxelles et la participation de la Belgique à la Conférence de Saint-Pétersbourg* (Brussels, Muquardt, 1875) 4. However, he played an even less prominent role at the Conference.

[136] E Benvenisti and D Lustig, 'Taming Democracy: Codifying the Laws of War to Restore the European Order, 1856–1874' (2017) Legal Studies Research Paper Series 28/2017, papers.ssrn.com/sol3/papers.cfm?abstract_id=2985781, 6.

[137] *Actes* (n 34) 8.

[138] J de Breucker, 'La Déclaration de Bruxelles de 1874 concernant les lois et coutumes de la guerre' (1974) 28 *La chronique de politique étrangère* 3, 15.

[139] *Actes* (n 34) 8.

[140] See also Crossland (n 108) 127.

[141] *Actes* (n 34) 29; 'a publicist who lays down his ideas in a review and a government responsible for its actions and words', 'the writer speaks of obligatory and universal service and proclaims its excellence' whereas 'the representative of a country expresses himself with prudence' (author's translation).

[142] ibid 27.

that the theoretical exposition was rooted in recent experience of war and also conformed with the understanding of military necessities.[143] Although Baron Jomini introduced the work of the commission to the plenary as having taken into consideration military necessity, humanitarianism and the science of international law,[144] a clear bias towards military representatives and considerations is evident in the proceedings.[145] Commenting on the Brussels Declaration, Rolin-Jaequemyns himself bemoaned the uneven representation of jurists at the Conference, as one of the three 'facteurs du droit international de la guerre: l'Armée, la Diplomatie, la Science'.[146] Other commentators believed that the dominance of military delegates was beneficial. Percy Bordwell, for instance, argued that their participation brought experience of contemporary warfare and thus practical knowledge of the situations to be regulated to the Brussels Conference, and, as a result, bestowed the rules with authority.[147] It was their understanding that seems to have shaped the different approaches to legitimate and lawful participation in hostilities, and prevented an agreement on a binding definition of the combatant status at the Brussels Conference.

C. The Hague Peace Conferences

Scholars have dismissed the 1874 Brussels Declaration as not having 'garnered widespread acceptance'[148] and that it 'was always likely to be a "shipwreck"'.[149] However, this appraisal may undervalue its significance for later developments in the laws of war. Vladimir Pustogarov argues that 'the objections of the [Brussels] Conference participants testified to the unreadiness of the ruling circles and public opinion in many countries to accept the very idea of codification' at the time.[150] Even so, according to him, the Conference contributed to a more receptive atmosphere for further efforts 25 years later.[151] The laws of war were again included on the agenda of the First Hague Peace Conference in 1899. The revision of the Brussels Declaration was one of the Conference's objectives, as stated in the programme distributed by the Russian government, who had initiated the event.[152] The adoption of a binding international agreement

[143] ibid 30.
[144] ibid 48.
[145] See, eg, ibid 30.
[146] Rolin-Jaequemyns, 'Chronique' (n 130) 90–91; see also W Besobrasoff, 'Extrait d'une note présentée par M. Besobrasoff' (1875) 7 *Revue de Droit International et de Législation Comparée* 529, 552.
[147] Bordwell (n 130) 111.
[148] Scheipers (n 11) 100.
[149] Nabulsi, *Traditions* (n 43) 8.
[150] Pustogarov, *Our Martens* (n 114) 113.
[151] ibid.
[152] *1899 Proceedings* (n 30) 50.

in the form of the 1899 Hague Regulations was in all likelihood the result of various (political) factors. Robert Kolb suggests that '[t]he persisting differences in national regulations combined with experiences with abuse, disputes and accusations of violation provided a strong impetus to an international "codification" of the law of warfare'.[153] In her study of *The Hague Conferences and International Politics, 1898–1915*, Maartje Abbenhuis emphasises that 'recent conflicts, including the Franco-Prussian War, the Sino-Japanese War and the Spanish-American War, brought out common concerns relating to the conduct of war',[154] and public expectations further informed governments.[155] Without negating these possible driving forces, the following will show that the normative context also played an increasing role in the negotiation of the laws of war at the turn of the century.

Unlike in 1874, the negotiation of the laws of war on land at the First Hague Peace Conference was largely limited to the discussion and confirmation of a previously established text, the Brussels Declaration. Similarly, at the Second Hague Peace Conference in 1907, the Second Commission responsible for the laws of war only debated proposed amendments to the 1899 Hague Regulations, rather than each individual rule or the regime as a whole. The changing normative environment transformed the discourse at the Conferences more generally. The deliberation of the laws of war, both in 1899 and in 1907, was accompanied by a narrative of a shared long-standing tradition to ameliorate war and to mitigate its consequences under law. This narrative appropriated national and international, successful and failed law-making attempts including, for example, the St Petersburg Declaration and the Brussels Declaration, and culminated in the Hague Peace Conferences themselves.[156] While the provisions of the Lieber Code were still not drawn upon in the negotiation of specific rules, the adoption of the instrument was incorporated into this account of ostensible progress leading up to the Hague Regulations. The narrative was seemingly shaping a collective identity of states based on a perceived history of norm-creation and norm-development, rather than a history of the conduct of wars. This identity construction even included states which had not participated at the earlier conferences on the laws of war. As the following chapters will show, a similar approach to the reaffirmation and development of the laws of war has been repeatedly adopted since then.

[153] R Kolb, 'The Main Epochs of Modern International Humanitarian Law since 1864 and Their Related Dominant Legal Constructions' in KM Larsen, CG Cooper and G Nystuen (eds), *Searching for a "Principle of Humanity" in International Humanitarian Law* (Cambridge, Cambridge University Press, 2013) 40.

[154] M Abbenhuis, *The Hague Conferences and International Politics, 1898–1915* (London, Bloomsbury, 2019) 86.

[155] ibid 100.

[156] See, eg, *1899 Proceedings* (n 30) 505–08 and 518; JB Scott (ed), *The Proceedings of the Hague Peace Conferences: The Conference of 1907 – Translation of the Official Texts*, vol 3 (Oxford, Oxford University Press, 1921) (hereafter *1907 Proceedings*) 1–2 and 97–98.

It is notable that Martens, presiding over the 1899 sub-commission responsible for the laws of war, delivered a speech on this constructed history not at the beginning of its work but rather in light of the difficulties that the question of the combatant status posed.[157] He thus countered the opening to this topic by the Belgian delegate Beernaert, who had conveyed his concerns over submitting invasion and national self-defence to a written code of laws. The issue of national self-defence, in particular, still proved emotive, and a few small state representatives resorted to narratives about their own and other small states' experience in promoting an expansion of the combatant status beyond members of the armed forces.[158] Beernaert, for example, depicted the defence of Belgium by its patriotic inhabitants as a result of its geographic idiosyncrasy and history, and a necessity for a small state.[159] Conversely, Alexander notes that Germany, 'which was still traumatized by the experience of fighting the *francs-tireurs* (free-shooters) of the 1870–1 Franco-Prussian War, was the most vigorously opposed to irregular combatants' and declared that 'fighting outside the state military was savage, inhumane, and unfair'.[160] States' experience of war thus still informed their focus and argumentation in the negotiations. However, the deliberation of the definition of the contested combatant status primarily centred on its formulation in the Brussels Declaration. The provisions on the combatant status and the *levée en masse* were adopted, and the continuing disagreement over legitimate and lawful participation in warfare was accommodated by the vague Martens Clause as a saving clause.[161] The additional emphasis of a shared history and need for regulations appears to have been persuasive enough, and prevented individual state or group identity narratives from dominating the debate. The prevailing normative discourse around the turn of the century may be seen as an indication for an increased willingness of the states to regulate warfare under a treaty.

The British delegate General Sir John Ardagh still declared his concern that the attempt of adopting an international convention would meet with the same challenges as the Brussels Declaration, voicing his preference for a non-binding declaration instead.[162] In response, Martens again endorsed a collective identity of states by explaining that the motivation behind the First Hague Peace Conference was the founding of a society among 'nations of the civilized world' or a 'mutual insurance association' for which the 'by-laws' would comprise the Brussels Declaration.[163] A similar persuasion strategy was unsuccessfully pursued by the Russian delegation in 1874, as noted above. Rolin-Jaequemyns,

[157] *1899 Proceedings* (n 30) 505–08, see also 518.
[158] ibid 502–05 and 551.
[159] ibid 503–04.
[160] Alexander, 'Genesis' (n 12) 364; see also *1899 Proceedings* (n 30) 552–53.
[161] See section I.A.
[162] *1899 Proceedings* (n 30) 517.
[163] ibid 518; the argument was repeated in the sub-commissions 'Report to the Conference', drafted by Edouard Rolin, the son of Gustave Rolin-Jaequemyns.

one of the principal founding members of the IDI, had already observed a movement towards the regularisation of international relations which entailed 'la transformation de la *société de fait* qui existe entre nations en une véritable *société de droit*' in 1873.[164] According to him, the development was manifested in diplomatic action and the engagement of individual legal scientists.[165] Indeed, Martti Koskenniemi also observes that Europe at the time was marked by '*l'esprit d'internationalité*, a new spirit that taught nations and races to follow certain common principles not only in their mutual relations but also in their domestic legislation'.[166] However, the shared values and norms of such a society, if it indeed existed, did not yet seem to extend to warfare at the time of the Brussels negotiations. The ideational and normative context had seemingly evolved by the time of the Hague Peace Conferences where the discourse appears to have been more generally influenced by a shared belief in the creation of a system of common norms and rules. Several European states had adopted national military codes since the Lieber Code and mostly following the 1874 Brussels Conference,[167] which may have contributed to a more conducive environment for an international agreement. Even if a collective identity of states may still not have existed then, a changing self-understanding of states seems to have enabled a mutual standard for how future wars should be fought.

The construction of a collective identity was seemingly limited to what were considered 'civilised' states, restricting the scope of the adopted international law in effect.[168] While scholarship in this period considered the relationship between 'civilised' armed forces and 'uncivilised' peoples, or the regulation of so-called 'barbarous forces',[169] the negotiations of the Hague Regulations are silent on these issues. Nevertheless, Mégret argues that the existence of a colonial '"constitutive other" … was central to the *emergence* of the laws of war' in which European states sought to distance themselves from the 'uncivilized', 'barbarian', 'savage' other.[170] He observes that the combatant status in particular reflects the Western idea of legitimate warfare at the exclusion of the

[164] G Rolin-Jaequemyns, 'De la nécessité d'organiser une institution scientifique permanente pour favoriser l'étude et les progrès du droit international' (1873) 5 *Revue de Droit International et de Législation Comparée* 463, 463.

[165] ibid 463–64.

[166] M Koskenniemi, *The Gentle Civilizer of Nations: The Rise and Fall of International Law 1870–1960* (Cambridge, Cambridge University Press, 2004) 13.

[167] Including Germany, Russia, France, the Netherlands, Switzerland, Denmark, Spain, Portugal; TE Holland, *The Laws of War on Land (Written and Unwritten)* (Oxford, Clarendon Press, 1908) 72–73; A Roberts and R Guelff, *Documents on the Laws of War*, 3rd edn (Oxford, Oxford University Press, 2010) 12–13; Benvenisti and Lustig, 'Monopolizing War' (n 96) 165.

[168] *1899 Proceedings* (n 30) 518; see also H Kinsella, *The Image Before the Weapon: A Critical History of the Distinction Between Combatant and Civilian* (Ithaca, Cornell University Press, 2011) 104–11.

[169] See, eg, Bluntschli, *Völkerrecht* (n 129) 298 and 314; A Pillet, *Les Lois actuelles de la Guerre* (Paris, A Rousseau, 1898) 40; L Oppenheim, *International Law: A Treatise, vol II: War and Neutrality* (London, Longmans, Green, and Co, 1906) para 82.

[170] Mégret, 'From "Savages" to "Unlawful Combatants"' (n 57) 267.

'uncivilized' other.[171] A narrow understanding of the application of the laws of war can also be inferred from the setting of the development of the rules in the European context, despite the increasing involvement of non-European states. Arthur Eyffinger observes that the US representative was surprisingly quiet in the sub-commission revising the rules on land warfare,[172] notwithstanding the appropriation of the perceived progress in the laws of war by American delegates and scholars following the Hague Peace Conferences. They asserted a direct link between the Lieber Code and the Declaration as well as Regulations and, additionally, stressed the influence of the United States of America on this basis.[173]

Another important distinguishing factor in the deliberations of the laws of war at the turn of the century compared to the Brussels Conference is that several lawyers actively participated as delegates in the two Hague Peace Conferences. Martha Finnemore describes the 'concentration of legal talent in what earlier would have been a political and diplomatic gathering' as 'unusual for its time'.[174] She believes that international law, which became professionally organized in the nineteenth century, exerted an increasing influence in international diplomatic assemblies.[175] Pustogarov asserts that '[a]s a whole the Conference assembled the cream of international lawyers'.[176] The sub-commission in charge of the laws of war on land, in particular, included prominent jurists. According to Eyffinger, it was even dominated by 'the international lawyers who held sway and dictated debate, not the military men'.[177] He acknowledges that in 1899, 'international lawyers were still mostly peremptorily dismissed by diplomats as "mere technicians" whose intrusion into their sacred realm was deemed unduly presumptuous'.[178] Yet their 'ius standi' in the Hague Peace Conferences had been facilitated by their 'firmly established doctrinal and personal links with parliamentarians and pacifists' by this time.[179]

Eyffinger believes that it was due to Martens' influence that the revision of the Brussels Declaration was included in the programme of the First Hague

[171] ibid 304–08.

[172] A Eyffinger, *The 1899 Hague Peace Conference: 'The Parliament of Man, the Federation of the World'* (The Hague, Kluwer Law International, 1999) 263.

[173] JB Scott, 'The Work of the Second Hague Peace Conference' (1908) 2 *AJIL* 1, 11; E Nys, 'Francis Lieber – His Life and His Works: Part I' (1911) 5 *AJIL* 84, 86; JH Choate, *The Two Hague Conferences* (New York, Kraus Reprint, 1969) 13; Seth Low provides a more tentative narrative of the relationship, S Low, 'The International Conference of Peace' (1899) 169 *The North American Review* 625, 632–33.

[174] M Finnemore, *The Purpose of Intervention: Changing Beliefs About the Use of Force* (Ithaca, Cornell University Press, 2003) 49.

[175] ibid 26.

[176] Pustogarov, *Our Martens* (n 114) 315.

[177] Eyffinger, *1899 Hague Peace Conference* (n 172) 263.

[178] A Eyffinger, *The 1907 Hague Peace Conference: 'The Conscience of the Civilized World'* (The Hague, JudiCap, 2007) 12.

[179] ibid.

Peace Conference in the first instance.[180] Martens himself seemed to consider the 1899 Hague Regulations as not only a success but as an adoption of the Brussels Declaration, his 'beloved child'.[181] He played a particularly prominent role at the 1899 Conference, being 'an acknowledged expert in the field' and having attended the Brussels Conference 25 years before.[182] The changing constitution of state representatives may have also influenced the dynamics of the law-making process in 1899 and 1907 where the existing normative framework was more significantly drawn on than state practice in war. In all likelihood, lawyers were driving the development towards a more technical legal debate. They may have themselves been empowered by the normative environment and the apparent receptiveness of states for a written code on the laws of war. The general acceptance of binding and non-binding international instruments afforded their normative argumentation legitimacy and persuasiveness.

The work of the epistemic community of international lawyers may have also been indirectly influential. While the Brussels Declaration was used as a working draft to facilitate the achievement of an agreement, occasional reference was also made to the IDI's 1880 Oxford Manual on the laws of war.[183] Eyffinger describes the influence of both instruments, despite their non-binding natures, as 'incisive none the less'.[184] The IDI had published the Oxford Manual as a possible 'basis for national legislation in each State'.[185] While its efforts remained inconsequential in this respect,[186] it may have shaped the understanding of some of the leading participants at the First Hague Peace Conference. Several state representatives in the sub-commissions in charge of regulating the laws of war and in the drafting committee in 1899, were members of the IDI and some had even been involved in the drafting of the Oxford Manual.[187] Its impact can possibly be seen in the rearranged structure of the Regulations. While individual provisions in the Manual resemble the Brussels Declaration, the IDI notably changed the order of the sections and articles. The Manual thus follows more closely Rolin-Jaequemyns's proposal that it would be more logical 'de commencer par le *droit des personnes*: qui fait la guerre et contre qui se fait-elle', namely combatants and non-combatants.[188] This structure is even more distinct in the Hague Regulations, which begin with a section 'On Belligerents'

[180] Eyffinger, *1899 Hague Peace Conference* (n 172) 38.
[181] Cited in Pustogarov, *Our Martens* (n 114) 178.
[182] Eyffinger, *1899 Hague Peace Conference* (n 172) 263.
[183] See, eg, *1899 Proceedings* (n 30) 422, 488 and 510–11; *1907 Proceedings* (n 156) 131.
[184] Eyffinger, *1899 Hague Peace Conference* (n 172) 260.
[185] Oxford Manual, Preamble.
[186] Nabulsi, *Traditions* (n 43) 9.
[187] Notably Martens and den Beer Poortugael; *1899 Proceedings* (n 30) 416; 'Un nouveau manuel pour les lois de la guerre' (1880) 11:44 *Bulletin International des Sociétés de Secours Aux Militaires Blessés* 163, 166; G Moynier, 'Rapport de M. Moynier' (1882) 5 *AIDI* 150, 150.
[188] Rolin-Jaequemyns, 'Chronique' (n 130) 96.

that identifies who qualifies as combatants and POWs. The reordering of the 1899 provisions was also justified as 'more methodological' in the sub-commission's report to the Plenary Assembly.[189]

Normative standards, however, were still drawn upon selectively. The Hague Peace Conferences relied primarily on sets of rules negotiated and adopted by states, namely the Brussels Declaration and later the 1899 Hague Regulations. No attention was paid to scholarly treatises which collated principles and rules of the laws of war.[190] It is also notable that awareness of, or possibly disposition to acknowledge, the role of the Lieber Code diverged significantly between the participants and even within national delegations. As a lawyer, Martens emphasised the significance of the Code as part of the context of efforts to regulate warfare by international agreement at the First Hague Peace Conference.[191] In contrast, the Russian diplomatic delegate Nelidow, president of the Second Hague Peace Conference, mentioned the instrument in a less celebratory manner in his opening speech. His remark that it was created by 'a professor – Dr. LIEBER, I believe' suggests the minor importance attached to the authorship of the instrument.[192] The framing of the negotiations within the context of a history of law-making more generally was primarily led by the lawyers Martens and Beernaert. Martens, in particular, has been described as having held a progressive view of international law and its evolution, believing 'that the system of international law was no longer built on the absolute sovereignty of states, but on the idea of an international community of which sovereign states were merely a part'.[193]

The concept of combatants enshrined in the Brussels Declaration and the Hague Regulations is virtually the same. Yet its deliberations at the 1874 and 1899 Diplomatic Conferences took different shapes. The former was hampered by the states' preoccupation with their experience of warfare in the past and expectations about future warfare, whereas the latter was set in a more conducive normative environment. The existence of an international set of rules, albeit non-binding, provided the delegates with a starting point and allowed a more technical debate. The apparent increased willingness of states to agree on international standards for the laws of war which would be implemented by their own armed forces was arguably reflected in the more legal nature of both

[189] *1899 Proceedings* (n 30) 51.

[190] See, eg, HY Halleck, *International Law; or Rules Regulating the Intercourse of States in Peace and War* (San Francisco, Bancroft & Co, 1861); Bluntschli, *Kriegsrecht* (n 112); DD Field, *Draft Outlines of an International Code* (New York, Baker, Voorhis & Co, 1872); WE Hall, *International Law* (Oxford, Clarendon Press, 1880); F de Martens, *Traité de Droit International, tome III* (A Léo tr, Paris, Chevalier-Marescq, 1887); Pillet (n 169).

[191] *1899 Proceedings* (n 30) 505–06.

[192] JB Scott (ed), *The Proceedings of the Hague Peace Conferences: The Conference of 1907 – Translation of the Official Texts*, vol 1 (Oxford, Oxford University Press, 1920) 47.

[193] L Mälksoo, 'F.F. Martens and His Time: When Russia Was an Integral Part of the European Tradition of International Law' (2014) 25 *EJIL* 811, 822.

the discourse and the selected state delegates. These changes in the setting and negotiations likely proved beneficial for the acceptance of individual rules on warfare, including the combatant status, even though they did not lead to an agreement.

II. CIVILIANS – THE ABSENCE OF A CONCEPT

It has been observed that '[t]he law of war of the nineteenth century was only marginally concerned with civilian persons and their protection', not least because they were 'thought to stand "outside" the war and hence, being aloof, not to be in need of any specific regulation'.[194] Kolb argues that the 'relative absence of the civilian' can, inter alia, be explained by

> the optimistic belief that land warfare, with its focus on professional armies, would barely impinge on civilians, and in those exceptional cases where it did, this impingement would in any case be inevitable (such as in besieged towns) so that the law would not be able to do much about it, except by special agreement between the belligerents.[195]

Nonetheless, individuals who do not qualify as combatants fall under a complex set of implied regulations and explicit protections under the Brussels Declaration and Hague Regulations. This section examines how these individuals were in fact considered as implicated in or affected by the conduct of war in the development of the early written laws of war. It explains which understandings of these individuals underpin the rules in the international instruments and their silences.

To begin with, it needs to be emphasised that the term 'non-combatant' is only employed in the provision declaring that '[t]he armed forces of the belligerent parties may consist of combatants and non-combatants', and that both categories have the right to POW status.[196] The Brussels *projet* specified that combatants would take an active and direct part in the operation of war, whereas non-combatants were involved in different administrative branches of the military. It also used the term for religious and medical military personnel and declared that these individuals enjoyed neutrality because of their role in treating the wounded and sick.[197] Due to their position in the armed forces, non-combatants were still exposed to the dangers of war. Knut Ipsen argues that the provision was the result of an awareness of the diversity in the constitution of the armed forces, rather than an intention to establish a non-combatant status

[194] Kolb, 'Main Epochs' (n 153) 38.

[195] ibid.

[196] Brussels Declaration, art 11; see also 1899 and 1907 Hague Regulations, art 3.

[197] *Actes* (n 34) 5–6; these were also occasionally referred to as 'personnages civils' who belong to the armed forces during the 1874 discussions, see 13 and 16.

in international law or to equate the status of non-fighting military personnel to 'civilians'.[198] Indeed, while the contemporaneous scholar Bordwell considered the provision in the Brussels Declaration as 'almost superfluous', he went on to state that 'it was deemed advisable to add in order to ensure to the noncombatant part of the army equal treatment with the combatant'.[199] Belonging to the armed forces and the right to POW status provided non-combatants with a protective shield,[200] whereas individuals who did not belong to the armed forces may have been subjected to more adverse treatment.

While the term 'non-combatant' in the Brussels Declaration should be understood in its literal, negative sense as comprising individuals who do not fight, it does not seem to have been extended to individuals who are not members of the armed forces. Best believes that the appropriation of the term for the military was 'severing the remainder of the population the more decisively from connexion with hostilities, in order (in effect) to ensure its taking no part in them'.[201] As Kolb observes, the law of this period, which he describes as 'the classical laws of war', 'focused on the military branch'.[202] The Brussels Conference was thus concerned with the classification and clarification of privileges, obligations and protections of members of the armed forces and those individuals lawfully participating in war – albeit not necessarily in combat. The prevailing understanding of the inter-state nature of war may have enabled the regulation of non-combatants in the military at the same time as it constrained the conceptualisation of individuals who do not belong to the armed forces.

Stephen Neff argues that, during this period, 'civilians' were regarded 'either as participants (i.e., as unwelcome meddlers) or as victims'.[203] Scheipers also observes that the nineteenth-century 'approach to the laws of war was as much about disciplining civilians as it was about "humanizing war" and protecting local populations against wanton cruelty'.[204] She suggests that 'strong narratives about the threats posed by irregular forces actually *hindered* the development of an unequivocal and protected status of the "civilian"' at the time.[205] A close reading of the records of the Diplomatic Conferences reveals that the creation of such a status was not even attempted or contemplated. By examining the various ways in which individuals who do not belong to the armed forces were recognised in the negotiations and in the international instruments of this period, this section first challenges the conventional narrative that the laws of war developed for the purpose of protecting 'civilians' as war victims. It then outlines how

[198] K Ipsen, 'Combatants and Non-Combatants' in Fleck (n 75) 109–10.
[199] Bordwell (n 130) 234.
[200] *Actes* (n 34) 31.
[201] Best, *Humanity* (n 1) 180.
[202] R Kolb, *Advanced Introduction to International Humanitarian Law* (Cheltenham, Elgar, 2014) 3.
[203] Neff (n 7) 190.
[204] Scheipers (n 11) 101–02.
[205] ibid 13.

individuals who do not belong to the armed forces were perceived as intruders in organised warfare and as threats for regular combatants. Lastly, it highlights the deliberation of individuals as enemy and neutral nationals at the 1907 Hague Peace Conference.

A. The Protection of War Victims?

The 1868 St Petersburg Declaration is often believed to have introduced the principle of distinction into conventional law.[206] Best points out that the treaty is commonly regarded 'as the premier proof-text of civilian immunity', even though it 'says nothing explicitly about the non-combatant'.[207] The existence of individuals who do not belong to the armed forces is no more than implied in its oft-cited preambular declaration that 'the only legitimate object which States should endeavour to accomplish during war is to weaken the military forces of the enemy'.[208] The silence has given rise to different interpretations in contemporary scholarship. According to Kolb, '[t]he civilians are envisioned as being completely alien to armed contest' and the relevant clause 'confirms implicitly that civilians are not to be made the object of attacks being outside the sphere of belligerent violence'.[209] He argues that considering only military personnel in explicit terms reflects the conceptual understandings of the time.[210] Conversely, Best paraphrases the preambular clause as meaning not only that individuals who do not belong to the armed forces 'ought not to be involved' but also, by implication, that their participation would amount to a self-imposed risk.[211] The status of these individuals is undefined and rendered nebulous by the silence in the St Petersburg Declaration.

The *travaux préparatoires* themselves do not suggest that individuals were generally meaningfully discussed as victims of warfare at the 1868 St Petersburg Conference. Although the published records only provide a summary account of the negotiations, the nature of the discourse appears to have been dominated by a technical debate concerning weapons of war and ammunition.[212] The explosive bullets were considered as barbarous if employed against 'les hommes' or

[206] See, eg, Neff (n 7) 190; OM Stern, *Gender, Conflict and International Humanitarian Law: A Critique of the 'Principle of Distinction'* (London, Routledge, 2018) 19; E Crawford, 'The Enduring Legacy of the St Petersburg Declaration: Distinction, Military Necessity, and the Prohibition of Causing Unnecessary Suffering and Superfluous Injury in IHL' (2018) 20 *Journal of the History of International Law* 544.

[207] G Best, *War and Law Since 1945* (Oxford, Clarendon Press, 1994) 43.

[208] St Petersburg Declaration.

[209] R Kolb, 'The Protection of the Individual in Times of War and Peace' in B Fassbender and A Peters (eds), *The Oxford Handbook of the History of International Law* (Oxford, Oxford University Press, 2012) 325.

[210] ibid; see also Kolb and Milanov (n 25) 534.

[211] Best, *War and Law* (n 207) 43.

[212] 'Protocoles Saint-Pétersbourg' (n 24).

'des êtres vivants' rather than ammunition wagons or carts.[213] However, the drafters were not concerned with establishing whether the bullets were used solely against members of the enemy armed forces or whether certain categories of persons should not be attacked in general. They neither delineated lawful participation in hostilities nor legitimate targets of attack. The principle that the object of war should only be the weakening of the military forces was guided by an understanding of military necessity and the humanitarian idea that individuals who participated in combat and had been rendered *hors de combat* should not suffer unnecessarily.[214] It can be inferred that the overarching aim was to reduce the suffering of individuals who are members of the armed forces without any attention being directed towards those who are not. The distinction between participants in warfare and an undefined 'other' seems to have been a matter of fact, and not of principle.

The Brussels Declaration does also not establish a general status for individuals who do not belong to the armed forces. Two contrasting views of war prevailed at the time of its drafting, '[l]es uns voudraient la rendre plus terrible pour qu'elle soit plus rare, d'autres voudraient en faire un tournoi entre les armées régulières avec les peuples pour simples spectateurs'.[215] The latter seemed to inform the discourse at the Brussels Conference, where individuals who do not belong to the armed forces would usually fall outside of the conception of the battlefield. The original *projet* declared as one of its 'principes généraux' that '[l]es opérations de guerre doivent être dirigées exclusivement contre les forces et les moyens de guerre de l'Etat ennemi, et non contre ses sujets, tant que ces derniers ne prennent pas eux-mêmes une part active à la guerre'.[216] The provision has been interpreted today as a 'recognition of the general legal principle mandating civilian immunity from attack' and 'the earliest formulation of this principle in an international legal instrument'.[217] However, the text only provides a more explicit protection for one particular category of individuals who are not members of the armed forces, namely nationals of the enemy state, on the condition of their non-participation. The inclusion of the principle in the *projet* indicates an awareness that peaceful citizens of a belligerent state may be affected by the hostilities. It is, therefore, all the more noteworthy that the principle was neither discussed at the Conference nor adopted in the final text of the Brussels Declaration.

[213] ibid 460.

[214] ibid generally.

[215] *Actes* (n 34) 7; 'some would like to render it more terrible, in order for it to become more rare, others would like to make it a tournament between regular armed forces, with the people as simple spectators' (author's translation).

[216] ibid 4; 'operations of war must be directed exclusively against the forces and means of making war of the enemy state, and not against its subjects, so long as the latter do not themselves take any active part in the war' (author's translation).

[217] Dowdeswell (n 10) 836.

Instead, the prohibition of attacks on or bombardment of undefended towns under Article 15 of the Brussels Declaration, which became Article 25 of the 1899 and 1907 Hague Regulations, has been interpreted as a central provision in the protection of individuals who do not belong to the armed forces. For example, Judith Gardam claims that the provision 'was in fact tantamount to a general rule recognizing civilians as an illegitimate target' since these individuals would usually not have been affected by warfare with the exception of bombardment.[218] Emily Gade also believes that it 'indicate[s] the recurrent and pervasive nature of the non-combatant immunity norm in international consciousness'.[219] Alexander offers a more persuasive explanation for the provision which reflects the deliberations at the Brussels Conference. According to her, '[i]f non-combatant citizens in open towns were exempted from this pressure [by bombardment or starvation] it was not because of their intrinsic status as non-combatants, but simply because no violence was needed to take an open town'.[220] Individuals who do not belong to the armed forces would have been spared on the basis of military necessity[221] and the de facto scope of the battlefield.[222]

Regarding defended towns, notifying the authorities of the intention of bombardment was deemed sufficient without requiring any further protective measures.[223] Having been provided with a chance to leave the town, the inhabitants could have removed themselves from the hostilities. However, as Alexander notes, the warning preceding bombardment may have also remained inconsequential since 'the convention places no obligation on the surrounding forces to allow the "useless mouths" to leave'.[224] Contemporaneous international legal scholarship indeed observed that the practice of not letting them leave besieged towns was justified in terms of military necessity.[225] Nor would a warning be required in a surprise assault or bombardment. Furthermore, as Lester Nurick points out, the obligation to spare as much as possible certain targets in sieges and bombardments refers only to buildings, but not to individuals who do not belong to the armed forces.[226] According to him, 'it is generally accepted that non-combatants within the zone of operations are not immune

[218] JG Gardam, *Non-Combatant Immunity as a Norm of International Humanitarian Law* (London, Martinus Nijhoff, 1993) 19.

[219] EK Gade, 'Defining the Non-Combatant: How Do We Determine Who is Worthy of Protection in Violent Conflict?' (2010) 9 *Journal of Military Ethics* 219, 224.

[220] Alexander, 'Genesis' (n 12) 364.

[221] MW Royse, *Aerial Bombardment and the International Regulation of Warfare* (New York, Harold Vinal, 1928) 153–63; C Jochnick and R Normand, 'The Legitimation of Violence: A Critical History of the Laws of War' (1994) 35 *Harvard International Law Journal* 49, 67.

[222] *cf* F Mégret, 'War and the Vanishing Battlefield' (2011) 9 *Loyola University Chicago International Law Review* 131.

[223] Brussels Declaration, art 16.

[224] Alexander, 'Genesis' (n 12) 364.

[225] See, eg, Oppenheim, *International Law, vol II* (n 169) para 157; Spaight (n 74) 174–80; A Pearce Higgins, *War and the Private Citizen* (London, P.S. King & Son, 1912) 48–49.

[226] L Nurick, 'The Distinction Between Combatant and Noncombatant in the Law of War' (1945) 39 *AJIL* 680, 683–84; see Brussels Declaration, art 17; 1899 and 1907 Hague Regulations, art 27.

from bombardment'.[227] Indeed, Louise Doswald-Beck stresses that 'during the bombardment of a defended city a distinction between civilians and military objects could not be made as such'.[228] Under these provisions, individuals who do not belong to the armed forces were considered as inhabitants of undefended or defended towns who may or may not be affected by the hostilities due to their location and military necessity. The term 'inhabitants' identified their position in a conflict between states; yet it provided no indication of a legal status or claim to protection.

In relation to belligerent occupations, individuals who do not belong to the armed forces were not only recognised as inhabitants but, more importantly, as the population of an occupied state. The provision of specific rules and protections which restrict the authority of the occupying power is conceivable in light of the increased engagement between the state and the enemy population during an occupation.[229] This relationship is more implicit in the formulation of the section in the Hague Regulations as being 'On military authority over hostile territory',[230] compared to 'On the military power with respect to private persons' in the Brussels Declaration.[231] The majority of the provisions in these sections concern the population as a collective, even with respect to the prohibition of forced participation in military operations against their own country and the compulsion to swear allegiance to the occupying power.[232] The German delegate Colonel Gross von Schwarzhoff emphasised at the First Hague Peace Conference that the prohibition referred 'only to the population as a whole and not to individuals'.[233] Only the 1907 Hague Regulations rephrased the provisions as applying to 'inhabitants'.[234]

Coercing the population into services for the occupying power was strongly opposed on the grounds that 'the inhabitant of the country would become a traitor to his native land', and thus 'despicable in his own eyes and in those of every man of spirit';[235] it would be 'immoral in the highest degree'[236] and a 'cruelty'.[237] The Dutch delegate Lieutenant General den Beer Poortugael forcefully rejected the measure arguing that inhabitants should not be compelled to commit treason

[227] Nurick (n 226) 684: see also Oppenheim, *International Law, vol II* (n 169) para 116; Higgins (n 225) 43.

[228] L Doswald-Beck, 'The Value of the 1977 Geneva Protocols for the Protection of Civilians' in MA Meyer (ed), *Armed Conflict and the New Law: Aspects of the 1977 Geneva Protocols and the 1981 Weapons Convention* (London, British Institute for International and Comparative Law, 1989) 141; see also Spaight (n 74) 158.

[229] Nabulsi, *Traditions* (n 43) 63.

[230] 1899 and 1907 Hague Regulations, s III.

[231] Brussels Declaration, arts 36–42.

[232] ibid arts 36–37.

[233] *1899 Proceedings* (n 30) 487.

[234] 1907 Hague Regulations, arts 44–45.

[235] *1907 Proceedings* (n 156) 98–99.

[236] ibid 120.

[237] ibid 127.

in a contest between states, which found widespread approval by other members of the responsible commission.[238] The prohibition, conversely, was described as being 'humanitarian' since it would 'respect the conscience' and 'legitimate sentiments of the inhabitants of an occupied region'.[239] To a lesser extent, it was also recognised that, in addition to the individuals' conscience, their life and safety would be endangered in case of non-compliance under the enemy state[240] and in relation to their own state due to treason.[241] These individuals who do not belong to the armed forces were again perceived and protected as patriotic members of a nation. Moreover, it was arguably indirectly the state which benefitted from the regulations, since a citizen providing information and guidance to the enemy state was deemed potentially more harmful than one enlisted in the enemy armed forces.[242] Although it is seemingly the relationship between the occupying force and the population in the occupied territory that is regulated under the provisions, it is questionable whether the rules were informed by concerns for the individuals' well-being or rather sovereign states' interest in their own self-defence.

Article 38 of the Brussels Declaration, which became Article 46 of the 1899 and 1907 Hague Regulations, appears to be an exception in the text since it provides the most direct protection for individuals who do not belong to the armed forces in occupied territory. It requires respect for '[f]amily honour and rights, and the lives and property of persons, as well as their religious convictions and their practice'. However, its original formulation in the *projet* still referred to 'la population pacifique' rather than 'persons'.[243] Furthermore, it is part of the general focus of the negotiations and adopted texts on the protection of primarily private property rather than on the individuals themselves. In her study of pillage and rape as closely associated practices in war, Tuba Inal notes the brevity of the consideration of 'family honours' compared to the detailed discussion on private property at the Brussels Conference.[244] This preoccupation with private property can also be seen in relation to a petition of the inhabitants of Antwerp which was submitted to the Brussels Conference to request the prohibition of the bombardment of residential areas even in fortified towns. The commission's response concluded with its firm belief that the humanitarian objective of the Conference would lead to the regulation of the means and methods of warfare to protect the private property of the 'inoffensive' citizens as

[238] ibid 11.
[239] ibid 9 and 134.
[240] ibid 11.
[241] ibid 132.
[242] ibid; for an examination of the debate whether civilians may voluntarily provide or be forced into providing information at the Brussels Conference see S Darcy, *To Serve the Enemy: Informers, Collaborators, and the Laws of Armed Conflict* (Oxford, Oxford University Press, 2019) 61–70.
[243] *Actes* (n 34) 6.
[244] T Inal, *Looting and Rape in Wartime: Law and Change in International Relations* (Philadelphia, University of Pennsylvania Press, 2013) 62–63.

far as military necessity permits.[245] While it took into consideration the principle declared in the *projet* not to direct warfare against peaceful citizens, no such conviction of safety, even conditional on military necessity, was expressed with regards to the life and wellbeing of individual persons.

Presiding over the responsible sub-commission at the First Hague Peace Conference, Martens repeatedly emphasised that the Brussels Declaration and proposed law was intended for the protection of the 'weak', 'unarmed', 'inoffensive', 'peaceful' and 'peaceable' population.[246] This may have been a reflection of his personal humanistic[247] or liberal belief in the protection of individuals.[248] Yet, in the proceedings of the Diplomatic Conference, it seems to have been no more than strategic rhetoric in his attempt to reach an agreement in the dispute over populations fighting in defence of their country, and, ultimately, to achieve the adoption of a treaty. Even David Traven, who reads a more deliberate distinction between combatants and 'civilians' into the negotiations at the Conference, observes the permissive nature of the law noting that 'Martens seems to suggest that *incidental* civilian casualties are permissible *provided that* they are justified by the exigencies of military operations'.[249]

It is indeed noticeable that individuals who do not belong to the armed forces, despite potentially being subject to the effects of warfare, were not generally perceived and discussed as victims of war in the negotiations. On one occasion at the Brussels Conference, the peaceful population was seen as being endangered by unorganised and unregulated resistance fighters,[250] rather than war as a whole. The deliberations at the diplomatic events show no indication of an intention to protect peaceful individuals who do not belong to the armed forces generally under the written laws of war. Instead, the delegates at the Hague Peace Conferences apparently believed that the assortment of rudimentary protections included in the Brussels Declaration and later 1899 Hague Regulations offered sufficient safeguards for such individuals.[251]

Overall, the discourse at the Brussels Conference and the Hague Peace Conferences, as well as the texts of the Brussels Declaration and Hague Regulations did distinguish between combatants and individuals who do not belong to the armed forces. However, they did not entail two concepts, each providing a status with distinct privileges, obligations and protections for a clearly defined category of persons. On the contrary, individuals who do not belong to the armed forces were largely excluded from the written laws of war,

[245] *Actes* (n 34) 55–56.
[246] *1899 Proceedings* (n 30) 506–07, 518 and 551.
[247] Ivanenko (n 118) 1718.
[248] Mälksoo (n 193) 823.
[249] D Traven, *Law and Sentiment in International Politics: Ethics, Emotions, and the Evolution of the Laws of War* (Cambridge, Cambridge University Press, 2021) 203.
[250] *Actes* (n 34) 28 and 34.
[251] See, eg, *1899 Proceedings* (n 30) 63 and 493–95; *1907 Proceedings* (n 156) 23, 127–28 and 136.

which was limited to the battlefield and occupied territory. The law was designed to regulate the relations between states and, primarily, their armed forces. The existence of individuals who do not belong to the armed forces was acknowledged, but a definition and a comprehensive set of safeguards protecting them from the consequences of warfare or regulating their treatment in the hands of a belligerent party were seemingly not believed to be necessary. If at all, these individuals were mainly recognised, and possibly protected, as belonging to a belligerent or occupied state and in the distinct ways in which they were implicated in warfare. This is also apparent in the reference to 'populations' in the Martens Clause in the Hague Regulations,[252] compared to its modern reformulation concerning 'civilians'.[253] While Pustogarov asserts that the replacement of the term 'did not change the content of the notion',[254] the subtle difference is, nonetheless, revealing of the understanding of individuals and the absence of a concept of civilians in the period of the early written laws of war. The binding and non-binding instruments adopted during these years 'neither used nor defined the category "civilian" explicitly, much less protected them'.[255]

The marginal engagement with individuals who do not belong to the armed forces as war victims cannot be explained on the basis of a lack of experience in the historical context.[256] In her analysis of the practices of occupying armies in the nineteenth century, Nabulsi shows how 'civilians' were affected, for example, by pillage, looting, requisitions, billeting, reprisals and hostage-taking.[257] Scheipers equally notes that 'the historical record confirms that regular troops' harsh, repressive responses to guerrilla warfare tended to be directed towards the civilian population' from the late eighteenth to the mid-twentieth century.[258] The recent Franco-Prussian War alone would have provided sufficient examples of situations in which innocent inhabitants had fallen victim to counter-measures against *francs-tireurs* and the *levée en masse*. The bombardment of Strasbourg in 1870 had also shown that improvements in weapons technology rendered an attack on individuals who do not belong to the armed forces a viable military strategy.[259] In his 1912 study on *War and the Private Citizen*, Alexander Pearce Higgins observed that 'in every war since 1870, whether by inevitable accident or design, considerable damage has been done to the persons and property of ordinary peaceful citizens'.[260] Yet the participants in the law-making processes

[252] 1899 Hague Regulations, Preamble; the English text of the 1907 Hague Regulations refers to 'inhabitants', while 'populations' in the authoritative French text remains unchanged.

[253] Protocol Additional to the Geneva Conventions of 12 August 1949, and Relating to the Protection of Victims of International Armed Conflicts (Geneva, 8 June 1977), art 1(2).

[254] VV Pustogarov, 'The Martens Clause in International Law' (1999) 1 *Journal of the History of International Law* 125, 128.

[255] Scheipers (n 11) 101, see also 104.

[256] Doswald-Beck (n 228) 138–40.

[257] Nabulsi, *Traditions* (n 43) ch 3.

[258] Scheipers (n 11) 13.

[259] Benvenisti and Lustig, 'Monopolizing War' (n 96) 162.

[260] Higgins (n 225) 46.

did not reflect on these practices, but focused instead on combatants. As Nabulsi remarks, '[t]he central problem engaging the lawmakers at The Hague was most emphatically *not* the protection of civilians'.[261]

By remaining largely silent on the vulnerability or need for protection of certain categories of individuals who do not belong to the armed forces, the negotiations at these Diplomatic Conferences also differ from their normative and ideational context. Kolb reminds the contemporary reader that '[f]or centuries the law attached protection to such concrete persons' as 'the elderly, women, children, priests, the insane' who were deemed 'innocent' in the sense of not participating in warfare, rather than 'to a general category of civilians'.[262] The Lieber Code, for example, specifically emphasised the exclusion of women and children from warfare,[263] and went on to regulate the 'protection of persons, and especially women'.[264] Contemporaneous international legal scholarship also stressed the particular care granted to individuals based on their gender and age.[265]

The Brussels Conference, on the other hand, only briefly identified particular parts of the population as 'des habitants inoffensifs, femmes, enfants, vieillards, infirmes' in the discussion of the regulation of sieges.[266] Yet the German delegate Major General von Voigts-Rhetz invoked this as an example against overly constraining rules. He argued that despite the cruelty of the position of these 'malheureux', no favourable treatment can be expected on the side of the besieging force.[267] Similarly, at the Second Hague Peace Conference, Lieutenant General den Beer Poortugael observed that '[i]f the enemy has invaded a certain country, it can send for the inhabitants, men and women, and interrogate them with threats of shooting them instantly if they do not give satisfactory information'.[268] In 1899, the extraordinary nature of *levées en masse* in the early nineteenth century was highlighted as comprising '[n]ot only able-bodied men, but also old men, children and women'.[269] While these categories of individuals were clearly conceived as being outside the normal conduct of war, an arguable immunity from attack was neither mentioned nor implied at the Conferences.

[261] K Nabulsi, 'Evolving Conceptions of Civilians and Belligerents: One Hundred Years After the Hague Peace Conferences' in S Chesterman (ed), *Civilians in War* (London, Lynne Rienner, 2001) 12; *cf* Traven (n 249) 199–204.

[262] Kolb, *Advanced Introduction* (n 202) 6.

[263] Lieber Code, arts 19 and 37.

[264] ibid s II.

[265] See, eg, Bluntschli, *Kriegsrecht* (n 112) 10 and 14; Holland, *Laws of War* (n 167) para 15.

[266] *Actes* (n 34) 10.

[267] ibid.

[268] *1907 Proceedings* (n 156) 120; see also 790, where the British delegate Sir Edward Fry illustrated the evils of land warfare among others as 'women and children fleeing before the enemy soldiers', yet not in an appeal for their protection from the effects of war under the law, but rather to counter the US delegates' concerns over the capturing of private property at sea.

[269] *1899 Proceedings* (n 30) 551.

This approach to individuals who do not belong to the armed forces may be due to the dominance of military personnel at the Brussels Conference, which, as argued above, also influenced the deliberation of the combatant status. De Breucker suggests that the *projet*, which was probably drafted by lawyers, reflects a more humanitarian understanding given its structural division into sections on belligerents and private persons. Yet he notes that the importance of this was not adequately emphasised by the Brussels Conference itself,[270] where military and diplomatic delegates led the negotiations.

Moreover, it needs to be stressed that participation at the event was confined to state delegations, preventing access for and the direct influence of non-state actors. Their non-participation was explicitly justified on the basis that the regulation of warfare touched upon the rights and interests of states.[271] According to Benvenisti and Lustig, the exclusion of non-governmental parties from the Conference was also 'the German precondition for coming to Brussels'.[272] Consequently, submissions by non-state actors were only admitted for deliberation if brought forward by one of the participating states,[273] possibly in a modified form. This rule affected the above-mentioned petition by the inhabitants of Antwerp who had requested that, according to the principle of humanity, the bombardment of quarters of inoffensive private persons in fortified towns should also be prohibited. When the Belgian delegation presented the petition to the Conference, it was only briefly discussed in accordance with states' military interests rather than humanitarian considerations. Major General von Voigts-Rhetz insisted that it would be impossible to satisfy the wish of the petitioners since it would amount to a restriction of one of the most efficacious means of attaining the object of war.[274] However, it is notable that the *projet*'s general principle on the apparent immunity of the enemy state's peaceful subjects was only mentioned in the Conference's response to this petition, without further elaboration.[275] It remains unknown whether a more active participation of non-state actors, including norm entrepreneurs, would have changed the discourse to comprise a more sustained examination of humanitarian ideals and how peaceful individuals experienced war. The nature of the negotiations at the Brussels Conference suggests that the deliberation of the laws of war was considered an endeavour of states, and essentially the domain of the armed forces. Wars were conceived as inter-state relations in which the interests of individuals, populations or private associations were largely inconsequential.

The discourse at the Hague Peace Conferences diverges in some respects from the negotiations at the Brussels Conference, most notably in the contributions of international lawyers. At the time, the work of jurists and publicists

[270] de Breucker (n 138) 18.
[271] *Actes* (n 34) 7.
[272] Benvenisti and Lustig, 'Monopolizing War' (n 96) 154.
[273] *Actes* (n 34) 18–19.
[274] ibid 9.
[275] ibid 55.

more generally seems to have been informed by different interpretations of individuals who do not belong to the armed forces, as well as the role of the laws of war in protecting them. A survey of international legal treatises during this period shows no common understanding of the principle of distinction as it is known today.[276] However, some international lawyers more clearly promoted a distinction between combatants and individuals who do not belong to the armed forces. A few even declared the immunity of the latter as long as they remained peaceful and, according to some, military necessity allowed it.[277] The IDI's Oxford Manual contained a similar provision to what is sometimes believed to have been an early example of the principle of distinction in the Brussels' *projet*, which was removed from the Declaration.[278] Moreover, it went even further by enshrining explicitly, as the only international instrument of the period, the general principle that '[i]t is forbidden to maltreat inoffensive populations'.[279] Annette Mailler proclaims in her doctoral thesis *De la distinction des combattants et non combattants comme base du droit de guerre*, published in 1916, that legal scholars at the time, albeit only citing Antoine Pillet as an authority, considered peaceful inhabitants not as enemies but as inviolable persons who should not be harmed.[280] According to her, the distinction formed the basis for the Brussels Declaration and the Hague Regulations; yet she merely briefly mentions Article 46 of the Hague Regulations on the respect for 'family honours and rights, individual lives and private property, as well as religious convictions and liberty' as embodying the respect for non-combatants.[281]

At the Hague Peace Conferences themselves, some international lawyers also seemed to believe that the Brussels Declaration and the revision of the laws of war 25 years later were informed by a principled distinction between combatants and individuals who do not belong to the armed forces. Lord Reay, a former president of the IDI, stated that

> war must in all possible measure be limited to the direct action of the armies, and that the belligerents must do all in their power in order not to expose the civil population to the evils or losses which would be avoidable. This was the master thought of the Convention of 1899.[282]

[276] See, eg, Halleck (n 190) 383; Field (n 190) para 750; Hall (n 190) para 18; notably in a chapter entitled 'de la distinction des combattants et des non-combattants', Mérignhac outlines the provisions on belligerents, *levée en masse* and the distinction between combatants and non-combatants in the armed forces, rather than the modern understanding of the principle of distinction, A Mérignhac, *Les lois et coutumes de la guerre sur terre d'après le droit international moderne et la codification de la Conférence de La Haye de 1899* (Paris, Chevalier-Marescq, 1903) 70–87.

[277] See, eg, Bluntschli, *Kriegsrecht* (n 112) 5 and 14; JS Risley, *The Law of War* (London, Innes & Co, 1897) 107–08; Pillet (n 169) 35 and 38; Holland, *Laws of War* (n 167) 17; Hall (n 190) paras 127–28.

[278] Oxford Manual, art 1 explanatory note.

[279] ibid art 7.

[280] A Mailler, *De la distinction des combattants et non combattants comme base du droit de guerre* (Paris, A Pedone, 1916) 44–45.

[281] ibid 55–56 and 90.

[282] *1907 Proceedings* (n 156) 39.

This retrospective reading of humanitarian considerations, including the protection of the civilian population, into the early written laws of war became even more entrenched over time, as the following chapters will argue. Yet, as the analysis of the drafting of the Brussels Declaration has shown, neither a principled distinction between combatants and all other individuals, nor an understanding of the law as fulfilling a protective function for peaceful bystanders was foundational for the rules adopted in 1874.

Furthermore, it is noteworthy that, at the two Hague Peace Conferences, the distinction between combatants and individuals who do not belong to the armed forces was almost exclusively drawn in the negotiation of rules other than the existing laws and customs of war on land. Major General Yermolow mentioned the distinction in passing in a speech on the opening of hostilities.[283] The above-cited quote by Lord Reay derives from the discussion of a special status for neutral persons in belligerent territory. Beernaert made a similar statement in response to a proposed provision on enemy nationals.[284] He also noted that the 1874 Brussels Declaration and 1899 Hague Regulations were formed on two main principles: 'It is forbidden to harm in any way populations who take no part in the military operations; and, even between combatants all unnecessary infliction of injury is forbidden'.[285] However, he presented this speech during the discussion of naval bombardment of undefended ports, towns and villages, rather than in the context of the laws of war on land. Another Belgian delegate and lawyer Jules Van den Heuvel framed the restriction of such naval bombardment as a requirement rooted in 'the right of innocent inhabitants [which] cannot be neglected'.[286] This proclamation appears to have found its way into the preamble of the 1907 Convention (IX) concerning Bombardment by Naval Forces in Time of War.[287] While it suggests that this aim would be achieved by applying the 1899 Hague Regulations on land warfare to the extent that it is possible analogously to naval warfare, the 1899 treaty itself is silent on the rights of inhabitants.

Individuals who do not belong to the armed forces were also occasionally portrayed as being outside the scope of hostilities in relation to certain (expected) developments in the conduct of warfare that raised new concerns and were not regulated by existing international instruments. In particular, the discussion of the prohibition of asphyxiating gases, and the discharge of projectiles and explosives from balloons had to rely on general principles, such as military necessity and humanity, in the absence of practical experience and established rules. Some delegates emphasised the likely effects of these methods

[283] ibid 4.

[284] ibid 111; on the discussion of neutral and enemy nationals at the Second Hague Peace Conference see further section II.C.

[285] *1907 Proceedings* (n 156) 543.

[286] ibid 349–50.

[287] (The Hague, 18 October 1907), Preamble.

on 'inoffensive inhabitants' and 'non-combatants'.[288] Although this may suggest that these individuals should not be affected by hostilities, notions of military necessity were predominant especially among the non-legal delegates. For example, the US delegate Seth Low afterwards declared that the possible harm for non-combatants constituted 'useless damage; that is to say, damage that does not advance at all the military object of the fighting'.[289] Nevertheless, the question arises whether the understanding of land warfare would have been shaped differently at the Hague Peace Conferences if it had not been constrained by the rules and conceptualisations of individuals in the Brussels Declaration.

As the above analysis of the concept of combatants has shown, international lawyers played an increasingly prominent and active role in the negotiations at the Hague Peace Conferences compared to the Brussels Conference. They introduced alternative understandings of individuals who do not belong to the armed forces into the discourse; yet these were not incorporated into the legal rules on land warfare. Despite these delegates' references to the Oxford Manual and international legal scholarship in addition to the Brussels Declaration,[290] the protection of individuals was not considered beyond the regulations in the 1874 instrument. Crawford notes that 'military and political figures' still dismissed the IDI's more humanitarian Oxford Manual 'as a scholarly work that seemed not to reflect existing trends in practice [which] might have been influenced by the fact that the Institute was an organisation of lawyers and jurists, rather than politicians and military personnel'.[291] The Brussels Declaration, on the other hand, achieved a comparatively higher degree of acceptance.[292] Its provisions were adopted without significant discussion and amendments. The prevailing technical debate on the laws of war on land at the First Hague Peace Conference may have not only facilitated the creation of conventional law, but also limited its content. Neither the international lawyers participating in the negotiations nor other delegates introduced more extensive guarantees into the treaty which may have reflected the understanding of these individuals as innocent bystanders or even victims.

The approach of military delegates at the Hague Peace Conferences suggests that they believed a more comprehensive protection regime was not required and that military necessity determined the fate of the individuals who do not belong to the armed forces. These individuals may have also still been perceived as naturally falling outside of the scope of war and thus not needing more specific safeguards under the written laws of war. International lawyers, on the other hand, may have seen the existing rules in the Brussels Declaration as reflecting principles and norms that were more prevalent in the international

[288] See, eg, *1899 Proceedings* (n 30) 280, 283 and 354; *1907 Proceedings* (n 156) 148.
[289] Low (n 173) 630.
[290] See, eg, *1907 Proceedings* (n 156) 131–32.
[291] Crawford, *Non-Binding Norms* (n 77) 58.
[292] ibid.

legal community than in the deliberations in 1874. Consequently, Beernaert's observations regarding the underpinnings of the 1899 Hague Regulations at the Second Hague Peace Conference more likely reveal his personal understanding of the laws of war, informed by his professional background knowledge, than an insight into the drafting history by one of the participating state representatives. Ultimately, the participating lawyers at the First Hague Peace Conference likely lacked the power, or possibly perceived need, to renegotiate the rules on individuals who do not belong to the armed forces entirely.

Overall, the deliberations at the conferences as well as the rules in the texts of the international instruments reveal the absence of a shared understanding of these individuals as victims of war who should be shielded from suffering its consequences by virtue of not being combatants. In relation to the laws of war on land, these individuals were neither discussed as inherently innocent or vulnerable nor as immune from attack. The various provisions which provide limited protections for individuals who do not belong to the armed forces have in common that they are not attached to a particular status of persons, but rather that they are conditional upon the individuals' situation and conduct. This reflects the more prevailing understanding of these individuals at the conferences as potential intruders and threats to organised warfare, as will be examined next.

B. The Regulation of Intruders and Threats

The conventional historical account regarding civilians under the laws of war does not commonly mention the 1864 Geneva Convention which is limited to the protection of wounded and sick combatants, and the neutrality of medical personnel and establishments. However, the drafting history of the treaty provides valuable insights into the perception of individuals who do not belong to the armed forces in the early attempts towards regulating warfare under international law. The 1864 Diplomatic Conference was marked by a contentious engagement with such individuals, which stands in contrast to its complacent approach to combatants. In particular, the delegates debated whether non-military individuals and entities, such as volunteers and private relief societies, should be permitted to treat wounded soldiers on the battlefield and whether an authorisation by a state party to the conflict would be required.[293] The experience in recent wars, including the Crimean War, had shown that individual volunteers, such as the 'compassionate nurse', may emerge on the battlefield.[294] State practice prior to the negotiation of the new regulations had provided no restrictions on medical and other non-military individuals who may have become

[293] 'Protocoles 1864' (n 16) 381–82.
[294] Benvenisti and Lustig, 'Monopolizing War' (n 96) 134.

involved in the treatment of wounded soldiers during and after the conduct of hostilities. At the same time, however, '[a]mbulance workers on and around the battlefield, apart from being far too new, had no conventional protection from fire …; local inhabitants who tried to succour vanquished sufferers were victimized by suspicious victors'.[295] The Geneva Convention, therefore, entered new grounds in enabling and constraining various individuals in their relation to the wounded soldiers in the field.

The issue of voluntary medical services had already been considered at the Geneva International Conference of 1863, where the International Committee for Relief to the Wounded, the predecessor of the International Committee of the Red Cross (ICRC), was founded. As Giovanni Mantilla remarks, the development of the laws of war in the early 1860s already followed what would become the ICRC's standard procedure of convening 'unofficial' meetings followed by law-making diplomatic conferences.[296] While the 1863 Conference promoted the creation of national committees for medical relief in times of war, it proposed a restrictive approach to voluntary services provided by individuals who do not belong to the armed forces. It declared that '[o]n the request or with the consent of the military authorities, Committees may send voluntary medical personnel to the battlefield where they shall be placed under military command'.[297] Societies evading governmental control were perceived as potentially posing a threat to the interests and well-being of the military and the wounded. Some state delegations cautioned vehemently against the lack of discipline, military organisation and competence among volunteers, as well as the danger of espionage. According to them, medical assistance for wounded soldiers should be left entirely to states.[298] The 1863 Conference, nevertheless, endorsed neutrality for voluntary nurses. Its recommendations were introduced at the Diplomatic Conference one year later by General Guillaume-Henri Dufour, a co-founder of the ICRC's predecessor who participated at the 1864 Conference as a Swiss delegate.[299] The working draft prepared for the Diplomatic Conference itself, however, did not mention voluntary nurses. The Prussian delegate Friedrich Loeffler not only drew attention to this omission but also declared that the

[295] Best, *Humanity* (n 1) 149.

[296] G Mantilla, *Lawmaking under Pressure: International Humanitarian Law and Internal Armed Conflict* (Ithaca, Cornell University Press, 2020) 37.

[297] Resolutions of the Geneva International Conference (Geneva, 26–29 October 1863) reprinted in Schindler and Toman (n 5), art 6.

[298] C Lueder, *La Convention de Genève au point de vue historique, critique et dogmatique* (Erlangen, Édouard Besold, 1876) 68–69; M Finnemore, 'Rules of War and Wars of Rules: The International Red Cross and the Restraint of State Violence' in J Boli and GM Thomas (eds), *Constructing World Culture: International Nongovernmental Organizations Since 1875* (Stanford, Stanford University Press, 1999) 157; F Bugnion, 'Birth of an Idea: The Founding of the International Committee of the Red Cross and of the International Red Cross and Red Crescent Movement: From Solferino to the Original Geneva Convention (1859–1864)' (2012) 94:888 *IRRC* 1299, 1317.

[299] 'Protocoles 1864' (n 16) 378.

lacuna should be filled.[300] Despite this acknowledgement and a brief preliminary debate on whether voluntary societies would be protected by virtue of being attached to hospitals or ambulances, the treaty remained silent on the issue.

In 1868 another Diplomatic Conference was convened to update the Geneva Convention by clarifying some provisions and expanding it to naval warfare. The Conference also saw a renewed attempt at including voluntary societies in the treatment and care of wounded soldiers. Following the same procedure as before, the recommendations of the ICRC's predecessor in 1867 indicate that it was one of the objectives of the *Projet de Convention* for the 1868 Conference to '[p]rise en considération, dans la loi, des sociétés de secours volontaires et de leurs délégués pendant la guerre'.[301] Yet the issue was again not submitted for revision and not incorporated into the formally adopted 1868 Additional Articles to the Geneva Convention.[302] Only the 1906 Geneva Convention, replacing the 1864 treaty, explicitly recognised private relief societies under strict conditions of military authorisation and control.[303]

In addition to voluntary relief societies, the involvement of inhabitants was also considered. The 1864 Geneva Convention provides that '[i]nhabitants of the country who bring help to the wounded shall be respected and shall remain free'.[304] In his 1901 study of the treaty, Gustav Münzel noted that these persons should have been generally spared.[305] However, only inhabitants who extend treatment and shelter to wounded military personnel were seemingly considered in need of protection from the consequences of belligerent conduct and occupation. More recent comments, nevertheless, suggest that the Convention was 'very liberal with regard to a population giving assistance to the wounded'.[306] The 1868 Additional Articles intended to limit the involvement of inhabitants further through a restrictive interpretation of the provision.[307] Although the instrument was approved by all the signatory states to the 1864 Geneva Convention,[308] it remained unratified and did not enter into force. Instead, the

[300] ibid 381.

[301] Lueder (n 298) 151; 'take into consideration under the law voluntary aid societies and their personnel during war' (author's translation).

[302] 'Protocoles des Conférences internationales tenues à Genève, en octobre 1868' (1875) 20 *Nouveau recueil général de traités* 400, 412.

[303] Convention for the Amelioration of the Condition of the Wounded and Sick in Armies in the Field (Geneva, 6 July 1906) (1906 Geneva Convention), arts 10–11.

[304] 1864 Geneva Convention, art 5.

[305] G Münzel, *Untersuchungen über die Genfer Konvention: eine Darstellung und Kritik des nach diesem Vertrage geltenden Landkriegsrechtes, mit einem geschichtlichen Überblick über die Bestrebungen bis zum Abschlusse des Vertrages und über die Versuche zu seiner Fortbildung* (Freiburg, G Ragoczy, 1901) 170.

[306] D Bujard, 'The Geneva Convention of 1864 and the Brussels Conference of 1874' (1974) 14:163 *IRRC* 527, 532.

[307] 'Protocoles Genève, 1868' (n 302) 412 and 418.

[308] 'Articles Additionnels à la Convention de Genève du 22 Août 1864; Signés à Genève, le 20 Octobre 1968' (1873) 18 *Nouveau recueil général de traités* 612, 612.

1906 Geneva Convention limited the 'special protection and certain immunities' for inhabitants to those acting upon the appeal and under the supervision of military authority.[309] Best argues that the 1864 Geneva Convention 'needed to be tightened up, and the authority of the military unmistakably restored' so that national volunteers would take 'their proper place within the national military organization; like soldiers, "subject to military laws and regulations"'.[310]

This hesitant, indeed reluctant, approach to safeguarding individuals who do not belong to the armed forces was informed by the prevalent scepticism and even hostility with which not only military officials but also some prominent humanitarians, such as Florence Nightingale, perceived private individuals at the time.[311] They were often portrayed as hyenas on the battlefield, and the authors of plunder and barbarous cruelty against the wounded combatants left behind.[312] The dismaying experience of the wars of 1866 and 1870–71, characterised by the abuse of wounded military personnel at the hands of inhabitants,[313] may have given further cause for reservation regarding the inclusion of private individuals in the care for the wounded and sick under the law.

The negotiation of the 1864 Geneva Convention and related subsequent instruments show the marginal yet contested role of individuals who do not belong to the armed forces. They did not acquire a protective status in their own right. Their non-military character was not a ground for protection, but rather for their exclusion from both the theatre of war and the scope of the Geneva Convention. The negotiation of the instruments reaffirmed the perceived inter-state character of war and thus the battlefield even after the cessation of hostilities. This understanding was likely informed by the nature of the law-making process itself, which inter alia constrained the norm entrepreneurship of the ICRC's predecessor. While the state delegations recognised its work at the 1864 Conference, the Committee was only admitted to participate in the role of an observer, unable to cast a vote.[314] Moreover, as mentioned above, its recommendations were not adopted without modification, but instead adapted to state interests in the working drafts. Benvenisti and Lustig accordingly portray the history of the laws of war in the second half of the nineteenth century as one of civil society's exclusion rather than success, and as supressing its vision for the codification movement.[315]

[309] 1906 Geneva Convention, art 5.

[310] Best, *Humanity* (n 1) 152.

[311] Crossland (n 108) 64 and 72–75.

[312] See, eg, J Naundorff, *Unter dem rothen Kreuz – Fremde und eigene Erfahrungen auf Böhmischer Erde und den Schlachtfeldern der Neuzeit* (Leipzig, Veit, 1867); Lueder (n 298) 267 and 333.

[313] Lueder (n 298) 268, 296 and 333.

[314] 'Protocoles 1864' (n 16) 380.

[315] E Benvenisti and D Lustig, 'Revisiting the Memory of Solferino: Knowledge Production and the Laws of War' in A Bianchi and M Hirsch (eds), *International Law's Invisible Frames: Social Cognition and Knowledge Production in International Legal Processes* (Oxford, Oxford University Press, 2021).

It should also be noted that the deliberation of the provisions, and thus the construction of individuals, was primarily conducted by medical military staff, who may have been protective of their own professional sphere. Both international lawyers and military officials criticised the 1864 Geneva Convention for the lack of consideration of their respective perspectives and interests.[316] The provisions were deemed insufficiently precise, and too accommodating of humanitarian ideals at the expense of military necessity and prudence.[317] Regarding the 1868 Additional Articles, Best even believes that they failed to achieve 'the same legal status and reputation' as the 1864 Geneva Convention partly due to 'the wariness and even resentment of the professional military interest at the humanitarians' intrusions into their affairs'.[318] Nevertheless, the 1864 treaty itself was adopted as a state-centric protection regime for combatants in which other individuals remain peripheral to the understanding of the battlefield.

The drafters of the Brussels Declaration were also concerned that individuals who do not belong to the armed forces may intrude in the organised warfare between regular armed forces. The 1874 Diplomatic Conference focused on their participation in hostilities, for example, in relation to the concept of combatants, as outlined above, rather than their position as innocent bystanders. While the existence of individuals who are not members of the armed forces are implied in various articles of the Brussels Declaration, the population in whole or in part only constitutes a defined category of persons in form of the *levée en masse*. The provision was notably originally placed in the section on 'des droits des parties belligérantes par rapport aux personnes privées' in the *projet*.[319] Indeed, the first three provisions in this section dealt with individuals fighting against an invading or occupying power.[320] Yet the understanding of these individuals and their participation in the hostilities was by no means uniform, as the above analysis with regard to the combatant status has shown. The delegations of small states in fact desired some involvement of the population in the defence of the country. Beernaert's impassioned speech at the First Hague Peace Conference further suggests that, in his view, the indolent bystander was a greater threat than the dutiful citizen fighting to defend their country against an invader.[321] General den Beer Portugael further argued that 'it is to the benefit of the populations to impose on them' the requirements of organised and disciplined warfare,[322]

[316] N Wylie, 'Muddied Waters: The Influence of the First Hague Conference on the Evolution of the Geneva Conventions of 1864 and 1906' in M Abbenhuis, CE Barber and AR Higgins (eds), *War, Peace and International Order? The Legacies of the Hague Conferences of 1899 and 1907* (Abingdon, Routledge, 2017) 56–57.

[317] See, eg, *Actes* (n 34) 18–20; Lueder (n 298) 351–52.

[318] Best, *Humanity* (n 1) 151.

[319] *Actes* (n 34) 6.

[320] ibid.

[321] *1899 Proceedings* (n 30) 504.

[322] ibid 549.

thus showing a concern for the protection of the population which *participates* in the hostilities in accordance with the laws of war, rather than the peaceful population.

Generally, however, the rudimentary forms of protection for individuals who do not belong to the armed forces were repeatedly emphasised as being conditional on their non-participation.[323] For instance, the prohibition of bombardments in the *projet* was not only limited to towns undefended by armed forces, but also by its inhabitants,[324] once again suggesting their capacity for violence. The formulation adopted in Article 15 of the Brussels Declaration stipulates that the towns 'are not defended' without specifying whether this only refers to the armed forces. The reiteration that individuals who do not belong to the armed forces are required to abstain from armed resistance during the negotiations[325] still suggests that the drafters believed that the inhabitants of the town had to remain peaceful to benefit from the protection. Twenty-five years later, Beernaert observed the constraining force of the Brussels Declaration on these individuals, noting that to achieve the instrument's humanitarian objective it was desired 'that populations be in some sort forbidden to mingle with the war'.[326] Colonel Gross von Schwarzhoff also proclaimed that if the condition of their peaceful conduct 'is not fulfilled, most of the guaranties provided in [*sic*] behalf of the inhabitants lose their reason for existence'.[327] The possibility that individuals who do not belong to the armed forces may participate in warfare, especially by violent means, seems to have been at the forefront of the drafters' minds, and the adopted rules reflect this concern. The deliberations at the Diplomatic Conferences, as well as the drafts and adopted provisions, show that it was not inconceivable for the armed forces to attack individuals who would today be considered 'civilians'; nor was it believed that the latter would necessarily abstain from participating in warfare.[328] Rather, if these individuals were aloof from warfare, it was on their own account; however, they might also 'be drawn in, whether voluntarily or by force of circumstance'.[329] The law itself did not shield them from suffering these consequences of war.

By insisting on their non-participation, individuals who do not belong to the armed forces were meant to be excluded from the battlefield. However, this was not only, or possibly not at all, pursued for their own benefit but rather to protect lawful regular combatants from what was perceived to be barbarian and cruel behaviour. While the understanding of non-military individuals was not generally embedded in ideas of innocence or immunity, a discourse of victimhood

[323] See, eg, *Actes* (n 34) 6, 9 and 34.
[324] ibid 5.
[325] ibid 9.
[326] *1899 Proceedings* (n 30) 502.
[327] ibid 552.
[328] cf Kolb, *Advanced Introduction* (n 202) 5.
[329] Alexander, 'Genesis' (n 12) 365.

surrounded combatants confronted with unchivalrous conduct.[330] In 1874, it was suggested that the *levée en masse* should carry arms openly thus protecting the resisting population itself from being treated more harshly if they were not distinguishable.[331] In contrast, the German delegation, which introduced the amendment in 1907, had argued for a similar requirement in 1899 seemingly to protect the regular armed forces who would otherwise 'find themselves in an unfavorable situation',[332] rather than to shield the population. In a lecture shortly after the Brussels Conference, Thomas Erskine Holland cited the Duke of Wellington as expressing the prevalent fear at the time that an individual may 'play the part of peaceful inhabitant and soldier by turns'.[333] Benvenisti and Lustig even argue that '[t]he Brussels Declaration was designed partly to protect armies – and their governments – from "patriotic insurrections" by foreign and domestic civilians'.[334] As Alexander observes '[t]he probability that citizens would not remain so [peaceful] was one of the principal concerns of jurists and governments at the time – certainly a much greater concern than the suffering of private citizens'.[335]

C. Neutral and Enemy Nationals

The deliberations at the Second Hague Peace Conference differed from the earlier diplomatic conferences in their increasing consideration of the nationality of individuals who do not belong to the armed forces.[336] In 1907, the Conference not only sought to regulate the rights and duties of neutral states, but also examined the status of neutral persons in the territory of belligerent parties. It is notable that the debate on the treatment of neutral persons was characterised by a more sustained engagement with particular situations in war compared to the deliberation of the Hague Regulations which relied upon the Brussels Declaration as a starting point. Similar to the negotiations of other newly introduced regulations in 1907, the discussion also seems to reflect to a greater extent the understandings and approaches in international legal scholarship.

The report on neutral persons in the territory of belligerents submitted to the Second Commission explained that the proposed rules were based on the idea that these individuals 'should remain, as far as possible, unaffected by the

[330] See, eg, *1899 Proceedings* (n 30) 552–53; *1907 Proceedings* (n 156) 16.
[331] *Actes* (n 34) 34.
[332] *1899 Proceedings* (n 30) 552.
[333] TE Holland, *A Lecture on the Brussels Conference of 1874, and other Diplomatic Attempts to Mitigate the Rigour of Warfare* (Oxford, Parker, 1876) 17–18.
[334] Benvenisti and Lustig, 'Monopolizing War' (n 96) 131.
[335] Alexander, 'Genesis' (n 12) 362.
[336] For an analysis of the significance of nationality for the protection of individuals see further S Landefeld, 'The Changing Significance of Nationality for the Protection of Civilians in the Hands of a Party to an International Armed Conflict' (2023) 28 *Journal of Conflict & Security Law* 501.

war. They shall not take part in it and they shall suffer the effects of it only so far as unavoidable'.[337] The proposition regarding the settlement of indemnities stipulated different timings for reparations for neutral nationals and nationals of the belligerent parties where the latter would be left until the conclusion of peace. While this differentiated scheme was defended as being grounded in practicalities,[338] some delegations rejected the creation of a special status for neutral nationals and the guarantee of more favourable treatment of their property. It was believed to be impossible in practice to draw a distinction based on nationality.[339] More importantly, some lawyers and military delegates believed that the nationality of private persons was inconsequential for their status due to the nature of war being a conflict between states, rather than individuals, thus echoing the Rousseau/Portalis doctrine. It was argued that a distinction based on nationality would be a step backward since the individuals were deemed to be protected as 'peaceful inhabitants' or 'non-combatants',[340] notwithstanding that no general protection regime had been established for them under the Hague Regulations. Indeed, the same delegates maintained that neutral nationals domiciled in a state should share with its residents the benefits of peace, as well as the burdens of war.[341] The French delegate and lawyer Louis Renault, for example, stressed that 'all individuals not taking part in hostilities should stand on a footing of absolute equality, whether it be a question of *protective* measures or of *rigorous* measures'.[342] The report itself emphasised that the '[t]he sole and immediate object of the project is not to favor foreigners as against the native population of the country where they live', but rather 'to minimize, so far as possible, the evil effects of war and to diminish, so far as circumstances permit, the number of persons called upon to suffer its hardships and burdens'.[343] It noted, however, that the international instrument could not regulate the relationship between belligerent states and their own subjects. These individuals were again regarded as citizens who owed a duty towards their states and were thus considered as naturally called upon for sustaining the war efforts and paying requisitions to the invading enemy state.[344]

The consideration of special treatment for neutral persons was closely related to the understanding of the nationals of the belligerent parties as enemies themselves. While it was submitted that '[t]he tie of allegiance which unites [neutral persons] to a neutral State creates in their favor a special status admitting of rights and duties', even if their domicile is in a belligerent state,[345] nationals

[337] *1907 Proceedings* (n 156) 60.
[338] ibid 139–42.
[339] ibid, see also 40.
[340] See, eg, ibid 38–39, 72–73 and 79–80.
[341] ibid 39, 72 and 79.
[342] ibid 141 (emphasis added).
[343] ibid 64; it is worth noting that the report was written by the Swiss delegate and lawyer Colonel Borel since Switzerland was one of the main supporters of the provision in question.
[344] ibid 64–65.
[345] ibid 187.

of belligerent states were perceived as 'enemies' due to their respective tie of allegiance to the enemy state. The engagement with 'populations' and 'citizens', both at the Brussels Conference and the First Hague Peace Conference, already showed an understanding of the individuals as belonging to a state. However, their classification as 'neutral' and especially 'enemy' persons additionally emphasised that their position was determined along the belligerent lines of inter-state relations. Even if they were not perceived as potential intruders and threats to organised warfare in a particular situation, nationals of the enemy state were regarded as belonging to the opposing belligerent party and were, therefore, generally considered enemies.

This understanding of individuals who do not belong to the armed forces was prevalent during the period of the early written laws of war. The Oxford Manual provided for a distinction 'between the individuals who compose the "armed force" of a State and its other "*ressortissants*"'.[346] International legal scholarship commonly referred to the nationals of a belligerent state as enemies, albeit sometimes as 'passive enemies' to distinguish them from combatants.[347] Alexander remarks that 'jurists were proud of the conceptual separation of the private citizen and the state military', but 'they often seem to mention the concept in order to limit it'.[348] As citizens or subjects of a belligerent state, 'they are unavoidably a part of their state and cannot expect much respite from its fortunes'.[349] The Lieber Code also seemed to accept that citizenship, as a link between the individual and the state, would not only render the person an enemy but also subject 'to the hardships of the war'.[350] In his exploration of 'A Different Sense of Humanity' in the Lieber Code, Giladi highlights how the individual was understood as a member of the collective society in a public war.[351]

The opinions of international lawyers, however, diverged from state practice in terms of the implications of enemy nationality for the individual's treatment.[352] Leading scholars such as Rolin-Jaequemyns and Bluntschli condemned the mass expulsion of enemy aliens in their publications,[353] and Martens believed that 'expulsion and persecution of enemy aliens were obsolete practices'.[354]

[346] Oxford Manual, art 1 explanatory note.

[347] See, eg, Halleck (n 190) ch XVII–XVIII; Bluntschli, *Völkerrecht* (n 129) 35 and 297; Field (n 190) paras 744–47; Oppenheim, *International Law, vol II* (n 169) paras 87–92 and 100; some scholars, on the other hand, defined enemy individuals based on their place of birth and place of residence, see Robert Phillimore (1854) cited in DL Caglioti, *War and Citizenship: Enemy Aliens and National Belonging from the French Revolution to the First World War* (Cambridge, Cambridge University Press, 2021) 18.

[348] Alexander, 'Genesis' (n 12) 362.

[349] ibid.

[350] Lieber Code, art 21.

[351] R Giladi, 'A Different Sense of Humanity: Occupation in Francis Lieber's Code' (2012) 94:885 *IRRC* 81, 107–08.

[352] Caglioti (n 347) 17–58.

[353] ibid 45–46.

[354] ibid 50.

Regarding state practice, on the other hand, Daniela Caglioti identifies the Franco-Prussian War as 'a watershed in national policies on civilians of enemy nationality' in her study on *War and Citizenship*.[355] She argues that it was the first time that 'governments identified foreign nationals as "enemies within" as standard practice'.[356] At the outbreak of the war, for example, '40,000 German men, women and children' had been expelled 'from Paris and the department of the Seine'.[357] Shortly after this war, the 1874 *projet* declared that hostilities should not be conducted against the peaceful nationals of the enemy state;[358] yet nationality did not feature prominently at the Diplomatic Conference and was not mentioned in the adopted Brussels Declaration.

The consideration of nationality as a ground for differentiated treatment was only introduced into the negotiations of the written laws of war at the Second Hague Peace Conference. This concern for the treatment of enemy aliens was likely triggered by recent state practice shortly before and since the First Hague Peace Conference. The Thirty-Day War between Turkey and Greece (1897) had seen the expulsion of Greeks from the Ottoman Empire.[359] During the Anglo-Boer War (1899–1902), civilians were interned in concentration camps and Britons were expelled from Transvaal.[360] During the Russo-Japanese War (1904–1905), Japanese nationals were subjected to adverse treatment which led to their flight and expulsion from the Russian Empire. In contrast, the Japanese government, striving for recognition as a member in the family of 'civilised' nations, proclaimed that it would respect and protect enemy aliens in its territory.[361]

At the Diplomatic Conference in 1907, the Japanese delegation proposed an article providing that '[t]he *ressortissants* of a belligerent, inhabiting the territory of the opposing party shall not be interned unless the exigencies of war make it necessary'.[362] The Italian delegate Count Tornielli suggested the extension of the provision to also forbid expulsion.[363] While these proposals first and foremost distinguished between individuals who do not belong to the armed forces based on their nationality, they also entailed an individualised approach to the treatment of enemy nationals. The Italian delegate explained that 'individuals may be expelled if their conduct is considered dangerous, it means to affirm that on the other hand expulsions *en masse* are forbidden'.[364] This restriction of expulsion, however, was rejected for interfering with the states' sovereign right to expel non-nationals.[365] According to Caglioti, '[t]he [Second]

[355] ibid 40.
[356] ibid.
[357] ibid.
[358] *Actes* (n 34) 4.
[359] Caglioti (n 347) 63.
[360] ibid 56.
[361] ibid 58–59.
[362] *1907 Proceedings* (n 156) 243.
[363] ibid 105.
[364] ibid 112.
[365] ibid 112 and 114.

Hague Peace Conference thus reaffirmed that expulsions, even mass expulsions, were outside of the sphere of international law and could not be regulated in a convention'.[366] The proposal on the internment of enemy nationals, on the other hand, was considered problematic since it was perceived as enabling the adverse treatment of 'inoffensive' individuals who do not belong to the armed forces, rather than protecting them.[367] The Japanese delegation ultimately withdrew the proposal on the understanding that Article 5 of the Hague Regulations was to be interpreted as meaning that, 'since it is permitted to subject prisoners of war to internment, the other *ressortissants* of the enemy State who are not prisoners cannot be interned'.[368] The Russian delegate Major General Yermolow also briefly proposed the creation of a separate chapter dedicated to the '*Ressortissants* of a belligerent in the territory of the adverse party'.[369] While the proposal was not further pursued, it foreshadowed developments in the inter-war period and after the Second World War.[370]

Caglioti observes that '[e]ven the recent experiences of the Anglo-Boar War and the Russo-Japanese War did not push delegates to completely rethink the logic on which the 1899 Convention was originally based'.[371] As argued above, the regulation and protection of individuals who do not belong to the armed forces in the Hague Regulations were taken from the Brussels Declaration without extending its protective shield. Moreover, it is worth noting that the discussion of the Japanese and Italian proposals briefly focused on the relevance of wars in colonial territories as recent experience that might have justified the suggested provisions.[372] The Belgian delegate Beernaert emphasised the absence of such internments in European wars, noting only two examples 'of Cuba and the Transvaal, which are not very commendable'.[373] Yet the Franco-Prussian War had shown that enemy nationals were also the subject of adverse treatment in Europe. Beernaert's consideration of 'internments or expulsions *en masse* as belonging to another age',[374] in retrospect, seems to have been too optimistic in light of developments during the two World Wars.[375] Ultimately, however, the self-perception of the respective actors determined which historical examples they drew on in the construction of warfare and its regulation.

Indeed, the European bias of the negotiations was also apparent in the discussion of nationality itself. The nationality link and thus the understanding of the individual through the prism of the state proved challenging with respect

[366] Caglioti (n 347) 62.
[367] *1907 Proceedings* (n 156) 111.
[368] ibid 113–14.
[369] ibid 132.
[370] See chapter 4, section II.A.
[371] Caglioti (n 347) 63.
[372] *1907 Proceedings* (n 156) 111–13 and 124.
[373] ibid 111.
[374] ibid 113.
[375] See chapter 4, section II.A.

to colonial territories in which individuals of various nationalities might have been assembled without a sentimental link to their country of nationality.[376] Lieutenant General den Beer Pootugael instead argued that, in the context of colonies, the sense of belonging and the link of loyalty did not stem from nationality but rather 'the bond of preservation, conservation, security, equality and fraternity which unites the civilized against the uncivilized in the face of a common danger'.[377] It was also pointed out that nationality legislation was missing in some states in the 'Far East' and that 'entire populations may be found in this part of the world whose citizenship is quite uncertain or might be changed at any moment by decisions too interested to be acceptable'.[378] Although nationality was thus acknowledged as not decisive for the perception of individuals in every situation, it was incorporated into the law.[379] This may have been due to the underlying preoccupation of the majority of delegations with European wars. The adopted written international code on warfare appears to have been essentially a European project.

III. CONCLUSION

A close reading of the drafting histories of the early written laws of war in the second half of the nineteenth and beginning of the twentieth century reveals that the rules and regulations were not informed by a principled clear distinction between combatants and 'civilians'. Instead, the law-making processes were riddled with struggles to reconcile different, sometimes contradictory, understandings of individuals in an agreed upon text.

Members of the regular armed forces were considered victims of war when wounded or sick, and when they were faced with the participation of irregular fighters and individuals who do not belong to the armed forces more generally. The obligations, privileges and protections associated with the combatant status were uncontested. Yet the question of which individuals would qualify as combatants under the laws of war was the subject of disagreement. States explicitly deliberated the personal scope of the combatant status at the Brussels Conference without finding common ground. This shows that the construction of shared meaning may not be possible at a Diplomatic Conference where states are informed by diverging interests. Although a legally binding definition was later adopted in the Hague Regulations, it does not reflect the understanding of combatants by all states who participated in the drafting. No agreement was achieved beyond the apparent incompleteness of the written laws of war.

[376] *1907 Proceedings* (n 156) 64 and 80.
[377] ibid 80.
[378] ibid 64.
[379] See especially Convention (V) Respecting the Rights and Duties of Neutral Powers and Persons in Case of War on Land (The Hague, 18 October 1907), ch III.

It remained unsettled whether outside of the conventional legal framework the involvement of the population in national defence that was commonly considered legitimate was also a lawful form of participation in warfare.

Adam Roberts suggests that 'the civilian hardly entered with an intact identity and clear protection' in the early treaties on the laws of war.[380] This chapter has argued that a concept of civilians, which deems individuals who do not belong to the armed forces to be innocent and vulnerable victims and protects them by virtue of their status of not being combatants, was indeed absent in this period. The silences in the international instruments at this time indicate that the perceived purpose of the laws of war was *not* to generally protect such individuals by shielding them from the consequences of warfare. The few guarantees that are included in the adopted texts reveal the various forms in which these individuals were understood in the context of war. They were recognised as affected, and potentially in need of protection, due to being inhabitants of particular locations, the population of a belligerent or occupied state, or nationals of a particular state. The designation of some individuals as 'peaceful' or 'inoffensive' seemingly removed them from the perceived scope of war, and thus commonly from the reach of the written laws of war.

Moreover, instead of being considered as victims of war, individuals who do not belong to the armed forces were primarily discussed in terms of their own involvement in warfare. Their active roles in providing assistance and care to the wounded and sick, as well as in participating in hostilities, gave rise to significant concerns among most states. Yet small states desired their participation, as dutiful citizens, in the countries' self-defence. These individuals thus became the focus of attention, either as intruders or potential threats to the organised conduct of war and the regular armed forces or, indeed, as legitimate and even lawful participants in national defence. Ultimately, no coherent, distinct conceptualisation of such individuals based on some shared characteristics can be discerned from the negotiations of the treaties. The mere fact that they neither belonged to the armed forces nor qualified as combatants did not provide them with a status that would have comprised distinct privileges, obligations or protections. The negotiations of the laws of war at the time did not lead to the creation of a status for everyone. They were characterised by the inclusion and exclusion of individuals from the scope of conventional law, which was chiefly designed to regulate and protect individuals who lawfully participate in warfare.

The absence of a status and general protection for 'civilians' has been sometimes explained with the prevailing understanding of the laws of war at the time as regulating the belligerent relation between states, and thus their regular armed forces. This narrow view of the law may have been facilitated by the nature of the law-making processes. The history of the instruments as well as

[380] A Roberts, 'The Civilian in Modern War' (2009) 12 *YIHL* 13, 35.

contemporaneous legal scholarship suggest that alternative understandings of individuals who do not belong to the armed forces existed, some of which had even been brought to the attention of the drafters. Nevertheless, the dominance of military officials and diplomats, as well as the exclusion of non-state actors especially at the Brussels Conference may have entrenched general assumptions about the institution of war and contributed to the non-engagement with individuals who were believed to be de facto outside of the battlefield. While the characterisation of actors, for example, as medical personnel, military officials, diplomats and international lawyers is necessarily a simplification, their argumentations during this period show certain differences in their understanding of individuals. They were informed by diverse ideational and normative frameworks of their time ranging from the understanding of professional, organised warfare and patriotism to emerging humanitarian ideals and the doctrine of international legal scholarship. The varying influence of their contributions to the negotiation of the early written laws of war also highlights the power imbalance between different participants in the law-making process.

Overall, the adoption of the 1864 Geneva Convention and the 1868 St Petersburg Declaration may have been facilitated by prevailing common assumptions about warfare as a tournament between states and their regular armed forces. In contrast, the actual engagement with the personal scope of the combatant status at the 1874 Brussels Conference gave rise to disagreement. Small and great military states were advocating divergent understandings of lawful participation in hostilities informed by either their experience of warfare in the past or an interest in rule-governed organised warfare in the future. Even though no agreement was achieved, the Brussels Declaration seems to have institutionalised certain understandings of individuals for the purpose of the laws of war. The First Hague Peace Conference introduced the Declaration's definition of combatants into conventional international law following a less sustained engagement with different forms of participation in warfare. Similarly, the rudimentary guarantees for individuals who do not belong to the armed forces in the Brussels Declaration were merely confirmed in the Hague Regulations. The framing of the First Hague Peace Conference as the continuation of a progressive history of law-making, and the growing influence of the normative context on the negotiations may have facilitated the adoption of conventional law; yet, at the same time, it constrained the rules' regulatory and protective scope. The understandings of individuals in warfare which underpin the rules in the 1899 and 1907 Hague Regulations were, therefore, arguably shaped in 1874 rather than at the Hague Peace Conferences.

4

The Inter-war Years and the 1949 Geneva Conventions

THE FOUR GENEVA Conventions of 1949 are generally considered to be a response to the evolution of warfare and the atrocities committed during the Second World War. The drafters at the 1949 Diplomatic Conference themselves declared their aim to address the gaps in the law that had been revealed by the recent war, especially regarding the protection of civilians.[1] Given the absence of a concept of civilians and a related protection regime in the 1907 Hague Regulations on the Laws and Customs of War on Land,[2] as discussed in the previous chapter, the fourth Geneva Convention Relative to the Protection of Civilian Persons in Time of War[3] (GC IV) constitutes the first treaty that is seemingly designed to protect civilians and, on account of this, prima facie fills the *lacuna*. Karma Nabulsi observes the common assumption 'in the literature that the catastrophic results of "total war" were the primary factor behind the introduction of this new convention', which reflects 'a new set of norms [that] had been created between 1939 and 1945'.[4] While the Second World War was undoubtedly an impetus for the adoption of the 1949 Geneva Conventions, this chapter argues that the conceptualisation of individuals in the law-making process resumed developments preceding the outbreak of the war.

Although GC IV introduces the term 'civilian' for the first time into the written laws of war, now also comprising international armed conflicts (IACs), its title is arguably misleading. It suggests that it would be 'a Convention for the protection of *all* civilians in *all* circumstances in time of war', as the UK delegate

[1] *Final Record of the Diplomatic Conference of Geneva of 1949*, vol II(A) (Berne, Federal Political Department, 1950) 10; the terms 'civilians' and 'individuals who do not belong to the armed forces' are used interchangeably in this chapter due to the emergence of the former term in the period under examination, see A Alexander, 'The Genesis of the Civilian' (2007) 20 *LJIL* 359.

[2] Annex to Convention (IV): Regulations Respecting the Laws and Customs of War on Land (The Hague, 18 October 1907) (1907 Hague Regulations).

[3] (Geneva, 12 August 1949).

[4] K Nabulsi, 'Evolving Conceptions of Civilians and Belligerents: One Hundred Years After the Hague Peace Conferences' in S Chesterman (ed), *Civilians in War* (London, Lynne Rienner, 2001) 11.

Joyce Gutteridge later observed.[5] The treaty, however, not only fails to define 'civilians', but also the majority of the provisions pertain to a narrow group of 'protected persons' identified under Article 4 GC IV. Only a small portion of the Convention, namely Part II providing for the 'General Protection of Populations against certain Consequences of War', applies to the population as a whole.[6] This chapter shows that these two dissimilar conceptualisations of individuals who do not belong to the armed forces built upon developments of the inter-war years. Civilians were already drastically bearing the consequences of the First World War, and various actors subsequently assumed the task of humanising warfare by promoting safeguards for civilians. In particular, they were concerned with protecting civilian enemy nationals from and during internment, as well as shielding the civilian population from the effects of war. While these two apparent strands of progress were pursued more or less simultaneously and sometimes even by the same actors, their influence on GC IV was not the same. This chapter argues that the inter-war processes and the remaining structural divide in GC IV suggest that a coherent legal concept of civilians was still not achieved by the end of this period.

The construction of different categories of civilian persons prior to and during the drafting of GC IV coincided with a shift in focus in the development of the laws of war generally. The emphasis was often deliberately on the protection of war victims rather than the regulation of organised warfare,[7] including combatant status. The definition of the prisoner of war (POW) status in the 1949 Geneva Convention Relative to the Treatment of Prisoners of War[8] (GC III) changed the concept of combatants only slightly. This chapter first briefly outlines this evolution and examines why the (re-)construction of combatants was pursued to a very limited extent. Since advances regarding civilians were more significant in this period, they are at the centre of the present analysis. Lastly, the chapter explores the understanding of individuals in the emerging law on non-international armed conflicts (NIACs). It provides a brief overview of the status and regulation of such conflicts prior to the Second World War, and appraises Article 3 common to all 1949 Geneva Conventions (CA3). Overall, this chapter challenges the novelty of the understanding of individuals in times of international and non-international armed conflicts as well as the emergence of the concept of civilians in the immediate aftermath of the Second World War.

[5] JAC Gutteridge, 'The Geneva Conventions of 1949' (1949) 26 *BYIL* 294, 319.

[6] GC IV, art 13.

[7] R Kolb, 'The Protection of the Individual in Times of War and Peace' in B Fassbender and A Peters (eds), *The Oxford Handbook of the History of International Law* (Oxford, Oxford University Press, 2012) 328; see also N Wylie and L Cameron, 'The Impact of World War I on the Law Governing the Treatment of Prisoners of War and the Making of a Humanitarian Subject' (2018) 29 *EJIL* 1327.

[8] (Geneva, 12 August 1949), art 4.

I. COMBATANTS – THE CONTINUATION OF A CONCEPT

While the first three 1949 Geneva Conventions protect different categories of war victims, the beneficiaries of these protection regimes are primarily combatants in specified situations of vulnerability. The combatant status, which identifies lawful participants in the conduct of hostilities, seems to permeate the rules of GC III especially, even though it is not mentioned as such. This is due to 'a merger of sorts between conditions for POW status and conditions expected of combatants generally',[9] which had already been achieved in the predecessor of GC III, the Convention Relative to the Treatment of Prisoners of War[10] adopted in 1929. This treaty delineated its scope of application *ratione personae* by referring to the 1907 Hague Regulations' qualification of combatants[11] instead of defining POWs. GC III does not mention the Hague Regulations expressly; yet it reproduces the relevant provisions in an amended and expanded form.[12] The same categories of persons are also identified as the beneficiaries of the Geneva Convention for the Amelioration of the Condition of the Wounded and Sick in Armed Forces in the Field[13] and the Geneva Convention for the Amelioration of the Condition of Wounded, Sick and Shipwrecked Members of Armed Forces at Sea.[14]

The 1929 POW Convention, the first multilateral treaty dedicated exclusively to regulating the treatment of POWs, significantly developed the laws of war in terms of the substantive protection of these individuals. At the same time, it reaffirmed the existing notion of who would qualify as a POW, and indirectly as a combatant, without changing it. The International Committee of the Red Cross (ICRC), which had initiated the law-making process after the First World War, declared in its preparatory work for the new treaty that it was beyond its competence to revise the first Chapter of the Hague Regulations.[15] At the 1929 Diplomatic Conference, the drafters themselves debated whether the application clause *ratione personae* should take the form of an express reference to the Hague Regulations or a reproduction of its terms, only tacitly relying on the treaty.[16] Either way, the meaning and scope of the combatant status as defined

[9] S Watts, 'Who Is A Prisoner of War?' in A Clapham, P Gaeta and M Sassòli (eds), *The 1949 Geneva Conventions: A Commentary* (Oxford, Oxford University Press, 2015) para 2.
[10] (Geneva, 27 July 1929) (1929 POW Convention).
[11] ibid art 1.
[12] GC III, art 4.
[13] (Geneva, 12 August 1949), art 13.
[14] (Geneva, 12 August 1949), art 13.
[15] 'Projet de Code des prisonniers de guerre, déportés, évacués et réfugiés' (1923) 5:56 *IRRC* 771, 778–79; the International Law Association's draft Regulations for the Treatment of Prisoners of War for combatants, unlike its recommendations for civilian POWs (see section II.A), also refrained from defining the term, ILA, 'Second Day's Proceedings: Treatment of Prisoners of War' (1921) 30 *ILA Reports of Conferences* 188, 237–46.
[16] *Actes de la Conférence diplomatique de Genève de 1929* (Geneva, Imprimerie du Journal de Genève, 1930) 444–45 and 461.

in the Hague Regulations was seemingly taken for granted. The 1929 POW Convention was regarded as building on previous achievements by completing, developing and enlarging the laws of war which had been elaborated before in Brussels and The Hague.[17] It merely expanded the scope of POW status to include military personnel involved in maritime and aerial warfare, subject to derogations,[18] since the Hague Regulations are limited to the armed forces on land. The inter-war law-making process was thus strongly rooted in the legal framework of the previous period.

The 1947 Commission of Government Experts, which formed part of the drafting process in the wake of the Second World War, was aware of the preference in 1929 'to refer back to the Hague Regulations' and the 'generally accepted' definition of combatants therein instead of adopting a potentially contradictory definition of POWs.[19] Yet the ICRC considered these provisions obsolete and inadequate in light of the changing nature of warfare, and expected a revision of the Hague Regulations in the future.[20] As a result, although the drafters of GC III at the 1949 Diplomatic Conference were in 'unanimous agreement' that the delineation of those eligible for POW status should be 'in harmony with the [Hague] Regulations',[21] the treaty provides a self-contained,[22] and partly novel definition of POWs.

The Stockholm Draft, which functioned as a working draft at the 1949 Diplomatic Conference, included 'members of voluntary corps which are regularly constituted' under the POW status,[23] without further elaboration. The negotiations later clarified that the phrase 'regularly constituted' entailed the four Hague criteria for combatant status, which were only discussed with respect to their formulation.[24] Article 4 GC III, nevertheless, abstains from merely referring to the 1907 provisions, due to the perceived need 'after such a long interval, to reaffirm those rules explicitly, so as to leave no doubt as to their validity'.[25] Persons belonging to a *levée en masse* are also included in the definition of POWs, although it was argued that this particular form of warfare 'had practically never arisen'.[26] Even the language of this rule in GC III was

[17] ibid 633.

[18] 1929 POW Convention, art 1(2).

[19] *Commission of Government Experts for the Study of Conventions for the Protection of War Victims – Preliminary Documents Submitted by the International Committee of the Red Cross, vol II, Geneva Convention of July 27, 1929, relative to the Treatment of Prisoners of War* (ICRC Library, CEG_1947_DOCPG_ENG_01) 3.

[20] ibid 3 and 16.

[21] *Final Record*, vol II(A) (n 1) 561.

[22] JS Pictet (ed), *The Geneva Conventions of 12 August 1949, Commentary III: Geneva Convention Relative to the Treatment of Prisoners of War* (Geneva, ICRC, 1960) (hereafter *GC III Commentary*) 51.

[23] *Final Record of the Diplomatic Conference of Geneva of 1949*, vol I (Berne, Federal Political Department, 1950) 73.

[24] *Final Record*, vol II(A) (n 1) 237, 414 and 479.

[25] ibid 237.

[26] ibid 239; although isolated cases in France and Greek were recognised.

trapped in its 1907 formulation. Article 4(A)(6) reproduces almost verbatim Article 2 of the Hague Regulations, employing the terminology of 'inhabitants' of a non-occupied territory. In comparison, the discussion regarding POWs otherwise mainly referred to 'civilians' and the 'civilian population', which were the common terms of the period, as further discussed below.[27] Instead of defining POWs *ab initio*, GC III thus reinforced and naturalised the combatant status as it had been enshrined in conventional law in the previous period, despite its then contested and non-exhaustive nature.[28]

This is partly due to the nature of GC III as a humanitarian protection regime for war victims rather than a regulatory system for the conduct of hostilities. Indeed, some novel elements in the 1949 definition of POWs are inconsequential for the concept of combatants. First, Article 4 also includes certain civilians. These are identified in a revised list of '[p]ersons who accompany the armed forces without actually being members thereof'[29] as well as '[m]embers of crews … of the merchant marine and the crews of civil aircraft of the Parties to the conflict, who do not benefit by more favourable treatment under any other provisions of international law'.[30] On the other hand, Article 33 excludes medical personnel and chaplains from POW status while guaranteeing them 'as a minimum the benefits and protection of the present Convention'.[31] Second, the explicit extension of the POW protection regime to demobilised military personnel in occupied territory and military personnel interned in neutral countries[32] provides safeguards in specific circumstances for individuals already recognised as combatants. These provisions were adopted as responses to ambiguities and *lacunae* in the law, which had become apparent during the Second World War.[33] They amended the scope of the POW status, yet not the concept of combatants.

The understanding of combatants, and thus of lawful participation in armed conflicts, nevertheless shaped the discussion of Article 4 GC III. The extension of POW status to '[m]embers of regular armed forces who profess allegiance to a government or an authority not recognized by the Detaining Power'[34] may appear to detach it from the requirement of state authority. Yet the debate centred on whether these forces were associated or 'fighting in conjunction with a State recognized as a regular belligerent'.[35] This proposed condition

[27] See section II.

[28] See chapter 3 section I.

[29] GC III, art 4(A)(4); cf 1907 Hague Regulations, art 13.

[30] GC III, art 4(A)(5); for a discussion of their POW status despite their perception as civilians see *Government Experts*, vol II (n 19) 24–28.

[31] cf 1907 Hague Regulations, art 3 which declares that non-combatant members of the armed forces 'have a right to be treated as prisoners of war'.

[32] GC III, art 4(B)(1)–(2).

[33] *GC III Commentary* (n 22) 6, 50 and 65–66.

[34] GC III, art 4(A)(3).

[35] *GC III Commentary* (n 22) 64.

indicates the presupposition that the laws of war only regulate relations between belligerent states. Combatants acquire their legitimacy and lawfulness from their connection to such a state. The first, commonly believed to be authoritative, *GC III Commentary* by the ICRC confirms this by declaring that, despite the rejection of an explicit requirement, the non-recognised authority should 'either consider itself as representing one of the High Contracting Parties, or declare that it accepts the obligations stipulated in the Convention and wishes to apply them'.[36] Hence, the conceptualisation of combatants very much remained state-centric and confined within the ideational structure of regulated and organised warfare.

Only the controversial inclusion of organised resistance movements under Article 4(A)(2) can arguably be considered as an indirect development of the concept of combatants. While such irregular fighters fell outside the scope of the written laws of war, the ICRC already ventured to protect them in accordance with the standards for the treatment of POWs during the Second World War.[37] The report of Committee II responsible for the drafting of the POW convention at the Diplomatic Conference consequently justified the 'important innovation' to include resistance movements under the regime as a response to the experience during the recent war.[38] The prolonged negotiation of their inclusion at the 1947 Conference of Government Experts and at the 1949 Diplomatic Conference proved, nonetheless, difficult and contentious, not least due to the underpinning disagreement on their right to participate in hostilities. The debate itself focused on the established Hague conditions applicable to militias and voluntary corps, as well as the proposed additional requirements of effective territorial control and the notification of the Occupying Power of their participation. Although these newly suggested conditions were not adopted, only those irregular fighters who resemble regular armed forces in their 'principal characteristics' qualify as POWs.[39] The additional requirement of 'belonging to a Party to the conflict', furthermore, links them to a state.[40] Partisans were thus indirectly legitimised as combatants if they fitted within the traditional understanding of organised inter-state warfare.

Various other forms of resistance remain excluded, such as *levées en masse* in occupied territory, as well as unorganised movements and individual resistance. The Italian and Israeli delegations advocated the protection of the civilian population, which was unable to organise itself before rising in defence of the country against the occupying power. Their proposals were rejected, however, inter alia for redefining the combatant status. The UK delegation in particular

[36] ibid 63.
[37] ibid 52.
[38] *Final Record*, vol II(A) (n 1) 562.
[39] *GC III Commentary* (n 22) 58.
[40] R Kolb, *Advanced Introduction to International Humanitarian Law* (Cheltenham, Elgar, 2014) 132.

declared that it would have been ultra vires for the Diplomatic Conference 'to examine and revise the definition of "combatant"'.[41] The existing laws of war thus constrained the construction of individuals for the purpose of GC III. This insistence on the established legal framework, and thus the status quo, may have also served a strategic aim in support of the political national interests of certain states.

The debate on recognising and protecting irregular fighters under the new POW convention was dominated by two opposing views, which partly resembled the discourse of the earlier period.[42] The two sides have been associated with the perspectives of the occupying and occupied powers.[43] Giovanni Mantilla rather observes a 'chasm between the "Liberated" (France and others in Western Europe, along with Eastern European countries) and "Liberator" countries (the United States and the UK, in particular)', linking the positions of states to their recent experience in the Second World War.[44] For example, the US delegate and lawyer Raymund Yingling, who 'had practical experience in legally administrating occupied territories',[45] declared that '[a]rmies of occupation should be protected against attacks by the civilian population',[46] echoing arguments made by the German delegation at the 1899 Hague Peace Conference. The UK delegation was also one of the strongest proponents of strict conditions for resistance movements.[47] During the discussion of Article 4, it was primarily represented by William Gardner, a member of the British War Office, which, according to Boyd van Dijk, was responsible for revising the POW Convention and took a hardline position maintaining 'a regressive and extrajudicial attitude with respect to treating irregulars'.[48] William Hitchcock explains the British position in light of its recent encounter with Zionist 'resistance' fighters in Palestine and its ongoing fight against 'a powerful anticolonial insurgency in Malaya'.[49] Van Dijk more generally argues that the Anglo-American drafters were affected by Cold War and decolonisation anxieties.[50] Even France, which had an interest in protecting partisans after

[41] *Final Record*, vol II(A) (n 1) 420–22.

[42] cf chapter 3, section I.

[43] *Final Record*, vol II(A) (n 1) 429; *GC III Commentary* (n 22) 49–50 and 53; G Best, *War and Law Since 1945* (Oxford, Clarendon Press, 1994) 128.

[44] G Mantilla, 'The Origins and Evolution of the 1949 Geneva Conventions and the 1977 Additional Protocols' in M Evangelista and N Tannenwald (eds), *Do the Geneva Conventions Matter?* (Oxford, Oxford University Press, 2017) 40.

[45] B van Dijk, *Preparing for War: The Making of the Geneva Conventions* (Oxford, Oxford University Press, 2022) 46.

[46] *Final Record*, vol II(A) (n 1) 425.

[47] See, eg, ibid 240–43.

[48] van Dijk, *Preparing for War* (n 45) 171–72.

[49] WI Hitchcock, 'Human Rights and the Laws of War: The Geneva Conventions of 1949' in K Iriye, P Goedde and WI Hitchcock (eds), *The Human Rights Revolution: An International History* (Oxford, Oxford University Press, 2012) 99.

[50] van Dijk, *Preparing for War* (n 45) 148.

the war, 'excluded anti-colonial guerrillas and other irregulars from these treaties'.[51] The limited admission to recognise some irregular fighters under the debated status was once again a compromise and 'an instrument to end a political deadlock'.[52]

On the other side, some submissions in favour of recognising organised resistance movements were seemingly still informed by the notion of patriotism,[53] although the self-identification of delegations as small states in need of popular defence remained exceptional.[54] The Soviet Union argued for a less strict approach to certain irregulars framing its submissions within the older discourse of 'just war' theory,[55] unlike the Russian delegations in the earlier period. Other arguments drew on norms and values of more recent standing. The Danish delegate Georg Cohn advocated the expansion of POW status to civilians acting in defence of their country against an *aggressor*.[56] The international law professor had long been promoting 'a world relieved of state aggression' by international law, not least through the non-recognition of conquest.[57] His attempt to persuade the other participants was framed in the language of current developments within the international legal system, namely the United Nations' outlawing of wars of aggression and the International Military Tribunals' judgments. This argument was, however, not accepted since the underlying principles were seen as belonging to two different fields of international law,[58] reflecting the long-held belief in the principle of equal application of the laws of war.[59] The advances in the *jus ad bellum* did not affect the concept of combatants and the applicable rules under the *jus in bello*. While it was seemingly taken for granted that the states participating at the Conference were bound by the same rules as members of the international community, a cross-fertilisation between the distinct areas of law was generally discouraged.

The discussion of the Danish proposal to protect civilians who are defending their country against aggression or illegal occupation, or are acting in their own self-defence also brought the POW status into association with the deliberation of the new rules on civilians. During the 1947 Conference of Government

[51] ibid 147.

[52] ibid 149.

[53] *Final Record*, vol II(A) (n 1) 242, 426 and 429.

[54] ibid 468.

[55] van Dijk, *Preparing for War* (n 45) 318–19.

[56] *Final Record*, vol II(A) (n 1) 240 and 425–26; see also *Final Record of the Diplomatic Conference of Geneva of 1949*, vol II(B) (Berne, Federal Political Department, 1950) 267–68.

[57] G Ben-Nun, *The Fourth Geneva Convention for Civilians: The History of International Humanitarian Law* (London, IB Tauris, 2020) 9 and 120–34.

[58] *Final Record*, vol II(B) (n 56) 269 and 408; *Conférence diplomatique 1949: sténogrammes de la Commission II, tome III* (20 July 1949) (ICRC Library, CD_1949_COMM2_CR35) 51; Gutteridge (n 5) 314.

[59] For a brief historical survey of the principle see A Roberts, 'The Principle of Equal Application of the Laws of War' in D Rodin and H Shue (eds), *Just and Unjust Warriors: The Moral and Legal Status of Soldiers* (Oxford, Oxford University Press, 2008) 230–37.

Experts, a collaborative approach to regulating and protecting irregular participants in warfare had already been specifically sought. Before entering into a debate, the POW Commission at this earlier conference referred the draft formulation of the POW status to the Civilian Commission, and invited interested members to attend its sessions on the question of partisans.[60] The Civilian Commission then also emphasised the importance of distinguishing between civilians and partisans, and examined the proposed POW definition in its deliberation of civilian internees.[61] Once the intersection between the work of the POW Committee and Committee III responsible for the protection of 'civilians' emerged again at the Diplomatic Conference, the Israeli delegate Major Steinberg argued that it 'should be referred to the Co-ordination Committee to decide whether a similar clause should be inserted in the Civilians Convention'.[62] The Civilian Committee's chairman Georges Cahen-Salvador, who upon request attended the work on POWs, held that the issue was of concern for both Conventions and suggested that the amendment could be submitted to his Committee. The Danish delegate Cohn declined, believing that it was a matter for the POW Convention alone. Yet his amendment was not voted on since other delegations deemed it a question for the regulation and protection of civilians, rather than combatants.[63] No further consultation between the two Committees is recorded in the *travaux préparatoires* on this issue.

The Diplomatic Conference's objective to also protect civilians appears to have had a constraining effect on the expansion of the POW status to civilians participating in hostilities, and even the POW Committee's engagement with the issue. The UK delegate Gutteridge declared that an amendment which regulates civilian self-defence under the POW convention 'would have the effect of abolishing the distinction between combatants and non-combatants'.[64] A binary understanding of combatants and civilians, however, finds no support in the general argumentations at the Conference nor the eventually adopted conventions. Proponents of an expansive protection of resistance fighters emphasised that certain individuals who do not belong to the armed forces were already recognised as combatants, such as the *levée en masse*, and had a right to POW status. On the other hand, a memorandum submitted to the Diplomatic Conference by the UK itself, while stressing the distinction, proclaimed that

[60] *Conférence d'experts gouvernementaux pour l'étude des Conventions protégeant les victimes de la guerre: procès-verbaux de la Commission II: révision de la Convention de 1929 relative au traitement des prisonniers de guerre*, vol III (ICRC Library, CEG_1947_COMM2_PV_01 and CEG_1947_COMM2_PV_05) 97 and 438.

[61] *Conférence d'experts gouvernementaux pour l'étude des Conventions protégeant les victimes de la guerre: procès-verbaux de la Commission III: condition et protection des civils en temps de guerre*, vol IV (ICRC Library, CEG_1947_COMM3_PV_01 and CEG_1947_COMM3_PV_03) 7–10 and 165–68.

[62] *Final Record*, vol II(A) (n 1) 426.

[63] ibid 426–27 and 434.

[64] ibid 426.

'private enemy individuals' who commit hostile acts would qualify neither as combatants nor civilians.[65] According to van Dijk, the Anglo-American delegations 'wished to create a gap in order to internationally codify their extra-judicial policies and prevent suspected communist agents from falling under the umbrella of humanitarian law'.[66] The Dutch delegate Captain Mouton observed more disapprovingly that the belief '[t]hat persons who do not fall under [Article 4 GC III] are automatically protected by other Conventions is certainly untrue' given the exclusionary nature of the definition of 'protected persons' under GC IV.[67] While the construction and protection of civilians was left to the Civilian Committee, members of the POW Committee seemingly perceived and desired different demarcating lines between combatants and civilians, as well as their respective privileges and protections.

As an alternative amendment, Cohn proposed a provision along the lines of the so-called 'Martens Clause' which would have provided a safety net for individuals involved in resistance or self-defence without being recognised as combatants. He asserted that the definition of POWs could not be read as depriving individuals who did not qualify under this status 'of the inherent rights of the human person and the right of legitimate self-defence against illegal acts'.[68] Small states at former conferences had resorted to similar arguments regarding self-defence in their attempt to improve the treatment of irregular fighters. Yet while they had requested the omission of an explicit reference to military justice, preferring instead the ambiguity of the unwritten laws of war,[69] Cohn sought an express declaration of the right to act in self-defence and humanitarian treatment. Its implication seems to be that every individual should have some form of protection under the written laws of war. Instead, Article 5 was adopted as a safeguard which provides that, if in doubt, the status of an individual should be determined by a competent tribunal.

Commentators today disagree on the influence of GC III on the combatant status. Emily Crawford asserts that 'the 1949 Diplomatic Conference adopted significantly expanded rules regarding combatants'.[70] Conversely, Sibylle Scheipers argues that conditions for belligerency in Article 4 GC III 'remained largely identical to those of the 1907 Hague Convention'.[71] Kubo Mačák

[65] *Draft of the 4 Geneva Conventions of 1949 and Proposals and Comments from Governments – Memorandum by the Government of the United Kingdom* (ICRC Library, CD_1949_DOCTRAV_ENG_06) 2.

[66] van Dijk, *Preparing for War* (n 45) 150, see also 177–78.

[67] *Final Record*, vol II(B) (n 56) 271; see further section II.A.iii; see also R Baxter, 'So-called Unprivileged Belligerency: Spies, Guerrillas, and Saboteurs' (1951) 28 *BYIL* 323, 328–29.

[68] *Final Record*, vol II(A) (n 1) 480.

[69] See chapter 3, section I.A.

[70] E Crawford, *The Treatment of Combatants and Insurgents under the Law of Armed Conflict* (Oxford, Oxford University Press, 2010) 51.

[71] S Scheipers, *Unlawful Combatants: A Genealogy of the Irregular Fighter* (Oxford, Oxford University Press, 2015) 144.

suggests that the provision should 'be understood as outlining which persons qualify as combatants',[72] whereas Anthony Rogers believes that it 'dealt with prisoner-of-war status and left untouched the rules on combatant status as set out in the Hague Regulations'.[73] It is argued here that, even though the focus lay on the protection of war victims rather than the regulation of the conduct of hostilities, the GC III definition of POWs constituted a reaffirmation of the understanding of combatants with a limited adaptation of the established law to new forms of warfare. Assumptions about the nature of the combatant status enshrined in the 1907 Hague Regulations were set against the contextualisation of the concept in light of the experience of the Second World War. However, proposals to advance the law accordingly were in tension with long-standing and emerging ideational and normative structures, as well as a bias of some states towards a narrow scope of protection. As a result, the understandings of individuals in the debate were to varying degrees influenced by a state-centric view of warfare, the drawing of a clear line between the *jus in bello* and *jus ad bellum*, and a more contested distinction between combatants and civilians.

II. CIVILIANS – THE EMERGENCE OF DIFFERENT CONCEPTUALISATIONS

Civilians had been affected by the Second World War in mainly three distinct ways: as enemy nationals in the territory of a belligerent state, as inhabitants of an occupied state, and as intentional or incidental victims of attacks, especially as a result of aerial bombardment.[74] After the war, the ICRC advocated the expansion of the laws of war to also protect civilians. However, the introductory note in the ICRC's *GC IV Commentary* remarks upon the challenge that the drafters of the post-war treaty were facing. Unlike POWs, civilians did not yet constitute a well-defined category of persons in the existing legal framework. Instead, it was necessary to conceptualise 'an unorganized mass of civilians scattered over the whole of the countries concerned'.[75] The task was further complicated by the need for 'a pre-emptive safeguard preventing individuals from becoming victims', whereas the first three 1949 Geneva Conventions protect 'people who had already become the victims of war'.[76] While civilians

[72] K Mačák, *Internationalized Armed Conflicts in International Law* (Oxford, Oxford University Press, 2018) 136.

[73] A Rogers, 'Combatant Status' in E Wilmshurst and SC Breau (eds), *Perspectives on the ICRC Study on Customary International Humanitarian Law* (Cambridge, Cambridge University Press, 2007) 106.

[74] Best (n 43) 115.

[75] JS Pictet (ed), *The Geneva Conventions of 12 August 1949, Commentary IV: Geneva Convention Relative to the Protection of Civilian Persons in Time of War* (Geneva, ICRC, 1958) (hereafter *GC IV Commentary*) 5.

[76] ibid.

were not defined or protected as such under any existing treaty by this time, various actors had already endeavoured to promote such protection in the inter-war years. This section highlights continuities and breaks between the pre-Second World War developments and the forms of conceptualising and protecting individuals who do not belong to the armed forces under GC IV.

A. Protection of Enemy Civilians

i. Civilian Prisoners of War

Although the suffering of civilians in times of war was not new, it reached an unprecedented scale in the First World War. Those affected by internment, deportation, evacuation and displacement were seen as especially in need of protection under international law. The Hague Regulations' rudimentary safeguards for individuals who are not members of the armed forces were silent on these matters. The 1907 Hague Peace Conference briefly considered civilian internment, yet agreed that the provision stating that POWs can be interned should be interpreted as *a contrario* precluding such measures against individuals who do not belong to the armed forces.[77] This supposed restraining force of the law proved insufficient during the war. Almost all warring states resorted to a policy of some form of internment or confinement for enemy civilians.[78]

Some states adopted bilateral agreements which regulated the treatment and exchange of POWs in the traditional sense, as well as individuals identified as 'civilian prisoners of war'.[79] The ICRC was also striving to provide protection for interned civilians, often referred to as civilian POWs,[80] thus expanding its field of action to a growing number of war victims. In addition to its *ad hoc* commitment during the war, it continued to promote the protection of interned civilians in a more permanent multilateral regime in the post-war years.[81] It created a special commission for the study of the situation of civilians in war,

[77] See chapter 3, section II.C.

[78] For a detailed study of the treatment of enemy nationals during the war, see DL Caglioti, *War and Citizenship: Enemy Aliens and National Belonging from the French Revolution to the First World War* (Cambridge, Cambridge University Press, 2021).

[79] See, eg, Agreement between Great Britain and Germany Concerning Combatant and Civilian Prisoners of War (The Hague, 2 July 1917); Agreement between the British and German Governments Concerning Combatant Prisoners of War and Civilians (The Hague, 14 July 1918); regarding agreements between the US and Germany, as well as Austria and Italy see F Ferrière, 'Projet d'une Convention internationale réglant la situation des civils tombés à la guerre au pouvoir de l'ennemi' (1923) 5:54 *IRRC* 560, 571.

[80] G Ador, 'Egalité de traitement pour les prisonniers de guerre militaires ou civils' (1915) 46:181 *Bulletin International des Sociétes de la Croix-Rouge* 5.

[81] N Wylie and S Landefeld, 'Prisoners of War, Civilians and the Post-World-War I Development of International Humanitarian Law' in I Rachamimov and R Kowner (eds), *Out of Line, Out of Place: A Global and Local History of World War I Internments* (Ithaca, Cornell University Press, 2022); see also van Dijk, *Preparing for War* (n 45) 59–64.

which inter alia considered agreements between states that dealt with civilians during and after the First World War.[82] In 1921, the first post-war International Red Cross Conference (International Conference) adopted a resolution which appealed to states to conclude, as soon as possible, a convention on POWs as well as civilians who had been deported, evacuated or become refugees, and already proposed relevant provisions.[83] While this resolution envisaged one code for both POWs and civilian victims of war, the appointed special commission believed it preferable to prepare two separate documents which were then submitted to the next International Conference in 1923.[84] This Conference adopted one resolution promoting a convention for the protection of POWs,[85] and a separate resolution regarding the 'situation des civils tombés au pouvoir de l'ennemi'.[86] Finally, the International Conference in 1925 changed the focus in terms of the title to the 'situation des non-combattants sur territoire ennemi'.[87] While it was considered a sequel to the earlier resolution, the ICRC deliberately excluded the civilian population in invaded and occupied territory from its scope[88] expecting more opposition from governments on these points.[89]

The 1929 Diplomatic Conference adopted the draft prepared by the ICRC on the treatment of POWs; yet no equivalent protection regime emerged for civilian POWs or civilians in the hands of the enemy more widely. Since the protection of civilians was deemed beyond the Conference's scope of competence,[90] the forgoing ICRC efforts resulted in no more than a unanimous resolution in the non-binding Final Act. It recommended

> that an exhaustive study should be made with a view to the conclusion of an international Convention regarding the condition and protection of civilians of enemy nationality in the territory of a belligerent or in territory occupied by a belligerent.[91]

[82] 'Documents Consultés', Archives du Comité International de la Croix-Rouge (AICRC) CR.119 GV; 'Tableau comparatif des conventions passées au cours de la guerre mondiale concernant les civils tombés au pouvoir de l'ennemi', AICRC CR.119.

[83] ICRC, *Dixième Conférence internationale de la Croix-Rouge* (Geneva, Imprimerie Albert Renaud, 1921) 218–19.

[84] A Durand, *History of the International Committee of the Red Cross: From Sarajevo to Hiroshima* (Geneva, Henry Dunant Institute, 1984) 237–38; see also van Dijk, *Preparing for War* (n 45) 60–61.

[85] ICRC, *Onzième Conférence internationale de la Croix-Rouge* (Geneva, Imprimerie ATAR, 1923) 198.

[86] ibid 200–01.

[87] ICRC, *Douzième Conférence internationale de la Croix-Rouge* (Geneva, Imprimerie de la "Tribune de Genève", 1925) 172–73.

[88] *Annexe au rapport général du Comité international de la Croix-Rouge: la situation des non-combattants tombés au pouvoir de l'ennemi* (ICRC Library, CI_1925_016_FRE_016_HD_Su) 5.

[89] *Memorandum concernant le problème des prisonniers civils et l'élaboration éventuelle d'un projet d'une Convention internationale règlant la situation des civils tombés à la guerre au pouvoir de l'ennemi* (1925), AICRC CR.119/7.

[90] *Actes 1929* (n 16) 555–56.

[91] Final Act of the Diplomatic Conference 1929 (Geneva, 27 July 1929) reprinted in D Schindler and J Toman (eds), *Laws of Armed Conflict: A Collection of Conventions, Resolutions, and Other Documents*, 4th edn (Leiden, Martinus Nijhoff, 2004) Recommendation VI.

The seeming demand for additional expert knowledge may suggest that the ICRC itself was perceived as no more than a norm entrepreneur which was unable to persuade states as the main actors of international law-making at the time. Alternatively, it may have been merely a rhetorical device diverting attention in order to avoid regulation.

Civilian POWs also became a concern of international lawyers.[92] The International Law Association (ILA) began the consideration of the treatment of POWs, including civilian POWs, at its first conference in the aftermath of the First World War in 1920.[93] It appointed a committee to study the issue which comprised persons who had been involved in the negotiation of related Anglo-German treaties as well as the commission for enquiries into war crimes.[94] This prior engagement of the members may explain certain similarities between the approach of states and the epistemic community of international lawyers, not least in the terminology of 'civilian POWs'. Yet the report on the topic submitted to the conference in advance argued that the status of civilian prisoners 'should have no military character'.[95] The 1924 report of the POW Committee also condemned 'the general practice of interning enemy civilians and, in particular, women'.[96] Instead, it recommended permitting individuals to remain peacefully in the country or to repatriate, limiting internment to 'individuals whom, for military reasons, it would be against the interests of the captor State to allow to leave the country'.[97] The Draft Regulations for the Treatment of Civilian Prisoners of War, adopted unanimously by the 1924 ILA Conference, were, nevertheless, modelled on the ILA's 1921 regulations regarding 'combatant prisoners'.[98]

The ICRC and ILA recognised their concurrent interest and studies regarding interned civilians. Indeed, the ICRC contacted the ILA for its assistance with establishing the relevant legal framework,[99] and considered the latter's 1924 conclusions in its subsequent examinations.[100] However, both non-state actors appeared initially hesitant with respect to their proper role in promoting the protection of civilians. The ILA's POW Committee excluded civilian POWs from its scope in 1921 due to the delicate nature of the subject.[101] Despite

[92] See, eg, GG Phillimore, 'Some Suggestions for a Draft Code for the Treatment of Prisoners of War' (1920) 6 *Transactions of the Grotius Society* 25.

[93] ILA, 'Third Day's Proceedings' (1920) 29 *ILA Reports of Conferences* 247.

[94] ILA, 'Report of the Prisoners of War Committee' (1924) 33 *ILA Reports of Conferences* 227, 237.

[95] ILA, 'Third Day's Proceedings' (n 93) 274.

[96] ILA, 'POW Committee' (n 94) 228.

[97] ibid.

[98] ibid 238.

[99] *Commission des 'civils' – procès verbal* (28 November 1923), AICRC CR.119 No 1.

[100] *Procès-verbaux des commissions: Commission I: examen du rapport general du Comité international* (ICRC Library, CI_1925_001_FRE_001) 2; *Annexe au rapport* (n 88) 3.

[101] ILA, 'Second Day's Proceedings' (n 15) 193, 220–21 and 236.

acknowledging that the question was one of 'high policy', it then provided recommendations for the treatment of civilian POWs in 1924, 'without attempting to lay down any binding rules'.[102] The ICRC delegate attending the 1924 ILA Conference explained that the ICRC itself still considered general *vœux* more preferable than a set of strict rules. It seemed wary of the subject 'qui touche directement aux intérets vitaux des Etats',[103] and which governments would reserve for themselves in light of political and military considerations involved.[104] Mantilla suggests that 'a series of early organizational challenges provoked (or reinforced) the ICRC's reluctance to confront prevailing sovereignty norms' and thus its conservatism.[105] Moreover, the regulation of civilians in the power of the enemy was seen as a matter for a diplomatic conference concerned with extending the 1907 Hague Regulations, thus falling outside the domain of the ICRC.[106] The fear that the regulation of war, including the status of civilians, might undermine the universal cause for peace was also continuously present during this period.[107] The non-state actors, however, increasingly overcame these qualms and early self-restraints. The ILA was not only willing to submit its 1924 Draft Regulations to any related diplomatic conference of states,[108] it, indeed, brought the issue of civilian POWs to the attention of the committee of legal experts of the League of Nations. Yet neither civilian POWs nor any other aspect of the laws of war can be found on the list of subjects of the work of the League's committee.[109] The epistemic community's attempts to regulate the treatment of interned civilians failed to result in the adoption of a treaty.

It is, nonetheless, important to examine the conceptualisation of individuals in these efforts more closely. Although it has been sometimes emphasised that individuals who accompany the armed forces without belonging thereto are civilians who qualify as POWs,[110] the term 'civilian POWs' became mainly a designation for a new category of interned individuals who were not yet recognised in the Hague Regulations and who were not (directly) associated with

[102] ILA, 'POW Committee' (n 94) 238.

[103] ibid 242–43; 'that touches directly on the vital interests of states' (author's translation).

[104] Durand (n 84) 238.

[105] G Mantilla, *Lawmaking under Pressure: International Humanitarian Law and Internal Armed Conflict* (Ithaca, Cornell University Press, 2020) 30.

[106] Letter from Girardet to Lescaze (23 November 1923), AICRC CR.119; *Commission des 'civils'* (n 99); *Memorandum* (1925) (n 89).

[107] R-M Frick-Cramer, 'Le Comité international de la Croix-Rouge et les Conventions internationals pour les prisonniers de guerre et les civils' (1943) 25:295 *IRRC* 567, 574.

[108] AK Kuhn, 'Report of the Stockholm Conference of the International Law Association, 1925' (1925) *Proceedings of the American Branch of the International Law Association* 22, 25.

[109] ILA, 'Report of the Codification Committee' (1926) 34 *ILA Reports of Conferences* 374, 374–76.

[110] See, eg, 1929 POW Convention, pt VII; GC III, art 4 includes these individuals but no longer emphasises their civilian character; cf the updated *GC III Commentary* refers to 'civilian prisoners of war', ICRC, *Commentary on the Third Geneva Convention* (ICRC, 2020) ihl-databases.icrc.org/ihl/full/GCIII-commentary, paras 1045–46.

the military. The adverse treatment of these civilians was commonly a result of their perception as potential participants in the hostilities. There is a noticeable similarity between this understanding and the earlier discourse at the Brussels and Hague Peace Conferences where inhabitants of a belligerent state or occupied territory were regarded by the opposing state as a constant threat.[111] Given mass conscription in many countries at the time, the internment of individuals subject to mobilisation followed similar objectives as the taking of combatant POWs, such as the weakening of the enemy's armed forces.[112] Attempts were made to distinguish civilians who can be mobilised from those who cannot, often illustrated as women, children and men who were sick or beyond the age of carrying arms. It was believed by some that these should be governed under different rules.[113] The complexity of civilians, and the difficulty of categorising and regulating them under a potential treaty, was thus emphasised in the deliberations.

Although individuals taken as civilian POWs were generally recognised as in some ways distinct, states resorted to an established measure for regular combatants against them. As a result, non-state actors responded with resolutions calling for the same protection for these civilians deprived of their liberty as for military POWs. As mentioned above, the ICRC's 1921 resolution contemplated a single convention proposing the same safeguards for military POWs and civilians.[114] Various of the bilateral agreements and non-state actors' proposals applied guarantees for POWs by extension or by analogy to interned civilians. They were thus shielded from more adverse measures which they may have otherwise faced. The actors did not significantly change their conceptualisation of warfare to create an entirely new concept which protects civilians; instead, they expanded an existing notion and the respective legal framework.

The terminology describing the (relatively new) phenomenon of interned civilians as civilian *POWs* also suggests that it was informed by the existing ideational framework for categorising individuals in times of war. This 'rather anomalous term' in a number of agreements on POWs has been explained on the basis of 'the necessity to provide a *modus operandi* for dealing with civilian internees who, at the time, were not the subjects of any humanitarian convention'.[115] Since individuals who do not belong to the armed forces were

[111] See chapter 3, section II.B.

[112] RM Frick-Cramer, 'A propos des projets de conventions internationales réglant le sort des prisonniers' (1925) 7:74 *IRRC* 73, 78; ICRC, *Dixième Conférence* (n 83) 218–20.

[113] Ferrière (n 79), although he notes that the distinction was often not made in practice, 564; Frick-Cramer, 'A propos' (n 112) 79; *Memorandum* (1925) (n 89); implied in the ILA Draft Regulations, ILA, 'POW Committee' (n 94) 229–31.

[114] ICRC, *Dixième Conférence* (n 83) 218–21; Renée-Marguerite Frick-Cramer, who was involved in the ICRC's work on civilians in the hands of the enemy, even criticised the distinction between regimes applicable to military and civilian POWs, Frick-Cramer, 'A propos' (n 112).

[115] 'Agreement between Great Britain and Germany Concerning Combatant and Civilian Prisoners of War' (1979) 60 *International Law Studies* 86, 86.

without a distinct status under the written laws of war, states may have resorted to the well-known term 'POWs' in referring to those who were interned on the basis of perceived military necessity. This introduced these civilians conceptually into a system of rules which regulated belligerent relations between states, and which was, consequently, confined to individuals associated with a party to the conflict. The qualification of individuals as *civilian* POWs distinguished these individuals from combatants as defined in the Hague Regulations. Unlike combatants they had no right to participate in the hostilities. Yet, as was noted by the ICRC special commission in 1923, '[l]e "civil" est totalement inconnu dans le droit international'.[116] The characterisation as 'civilian', therefore, did not invoke a particular status in the context of war and under the written laws of war.

ii. Enemy Civilians[117]

Some international agreements referred to 'interned civilians' without designating them as POWs.[118] As mentioned above, the ICRC itself modified its terminology in a series of resolutions it adopted throughout the early 1920s while its focus remained primarily on civilian internees. At the 1929 Diplomatic Conference, the Belgian delegate and legal expert Joseph de Ruelle argued that 'la conception du prisonnier civil est une conception généralement réprouvée par le droit des gens. C'est plutôt le traitement des civils que le traitement des prisonniers civils qu'il convient de prévoir'.[119] The *travaux préparatoires* of the Conference show that the term 'prisoners' was deliberately omitted from the text of the resolution as a result.[120] The expressed concern for 'civilians of enemy nationality in the territory of a belligerent or in territory occupied by a belligerent' instead was a precursor of the conceptualisation of civilians in terms of nationality and *ratione loci* in later instruments.

The shift from 'civilian POWs' to 'enemy civilians' may seem prima facie an expansion of the scope of regulations beyond internment to other measures of warfare and consequences of war, while simultaneously limiting the personal scope to exclusively civilians of enemy nationality. However, this apparent evolution in terms may obscure the continuation of ideas. Although the

[116] 'Question des civils évacués et déportés' (1923), AICRC CR.119; 'the "civilian" is completely unknown in international law' (author's translation).

[117] For a more detailed analysis see S Landefeld, 'The Changing Significance of Nationality for the Protection of Civilians in the Hands of a Party to an International Armed Conflict' (2023) 28 *Journal of Conflict & Security Law* 501.

[118] See, eg, Treaty of Peace between the Allied and Associated Powers, of the one Part, and Germany, of the other Part (Paris, 28 June 1919); Agreement between Germany and the Russian Socialist Federal Soviet Republic (Berlin, 19 April 1920).

[119] *Actes 1929* (n 16) 510; 'the conception of the civilian prisoner is a conception that is generally reproached by the laws of nations. It is rather the treatment of civilians than the treatment of civilian prisoners that should be provided for' (author's translation).

[120] ibid.

notion of civilian POWs was largely invoked and discussed without mentioning the nationality of the individuals concerned, it seems to have been designed for non-nationals, and primarily *enemy* civilians who hold the nationality of the opposing belligerent state. The nationality requirement was unsuccessfully challenged as a criterion for the status and treatment of individuals at the 1924 ILA Conference for being an insufficient or inadequate indicator of affiliations.[121] During the negotiations it was emphasised that the scope of the articles was restricted to aliens, despite having acknowledged that states' own nationals had also been interned during war.[122] The ILA draft regulations themselves define civilian POWs as 'persons belonging to an enemy State'.[123]

International legal literature had long considered the issue of enemy nationals, even though the notion was largely absent from most of the discourses leading to the early written laws of war.[124] The formal legal bond to the opposing belligerent state was conceived as confirming the enemy character of the individual, based on the formal concept of allegiance, as well as an assumed affinity and loyalty. The prevalent idea of 'total warfare', and 'the resulting mobilization in wartime of all resources and energies of each belligerent state for the purpose of the conflict has served to give general force' to the notion of enemy nationals.[125] Enemy nationals have also experienced economic hardship, discrimination, vilification and even attacks by the public. Enemy nationality thus not only served to identify the adversary, but also individuals who were at risk of arbitrary treatment and the abuse of power. Individuals were still regarded as an extension of the state. Unlike in the previous period, however, their vulnerability and perception as a threat was not determined by their position inside or outside of the battlefield since entire countries were seen as directly or indirectly affected by war. The only territorial consideration was whether enemy civilians were in belligerent or occupied territory.

Enemy nationality was, consequently, adopted as the essential criterion underlying proposed protection regimes for civilians in the power of a belligerent state during the inter-war years. The most well-known instrument in this respect was the Draft International Convention on the Condition and Protection of Civilians of Enemy Nationality Who Are on Territory Belonging to or Occupied by a Belligerent.[126] It was prepared by a special committee constituted under the auspices of the ICRC, and adopted at its 1934 International Conference in Tokyo. This so-called Tokyo Draft seemingly defined the envisaged beneficiaries as 'civilians': in addition to the nationality requirement, individuals had to fulfil the negatively formulated condition of 'not belonging to the land, maritime

[121] ILA, 'POW Committee' (n 94) 240 and 255–56.
[122] ibid 244.
[123] ibid 229.
[124] See chapter 3, section II.C.
[125] M Greenspan, *The Modern Law of Land Warfare* (Berkeley, University of California Press, 1959) 44.
[126] (Tokyo, 29 October 1934) reprinted in Schindler and Toman (n 91).

or air armed forces of the belligerents, as defined by international law, and in particular by Articles 1, 2 and 3' of the 1907 Hague Regulations.[127] Yet their enemy nationality, rather than their status as 'civilians', was the determinative condition for their protection under the proposed rules. They were primarily considered in terms of their association with the enemy state.

The Tokyo Draft arguably continued the conceptualisation of some individuals as civilian POWs, albeit not using that term, since it partly relied on the application of the 1929 POW regime by analogy.[128] Military considerations behind the taking of civilian POWs are reflected in the Draft's explicit justifications for internment and the restriction of departure from the state's territory. Internment of enemy civilians was limited to, yet permitted for, three identified categories of persons comprising 'civilians eligible for mobilization' under specified conditions, 'where the security of the Detaining Power is involved', and 'where the situation of the enemy civilians renders it necessary'.[129] Enemy civilians were thus primarily constructed as a potential threat to state security. However, they were simultaneously seen as vulnerable to adverse wartime measures which were deemed in need of regulation. The committee preparing the text for the 1934 International Conference had considered limiting the scope of the instrument to enemy civilians in belligerent territory given the existing legal framework for occupied territory.[130] Nevertheless, the Tokyo Draft also addressed the latter by referring to the (rudimentary) safeguards in the 1907 Hague Regulations and expanding them slightly.[131]

Since governments were slow to react, or responded decidedly negatively, to the Tokyo Draft,[132] the outbreak of the Second World War prevented the diplomatic conference intended to be held in 1939 to discuss the instrument from taking place.[133] Despite the failure to adopt a binding international instrument, the ICRC appealed to the belligerent states to adhere to the Tokyo Draft during the next war. However, states only agreed to apply the POW regime by analogy to civilian internees,[134] suggesting that states were more willing to endorse the earlier conceptualisation and more narrow regulation of civilian POWs. As van Dijk observes, even if the Tokyo Draft 'had been applied faithfully during World War II, it would not have protected numerous civilians, such as American-Japanese internees (as the state's own nationals), Italian Jews (co-belligerent nationals), Poles (denationalized persons), or German Jews (stateless individuals)'.[135]

[127] ibid art 1(a).
[128] ibid art 17.
[129] ibid art 15.
[130] 'Commission des Civils, Séance du 27 février 1934' (1934), AICRC CR.119.
[131] Tokyo Draft, arts 18–19.
[132] Durand (n 84) 292.
[133] *GC IV Commentary* (n 75) 4.
[134] ibid 5 and 372.
[135] B van Dijk, 'Human Rights in War: On the Entangled Foundations of the 1949 Geneva Conventions' (2018) 112 *AJIL* 553, 563.

iii. 'Protected Persons' under the Fourth Geneva Convention

The main protection regime of GC IV applies to 'protected persons', defined in Article 4 as individuals 'who at a given moment and in any manner whatsoever, find themselves, in case of a conflict or occupation, in the hands of a Party to the conflict or Occupying Power of which they are not nationals'. In addition to this nationality requirement, the scope of application is further delimited by the relationship between the state in whose powers the individuals find themselves and their state of nationality, namely whether they are enemies, allies or neutral. The provision is commonly understood as referring to two main categories of persons who are in need of protection against arbitrary treatment at the hands of the enemy: '(1) *enemy nationals* within the national territory of each of the Parties to the conflict and (2) *the whole population* of occupied territories (excluding nationals of the Occupying Power)'.[136]

An earlier draft of the 'Civilian Convention' in the post-Second World War law-making process also specified the *civilian* status of the beneficiaries as meaning persons 'not belonging to the armed forces, as defined in the Convention relative to the treatment of Prisoners of War'.[137] At the 1949 Diplomatic Conference, Pierre Majerus, a delegate of Luxemburg and lawyer, argued that 'it would seem essential to define what was meant by the term "civilians" as opposed to "military", and so avoid the use of the expression "protected persons"'.[138] Nonetheless, Article 4 only implies the civilian character of individuals who fall under the definition of 'protected persons' and the corresponding guarantees. Its reference to the other three 1949 Geneva Conventions seems to be designed to prevent an overlap of their respective protection regimes rather than a requirement of non-combatancy. While the title denotes the protection of civilians as the Convention's objective, the beneficiaries of GC IV's main protection regime are defined and almost exclusively constructed based on nationality and thus their formal link to a state.[139]

In a scholarly commentary, Nishat Nishat argues that the rationale behind the GC IV protection regime is the same as for the other three 1949 Geneva Conventions, namely that 'those who find themselves in the hands of the *enemy* ought to be protected'.[140] Indeed, the focus of the deliberations for a new Civilian Convention at the 1947 Conference of Government Experts mirrored the inter-war developments. While the draft convention contained a provision guaranteeing all other non-nationals 'treatment at least as favourable', the primary intended beneficiaries were enemy nationals.[141] Not only was Part I

[136] *GC IV Commentary* (n 75) 46.

[137] *Report on the Work of the Conference of Government Experts for the Study of the Conventions for the Protection of War Victims* (Geneva, ICRC, 1947) 272–73.

[138] *Final Record*, vol II(A) (n 1) 621–22.

[139] For a historisation and critique of the nationality requirement see Landefeld (n 117).

[140] N Nishat, 'The Structure of Geneva Convention IV and the Resulting Gaps in that Convention' in Clapham, Gaeta and Sassòli (n 9) para 1 (emphasis added).

[141] *Report – Government Experts* (n 137) 272–75.

entitled 'Protection of Civilian Enemy Aliens in Time of War', the draft also included a separate chapter on 'Rules concerning Civilian War Internees'.[142] The personal scope and largely analogous application of regulations on the treatment of POWs is unsurprising given that the Tokyo Draft functioned as a working draft. The Stockholm Draft, adopted by the 1948 International Conference, expanded the regime to all non-nationals.[143] Yet some delegations at the Diplomatic Conference again advocated limiting the safeguards to enemy nationals, excluding neutral nationals in particular.[144] These influential states, which strove to reduce their obligations under the new protection regime, thwarted attempts to create a more inclusive, and thus humanitarian treaty.[145] Although Article 4 defines 'protected persons' in broader terms, thus seemingly moving away from the conceptual underpinnings of the inter-war draft rules, enemy nationals were still at the centre of the deliberations.

As mentioned above, enemy nationals were perceived as enemies themselves due to the assumed allegiance to the state of their nationality, and hostile disposition towards the state in whose power they were. The ICRC *GC IV Commentary* highlights that, at the time the treaty was drafted, it was commonly believed that 'every enemy national is a potential soldier and his internment becomes understandable' due to 'the general adoption of a system of compulsory military service'.[146] The concern with 'total war' more generally, and thus the possibility of civilians directly or indirectly contributing to the war efforts, is evident in the drafting history of GC IV.[147] The report of the Civilian Committee at the Diplomatic Conference, for example, emphasised that '[m]odern warfare does not take place on the battlefields alone; it also filters into the domestic life of the belligerent'.[148] While GC IV addresses the (presumed) differentiated treatment of enemy aliens, it abstains from explicitly stipulating these motivating forces.

The adopted treaty text itself, nonetheless, reflects the underlying concern with enemy nationals. Part III of GC IV regulates security and control measures that have been historically adopted against enemy nationals who are regarded as a threat to the security of the state in whose territory they are, or the occupying power. These include the refusal to leave the territory, assigned

[142] ibid 272, 294–96 and 306–29; the responsible commission at the 1946 Preliminary Conference was even in favour of a single convention for the protection of POWs and civilians, *Report on the Work of the Preliminary Conference of National Red Cross Societies for the Study of the Conventions and of Various Problems Relative to the Red Cross* (Geneva, ICRC, 1947) 92–93.

[143] *Final Record*, vol I (n 23) 114 and 119.

[144] *Final Record*, vol II(A) (n 1) 814; see also *UK Memorandum* (n 65) 3–4.

[145] Landefeld (n 117).

[146] *GC IV Commentary* (n 75) 232.

[147] See, eg, *Commission of Government Experts for the Study of Conventions for the Protection of War Victims – Preliminary Documents Submitted by the International Committee of the Red Cross, vol III, Condition and Protection of Civilians in Time of War* (ICRC Library, CEG_1947_DOC_PROTCIV_ENG) 5; *Conférence d'experts gouvernementaux*, vol IV (n 61) 17–20; *Report – Government Experts* (n 137) 278; *Final Record*, vol II(A) (n 1) 654.

[148] *Final Record*, vol II(A) (n 1) 814.

residence and internment, as well as punishment. Even the special clause for the protection of enemy refugees under Article 44 demonstrates that individuals were essentially constructed according to the belligerent relations of the state of their nationality. During the Second World War, some states had distinguished between 'real enemies' and 'friendly enemies' – the latter term designating refugees from an opposing belligerent state.[149] States were encouraged 'to take into consideration a whole set of circumstances which may reveal what might be called the "spiritual affinity" or "ideoloigcal [*sic*] allegiance"' of the individual refugee with de jure nationality.[150] While this indirectly challenges the enemy character inferred from the formal link to the opposing belligerent state, the rebuttable characterisation as enemies indicates the prevalent understanding of civilians as being informed by their nationality. These safeguards reveal the engrained collective understanding of individuals on the basis of their nationality, on the one hand, and an individualised assessment of their situation, on the other, as the opposing driving forces during the drafting process.

Article 5, furthermore, shows that beneficiaries of the treaty regime were not only regarded as vulnerable, but also as potential threats. The provision was specially introduced as a derogation clause in response to the perceived insufficient protection for states against spies, saboteurs and traitors.[151] Yet it permits adverse treatment only when the party to the conflict 'is satisfied that an individual protected person is definitely suspected of or engaged in activities hostile to the security of the State'. It needs to be emphasised that Article 5 derogates from certain 'rights and privileges' under GC IV without depriving individuals of their status as 'protected persons' or placing them outside the scope of the treaty as a whole.[152] Consequently, while the provision may have been intended to repress participation in warfare, the status as 'protected person' is not conditional upon peaceful or inoffensive conduct.[153]

Indeed, an earlier draft which limited the scope of the treaty *ratione personae* to individuals 'who take no active part in hostilities' was discarded prior to the 1949 Diplomatic Conference.[154] The ICRC's pamphlet on *Remarks and Proposals* submitted to the Conference observed that the definition of 'protected persons' was framed as to 'cover those who commit hostile acts whilst not being regular combatants, such as *saboteurs* and *francs-tireurs*'.[155] The French proposal to include partisans under the Civilian Convention[156]

[149] *GC IV Commentary* (n 75) 263.
[150] ibid 264; see also *Final Record*, vol II(B) (n 56) 412.
[151] *Final Record*, vol II(A) (n 1) 796 and 814.
[152] A-L Graf-Brugère, 'The Derogation Clause' in Clapham, Gaeta and Sassòli (n 9) para 6.
[153] cf chapter 6, sections III.A–III.B.
[154] *Revised and New Draft Conventions for the Protection of War Victims – Remarks and Proposals Submitted by the International Committee of the Red Cross* (Geneva, ICRC, 1949) 68.
[155] ibid.
[156] Ben-Nun (n 57) 46–52.

was, however, not followed since the Government Experts incorporated them under the POW status instead.[157] The Civilian Committee at the Diplomatic Conference itself only marginally considered the possible participation of civilians in hostilities. Its approach thus differed from the expectations voiced by the POW Committee, which abstained from considering individuals acting in self-defence, believing that the issue fell under the Civilian Convention.[158]

The discrepancy in the Committees' approaches may have been due to their diverse compositions. Only three delegates are documented in the *Final Records* of the Conference as having actively participated in both discussions on the definition of POWs and civilian 'protected persons'. One of these, the UK delegate Brigadier Kenneth Page, seemed to suggest in line with the general UK position that 'illegitimate bearers of arms' still fall outside of the scope of the written laws of war, while admitting that they 'should no doubt be accorded certain standards of treatment'.[159] Although he drew a distinction between combatants and civilians and their respective rights and obligations at the outset of the Civilian Committee's work, no discussion of this distinction or an interrelation between the two categories of persons followed. He was also the only participant to assert that civilians in occupied territory had a 'duty to behave in a peaceful manner and not take part in hostilities',[160] while Colonel William Roy Hodgson hinted at the duties and obligations of civilians generally.[161] Van Dijk rightly observes that the *travaux* contain 'heavily edited' minutes, and some 'key decisions, these reports indicate, were made informally, or at least not in public rooms in which minutes were taken'.[162] Ultimately, however, as Scheipers remarks, GC IV 'did not spell out conditions for lawful acts of resistance against the occupier', although it 'did include far-reaching protections for civilians in occupied territory and was intended to curb the excesses of the suppression of armed resistance and anti-partisan warfare'.[163] The Civilian Commission generally does not appear to have contemplated the distinction between combatants and civilians, or sought to protect the latter in contradistinction to the former.

'Protected persons' were also not meaningfully constructed at the Diplomatic Conference as deserving protection by virtue of being human,[164] despite some contemporary scholarship interpreting the treaty as being informed by human

[157] *Report – Government Experts* (n 137) 273.

[158] See section I.

[159] *Final Record*, vol II(A) (n 1) 620–21.

[160] ibid 621; see also comments by his fellow UK delegate William Gardner in the discussion of the expansion of the POW status in the POW Committee, ibid 420.

[161] *Conférence diplomatique 1949: sténogrammes de la Commission III, tome I* (26 April 1949) (ICRC Library, CD_1949_COMM3_CR02) 47.

[162] van Dijk, *Preparing for War* (n 45) 23.

[163] Scheipers (n 71) 144.

[164] cf chapter 5, section III.

rights thinking.[165] In the absence of a preamble, the *GC IV Commentary* identifies CA3 and Article 27 GC IV as enshrining the underlying principles and ideas upon which all four Geneva Conventions are founded, namely 'respect for the human person and the inviolable character of the basic rights of individual men and women'.[166] However, the former applies to NIACs and the latter contains 'general observations' regarding the treatment of 'protected persons' only. Moreover, as Helen Kinsella remarks, '[t]he discussion about a potential Preamble to the IV Convention reveals some of the delegates' struggles to root the protection of civilians in a common identifiable ground'.[167] The reference in most proposals to dignity and the respect for the human person proved less controversial than religious allusions regarding the divine origin of man.[168] Yet this humanitarian ideal was arguably subdued in the negotiation of the guarantees themselves. Neither the delineation of the scope of application *ratione personae* nor individual provisions were noticeably discussed with reference to the dignity of the person, excepting special safeguards for women.[169]

The drafters of GC IV were instead concerned with the protection of particular categories of civilian persons. Beyond the primary focus on enemy nationals, as noted above, the vulnerable position of refugees with de jure enemy nationality, children and women was highlighted in the discussions and prompted the adoption of certain safeguards. Their preferential treatment under the treaty was partly shaped by non-state actors, such as the International Union for Child Welfare, the International Council of Women and the International Abolitionist Federation, as well as the International Refugee Organisation. The International Union for Child Welfare had already cooperated with the ICRC before the Second World War, and the respective GC IV provisions followed its earlier attempts of promoting a special convention for the protection of children in war.[170] At the 1938 International Conference, the ICRC extended its regard for the effects of war on children to women as vulnerable groups.[171] At the 1949 Diplomatic Conference itself, the International Refugee Organisation and the Israeli delegation protested that the nationality requirement for 'protected persons' would likely affect refugees and de facto stateless persons in a negative manner.[172] They thus accomplished the inclusion of the clause

[165] See, eg, Hitchcock (n 49); van Dijk, 'Entangled Foundations' (n 135); van Dijk himself notes in his later monograph that 'the leading drafters of the Civilian Convention', naming in particular Pilloud, Pictet and Cahen-Salvador, 'initially adopted human rights thinking but ultimately rejected incorporating its discourse and principles within the Convention's text', van Dijk, *Preparing for War* (n 45) 54–56.

[166] *GC IV Commentary* (n 75) 14 and 199–200.

[167] H Kinsella, *The Image Before the Weapon: A Critical History of the Distinction Between Combatant and Civilian* (Ithaca, Cornell University Press, 2011) 116.

[168] *Final Record*, vol II(A) (n 1) 691–97 and 777–82.

[169] ibid 644.

[170] *GC IV Commentary* (n 75) 285.

[171] ICRC, *Sixteenth International Red Cross Conference* (Geneva, ICRC, 1938) 104.

[172] *Final Record*, vol II(A) (n 1) 653, 658 and 660.

on the treatment of refugees with enemy nationality.[173] While the Conference may have dealt with these categories of civilians without the intervention of non-state actors, they arguably sustained the delegates' engagement with the situation of these individuals. They drew the states' attention to the necessity of providing special guarantees and reformulated draft provisions. Not all non-state actors were permitted to participate in the debates directly as observers or experts.[174] Yet even their written communications seem to have influenced states' shared understanding of who would be in need of what kind of protection. Compared to the period of the early written laws of war, non-state actors had become agents in the process and more powerful in constructing individuals for the purpose of regulating warfare.

Emphasising these victim groups may have, however, drawn the attention away from a more consistent consideration of the nature and status of civilians generally. The majority of individuals themselves were voiceless, and the general plight of civilians in time of war remained unspoken. Although Joseph Kunz, for example, hailed the protection of stateless persons under GC IV as 'an innovation and great progress in international law',[175] their inclusion in Article 4 is no more than implied in the negative definition of 'protected persons' as non-nationals. An explicit reference which recognised their need for protection in an earlier draft was removed,[176] and no consensus existed among the delegations in 1949 with respect to the position of stateless persons.[177] Without an advocacy network promoting their wellbeing, these individuals were not constructed for the purpose of the protection regime; paradoxically, the absence of representation at the inter-state level constitutes the very reason for their vulnerability and need for protection under international law.

The conceptualisation of individuals and the formulation of their protection in the treaty text remained ultimately the prerogative of states. They considered their own nationals as not in need of the safeguards provided for 'protected persons'.[178] The common understanding of the *domaine réservé* of states which curtailed the reach of international law also excluded these individuals from the scope of application *ratione personae* of GC IV. Given that the protection of wounded and sick soldiers has applied to a belligerent party's own armed forces since the first Geneva Convention of 1864,[179] the seemingly inevitable exclusion of states' own nationals may be questionable. Yet by limiting the main

[173] GC IV, art 44.

[174] Notably, the International Refugee Organisation was admitted as an observer.

[175] JL Kunz, 'The Geneva Conventions of August 12, 1949' in GA Lipsky (ed), *Law and Politics in the World Community: Essays on Hans Kelsen's Pure Theory and Related Problems in International Law* (Berkeley, University of California Press, 1953) 310.

[176] See Landefeld (n 117).

[177] See, eg, *Final Record*, vol II(A) (n 1) 621 and 793.

[178] See, eg, ibid 814.

[179] Convention for the Amelioration of the Condition of the Wounded in Armies in the Field (Geneva, 22 August 1864) art 6.

protection regime to non-nationals, the treaty remains faithful to the traditional principle of non-interference under international law, except in the particular situation of refugees.[180]

The essentially state-centric discourse had indeed arguably acquired a new dimension and restraining influence at the 1949 Diplomatic Conference compared to the inter-war years. This can be seen in the unprecedented significance of the nationality requirement for allied and neutral nationals which delineates the position of individuals within the belligerent relations between states and within the international legal system. Article 4 paragraph 2 suggests that the individuals' vulnerability and merit for benefitting from the main GC IV protection regime derive from the lack of operative diplomatic relations between states rather than the situations experienced by the individuals. It provides a subsidiary protection mechanism for allied and neutral civilians which comes into operation when ordinary inter-state mechanisms are unavailable.[181] The protective scope of the treaty was thus limited by the ambit of other fields of international law, primarily the protection of individuals under the laws of peace, including diplomatic protection.[182] Moreover, nationals of non-contracting states are also excluded, indicating a lingering deference to the traditional principle of reciprocity in international law and in particular the laws of war. The protection of individuals where the state of nationality has not ratified the treaty was rejected as unreasonable, unfair and inappropriate since the Convention was apparently regarded as providing transactional obligations between states.[183] Such legalistic approaches had been absent in the efforts of non-state actors who followed humanitarian ideals and may have been less concerned with tailoring protection in accordance with states' legal relations during the inter-war years.

However, not all states and individual delegates supported a restrictive approach as the conflicting opinions on the balancing of the interests of individuals and states in the deliberations show.[184] The Bulgarian delegate and lawyer Nissim Mevorah stressed the need to protect 'elementary human rights'.[185] In contrast, the Australian delegate Colonel Hodgson rejected a remark by the French delegate and lawyer Andrée Jacob that 'the object of the Convention was to provide for the protection of persons, and not to safeguard the rights of States', emphasising the latter instead.[186] The divergent views of the delegations reflect different understandings of the role and scope of the laws of war,

[180] *GC IV Commentary* (n 75) 46.

[181] E Salmón, 'Who Is a Protected Civilian?' in Clapham, Gaeta and Sassòli (n 9) para 38.

[182] *GC IV Commentary* (n 75) 621; *Final Record*, vol II(A) (n 1) 794.

[183] See, eg, *Final Record*, vol II(A) (n 1) 794; *Final Record*, vol II(B) (n 56) 375–77; *Conférence diplomatique 1949: sténogrammes de la Commission III, tome IV* (18 July 1949) (ICRC Library, CD_1949_COMM3_CR48) 16, 23 and 25–26.

[184] See, eg, *Final Record*, vol II(A) (n 1) 796–98; *Final Record*, vol II(B) (n 56) 377–83.

[185] *Final Record*, vol II(A) (n 1) 797.

[186] ibid 622.

and, consequently, the purpose of the Civilian Convention.[187] The UK delegate Brigadier Page seemingly portrayed the treaty as a substitute for ordinary protection under international law provided by diplomatic processes.[188] The Swiss and Scandinavian delegates, in contrast, conceived it as offering supplementary safeguards to diplomatic protection, which, according to the Swiss delegate, 'could only be regarded as an advantage'.[189] Stressing that the humane treatment of the civilian population was the objective of the treaty, the Soviet Delegate Dmitrievitch Morosov rejected the idea that '[t]he application of these humanitarian provisions' should be conditional upon 'race or nationality', and the state of nationality being a party to the convention.[190]

Various explanations have been advanced for the representatives' and delegations' disparate arguments. Geoffrey Best accords the difference in approaches to the realism of military officials and diplomats in response to humanitarian demands.[191] Gilad Ben-Nun describes Mevorah and Cahen-Salvador as being driven by 'their unabating desire for a universal and all-encompassing purview for the Civilian Convention, based on their *personal* experiences as drafters who had also been Holocaust survivors a mere four years prior to GC-IV's making'.[192] More generally, he suggests that the Nordic and Soviet bloc states were 'harbingers of universalism' at the Conference, who 'wished for an all-encompassing convention that would be applicable to all people, under all circumstances, in all places'.[193] The benevolent disposition of the Soviet Union delegation has, however, been questioned. Van Dijk notes that UK and US representatives complained that the Soviet delegation 'assumed the role of a "great humanitarian" by trying to embarrass particularly those "who oppose[-d] working drafts on practical and legal grounds"'.[194] In his recent study of UK and US attitudes towards the drafting of the 1949 Geneva Conventions, he suggests that the Anglo-American delegations themselves 'regularly pushed for the most regressive solutions and opposed further restrictions on regulating occupation'.[195]

While the UK's position may indeed 'be at least partly explained by Cold War and imperial politics',[196] the nationality requirement appears to have served as a useful tool in its deliberate attempt to limit states' obligations under GC

[187] cf K Mačak and E Policinski, 'In Pursuit of a Treaty's Soul: A Study of the Object and Purpose of the Fourth Geneva Convention' (2024) 73 *ICLQ* 385, 408.

[188] *Final Record*, vol II(A) (n 1) 620; this understanding was also promoted after the adoption of the treaty by Gutteridge (n 5) 322.

[189] *Final Record*, vol II(A) (n 1) 621, see also 793–94.

[190] *Final Record*, vol II(B) (n 56) 375–76.

[191] Best (n 43) 104–05.

[192] Ben-Nun (n 57) 109.

[193] ibid 106.

[194] B van Dijk, '"The Great Humanitarian": The Soviet Union, the International Committee of the Red Cross, and the Geneva Conventions of 1949' (2019) 37 *Law and History Review* 209, 227.

[195] van Dijk, *Preparing for War* (n 45) 6.

[196] ibid 315.

IV and thus its protective scope. National interests may have informed the construction of individuals as enemy, co-belligerent and neutral nationals, and stirred the negotiations and the eventually adopted text towards the exclusion of various categories of civilians from the 'protected person' concept. Yet the success of this strategy was arguably due to the absence of a civilian concept and the reliance on nationality instead as an established criterion for recognising individuals in the context of inter-state armed conflicts and under international law. While civilians were no longer commonly believed to fall outside of the scope of war, the understanding of civilians and their position under the laws of war was determined on the basis of nationality. The main protection regime of GC IV, ultimately, only provides some protection for those who qualify under the exclusionary, legalistic concept of 'protected persons'.

B. Protection of the Civilian Population

i. The Regulation of Means and Methods of Warfare

The First World War had devastatingly shown that civilians were no longer, if they ever were, outside of the theatre of war. The regulation or prohibition of some novel forms of warfare – aerial warfare in particular – was consequently deliberated during the inter-war years with the intention of protecting civilian populations. The most prominent effort to create an international agreement on aerial warfare was the 1923 Hague Rules concerning the Control of Wireless Telegraphy in Time of War and Air Warfare (Hague Draft Rules).[197] Although the instrument was never adopted as a treaty, it has been described as 'an authoritative attempt to clarify and formulate rules of law governing the use of aircraft in war'[198] and as influential for the further development of international law.[199]

The proposed regime for the regulation of air bombardment is set out in Chapter IV of the Hague Draft Rules on 'Hostilities'. Article 24 stipulates limitations on the basis of intent, including the prohibition of terrorising the civilian population, and the nature of the targets, only allowing bombardment 'directed against a military objective'. While these 'legitimate' objectives are enumerated exhaustively, the civilian population is not defined. Furthermore, the Draft Rules differentiate the 'bombardment of cities, towns, villages, habitations and

[197] Reprinted in Schindler and Toman (n 91).

[198] H Lauterpacht (ed), *International Law: A Treatise by L Oppenheim, vol II: Disputes, War and Neutrality*, 7th edn (London, Longmans, Green and Co, 1952) para 214*b*.

[199] HM Hanke, 'The 1923 Hague Rules of Air Warfare: A Contribution to the Development of International Law Protecting Civilians from Air Attack' (1993) 33:292 *IRRC* 12; C Wilke and H Doutaghi, 'Legal Technologies: Conceptualizing the Legacy of the 1923 *Hague Rules of Aerial Warfare*' (2024) 37 *LJIL* 88; in line with the overarching approach of the book, this chapter focuses on the instrument's influence on conventional rather than customary international law.

buildings' with respect to their proximity to 'operations of the land forces'. In the absence of armed forces, the presence of a designated 'military objective' does not render the attack lawful if 'an undiscriminating bombardment of the civil population would result therefrom'. Conversely, a proportionality analysis is required where the criterion of 'the immediate vicinity of the operations of the land forces' is fulfilled. Amanda Alexander concludes that '[i]t was agreed that the distinction between combatant and non-combatant did not mean that the presence of non-combatants would render military objectives immune from attack'.[200]

The Hague Draft Rules apply 'different standards to different areas' since the drafters perceived the frontline and 'the erstwhile "peaceful" areas in the rear' differently.[201] While this distinction was common in scholarship, James Molony Spaight, a leading authority on aerial warfare at the time, additionally acknowledged that '[w]arships and aircraft carry … their own zones of operations with them; they create their battle zones as they go'.[202] Hays Parks also remarks that '[t]he battlefield was extended by the industrialization of nation-states and by a capacity for attack of military objects beyond artillery range'.[203] Although not confined to the battlefield alone, the spatial distinction in the Draft Rules reveals the continuing traditional territorial understanding of war unaffected by the nature of modern warfare. Civilians were still seemingly protected depending on their location inside or outside of the battlefield. It was believed that civilian suffering would be avoided due to their evacuation or flight from the combat zone or, alternatively, it would be self-imposed given their supposed awareness of the risk.[204]

Nevertheless, the Hague Draft Rules also protect 'the specific idea of the *civilian* as conceived during the [First World War]'.[205] The understanding of individuals as civilians appears to have a constraining effect on the conduct of hostilities under the instrument. Sparing civilians was no longer a practical consequence of the limits of technology and military necessity,[206] but seemingly a normative imperative. Accordingly, the limits of legitimate warfare were partly

[200] A Alexander, 'The "Good War": Preparations for a War against Civilians' (2019) 15 *Law, Culture and the Humanities* 227, 244–45.

[201] Hanke (n 199) 23; see also Commission of Jurists, 'General Report' (1938) 32 *AJIL Supplement* 1, 22; JB Moore, *International Law and Some Current Illusions and other Essays* (New York, The Macmillan Company, 1924) 195 and 199.

[202] JM Spaight, 'Air Bombardment' (1923–24) 4 *BYIL* 21, 28–29.

[203] WH Parks, 'Air War and the Law of War' (1990) 32 *Air Force Law Review* 1, 32; for an examination of the concept of the battlefield see F Mégret, 'War and the Vanishing Battlefield' (2011) 9 *Loyola University Chicago International Law Review* 131.

[204] JW Garner, 'International Regulation of Air Warfare' (1932) 3 *Air Law Review* 103, 123; Hanke (n 199) 23; see also chapter 3, section II.A.

[205] Alexander, 'Genesis' (n 1) 360.

[206] MW Royse, *Aerial Bombardment and the International Regulation of Warfare* (New York, Harold Vinal, 1928) 150–54; C Jochnick and R Normand, 'The Legitimation of Violence: A Critical History of the Laws of War' (1994) 35 *Harvard International Law Journal* 49, 78.

determined by the classification of persons and objects as military or civilian, and not only the de facto territorial scope of the theatre of war. This is, for example, noticeable in the move away from the notion of 'undefended towns' in the earlier period, to the identification of 'military objectives' in the regulation of attacks under the Draft Rules. Various commentators emphasised the inoperability of the 'undefended' criterion in aerial warfare.[207] Parks observes that the responsibility to avoid harming civilians was shifted from the defending to the attacking state.[208] Christiane Wilke and Helyeh Doutaghi, on the other hand, note that civilians themselves remained partially accountable since Article 25, for example, required that protected medical, religious and historic buildings were marked with a sufficiently visible sign to shield them from attack.[209] While the laws of war were still permissive, their conceptualisation moved increasingly from having an enabling effect on warfare wherever the belligerent sides encountered each other, to acquiring a more constraining force.

This underlying belief in the constraining power of international law may have been due to the nature of the actors involved. The Hague Draft Rules were prepared by a Commission of Jurists which had been instituted by the 1922 Washington Conference on the Limitation of Armaments. Despite the Commission's name, the legal experts were supported by military technical advisers belonging to the armed forces of the respective states as well as diplomats. The delegations included such eminent experts on aerial warfare and the laws of war as Spaight, Rear Admiral William Ledyard Rodgers and Albert de Geouffre de Lapradelle.[210] Rodgers, an adviser for the American delegation, observed a division between the jurists and technical advisers, deploring the former's inexperience 'with the art and practice of war' and undue faith in the constraining power of the laws of war.[211] Contemporaneous commentators[212] and international legal scholars today[213] ascribe the non-adoption of the Hague Draft Rules as law to the overly idealistic approach of the jurists behind them. Yet Rodgers himself recounted the influential role that the technical advisers played and described the rules as 'practicable and reasonable'.[214] More recent studies of the instrument also note that the involvement of military experts was likely 'robust',[215] and that the rules were consistent 'with the existing military

[207] See, eg, Spaight, 'Air Bombardment' (n 202) 22; Garner (n 204) 118–19; R Gallopin, 'La protection des civils en temps de guerre et la notion de l'objectif militaire' (1939) 21:247 *IRRC* 545, 547.
[208] Parks (n 203) 34.
[209] Wilke and Doutaghi (n 199) 98.
[210] Moore (n 201) 182–83.
[211] WJ Rodgers, 'Laws of War Concerning Aviation and Radio' (1923) 17 *AJIL* 629, 633.
[212] See, eg, FE Quindry, 'Aerial Bombardment of Civilian and Military Objectives' (1931) 2 *The Journal of Air Law* 474.
[213] See, eg, Parks (n 203) 31; Jochnick and Normand (n 206) 83–84; Alexander, '"Good War"' (n 200) 244.
[214] Rodgers (n 211) 634.
[215] Wilke and Doutaghi (n 199) 95.

practices of states and international law'.[216] David Traven further suggests that the Commission's aim was to determine the applicability of existing rules and need for change in light of new military technologies, rather than to create a treaty.[217]

It should also be noted that the confidence in the laws of war was not universally shared even among international lawyers at the time. The period is generally known for the silence in scholarship with respect to this area of law, a pessimistic outlook on the viability of regulating warfare under legal rules, and a distrust towards the continuing existence of a legal framework for the conduct of war which could endanger the cause of peace.[218] One of the Commission's legal experts, Jonkheer van Eysinga, himself later avowed in response to an ICRC's enquiry whether international legal rules protecting the civilian population from air bombardment would be possible that such protection would not be 'realizable in practice'.[219] It is, nonetheless, noticeable that the Draft Rules seem to have been inspired by a belief in the value of international law that extends beyond an affirmation of military necessity.

Other actors in the epistemic community of lawyers were also concerned with the regulation of aerial warfare.[220] The ILA held a Conference on Aviation in 1922 where its Aviation Law Committee already restricted aerial warfare to military objectives and prohibited '[a]erial attack upon any town, village, or place, with the sole purpose of terrorising the civil population'.[221] It thus employed the same new language and ideas as the drafters of the Hague Draft Rules. The 1924 report of the ILA Committee in fact mentions that 'a great part of the Rules … was based upon the proposals which were sent to the Jurists Commission' by the ILA.[222] However, while it is unknown whether it was a deliberate step by the governments, the official representatives of six world powers in the Commission of Jurists were not drawn from the international lawyers considering the same issue in the ILA in 1922. At its 1924 conference, the ILA not only debated its own 1922 draft but also the Hague Draft Rules on air bombardment.[223] It amended its earlier draft provisions, for example, to include

[216] D Traven, *Law and Sentiment in International Politics: Ethics, Emotions, and the Evolution of the Laws of War* (Cambridge, Cambridge University Press, 2021) 225.

[217] ibid.

[218] See, eg, JL Kunz, 'Plus de lois de la guerre?' (1934) 41 *Revue générale de droit international public* 22; *GC IV Commentary* (n 75) 4; Alexander, '"Good War"' (n 200).

[219] H Lauterpacht, 'The Problem of the Revision of the Law of War' (1952) 29 *BYIL* 360, 368.

[220] The Institut de Droit International had adopted a resolution regarding air law, including aerial warfare, in 1911, IDI, 'Textes votés à la Session de Madrid (1911): Sur le régime juridique des aérostats' (1911) 24 *AIDI* 346, 346; yet it refrained from considering the laws of war during the inter-war years, JL Kunz, 'The Chaotic Status of the Laws of War and the Urgent Necessity for Their Revision' (1951) 45 *AJIL* 37, 39.

[221] ILA, 'Report of the Aviation Law Committee' (1922) 31 *ILA Reports of Conferences* 211, 213–14.

[222] ILA, 'Report of the Aerial Law Committee' (1924) 33 *ILA Reports of Conferences* 113, 120.

[223] ibid 131–45.

the prohibition of indiscriminate bombardment in the vicinity of military objectives, to reformulate the prohibition of terrorising the civilian population, and to redefine military objectives to reflect the Hague Draft Rules.[224]

The ILA resumed its engagement with the protection of civilian populations 'against new engines of war' at its 1936 conference.[225] It adopted a Draft Convention in 1938 which enshrined a combination of earlier regulations regarding undefended towns and provisions resembling the Hague Draft Rules.[226] It was, indeed, acknowledged in the proceedings that the instrument was not only informed by existing treaties, namely the 1899 and 1907 Hague Regulations, but also 'draft Conventions and Projects which have never come into force as international treaties', including the Hague Draft Rules as well as the so-called Monaco Draft,[227] which is further discussed below.[228] While the reliance on non-binding instruments, some of which had been adopted by non-state actors, may be generally less surprising and uncontroversial for the ILA in comparison to states, it is also notable that an overlap now existed in the persons involved. In particular, de Lapradelle, a professor of international law who had been a delegate for France at the Commission of Jurists, served as the president of the ILA in 1936 and the chairman of the ILA committee responsible for the protection of civilian populations in 1938. This may further explain the legacy of the Hague Draft Rules within the epistemic community of international lawyers.

Other actors reaffirmed existing law and resorted to the declaration of principles rather than the drafting of comprehensive sets of rules and regulations for the protection of civilians. At its International Conference in 1921, the ICRC adopted a resolution on the limitation of warfare which required a strict application of Article 25 of the Hague Regulations prohibiting the attack or bombardment of undefended towns. It also declared that aerial warfare should be limited to military targets to exclude civilian populations as much as possible from bearing the consequences of this new form of warfare.[229] The ICRC had already demanded the same measures in a letter to the League of Nations calling for the limitation of war in 1920.[230] The 1932 Disarmament Conference under the auspices of the League of Nations concluded its first phase stating that '[a]ir attack against the civilian population shall be absolutely prohibited'.[231]

[224] ibid 118–19.

[225] ILA, 'Protection of Civil Populations against New Engines of War' (1936) 39 *ILA Reports of Conferences* 251.

[226] Draft Convention for the Protection of Civilian Populations against New Engines of War (3 September 1938) (1938 ILA Draft Convention) reprinted in Schindler and Toman (n 91), arts 2–5.

[227] ILA, 'Protection of Civilian Populations against New Engines of War' (1938) 40 *ILA Reports of Conferences* 37, 39–40.

[228] See section II.B.ii.

[229] ICRC, *Dixième Conférence* (n 83) 216.

[230] ICRC, 'Limitation de la guerre – Lettre du Comité International de la Croix-Rouge à l'Assemblée de la Société des Nations' (1920) 2:24 *IRRC* 1348.

[231] 'The Disarmament Conference: Conclusion of the First Phase' (1932) 9:3 *Bulletin of International News* 3, 11.

Similarly, the League of Nations adopted a resolution in 1938, in the context of the Spanish Civil War and the Sino-Japanese War,[232] which declared:

(1) The intentional bombing of civilian populations is illegal;
(2) Objectives aimed at from the air must be legitimate military objectives and must be identifiable;
(3) Any attack on legitimate military objectives must be carried out in such a way that civilian populations in the neighbourhood are not bombed through negligence.[233]

Besides the Hague Regulations and the Hague Draft Rules, the negotiation of the resolution took into account a recent statement by the UK Prime Minister Neville Chamberlain in the House of Commons from which the three principles were derived.[234] The League of Nations apparently believed that 'the prohibition on the bombing of civilians was a recognized and established principle of international law and its affirmation would merely reiterate a rule that governments were bound to respect'.[235]

This notion of civilian immunity from attack was indeed frequently invoked during the inter-war years and seemed to imply the principle of distinction. It is noticeable that both supporters of the restriction of aerial warfare[236] as well as sceptics[237] mentioned the distinction between combatants and civilians in their argumentation. They followed disparate lines of reasoning: the former proclaimed that the distinction needed preserving and strengthening through the adoption of new rules regulating aerial warfare; the latter considered the distinction obsolete in light of modern forms of warfare and 'total war'. Both apparently believed that the distinction had informed the laws of war in the past. This arguably anachronistic reading of the law, which reoccurred in later periods,[238] was facilitated by the silence in the earlier period. The absence of an explicit reliance on the principle of distinction or a principled exclusion of civilians from warfare seems to have been retrospectively understood as implying its

[232] In the same context, the ICRC adopted a resolution on the 'protection of civilians against air raids', which was, however, only aimed at the protection of 'helpless women and children and aged civilians', ICRC, *Sixteenth Conference* (n 171) 103.

[233] Resolution for the Protection of Civilian Populations against Bombing from the Air in Case of War (30 September 1938) reprinted in Schindler and Toman (n 91), art I.

[234] League of Nations, 'Third Committee of the Nineteenth Ordinary Session of the Assembly (Reduction and Limitation of Armaments)' (1920–1946) *League of Nations Official Journal Special Supplement* 7.

[235] M Lippman, 'Aerial Attacks on Civilians and the Humanitarian Law of War: Technology and Terror from World War I to Afghanistan' (2002) 33 *California Western International Law Journal* 1, 13–14.

[236] See, eg, Moore (n 201) 200; ILA, 'New Engines' (1938) (n 227) 39; JM Spaight, 'Non-Combatants and Air Attack' (1938) 9 *Air Law Review* 372; regarding the regulation of warfare generally, see Kunz, 'Plus de lois' (n 218) 38.

[237] See, eg, E Colby 'Laws of Aerial Warfare' (1926) 10 *Minnesota Law Review* 207; L Nurick, 'The Distinction Between Combatant and Noncombatant in the Law of War' (1945) 39 *AJIL* 680, 689–96.

[238] See chapters 5 and 6.

taken-for-granted nature at the time. Alexander observes a similar development regarding the 'genesis' of the civilian. She argues that during the First World War, 'although the civilian had only just begun to be envisaged as a vulnerable group, this term was already described as an established and accepted measure of civilized warfare and adherence to the laws of war'.[239] She explains that the lawyers involved in this process supported the claim that civilians should be protected by means of 'a rhetorical slip that is often found in international law, and stated that they *were already* protected'.[240] The participating actors seemed to portray *lex ferenda* as *lex lata*.

The protection of civilians was the shared aim of these various actors despite their disagreement on the regulatory approach. This common standard for the directedness of the law was seemingly driving the debate of new rules. The discourse had thus changed significantly compared to the Brussels and Hague Peace Conferences where protecting individuals who do not belong to the armed forces from the consequences of warfare was not itself an objective, but appears to have been no more than an afterthought.[241] However, framing the proposed rules as reintroducing civilian immunity which had been lost in recent wars failed to provide a better understanding of civilians themselves. The discourse surrounding the regulation of aerial warfare was missing a sustained and coherent engagement with the meaning of the notion. Individuals protected as civilians or as part of the civilian population were merely implicitly constructed as innocent and vulnerable.

Indeed, while this idea of the civilian had seemingly become naturalised, a closer reading of the efforts and their context suggest that the understanding of civilians was not monolithic or uncontested. In her historical study of the concept of civilians, Alexander argues that civilians were simultaneously seen as victims, as well as valuable targets for attack.[242] In the context of so-called 'total war', individuals who do not belong to the armed forces were characterised as active participants in the war efforts beyond the immediate conduct of hostilities. Certain individuals were deemed to be of a 'quasi-military nature' and 'regarded as auxiliary services of the armies while at work', for instance, in munition factories.[243] The surrounding debate about the blurring line between combatants and civilians, nonetheless, suggests an underlying belief that attacking the latter would be illegitimate. Wilke and Doutaghi still contend that the perception of civilians in need of protection was limited to those who were white, 'civilised' and European.[244]

[239] Alexander, 'Genesis' (n 1) 369.
[240] ibid 373.
[241] See chapter 3, section II.A.
[242] Alexander, 'Genesis' (n 1).
[243] Parks (n 203) 42; see also Garner (n 204); Spaight, 'Non-Combatants' (n 236); Nurick (n 237) 693–94; Alexander, '"Good War"' (n 200) 243; Wilke and Doutaghi (n 199) 101–04.
[244] Wilke and Doutaghi (n 199) 99–100.

Although the need for a definition of the 'civilian population' was occasionally emphasised in the proceedings and by commentators, only the 1938 ILA Draft Convention provides one.[245] The ICRC Commission on 'Limitation de la guerre' called for a demarcation between the armed forces and the civilian population shortly after the First World War,[246] yet without any results. Spaight argued that the principle of civilian immunity would be weakened, and even 'dangerous', without a definition of its personal scope.[247] Jean Pictet also declared that, in order to provide the prohibition of the intentional bombardment of the civilian population with practical value, 'il faudrait définir clairement les catégories de personnes qui font partie de la population civile'.[248] He further noted that, since civilian immunity from attack was not expressly formulated in the written laws of war, although it was believed to be a part of the laws of nations,[249] it would have been advantageous 'à confirmer ce principe par une disposition du droit écrit'.[250] However, the deliberation of safeguards for civilians against the effects of warfare among non-state actors did not lead to the adoption of conventional law. While a distinction between combatants and the civilian population was more prevalent in these efforts regarding the conduct of hostilities compared to the debate on civilian POWs and enemy civilians, the meaning of 'civilians' – especially the personal scope of individuals who would qualify as such – was not clearly established in the process.

ii. Safety Zones and Localities

Another form of protection advocated during the inter-war years was the creation of zones, areas or localities under various labels, which were intended to shield individuals therein from the consequences of war. This second development embraced the territorial understanding of war and the idea of spatial protection more fully. The ICRC traces the origin of hospital and safety zones and localities back to Henri Dunant, who promoted the idea in the context of the Franco-Prussian War.[251] In 1929, the French surgeon-general Georges Saint-Paul 'drew up a plan for setting aside places of refuge to shelter not only wounded and sick members of the armed forces, but also sick civilians and certain other categories of civilians'.[252] Two years later, he founded the *Association Internationale des*

[245] The 'civilian population' is defined as 'all those not enlisted in any branch of the combatant services nor for the time being employed or occupied in any belligerent establishment as defined in Article 2', 1938 ILA Draft Convention, art 1.

[246] ICRC, *Dixième Conférence* (n 83) 142.

[247] Spaight, 'Non-Combatants' (n 236) 372 and 376.

[248] JS Pictet, 'La protection juridique de la population civile en temps de guerre' (1939) 21:244 *IRRC* 268, 283; 'the categories of persons which are part of the civilian population should be clearly defined' (author's translation).

[249] ibid 270–71.

[250] ibid 274; 'to confirm this principle in a written legal provision' (author's translation).

[251] *GC IV Commentary* (n 75) 121.

[252] ibid.

Lieux de Genève, 'for the purpose of giving publicity to the plan and encouraging its realization'.[253] Probably the most well-known effort, however, is a draft convention adopted in Monaco in 1934 by a commission of military doctors and lawyers, which had been called into being by the International Committee of Military Medicine and Pharmacy (ICMMP).[254]

The 1934 Monaco Draft has become especially renowned for the creation of safety zones and localities for civilians. Indeed, it was initiated by the ICMMP's finding at its 1933 Congress that more effective measures were necessary to protect the civilian population from future warfare.[255] However, the Draft only stipulates the transformation of undefended towns into security towns for the civilian population by extending the special status of military sanitary towns to them.[256] The remaining guarantees for the civilian population regulate cases of invasion and occupation, as well as acts of war.[257] The Draft also makes a principled declaration that '[t]he civil population shall be left out of any form of hostilities',[258] and it delineates legitimate targets of attack, including 'defended towns'.[259] It thus combines the language and ideas of the Hague Regulations and the Hague Draft Rules, both of which were referred to in the deliberations.[260]

The provisions regarding 'security towns' can be described as distinctly humanitarian. This novel form of protecting civilians implicitly relied on states' interest to safeguard their own populations in time of war. Furthermore, the silence with respect to the scope of application *ratione personae* suggests that all individuals habitant or located in the town benefit from its immunity without distinction. While civilians may have been considered as vulnerable, their protection in security towns derives from their territorial position. Hence, it needs to be emphasised that the immunity is attached to the zone, rather than the individuals. Indeed, the definition of the civilian population in the Monaco Draft, as including 'all persons who are not enlisted in the army',[261] seems to be primarily relevant for the regulation of attacks and not for security towns.

The proposed security and sanitary towns are believed to be related to the idea of the 'lieux de Genève', being 'structured territorially as bounded areas cleared of military activity and equipment, agreed to by all parties to a conflict',

[253] ibid 122.
[254] 'First draft Convention adopted in Monaco (Sanitary cities and localities), 27 July 1934' (ICRC) ihl-databases.icrc.org/applic/ihl/ihl.nsf/Treaty.xsp?action=openDocument&documentId=206E646653AB8F30C12563CD002D69E3 (Monaco Draft).
[255] *Vers l'humanisation de la guerre: Compte rendu des travaux de la Commission réunie par S.A.S. le Prince de Monaco (Février 1934) – Délibérations et Conclusions* (1934) 13.
[256] Monaco Draft, pt IV art 6.
[257] ibid arts 3–5.
[258] ibid art 1.
[259] ibid arts 4–5.
[260] *Vers l'humanisation* (n 255) 40.
[261] Monaco Draft, pt IV art 2.

and 'administered by a humanitarian organization such as the ICRC or by a neutral country's military medical services'.[262] They have been regarded as an extension of Articles 6 and 7 of the 1929 Geneva Convention on wounded and sick members of the armed forces which provide for medical formations and establishments in the field, the immunity of which is contingent on their non-participation in harmful acts towards the enemy.[263] The neutralisation of ambulances and military hospitals can be already found in Article 1 of the 1864 Geneva Convention. On the other hand, de Lapradelle, a member of the Commission in Monaco, remarked that the idea of security zones was built upon the traditional understanding of undefended towns which should not be subjected to bombardment.[264] Both interpretations relate the notion of security towns to existing rules and traditions which had already been firmly established in the ideational and normative structures of the laws of war.

The continuation of these ideas in the Monaco Draft may have been influenced by the professional values and interests of the medical doctors and lawyers who were drafting the project. While both types of actors had been involved in the development of so-called 'Geneva Law', protecting war victims who were in the power of the enemy, the legal experts, in particular, may have influenced the Monaco Draft's rules beyond the creation of humanitarian zones. Indeed, according to René Clémens, the Commission's medical members initially opposed a broad protection regime for the civilian population, preferring instead to confine the deliberations to 'des problems d'ordre sanitaire'.[265] It is noteworthy that de Lapradelle, who had participated in the preparation of the Hague Draft Rules, was explicitly noted as a representative of the legal perspective in Monaco in the negotiation of the protection of the civilian population.[266] Van Dijk argues that the legacy of his involvement in the former 'can be easily discovered in the final text agreed upon by the participants' in Monaco.[267] Although a diplomatic conference hosted by the Belgian government to discuss the proposals was contemplated, 'the lack of Great Powers' support for this attempt to regulate air bombing at a time of rising international tensions' meant the end of these plans.[268]

Aware of the work of the ICMMP's Commission, the ICRC adopted a resolution at its 1934 International Conference to study the question of

[262] M Kleinfeld, 'Too Difficult to Protect: A History of the 1934 Monaco Draft and the Problem of Territory for International Humanitarian Law' (2015) 33 *Environment and Planning D: Society and Space* 592, 597.

[263] ibid 600; *Report on the Proposed Convention for the Establishment of Hospital Towns and Areas* (ICRC Library, CI_1938_DOC15_ENG) 18; regarding sanitary towns, see *Vers l'humanisation* (n 255) 20–21.

[264] ILA, 'New Engines' (1938) (n 227) 81; regarding security towns, see *Vers l'humanisation* (n 255) 40.

[265] R Clémens, *Le projet de Monaco: le droit et la guerre, villes sanitaires et villes de sécurité, assistance sanitaire internationale* (Paris, Libraire du Recueil Sirey, 1937) 31–32.

[266] *Vers l'humanisation* (n 255) 39.

[267] van Dijk, *Preparing for War* (n 45) 214.

[268] ibid 215.

zones or towns protecting military wounded and sick, as well as the civilian population.[269] Yet, according to van Dijk, the ICRC was concerned 'that such measures might be ineffective against air bombing and that cooperation in such a politically sensitive area might undermine their neutrality, if not lead to encroachments on the Geneva Conventions'.[270] Indeed, three years later, the ICRC declared in a circular that it would no longer consider security towns for civilians, which it might instead return to in the future.[271] The 1938 report of the appointed Commission of Experts justified this decision by stating that hospital towns for military wounded and sick were more closely related to the Geneva Conventions and the objectives of the ICRC.[272] The 1938 International Conference did also not pursue an extension of the Geneva Conventions to protect civilians in light of an insistence on the ICRC's narrow role, and the diplomacy surrounding the Conference more generally.[273] The National Red Cross Societies merely adopted an unanimous resolution appealing to states, 'in all areas where civilian lives are liable to be endangered by any military operations, to arrange for the evacuation of women and children into zones of immunity under Red Cross protection'.[274] The ICRC's separate effort to convene a diplomatic conference to institutionalise military hospital zones in treaty form was precluded from taking place by the outbreak of the Second World War. Nevertheless, it promoted the adoption of agreements between belligerent parties for the benefit of not only combatants but also civilians during the war. The proposals were met with some 'replies which were favourable in principle', yet without practical effect.[275]

The ICRC's humanitarian interests were likely counteracted by its experience with states in caring for vulnerable groups. Although the ICRC 1938 draft rules on military hospital towns declared that civilian populations habitant therein 'shall be governed by the general principles of international law', it was feared that an overambitious attempt to extend the protection might undermine the overall project.[276] The constraint appears to have been to some extent self-imposed, given the ICRC's simultaneous efforts regarding the protection of enemy civilians. Yet the protection of civilians in occupied territory had also been initially excluded from its endeavours for similar reasons. The ICMMP had likewise decided to send to the Committee only those matters in the Monaco

[269] ICRC, *Quinzième Conférence internationale de la Croix-Rouge* (Tokyo, Kokusai Shuppan Insatsusha, 1934) 261.

[270] van Dijk, *Preparing for War* (n 45) 215.

[271] ICRC, 'Projet de création de villes sanitaires' (1937) 19:220 *IRRC* 401, 406.

[272] *Report – Hospital Towns* (n 263) 3; reaffirmed in ICRC, *Sixteenth Conference* (n 171) 77–78.

[273] R Gill, 'The 1938 International Committee of the Red Cross Conference: Humanitarian Diplomacy and the Cultures of Appeasement in Britain' in N Wylie, M Oppenheimer and J Crossland (eds), *The Red Cross Movement: Myths, Practices and Turning Points* (Manchester, Manchester University Press, 2020).

[274] ICRC, *Sixteenth Conference* (n 171) 103.

[275] *GC IV Commentary* (n 75) 123.

[276] *Report – Hospital Towns* (n 263) 14 and 28.

Draft which were of its concern,[277] implying the limits of the ICRC's scope of action. Conversely, the Monaco Draft, as a medical-juridical collaboration, was arguably deliberated in a social environment that was less affected by the traditional interests of states.

A similar inhibition of the ICRC can be found in the discussion of extending the protection of military hospitals as well as military wounded and sick to their civilian equivalents. At the time, only Article 27 of the Hague Regulations could be seen as providing a rudimentary shield for civilian hospitals in relation to sieges and bombardments subject to specified conditions. In the absence of a specific protection regime, some states resorted to the militarisation of civilian hospitals and their utilisation for the care and treatment of wounded and sick members of the armed forces. This practice was enabled under a broad reading of the Geneva Convention, arguing that 'the presence of civilians in military hospitals does not deprive them [the hospitals] of protection'.[278] In contrast, under a narrow interpretation, civilians were perceived as potentially undermining the immunity of military medical personnel and institutions under the laws of war. The 1929 Diplomatic Conference rejected the extension of the Geneva Convention for the protection of wounded and sick members of the armed forces to wounded and sick civilians.[279] A commission, established by the ICRC to study the revision of the treaty in 1937, took the limited step of preventing the cessation of the immunity of military medical establishments and personnel when caring for civilians, albeit not extending the immunity to the wounded and sick civilians themselves.[280] At the 1938 International Conference, it was suggested that enhancing the protection for civilian hospitals should instead be pursued through an amendment of the Hague Regulations.[281] The legal framework and the debates demonstrate that the distinction between military personnel and civilians was central to the understanding of war and the laws of war. Yet civilians were not conceptualised beyond the mere differentiation from military individuals. The discourse does not suggest different systems of immunity from attack pertaining to the wounded and sick combatants and the medical personnel attending to them, on the one hand, and civilians, on the other. Instead, the presence of *unprotected* civilians was seemingly perceived as interfering with and possibly even undermining the protection regime of the first Geneva Conventions.

[277] ibid 2; the perceived competence of the ICRC was limited to the existing Geneva Conventions and thus sanitary towns and localities as well as POWs, whereas the protection of the civilian population was regarded as related to the Hague Regulations, 'Réunions du Comité Permanent des Congrès Internationaux de Médecine et de Pharmacie militaires. 26, 27 et 29 juin 1934' (6 Février 1936) *Annexe au Journal de Monaco* 5, 6.

[278] *Commission of Government Experts for the Study of Conventions for the Protection of War Victims – Preliminary Documents Submitted by the International Committee of the Red Cross, vol I, Revision of the Geneva Convention and related Treaty Provisions* (ICRC Library, CEG_1947_DOC_CGREV_ENG) 80.

[279] ibid 79.

[280] *Report – Government Experts* (n 137) 26.

[281] ICRC, *Sixteenth Conference* (n 171) 78.

The ILA emerged as a third important actor deliberating safety zones for the protection of civilian populations at its 1936 and 1938 Conferences. The 1938 ILA Draft Convention formulates rules for the establishment of such zones,[282] in addition to the regulation of means and methods of warfare, as discussed above. It transformed the general notion of safety zones into a set of detailed regulations concerning the individuals protected therein, and their administration. Besides this legalistic measure, the ILA combined the humanitarian rationale for the creation of safety zones with understandings of military necessity. For instance, Kornelius Jansma, a member of the ILA drafting committee, declared that 'we do not appeal to the conscience of the belligerent, but merely to his interest'.[283] The ILA stressed the absence of a military value in attacking certain categories of civilians which would be protected in the safety zones since they were considered as 'purely inoffensive parts of the civil population'.[284] The identification of these 'non-belligerents *par excellence*' in the discussions[285] and in Article 12 of the Draft Convention constructs particular parts of the civilian population as innocent, rather than the civilian population as a whole. Although the provision initially refers to 'inhabitants of a safety zone', its immunity is intended for groups characterised primarily by age and gender, rather than civilian status.[286] The ILA's approach also shows traces of the emphasis on 'peaceful' and 'inoffensive' individuals who do not belong to the armed forces which had been prevalent in the early written laws of war.[287] It appears to have spoken two different languages of humanitarian ideals and military necessity, probably in order to render the idea of safety zones persuasive for the widest possible audience.

Since safety zones were sometimes deliberated alongside general principles regulating the means and methods of warfare, the concern was voiced that they would undermine general civilian immunity that some believed the laws of war provided for.[288] For instance, it was debated at the League of Nations whether the creation of zones explicitly excluded from bombardment might suggest that other towns and localities could be attacked or that the civilian population outside of those zones would be subject to less protection.[289] Others decisively discarded such fears.[290] Rather than substituting general rules which prohibit direct attacks against civilians, the creation of safety zones was argued as an

[282] 1938 ILA Draft Convention, arts 10–21.

[283] ILA, 'New Engines' (1936) (n 225) 280.

[284] ibid 255–56.

[285] ibid 267.

[286] Some ILA members opposed this approach which neglects parts of the population, see, eg, ILA, 'New Engines' (1938) (n 227) 73.

[287] See chapter 3, section II.A.

[288] ILA 'New Engines' (1936) (n 225) 268–69; ILA, 'New Engines' (1938) (n 227) 69 and 72; *XVIth International Red Cross Conference – IInd Commission: Summary of the Discussions of the Legal Commission* (ICRC Library, CI_1938_COMMJUR_ENG) 27.

[289] League of Nations (n 234) 34–35.

[290] ibid 35; ILA, 'New Engines' (1936) (n 225) 256; ICRC, *Sixteenth Conference* (n 171) 81.

additional, subsidiary safeguard. Yet the latter did not rely on the distinction between legitimate and illegitimate objectives but instead made 'such a differentiation irrelevant'.[291] The conceptualisation of such zones and the protection of civilians therein, therefore, did not derive from civilian immunity but followed different ideational traditions.

Even the actors advocating this form of protection could not agree on a shared understanding of the individuals shielded from attack in a specially designated area. A personal overlap existed in the discussions in the various forums. All three actors – ICMMP, ICRC and ILA – welcomed or sent delegates to the meetings of the other organisations and some individuals were members of more than one organisation.[292] De Lapradelle and Colonel Jules Voncken, in particular, were part of the ICMMP's and the ICRC's commissions and participated in the ILA conferences. The ICRC and ILA vowed to cooperate with the ICMMP in their pursuits of projects similar to the Monaco Draft. The president of the ILA, de Lapradelle, highlighted the influence of the 1934 Monaco Conference on the 1938 ILA Draft Convention.[293] Yet, ultimately, the initial humanitarian proposal of the Monaco Draft could not influence the construction of civilians by the other actors as being in need of protection generally and finding sanctuary in security zones without distinction. Instead, the institutional identities of these non-state actors continued to inform their respective drafts.

iii. The Protection of Civilians against Consequences of War under the Fourth Geneva Convention

Following the Second World War, the ICRC believed that the recent war had 'revealed in tragic fashion another aspect of the situation of Civilians, for which a remedy must if possible be found', namely 'the blind effects of modern mass warfare'.[294] It, therefore, advocated the extension of the Civilian Convention beyond the ambit of the Tokyo Draft. Its *Remarks and Proposals* submitted to the Diplomatic Conference suggested that the new instrument would be inspired by the notion of civilian immunity. It proposed an alternative preamble to the Stockholm Draft which confirmed 'that the civilian population must remain outside all warlike operations, in so far as military requirements allow'.[295] This principle, however, is not substantiated in the treaty text. While the title of Part II GC IV declares as its objective the 'General Protection of Populations against Certain Consequences of War', it abstains from regulating the means

[291] Lauterpacht, 'Law of War' (n 219) 371.

[292] See, eg, ICRC, 'Congrès convoqué par la Commission d'études medico-juridiques' (1936) 18:207 *IRRC* 213, 214; ICRC, 'Commission d'experts réunie en vue d'élaborer un projet de convention pour la création de localité et zones sanitaires' (1938) 20:238 *IRRC* 929; ILA, 'New Engines' (1938) (n 227) 37 and 57.

[293] ILA, 'New Engines' (1936) (n 225) 262–63.

[294] *Government Experts*, vol III (n 147) 40.

[295] *Remarks and Proposals* (n 154) 66–67.

and methods of warfare. Best argues that the regulation of air bombardment, especially of an atomic kind, had not been included in the Stockholm Draft and on the Diplomatic Conference's agenda due to its political nature.[296] Olivier Barsalou suggests that the US, in particular, feared the condemnation of its own practice during the recent war and wished to avoid limiting its warfare in the future.[297] A draft resolution submitted to the Conference by the Soviet Union delegation regarding bacteriological, chemical and atomic weapons as well as mass extermination of populations was inter alia rejected for falling outside of its competence.[298] By introducing special zones of protection for civilians into conventional law,[299] GC IV instead institutionalised the inter-war efforts regarding sanctuaries for civilians.

By this time, the ICRC regarded safety zones as falling into the ideational framework within which the Diplomatic Conference was conducted. It argued that their creation 'rests on the fundamental principle of the Geneva Convention …: the protection, even in the theatre of war, of certain persons who are entitled to immunity, because they are incapable of harming the enemy'.[300] Yet this principle does not seem to encompass all civilians. Article 13 defines the scope of application *ratione personae* of Part II as pertaining to 'the whole of the populations of the countries in conflict'. The civilian character of the population and its individual members is still only implied. More importantly, several of the provisions further distinguish between different parts of the population which are the designated beneficiaries of special protection. 'Hospital and safety zones and localities' provide permanent shelter 'for the weakest categories among the population', whereas 'neutralized zones' provide a more inclusive protection on a temporary basis.[301] Article 15 classifies two categories of beneficiaries of neutralised zones: 'wounded and sick combatants or non-combatants', where the latter can be assumed to belong to the armed forces due to the second category comprising 'civilian persons who take no part in hostilities, and who, while they reside in the zones, perform no work of a military character'. The idea of neutralised zones thus shows a similarity with the former concept of 'undefended towns'. Unlike Article 25 of the Hague Regulations, it identifies the individuals protected in the area. Nevertheless, immunity is still attached to the zone rather than the individuals.

The provision's specification of civilians who are deemed worthy of shelter in zones of immunity still resembles the notion of 'peaceful' and 'inoffensive'

[296] Best (n 43) 109.

[297] O Barsalou, 'Preparing for War: The USA and the Making of the 1949 Geneva Conventions on the Laws of War' (2018) 23 *Journal of Conflict & Security Law* 49, 63–64; see also van Dijk, *Preparing for War* (n 45) ch 5.

[298] *Final Record*, vol II(B) (n 56) 498; for a more detailed study of the politics surrounding the resolution see van Dijk, *Preparing for War* (n 45) 237–48.

[299] GC IV, arts 14–15.

[300] *Report Concerning Hospital and Safety Localities and Zones* (ICRC Library, CEG_1947_LOCSAN_RAP_ENG) 5.

[301] *GC IV Commentary* (n 75) 131.

inhabitants in the early written laws of war. The *GC IV Commentary* suggests that it was the objective of GC IV Part II 'to shield certain categories of the population who, by definition, take no part in the fighting: children, women, old people, the wounded and the sick'.[302] Kinsella argues that 'the basic justification for the protection of civilians has been grafted on that for the protection of wounded, sick, and captured combatants. In each case, the defining characteristics of harmlessness are dependency and vulnerability'.[303] Unlike for combatants protected under the first three Geneva Conventions, however, these characteristics are perceived as being 'essential' to 'children, women, and old people'.[304] Only certain categories of civilians were thus constructed as not taking part in the conduct of hostilities by their very nature. Several of the safeguards focused on the specific needs of these categories of individuals rather than the entire population as a result.

Gutteridge argued that the limited protection under Part II for only civilians who 'are taking no active part in the war effort' was an indication that 'these provisions take into account the wearing away of the distinction between combatants and non-combatants'.[305] Yet this distinction is arguably essential since it deterred the authors of the 1949 Geneva Conventions from incorporating wounded and sick military personnel and civilians, as well as POWs and civilian internees, in joined instruments. The protection of both collectively in the same instrument was still contemplated during the early stages of the post-Second World War law-making process,[306] but ultimately rejected. Individuals were excluded from the revised existing legal protection regimes as 'civilians'. However, GC IV Part II introduced into the written laws of war different categories of individuals who do not participate in the conduct of hostilities and war efforts, by providing them with special safeguards. They were perceived to be in need of different forms of protection, but not because they were civilians.

Furthermore, the inclusion of states' own nationals under Part II was deemed such an exceptional 'derogation from the general principles of the Convention that it was necessary, in Article 4, to make an explicit reservation' regarding its provisions.[307] While admitting that it diverges from the traditional understanding of international law, the Civilian Committee's report to the Plenary Assembly pointed out that 'the scope of that law is gradually becoming wider'.[308] It implied advances in international law towards regulating the

[302] ibid 118.
[303] Kinsella (n 167) 122.
[304] ibid.
[305] Gutteridge (n 5) 321.
[306] See, eg, *Report – Preliminary Conference* (n 142) 16–18 and 92–94; *Report – Government Experts* (n 137) 9–11 and 332.
[307] *GC IV Commentary* (n 75) 119.
[308] *Final Record*, vol II(A) (n 1) 816.

internal relations between states and their citizens, as can be seen in the report's stated example of the, albeit non-binding, Universal Declaration of Human Rights (UDHR). Although the report was intended to present the work of the entire Committee, the argumentation may have reflected the view of its author, Colonel Claude du Pasquier, a professor of law and delegate for Switzerland.

Instead of adopting this humanitarian and progressive approach, the majority of state delegates explicitly and decidedly objected to the laws of war's interference in internal affairs. While the adverse belligerent party would be required to recognise the protective zones, the responsibility to establish them lies on the state under attack rather than the attacker. It was primarily this reliance on states' interest in protecting their own civilian populations that proved more difficult at the 1949 Diplomatic Conference than during the humanitarian attempts to develop the law during the inter-war years. Reservations against a mandatory system of safety zones were also raised on the ground that governments themselves were best placed to adopt measures in accordance with the particular circumstances of their countries.[309] As a consequence, the provisions do no more than state that governments 'may' create the respective protected areas. Similar to the regulation of the treatment of 'protected persons', the law-making process was constrained by the perceived scope of international law in the inter-state system and states' sovereign powers.

The discussions at the Diplomatic Conference focused on technical issues rather than historical examples. The adoption of at least permissive provisions for safety zones may have, nonetheless, been facilitated by the humanitarian attempts and discourse of some actors prior to and during the conference. The ICRC seemingly tried to increase the persuasiveness of the proposals by reminding delegations throughout the drafting stages of the history of the idea, starting with Dunant. It referred to its own efforts in this respect, declaring that the provisions were consistent with its 1938 Draft Convention on Hospital Localities and Zones.[310] Moreover, successful and more disappointing experiences with such zones in recent years were invoked in its 1946 report on hospital and safety zones and during the negotiations.[311] Other efforts by the ICRC[312] and non-state actors promoting a range of safeguards against modern forms of warfare in the inter-war years, on the other hand, went unnoticed.

[309] ibid 626–29.

[310] *Report – Preliminary Conference* (n 142) 65; *Report – Government Experts* (n 137) 26–27; *Final Record*, vol II(A) (n 1) 627.

[311] *Final Record*, vol II(A) (n 1) 628 and 784; *Localities and Zones* (n 300) 8–10.

[312] For a survey of the ICRC's engagement with the protection of civilians in the inter-war years see also R Gallopin, 'Action des Conférences internationales de la Croix-Rouge et du Comité international de la Croix-Rouge dans le domaine de la protection des civils en temps de guerre' (1939) 21:244 *IRRC* 287; B Holmes, 'The *IRRC* and the Protection of Civilians, c. 1919–1939' (2018) 100:907/908/909 *IRRC* 115.

Although 'the ICRC's moral authority in the eyes of key states was severely weakened' after the Second World War,[313] the Committee itself took a leading role in the law-making process by preparing working drafts and being actively present as an expert at the Diplomatic Conference. Its distinct role, compared to other non-state actors who participated as observers, was due to its recognised unique expertise and competence.[314] In contrast, the ICMMP was admitted neither as an observer nor as an expert. It was acknowledged at the outset of the Diplomatic Conference, as well as in the 1946 report, that the Committee had 'already made a definite and important contribution to the preparation and study of the Conventions', and it was suggested that it might be invited on an *ad hoc* basis where its advice would be valuable.[315] Paul de Geouffre de Lapradelle, a delegate of Monaco, continued to persistently emphasise the relation between the provisions on safety zones in the draft Civilian Convention and the Monaco Draft, asserting that the former 'were the outcome' of the latter.[316] Yet his repeated calls for the ICMMP's involvement were unsuccessful.[317] The Committee's absence and the other state delegations' silence on the Monaco Draft may have been due to the instrument's origin as a project of a non-state actor other than the ICRC. Moreover, it may have been informed by states' likely hesitation towards the Draft's additional regulations on methods of warfare and its sanction regime in the case of violations.

Best describes the Monegasque delegate as a 'vigorous and influential French law professor' who was also 'a weighty spokesman for that most persistent of pressure-groups, the [ICMMP]'.[318] Additionally, this member of 'a distinguished dynasty of international lawyers',[319] was the son of Albert de Lapradelle, who had been a member of the Commission behind the Monaco Draft. His personal affiliation with the 1934 document and professional values may have informed his more principled approach towards safety zones. He not only stressed their humanitarian value marking 'a progressive step in human rights',[320] but also tried to assuage proclaimed concerns about the possibility of international regulations affecting domestic affairs and laws by pointing at existing conventions and the UDHR.[321] However, the influence of his eminent father in participating inter alia in the 1923 Hague Conference, the 1934 Monaco Commission, the 1936 and 1938 ILA Conferences, and the 1938 ICRC Commission of Experts

[313] H Lovat, *Negotiating Civil War: The Politics of International Regime Design* (Cambridge, Cambridge University Press, 2020) 128.
[314] *Final Record*, vol II(A) (n 1) 15.
[315] ibid 16; *Localities and Zones* (n 300) 1–2.
[316] *Final Record*, vol II(A) (n 1) 626.
[317] ibid 15–17 and 31–33.
[318] Best (n 43) 97.
[319] ibid 80.
[320] *Final Record*, vol II(A) (n 1) 626.
[321] ibid 628; *Conférence diplomatique 1949: sténogrammes de la Commission III, tome I* (27 April 1949) (ICRC Library, CD_1949_COMM3_CR03) 48–51.

may have been more instrumental in the environment of norm entrepreneurs and the epistemic community of international lawyers. The agency of individuals at the Diplomatic Conference seems to have been generally more subdued in light of the required shared understanding of states. Indeed, Pictet suggests that individual delegates in 1949 had less control over the outcome than at the Hague Peace Conferences due to changes in the nature of the treaty-making process.[322] They may, however, have had more weight behind the scenes, especially in their relationship with their respective governments, as revealed in the biographical and archival research by Ben-Nun and van Dijk.[323] Nevertheless, binding obligations requiring states to protect their own civilian populations were not achieved, and the safeguards for civilians against the consequences of war remained limited.

C. Was there a Concept of Civilians by 1949?

By the time GC IV was adopted, it was generally agreed that individuals who do not belong to the armed forces may be negatively affected by the consequences of war. Alexander persuasively argues that the 'genesis' of the civilian was during the First World War.[324] It is remarkable how quickly the term was firmly established in the language and understanding of actors. They started to consistently refer to these individuals as 'civilians', 'civilian persons' or collectively the 'civilian population(s)'. These terms also increasingly replaced the occasional description of such individuals as 'non-combatants', which instead once more designated individuals belonging to or associated with the armed forces without fulfilling a combat function.[325] This language suggests an unquestioned shared understanding of the meaning of the 'civilian population' which had been naturalised in the discourse on individuals who do not belong to the armed forces. The various expressions of 'civilians' seem to have consolidated incoherent formations of such individuals in a social concept, which usually already implied their peaceful nature without the need of an explicit designation as such. This construction of civilians was, however, only achieved by implication rather than by explicit negotiation in the attempts to develop the laws of war.

The actors involved in drafting non-binding and binding instruments during the inter-war years and in the aftermath of the Second World War seemingly believed that, *de lege ferenda*, civilians were spared from suffering the consequences of war. It was generally agreed that civilians *should* be outside of the scope of hostilities, although they often were not in practice. As the above

[322] J Pictet, 'The Formation of International Humanitarian Law' (1985) 25:244 *IRRC* 3, 11.
[323] Ben-Nun (n 57); van Dijk, *Preparing for War* (n 45).
[324] Alexander, 'Genesis' (n 1).
[325] See, eg, *Final Record*, vol II(A) (n 1) 68, 239, 256, 414, 422 and 850.

analysis has shown, however, actors disagreed on *how* civilians should be or were already protected in times of war, and different forms of protection were considered for diverse categories of civilians. Only certain types of civilians were regarded as inherently vulnerable and innocent, and consequently in need of certain protections. Other individuals falling under the overarching term were still perceived as potential participants in armed conflicts, or contributors to the war efforts.

The drafters of GC IV ultimately believed that civilians required a separate protection regime; yet the status and protection of these individuals was not unified under the law. Despite the adoption of a 'Civilian Convention', a clear legal status comprising such essential elements as privileges, obligations and protections commonly associated with the designation as 'civilian' did still not exist. The term fulfilled a descriptive rather than a prescriptive function. Civilians had become incorporated into the common understanding of warfare, but no coherent legal concept of civilians was established in the written laws of war.

III. INDIVIDUALS IN NON-INTERNATIONAL ARMED CONFLICTS

A 'revolutionary' development,[326] and possibly one of the most difficult achievements of the 1949 Diplomatic Conference, was the adoption of Article 3 common to all four Geneva Conventions. It was part of the post-Second World War endeavour to extend international legal protection to a larger number of victims of armed conflicts. The written laws of war until then had been limited to wars, which, under traditional international law, had a technical meaning and legal significance for the relations of belligerent states inter se as well as their interactions with neutral states. The 1949 Geneva Conventions moved away from the institution of war by expanding the scope of the conventional law to the regulation of IACs between states, as well as NIACs where at least one belligerent party is a non-state actor. Yet, as this section will argue, the conceptualisation of individuals did not evolve in line with these newly regulated situations. The continuing statist understanding of warfare and the laws of war, as reflected in the narrowly defined respective 'protected persons' status under GC III and GC IV, inhibited the extension of the Conventions to NIACs.

A. Civil Wars and the Laws of War before the Second World War

As chapter three has shown, the period of the early written laws of war was shaped by a belief in the institutional character of war, and the consideration

[326] F Siordet, 'Les Conventions de Genève et la guerre civile' (1950) 32:374 *IRRC* 104, 105; L Moir, *The Law of Internal Armed Conflict* (Cambridge, Cambridge University Press, 2002) 88.

of the use of force as a sovereign prerogative of states. Armed conflicts between states and non-state actors could, nevertheless, exceptionally become subject to the laws and customs of war. Their legal regulation 'was ad hoc in character and took two principal forms – recognition of belligerency and regulation through bilateral agreement or unilateral declaration'.[327] Recognition of belligerency acknowledged that the hostilities had reached a scale and intensity similar to inter-state war and had the potential of affecting the interests of what are commonly referred to as third states in the literature.[328] It required non-state actors to resemble states in their nature, capacity and conduct. Belligerency could only be conferred given the 'existence of a *de facto* political organization of the insurgents, sufficient in character, population and resources, to constitute it, if left to itself, a State among the nations, reasonably capable of discharging the duties of a State', as well as 'the actual employment of military forces on each side, acting in accordance with the rules and customs of war'.[329] Anthony Cullen suggests that civil war was regarded as a conflict between the established de jure government and an alternative internal de facto government.[330] Laura Perna further observes that 'states were ready to consider the possibility of applying the law of war to non-international armed conflicts only if the organized armed groups could fulfil the conditions required to obtain "belligerent status"'.[331] Other forms of internal violence, such as rebellion and insurgency, remained within the domain of domestic law, although it was within the states' discretion to apply the rules and principles of the laws of war to insurgency on an *ad hoc* basis.[332]

The Institut de Droit International adopted a declaration which reaffirmed the doctrine of belligerency in 1900. According to this instrument, the parent state had an unconditional discretionary right to recognise the belligerency of insurgents, whereas outside states could only do so if the criteria of territorial control and governance, a degree of organisation and military discipline in the armed forces, and the conduct of operations in accordance with the laws and customs of war were met.[333] However, it also advocated that, short of the recognition of belligerency, the state party could apply humanitarian rules without

[327] S Sivakumaran, *The Law of Non-International Armed Conflict* (Oxford, Oxford University Press, 2012) 9.

[328] *GC III Commentary* (2020) (n 110) para 394; for a critique of the terminology of 'third states' see D Kritsiotis, 'Intervention and the Problematisation of Consent' in D Kritsiotis, O Corten and GH Fox, *Armed Intervention and Consent* (Cambridge, Cambridge University Press, 2023) 37–41.

[329] H Wheaton, *Elements of International Law*, 8th edn (RH Dana ed, Boston, Little, Brown, and Company, 1866) 35.

[330] A Cullen, *The Concept of Non-International Armed Conflict in International Humanitarian Law* (Cambridge, Cambridge University Press, 2010) 17.

[331] L Perna, *The Formation of the Treaty Law of Non-International Armed Conflicts* (Leiden, Martinus Nijhoff, 2006) 49.

[332] Cullen (n 330) 8–13.

[333] IDI, 'Droits et devoirs des Puissances étrangères, au cas de mouvement insurrectionnel, envers les gouvernements établis et reconnus qui sont aux prises avec l'insurrection' (1900) 18 *AIDI* 227, 228–29.

affecting the status of the insurgents. A similar proviso was already included in the so-called Lieber Code,[334] and became a requisite for the regulation of NIACs in subsequent documents.

Notwithstanding these qualifications, states were reluctant to recognise the belligerency of non-state actors in their own territory, and the practice had come into disuse by the time the 1949 Geneva Conventions were adopted. Sandesh Sivakumaran attributes this averseness to two main reasons:

> First, the war-making power was considered a sovereign prerogative and, accordingly, only states could declare and fight wars. To upgrade violence that involved non-state armed groups to the category of war, even civil war, was deemed to be upgrading the legal status of rebels. Second, situations of internal violence were considered to be within the *domaine reservé* of states and therefore a matter for the affected state alone.[335]

With the recognition of belligerency by the territorial state, the law regulating international warfare, including combatant immunity and POW status, applied.[336] Although non-state actors lost their status as belligerents upon their defeat, subjecting them to national criminal law instead,[337] the notion of legitimate and lawful participation in hostilities embedded in the laws of war clashed with states' self-interest. This shows that the traditional understanding of war remained unchallenged, and the rules of warfare did not evolve conceptually in their application to non-state actors. It is noteworthy that these early considerations of the regulation of NIACs under international law, similar to the negotiation of written laws of war at the time, focused on participants in hostilities. Other individuals who may be affected by the armed conflict without being actively involved were not mentioned. Only the Lieber Code draws a distinction between 'loyal' and 'disloyal citizens'. It further differentiates the latter based on the nature of their assistance short of fighting and stipulates required and permitted measures against them.[338]

The issue of the status of members of the populations who take up arms was raised during the first deliberation of a possible international agreement regarding civil wars and insurrections under the auspices of the ICRC at its 1912 International Conference.[339] The ICRC had already pursued relief operations in internal conflicts alongside national Red Cross societies despite lacking an official mandate for these services.[340] The initiative to discuss the matter at

[334] General Orders No 100: Instructions for the Government of Armies of the United States in the Field (24 April 1863) (Lieber Code) arts 152–53.

[335] Sivakumaran (n 327) 9.

[336] ibid 16.

[337] L Oppenheim, *International Law: A Treatise, vol II: War and Neutrality* (London, Longmans, Green, and Co, 1906) para 59.

[338] Lieber Code, arts 155–56.

[339] ICRC, *Neuvième Conférence Internationale de la Croix-Rouge* (Washington, The American Red Cross, 1912) 200.

[340] Moir (n 326) 22.

the International Conference came from the American Red Cross society. It proposed to extend Red Cross assistance during civil disturbances beyond the wounded and sick to 'non-combatants', seemingly understood, according to its literal meaning, as individuals who are not fighting.[341] Yet the conceptual framework of war, including the status of belligerent parties and individual fighters, prevailed and rendered international involvement in internal conflicts unimaginable. The rapporteur who represented the majority view of the responsible Commission highlighted that the proposal broached the sensitive subject of irregular fighters, and suggested that the conditions for combatant status under the 1907 Hague Regulations would likely not be achieved in a civil war. The delegate of the American Red Cross and lawyer Joshua Reuben Clark, Jr tried to reassure the Conference in vain that the proposal was merely concerned with relief for humanitarian suffering. It was decided that the report should not be discussed and voted upon.[342] Ultimately, the proposal was rejected due to 'a mix between risk aversion among the imperiled European powers and states' broadly shared fear of legitimizing rebels through international principles'.[343]

Only after the First World War, at its 1921 International Conference, did the ICRC adopt a resolution which declared that all victims of civil war should be entitled to humanitarian assistance, without drawing a distinction between the beneficiaries.[344] The delegate of the (old) Russian Red Cross Georges Lodygensky argued that political prisoners constituted a new category of persons in civil wars and should be treated like POWs consistent with the 1907 Hague Regulations.[345] While the Conference included the humane treatment of these individuals in its resolution, it changed the language to avoid an explicit reference to POWs, and thus the contentious status associated with lawful combatants. It was believed that 'textual references to rebels as "belligerents" and "prisoners of war," … might prematurely legitimate an uprising in its early stages and deprive a government of its legal ability to quell it'.[346] As a result, the resolution proclaimed that political prisoners should be treated according to the principles which had *inspired* the drafters of the 1907 Hague Regulations.[347]

A resolution adopted at the 1938 International Conference went even further. It called for 'the application of humanitarian principles which were formulated' in the 1929 Geneva Convention and 1907 Hague Regulations. The general attitude appears to have moved towards a willingness to apply the principles enshrined in the conventional law itself, and not merely those which

[341] ICRC, *Neuvième Conférence* (n 339) 45–48.
[342] ibid 200–03.
[343] Mantilla, *Lawmaking* (n 105) 52.
[344] ICRC, *Dixième Conférence* (n 83) 217.
[345] ibid 162.
[346] Mantilla, *Lawmaking* (n 105) 56.
[347] ICRC, *Dixième Conférence* (n 83) 218.

inspired its drafters. The resolution specifically referred to 'the wounded, the sick, and prisoners of war', and promoted 'humane treatment for all political prisoners' as well as 'respect of the life and liberty of non-combatants'.[348] Yet the list of beneficiaries was arguably still not referring to or creating distinct legal statuses for individuals in a civil war. While a distinction had been drawn between 'civilians and military' persons in the draft resolution,[349] these terms were seemingly used as descriptors and did not invoke specific privileges and obligations. The resolution merely sought recognition and permission for Red Cross intervention and assistance in civil wars.

The draft resolution had engaged with the situation of peaceful 'non-combatants', also referred to as 'civilians', in more detail. It had expanded upon the protections which should be afforded to these persons comprising, for example, communication and freedom to leave their place of residence, as well as freedom from retaliation.[350] Nevertheless, civilians who were not actively participating in the civil war were not shown to be a significant concern for the actors involved in the deliberations. Rather, their protection appears to have emerged as part of the universal humanitarian assistance offered to everyone. Political prisoners, who were understood as 'people who had been arrested on account of their political opinions', and not 'persons directly involved in the fighting', were the exception.[351] The engagement with this category of individuals arguably resembles the inter-war approach to civilian POWs demanding protection for those who were interned due to being perceived as endangering national security. Their consideration in the proposal stemmed not from a right to fight, but the security measures adopted against them and, consequently, the risk of abuse. Their conceptualisation thus corresponded to the understanding of POWs as war victims, rather than combatants who are lawfully participating in the hostilities. Yet the approach to civilian POWs in IACs and political prisoners in NIACs differed in terms of the grounds for their protection. The former were commonly subjected to adverse treatment and safeguards due to their nationality which associated them with the opposing belligerent party. Political prisoners, on the other hand, were interned based on their own conduct or ideology.

The fear that an international instrument may imply the recognition of insurgents continued to exist. Although the deliberations largely refrained from any reference to the status of individuals under the laws of war, the combatant status appears to have been an inherent consideration. The debate involved the unspoken question whether the proposed regulations were creating rights for individuals (possibly even without obligations), or whether humanitarian assistance could be provided without distinction based on a person's (inferred)

[348] ICRC, *Sixteenth Conference* (n 171) 104.
[349] *Role and activities of the Red Cross in time of civil war* (ICRC Library, CI_1938_010_ENG_012_HD_Ra) 13.
[350] ibid 13.
[351] *XVIth International Conference* (n 288) 32.

status. Humanitarian protection under the previously adopted written laws of war was indeed primarily tied to the individual's status as wounded and sick soldier, or POW, as well as the state of war itself, which may explain the prevalent uneasiness. The attempt to extend humanitarian assistance to individuals in civil war portrayed them as victims or 'humanitarian subjects', in accordance with Neville Wylie and Lindsey Cameron's notion of persons 'whose treatment was based on an understanding of their humanitarian needs'.[352] This seemingly facilitated the adopted compromise texts in the later resolutions during the inter-war years which avoided creating or expanding a distinct status.

More generally, the repeated reference to the principles which inspired or are part of a convention suggests that the same underlying norms and ideas should inform the protection of individuals in international and non-international armed conflicts. Van Dijk argues that this proposed 'application of the treaty's "moral" principles, not its legal provisions' amounts to 'a "splitting idea" that would continue to resonate in Red Cross circles'.[353] Indeed, it was again invoked in the drafting of CA3.

B. Common Article 3 of the 1949 Geneva Conventions

Following the Second World War, and more importantly the Spanish Civil War, the law-making process returned to the issue of protecting victims of NIACs under international law. The participants at the 1949 Diplomatic Conference were unable to agree on extending the full or even partial protection of the Geneva Conventions to individuals in such conflicts. Instead, CA3 forms a 'Convention in miniature'[354] which provides minimum standards for humane treatment. The reasons for this approach are multifaceted,[355] and exceed the scope of this section. Yet a brief engagement with the provision's drafting history is necessary to understand its scope of application *ratione personae* which differs from the concepts of protected persons under the Geneva Conventions' protection regimes for IACs.

Throughout the preparatory stages of the post-Second World War treaties, the draft texts varied between applying either the principles of the conventions[356] or the conventions in full, often subject to the condition of reciprocity, to internal conflicts.[357] These two alternative approaches formed the basis of the

[352] Wylie and Cameron (n 7).
[353] van Dijk, *Preparing for War* (n 45) 108.
[354] *GC IV Commentary* (n 75) 34.
[355] For historical analyses see, eg, Ben-Nun (n 57); Mantilla, *Lawmaking* (n 105); van Dijk, *Preparing for War* (n 45).
[356] *Report – Government Experts* (n 137) 8, 103 and 272; *Report – Preliminary Conference* (n 142) 15, regarding the wounded and sick.
[357] *Final Record*, vol I (n 23) 47, 61, 73, 113; *Report – Preliminary Conference* (n 142) 70, regarding POWs and civilians.

disagreement in the Joint Committee at the Diplomatic Conference, which was mandated with the deliberation of provisions common to all four Conventions. However, they were both informed by the same, unspoken presupposition that the regulation of NIACs is achieved by considering these conflicts by analogy with war. The question was to what extent the existing legal framework should be applied to a different type of conflict. The debate abstained from contemplating rules specifically designed for the non-international character of the situations that were to be regulated. Differences between inter-state and civil wars were rarely raised and a contextualised approach called for.[358] Instead, the negotiations focused more on the technicalities and practicalities of applying the laws of war to NIACs, without challenging the inherent inter-state nature of the rules themselves.

The 1948 Stockholm Drafts proposed that 'each of the Parties to the conflict shall be bound to implement the provisions of the present Convention, subject to the adverse party likewise acting in obedience thereto'.[359] The definition of protected persons in the POW draft convention, unlike the equivalent provision in the civilian draft convention, notably failed to clarify how the status was intended to apply to NIACs. Indeed, combatant status, and even POW status were seldom mentioned during the debate. The Italian delegate and professor of law Adolfo Maresca argued that the term POWs could not be attached to insurgents since it 'was a definite concept according to the rules of warfare'.[360] Yet some of the given examples of inapplicable provisions, such as army pay, emphasised the technical nature of the regulation of POWs, rather than more general political concerns.[361] The significance of the notions of legitimate and lawful participation in hostilities can, nonetheless, be inferred from the discussion of the doctrine of belligerency.

The scope of application *ratione materiae* proved the subject of such fundamental disagreements that the Diplomatic Conference was at risk of adopting no protection for victims of NIACs. The Stockholm Drafts referred to 'cases of armed conflict not of an international character' without providing a definition. Some state delegations were concerned that the scope of the provision was drawn too widely. They feared 'that the Article would cover all forms of insurrection, rebellion and civil disorder, compelling a government in the throes of internal conflict to apply conventions concluded for the regulation of war', which Lindsay Moir points out may include 'granting belligerent status to insurgents who may be no more than a small group of rebels'.[362] Consequently, the US and Canadian delegations suggested limiting its application to cases in which the parent state recognised belligerency.[363]

[358] *Conférence d'experts gouvernementaux*, vol IV (n 61) 190–91.
[359] *Final Record*, vol I (n 23) 73 and 113.
[360] *Final Record*, vol II(B) (n 56) 99.
[361] ibid 13 and 99.
[362] Moir (n 326) 24.
[363] *Final Record*, vol II(B) (n 56) 12–13.

These proposals, as well as others which did not explicitly require the recognition of belligerency, advocated conditions for the non-state party to the armed conflict which demanded characteristics similar to a state and its regular armed forces.[364] They were still 'reminiscent of the traditional doctrine of recognition of belligerency'.[365] This was reflected in the first and second draft by the first Working Party which was created for the deliberation of the provision, and was dominated by the states which had adopted this narrow approach.[366] Mantilla notes that recognition of belligerency as a requirement was ultimately rejected given its implications for the status of the opposing party and the armed conflict, as well as the repercussions this would have for the insurgent party's relations with outside states.[367] However, the doctrine still continues to exist under customary international law alongside the 1949 Geneva Conventions,[368] which may lead to the application of the full Conventions if the parties to the conflict agree to this.

The conditions of military organisation, command authority and compliance with the laws of war which were proposed for applying the Conventions to non-state actors resemble the Hague criteria for combatants. The additional requirement of territorial control was also suggested during the debate on extending the POW status to organised resistance movements in the negotiation of GC III.[369] Yet the drafters of CA3 appear to have considered the belligerent party as a whole, 'qualifying the kind of "adverse Party" which would bring into force the Conventions',[370] rather than individual persons and their POW or combatant status. While state delegates were concerned that applying the Conventions to NIACs 'would appear to give the status of belligerents to insurgents, whose right to wage war could not be recognized',[371] they were challenging the belligerent status of 'insurgents' or 'rebels' as a collective entity. This seems to have precluded a more thorough deliberation of the status of the individual members of such a party.

State delegations were again apprehensive that, by expanding POW protection to participants in NIACs, legitimacy and lawfulness were conferred on the hostile non-state party. This was seen as undermining the legitimacy of the state's de jure government, especially in the context of an insurrection, an unstable government or secession.[372] Dieter Fleck observes that states' opposition to the regulation of internal conflicts was based not only on the 'implications for the status of parties to the conflict' itself, but also resultant 'restrictions

[364] ibid 12–13, 15 and 41–42.
[365] Moir (n 326) 40.
[366] *Final Record*, vol II(B) (n 56) 129.
[367] Mantilla, *Lawmaking* (n 105) 75.
[368] R McLaughlin, *Recognition of Belligerency and the Law of Armed Conflict* (Oxford, Oxford University Press, 2020) 210–11.
[369] See section I.
[370] Cullen (n 330) 32–33.
[371] *Final Record*, vol II(B) (n 56) 10.
[372] Crawford (n 70) 73.

on their ability to sanction individuals under domestic law for their belligerent acts'.[373] Insurgents were considered criminals under domestic laws, and it was commonly believed that the official government should have the power to repress the resistance with all its force. Some state delegations even voiced their concern that the provision of humanitarian safeguards may incite or embolden insurgency.[374] The participation of insurgents and, indeed, their resort to hostilities were emphasised as 'undemocratic methods' in internal politics,[375] lacking the perceived legitimacy of the population's self-defence against an invading foreign power.

Supporters of the Stockholm Draft, however, argued that some 'who are regarded as rebels are in actual fact patriots struggling for the independence and the dignity of their country'.[376] The Norwegian delegate Frede Castberg proposed that members of the armed forces of a revolutionary government should not be prosecuted for their participation in the hostilities.[377] While this suggestion proved unsuccessful, CA3 comprises 'fair trial safeguards that offset the traditional (criminal) treatment given to rebels under domestic treason laws'.[378] As the first *GC III Commentary* emphasises, it still 'leaves intact the right of the State to prosecute, sentence and punish according to the law'.[379] Moreover, it includes the proviso that the legal status of the parties to the armed conflict is not affected.

The eventually adopted text of CA3, consequently, avoids the language of combatants and POWs. Instead, it specifies 'members of armed forces who have laid down their arms and those placed *hors de combat*' as beneficiaries of its safeguards. It has become the subject of debate whether the provision refers to the armed forces of states as well as non-state actors in NIACs.[380] The new *GC III Commentary* published by the ICRC in 2020 interprets it as referring to both given that obligations are conferred on 'each Party to the conflict' and the plural use of 'armed forces' in the text.[381] Bianca Maganza argues that the invocation of regular organised armies in the Article stems from the historical context in which it was adopted. She notes that parties on both sides of a civil war, at the time, often comprised professional militaries which may have been 'very similar in size, discipline, means, and training'.[382] Indeed, the opposing non-state actor

[373] D Fleck, 'The Law of Non-International Armed Conflict' in D Fleck (ed) *The Handbook of International Humanitarian Law*, 4th edn (Oxford, Oxford University Press, 2021) 643.

[374] *Final Record*, vol II(B) (n 56) 10–11 and 327–30.

[375] ibid 15.

[376] *GC IV Commentary* (n 75) 31.

[377] *Final Record*, vol II(B) (n 56) 44.

[378] Mantilla, *Lawmaking* (n 105) 58.

[379] *GC III Commentary* (n 22) 40.

[380] See chapter 6, section III.D.

[381] *GC III Commentary* (2020) (n 110) para 564.

[382] B Maganza, 'Unveiling Common Article 3 to the Geneva Conventions: Contingency, Necessity, and Possibility in International Humanitarian Law' in I Venzke and KJ Heller (eds), *Contingency in International Law: On the Possibility of Different Legal Histories* (Oxford, Oxford University Press, 2021) 344–45.

commonly consisted of a dissident part of the government's armed forces. Yet the formulation was also based 'on the previous, deeply-rooted limitation of the conceptual scope of [international humanitarian law] to Western, structured, inter-state models of waging war.'[383] According to Maganza, while the phrase was 'not directly aimed at leaving particular kinds of conflicts outside the area of applicability of CA3', it inadvertently had this effect due to the Western-centric origins of the laws of war.[384] As the discussion of the doctrine of recognition of belligerency above already suggested, the drafters relied on a construction of participants in hostilities similar to the understanding of belligerents in IACs.

The reference to 'persons taking no active part in the hostilities' in CA3, on the other hand, has been interpreted to 'quintessentially include those who are not members of the armed forces, i.e. civilians'.[385] However, as section II above suggests, the protection of *all* civilians was not at the forefront of the drafters' minds during the post-Second World War process. At the Conference of Government Experts, the Belgian delegate and lawyer Maurice Bourquin already pointed out that the safeguards for civilians would have to be adapted to the special situation of civil wars since one of the characteristics of the beneficiaries of the draft civilian convention was that they were non-nationals.[386] The Stockholm Draft, which envisaged the application of the entire Civilian Convention to NIACs, resolved the definitional difficulty of the status of 'protected persons' by declaring that the regulations would apply to states' own nationals in such conflicts.[387] The ICRC additionally noted in its *Remarks and Proposals* that the provision was deliberately widely drawn as to include individuals who participate in the hostilities but are not covered by the other Geneva Conventions.[388]

Many state delegations at the Diplomatic Conference, however, opposed this approach. Although the concern about a state's diminished ability to supress uprisings was also voiced in this context,[389] arguments for the non-application of GC IV to NIACs were not usually framed as preventing an undue interference in domestic affairs. Instead, the presented reasons were of a more technical nature. Nationality and territoriality were so ingrained in the understanding of civilian 'protected persons' that some delegates rejected the extension of the regime to NIACs on this ground. For example, despite acknowledging the ICRC's proposed adjustment for such conflicts, the UK delegate George Hart

[383] ibid 346.
[384] ibid 345.
[385] JK Kleffner, 'The Beneficiaries of the Rights Stemming from Common Article 3' in Clapham, Gaeta and Sassòli (n 9) para 7.
[386] *Conférence d'experts gouvernementaux*, vol IV (n 61) 192–93.
[387] *Final Record*, vol I (n 23) 114.
[388] *Remarks and Proposals* (n 154) 68.
[389] See, eg, *Final Record*, vol II(B) (n 56) 13 and 42.

bluntly stated that civilians on either side of the armed conflict would not be non-nationals. He later pointed out the difficulties of applying the Stockholm Draft to the colonial context since it might extend the provisions to 'nationals of the home country'.[390] Relying on the adversarial nature of the 'protected person' status, the Canadian delegate Max Wershof remarked that it would be 'inconceivable' to apply the safeguards to citizens who favoured the revolutionary government without being in its de facto territory.[391] Ultimately, the exclusionary nature of the concept of civilian 'protected persons' appears to have been part of the reason, or at least the argument, why GC IV was not extended in full or in part to victims of NIACs.

Interestingly, nationality was still deliberately omitted as a prohibited ground of discrimination, suggesting that it plays a role even for the humanitarian safeguards under CA3. The French delegation, for instance, noted during the negotiations that governments may legitimately and lawfully distinguish between nationals and aliens in their response to an individual's participation in a NIAC.[392] On the other hand, Frédéric Siordet, who participated as an ICRC representative in the deliberation of the Article, argued in a subsequent publication that the justification for the omission in terms of the more severe treatment of aliens relates only to the lawful repression of criminal acts and not the degree of pain inflicted.[393] The non-inclusion of nationality has thus been interpreted as not affecting the humanitarian treatment of the individual.

It needs to be emphasised that CA3 refers to neither combatants nor civilians in the delineation of its scope of application *ratione personae*. Inadvertently, the 'Convention in miniature' appears to adopt a new approach distinct from the then existing legal framework. As '[p]ersons taking no active part in the hostilities', its beneficiaries are identified on the basis of their conduct rather than their status as in the protection regimes for IACs.[394] They have in common that they are perceived to be outside of the scope of fighting, and vulnerable due to their particular circumstances. This is even though the negotiations themselves did not focus on a distinction between individuals who participate in the hostilities, and those who remain peaceful. Indeed, the delegations failed to engage in any sustained manner with the varieties of ways in which individuals who are not fighting are nonetheless involved in or affected by NIACs. It seems to be a humanitarian concern for the well-being of all war victims which informs CA3.

In its continued strive to provide some form of protection to victims of NIACs, the ICRC justified the proposed application of the Geneva Conventions to such conflicts on the basis of the treaties' humanitarian nature. Henry Lovat

[390] ibid 41–42.
[391] ibid 13.
[392] ibid 94.
[393] Siordet (n 326) 206.
[394] Kleffner (n 385) para 5.

suggests that 'the appeal to humanitarian principles with respect to Common Article 3 appears to have been effective largely because it echoed … the humanitarian Zeitgeist of the negotiations'.[395] Yet the debate in the Joint Committee was characterised by a tension between the sovereign rights of states and rights of individuals which mirrors the above-mentioned discussion of civilian 'protected persons'.[396] Some delegations were concerned that applying the new Geneva Conventions in full to NIACs would strike the balance too much in favour of individuals. The UK delegate Sir Robert Craigie, for example, believed that the application of the Civilian Convention especially 'would strike at the root of national sovereignty and endanger national security'.[397] Conversely, the Hungarian and Romanian delegations declared that the Geneva Conventions' objective should be the protection of individuals to the greatest extent possible. Another advocate of humanitarian protection was the Norwegian delegate Castberg,[398] who, according to van Dijk, sought 'to apply human rights in interstate and intrastate wars'.[399] Nevertheless, a human rights discourse was also largely absent in this Committee, despite CA3 often being regarded today as the epitome of human rights thinking in international humanitarian law. Instead, the 'rights' of individuals were primarily invoked in opposition to the rights of States, emphasising the need to protect the latter.[400] A speech by the Mexican delegate Pedro de Alba, who had also been involved in the drafting process of the UDHR, forms an exception in this regard.[401] Additionally, the humanitarian motivation of the Soviet Union delegation, for example, has been again questioned in this context.[402] Mantilla still believes that social pressure and opprobrium compelled the UK and French delegations to relinquish their opposition to the regulation of NIACs in the end.[403]

Others have noted the persuasiveness of individual delegates in the negotiations of NIACs. According to Lovat, de Lapradelle commanded attention based on his perceived moral authority and technical expertise as an international lawyer.[404] The Monegasque delegate argued that civil wars could indeed fall under the realm of international law, noting the 1928 Convention on Duties and Rights of States in the Event of Civil Strife, signed by American states in Havana, as an example of a treaty applying to internal situations.[405] He and the Greek delegate and lawyer Rico Agathocles also explained how non-state

[395] Lovat (n 313) 131.
[396] See section II.A.iii.
[397] *Final Record*, vol II(B) (n 56) 10.
[398] ibid 11.
[399] van Dijk, *Preparing for War* (n 45) 111.
[400] See, eg, *Final Record*, vol II(B) (n 56) 10 and 12–13.
[401] ibid 333.
[402] Mantilla, *Lawmaking* (n 105) 84.
[403] ibid 59–60.
[404] Lovat (n 313) 129.
[405] *Final Record*, vol II(B) (n 56) 14; the main objective of the treaty was 'to prevent foreign states from supporting insurgents', Schindler and Toman (n 91) 1181.

actors would be bound by the rules of a treaty given the 'super-contractual' or law-making character of the Conventions, the Contracting Parties' obligation to respect and to ensure respect for the Conventions, and insurgents being bound as nationals of a member state.[406] They thus responded to the concern that the Conventions' obligations would not extend to insurgents, which those states trying to limit their application and even humanitarian principles to NIACs had raised repeatedly.

The eventually adopted provision ensued from a proposed amendment by the French delegation. It was a modified version of the Civilian Convention's draft preamble which had been prepared at the time by a Working Party under the chairmanship of the French delegate Cahen-Salvador, but ultimately removed. As a compromise for the seemingly unresolvable disagreement between delegations emphasising the rights of states and humanitarian advocates, CA3 was confined to basic humanitarian safeguards, which, however, apply to a wider range of conflicts. It provides no more than minimum standards of humane treatment prohibiting murder, torture and cruel treatment, hostage-taking, outrages upon personal dignity and summary justice. It is based on the belief that the Geneva Conventions are informed by certain humanitarian principles which are universally applicable. Yet its main significance for the conceptualisation of individuals lies in the removal of the traditional status-based approach from the perception and design of protection, as well as the non-distinction between victims of NIACs.[407]

IV. CONCLUSION

While the Second World War was likely an impetus for the revision of the laws of war and the creation of a 'civilian convention', the construction of individuals in the context of war and IACs in the drafting of the 1949 Geneva Conventions was not (entirely) new. It was informed and constrained by ideational and normative developments that preceded the outbreak of the war. The understanding of combatants in the Hague Regulations, especially, was naturalised in the explicit and implicit endorsement of its qualifying conditions in the two successive POW Conventions in 1929 and 1949. The conduct of partisan warfare during the Second World War would have provided the drafters of the 1949 Geneva Conventions with an occasion to reconsider the participation in hostilities of individuals who do not belong to the armed forces. Yet an examination of individuals acting in self-defence was largely excluded from the discourse relating to combatants without being taken up in the drafting of GC IV.

[406] *Final Record*, vol II(B) (n 56) 79 and 94; the ICRC delegate and lawyer Siordet concurred with the opinion.

[407] See further chapter 5, section III.

The concept of combatants was reaffirmed as its personal scope evolved only slightly by including a new form of warfare within the traditional understanding of combatants.

After the emergence of 'civilians' in the First World War, various actors were deliberating rules, or at least principles, which would further humanise the laws of war by alleviating the suffering of the civilian population. Their negotiations were seemingly informed by a distinction between combatants and civilians. However, this construction of difference did not entail or lead to a legal status for all civilians and their protection. Attempts to regulate the means and methods of warfare during the inter-war years provided the distinction with its most concrete form, but then reached a temporary dead end. Civilians were instead further distinguished into different categories. These were, for example, considered with respect to their distinct relation to belligerent states, the kind of hardship experienced by them, reasons for their innocence or vulnerability, but also the legitimacy of adverse measures adopted against some of them. The consequent guarantees for the various categories of civilians largely evolved from existing protections for combatants. In the safeguards provided, civilians were not juxtaposed with combatants, but likened to the latter in vulnerable positions as POWs, or wounded and sick members of the armed forces. The dichotomy between combatants and civilians implied in the division between the first three 1949 Geneva Conventions regulating the treatment of wounded, sick and shipwrecked combatants as well as POWs, on the one hand, and GC IV, on the other, is arguably more apparent than real.

The underlying agreement that individuals referred to as 'civilians' may become victims of war, even though they should remain outside of it, may have generally shaped the law-making processes. It entailed social norms and values which determined the directedness of the efforts frequently pursued by the same actors. Nevertheless, the apparent struggle and discrepancies in conceptualising civilians for the purpose of the laws of war in these long and multifaceted processes arguably reveals the absence of a shared understanding among the participating actors regarding which individuals should be protected and how. Moreover, states themselves remained inactive so that no binding agreement was adopted on the matter until 1949. GC IV was then informed by diverse developments during the inter-war years and still comprises disparate, exclusionary protection regimes which each conceptualise individuals who do not belong to the armed forces differently.

It is commonplace to criticise the development of the laws of war for its retrospective nature in response to atrocities in past wars.[408] Additionally, this chapter has shown that, when new treaties are adopted, they are developed

[408] R Kolb and K del Mar, 'Treaties for Armed Conflict' in A Clapham and P Gaeta (eds), *The Oxford Handbook of International Law in Armed Conflict* (Oxford, Oxford University Press, 2014) 52; other scholars suggest that the 1949 Geneva Conventions were also a preparation for future war, see Barsalou (n 297); van Dijk, *Preparing for War* (n 45).

within constraining existing ideational and normative frameworks. Various actors were pleading for the adoption of rules and regulations which they believed would enable them to return to assumed standards and practices of earlier times. Yet, rather than a vague common appreciation of the past, it was a more clearly defined system of laws that primarily shaped the process. The creation of protection regimes for civilians were grafted upon ideas which had emerged, and which had been partly institutionalised, in the period of the early written laws of war and the inter-war years. Similarly, instead of trying to conceptualise individuals in the context of NIACs, the drafters discussed whether the law on IACs could be applied in whole or in part to these conflict situations. The debate focused on technical rules which had been designed for inter-state relations, and in which privileges and protections for individuals were conditional on distinct legal statuses that were contingent on narrow criteria. The progress made in protecting POWs and civilians, and regulating NIACs after the Second World War was thus not only limited by political struggles among the drafters,[409] but also conceptual constraints on understanding individuals in armed conflicts.

The influence of the normative framework on the law-making process may have been partly due to the increasing involvement of international lawyers. The epistemic community attempted to facilitate the development of the laws of war more actively in the inter-war years, and its more successful efforts were notably rooted in existing law. In comparison to the earlier period, legal experts also had a growing presence in diplomatic conferences, and even in the leadership of state delegations, although the nature and size of delegations still varied.[410] Yet, as other historical studies have shown,[411] their approaches were not only shaped by their professional backgrounds. More importantly, the power of individual representatives may be questionable since state interests still prevailed in the law-making process. Notably, arguments drawing on existing laws and concepts were also exploited in this regard, including by lawyers, to deliberately limit the scope of the treaties and thus state obligations in a complex political and historical context. Other humanitarian actors and perspectives appear to have been less influential in the formal law-making process, with the exception of the adoption of CA3. Human rights thinking in the post-Second World War environment, which has been sometimes emphasised in scholarship today, did not significantly shape the understanding of individuals, which was instead still entrenched in a state-centric view of armed conflicts and the laws of war.

[409] See, eg. van Dijk, *Preparing for War* (n 45).
[410] See also ibid 44–48.
[411] See, eg, Ben-Nun (n 57).

5

From the 1949 Geneva Conventions to the 1977 Additional Protocols

WHILE THE 1949 Geneva Conventions were welcomed at the time of their adoption as significant progress in the laws of war, disillusionment followed shortly after. The International Committee of the Red Cross (ICRC), one of the driving forces behind the just adopted treaties, pursued the further improvement of what became increasingly known as international humanitarian law (IHL)[1] as early as the 1950s. Yet it was not until 25 years after the adoption of the post-war treaties that a Diplomatic Conference on the Reaffirmation and Development of International Humanitarian Law Applicable in Armed Conflicts was convened. After a prolonged process, the Protocol Additional to the Geneva Conventions of 12 August 1949, and relating to the Protection of Victims of International Armed Conflicts (AP I) and the Protocol Additional to the Geneva Conventions of 12 August 1949, and Relating to the Protection of Victims of Non-International Armed Conflicts (AP II) were adopted on 8 June 1977.

Among the most significant developments for which the 1977 Additional Protocols have been commended and condemned are the protection of the civilian population from the effects of warfare, the evolution of the combatant and prisoner of war (POW) status, and the regulation of non-international armed conflicts (NIACs) beyond the minimum guarantees in Article 3 common to all 1949 Geneva Conventions (CA3).[2] Moreover, AP I explicitly enshrined the principle of distinction between combatants and civilians for the first time in a legally binding international instrument. This has even been described as '[p]robably the most valuable contribution of the 1977 Protocols'.[3] The principle

[1] The change in terminology from the laws of war to IHL only occurred gradually throughout the period under analysis in this chapter. However, for consistency, the latter term is used except when referring exclusively to the law up to 1949. For an analysis of the emergence of the term 'international humanitarian law' see A Alexander, 'A Short History of International Humanitarian Law' (2015) 26 *EJIL* 109.

[2] See, eg, ibid 125; H-P Gasser, 'Some Legal Issues Concerning Ratification of the 1977 Geneva Protocols' in MA Meyer (ed), *Armed Conflict and the New Law: Aspects of the 1977 Geneva Protocols and the 1981 Weapons Convention* (London, British Institute for International and Comparative Law, 1989) 82–85.

[3] L Doswald-Beck, 'The Value of the 1977 Geneva Protocols for the Protection of Civilians' in Meyer (n 2) 137.

of distinction appears to inspire both the definition of civilians, and the reformulated conditions for combatant status in AP I. The resultant circular definitions in the text may prevent an understanding of each concept in its own terms. It has been criticised that 'neither category stands forth independently'.[4]

Although AP I thus frames the civilian and combatant status as interrelated, this chapter argues that they were not constructed in unison and were only partially informed by the principle of distinction. It examines the concepts of 'civilians' and 'combatants' separately to reveal the different dynamics at play in the conceptualisation of individuals protected and regulated under the law. Section I, on the concept of civilians, shows that the notion in both Protocols was not meaningfully considered and discussed during the official law-making process in the 1970s. Conversely, section II suggests that the negotiation of the combatant status took place primarily at the Diplomatic Conference itself. It examines how the concept was shaped by the disparate discourses of two different groups of actors, both of which engaged in distinct arguments of the time. Additionally, it addresses the absence of the concept of combatants in AP II. At the same time as the concepts of civilians and combatants were consolidated and renegotiated, the conceptualisation of individuals also evolved into a different direction. Section III, therefore, analyses the partial movement away from the categorisation of individuals in armed conflicts and towards their protection as human beings instead.

I. THE CONCEPT OF CIVILIANS

Following the adoption of the 1949 Geneva Conventions, the ICRC was especially concerned with protecting the civilian population from the effects of hostilities through the regulation of means and methods of warfare. Other non-state actors – including the Institut de Droit International (IDI) and the International Law Association (ILA), which resumed its inter-war efforts – also dedicated themselves to studying the lasting relevance of the laws of war, or the need for its revitalisation.[5] The law regarding the conduct of hostilities itself, sometimes described as 'Hague Law', had not been significantly advanced since the 1907 Hague Regulations,[6] and was often regarded as obsolete. AP I attends

[4] H Kinsella, *The Image Before the Weapon: A Critical History of the Distinction Between Combatant and Civilian* (Ithaca, Cornell University Press, 2011) 142.

[5] See, eg, IDI, 'Reconsidération des principes du droit de la guerre' (1957) 47:1 *AIDI* 323; IDI, 'Le problème que pose l'existence des armes de destruction massive et la distinction entre les objectifs militaires et non militaires en général' (1967) 52:2 *AIDI* 1; ILA, 'Committee on the Charter of the United Nations' (1962) 50 *ILA Reports of Conferences* 157; see also D Bindschedler-Robert (ed), *Report of the Conference on Contemporary Problems of the Law of Armed Conflicts* (New York, Carnegie Endowment for International Peace, 1971).

[6] Annex to Convention (IV) Regulations Respecting the Laws and Customs of War on Land (The Hague, 18 October 1907) (1907 Hague Regulations).

to this area of law. Furthermore, for the first time in the history of conventional IHL, it provides a definition of 'civilians' and the 'civilian population', and establishes a comprehensive regime to shield them from the consequences of hostilities.[7] It thus seems to fill the gap which had been left by earlier treaties.[8]

Article 50 AP I defines civilians negatively as persons who qualify neither for the combatant components of the POW status under the 1949 Geneva Convention on POWs (GC III) nor as members of the armed forces under AP I. As part of a binary, '[c]ivilians are what combatants, members of armed forces, are not'.[9] The ICRC's official *Commentary on the Additional Protocols* argues that the negative definition of civilians 'is justified by the fact that the concepts of the civilian population and the armed forces are only conceived in opposition to each other'.[10] It suggests that the clear binary opposition renders the definition of the civilian population more precise.[11] The dichotomous relationship between the two categories is further enshrined in Article 48 which declares the principle of distinction: 'the Parties to the conflict shall at all times distinguish between the civilian population and combatants and between civilian objects and military objectives and accordingly shall direct their operations only against military objectives'. The same provision frames the respect for and protection of civilians as the *raison d'être* of the principle of distinction. This objective can be further deduced from the inclusion of the provision as a 'basic rule' in the protection regime for the civilian population rather than the 'methods and means of warfare' generally.[12]

The abstract formulation of the principle of distinction in Article 48 is then elaborated – 'in often minute detail' – in the subsequent articles of Part IV Section I AP I which 'lay down rules for the general protection of civilians and civilian objects'.[13] Article 51, its central provision entitled 'Protection of the civilian population', lays the foundation for what is known as civilian immunity. It not only declares the general principle that '[t]he civilian population as such, as well as individual civilians, shall not be the object of attack';[14] it additionally 'reaffirms, clarifies and supplements certain rules derived from that principle'.[15]

[7] AP I, pt IV.
[8] See chapters 3–4.
[9] Kinsella (n 4) 142.
[10] Y Sandoz, C Swinarski and B Zimmermann (eds), *Commentary on the Additional Protocols of 8 June 1977 to the Geneva Conventions of 12 August 1949* (Geneva, Martinus Nijhoff, 1987) (hereafter *Additional Protocols Commentary*) para 1914.
[11] ibid paras 1911–14.
[12] cf AP I, art 35.
[13] F Kalshoven, 'Reaffirmation and Development of International Humanitarian Law Applicable in Armed Conflicts: The Diplomatic Conference, Geneva, 1974–1977; Part II' (1978) 9 *NYIL* 107, 108.
[14] AP I, art 51(2).
[15] M Bothe, KJ Partsch and WA Solf, *New Rules for Victims of Armed Conflicts: A Commentary on the Two 1977 Protocols Additional to the Geneva Conventions of 1949*, 2nd edn (Leiden, Martinus Nijhoff, 2013) 340.

However, the article also delineates the limits of this immunity providing for its suspension 'for such time as they [the civilians] take a direct part in hostilities'.[16] The general protection for the civilian population thus consists mainly of 'a prohibition on making them the object of direct attack, and a requirement to avoid unacceptable collateral loss or damage as a result of attacks on military objectives'.[17] The protection regime for the civilian population in NIACs mirrors the equivalent sections in AP I – but in a significantly abbreviated form.[18]

A. The New 'Established' Law

With the adoption of AP I, 'the civilian emerged as an identifiable legal concept, defined and codified in an international instrument'.[19] While this doubtlessly constituted a milestone in IHL, the drafters of the Additional Protocols framed it as a continuation of existing law. The ICRC acknowledged in its *Additional Protocols Commentary* that the definition of civilians in AP I was 'novel and not definitive'; yet 'the delegates accepted it as uncontroversial'.[20] Despite the absence of a definition or even an implicit distinct understanding of civilians in conventional IHL at the time, the drafters of the Additional Protocols did not significantly engage with the meaning of the concept. The silence in the negotiations regarding the personal scope and presumed immunity from direct attack suggests that these were undisputed elements of the concept of civilians. This is further supported by the consistent use of language during the drafting process and in the treaty referring to 'civilians' and the 'civilian population'. The general non-engagement with the meaning of civilians, however, conceals the divergence of views prior to and at the Diplomatic Conference.

Various draft instruments presented different definitions and understandings of 'civilians' over the years. Non-state actors during the inter-war period seemingly promoted a status-based approach, generally referring to civilians and the civilian population as comprising individuals who were not members of the armed forces.[21] In contrast, post-1949 draft regulations additionally excluded

[16] AP I, art 51(3).

[17] Kalshoven, '1974–1977, Part II' (n 13) 113.

[18] AP II, pt IV; cf AP I, pt IV ss I–II.

[19] C Garbett, *The Concept of the Civilian: Legal Recognition, Adjudication and the Trials of International Criminal Justice* (Abingdon, Routledge, 2015) 61.

[20] A Alexander, 'International Humanitarian Law, Postcolonialism and the 1977 *Geneva Protocol I*' (2016) 17 *Melbourne Journal of International Law* 15, 29.

[21] First draft Convention adopted in Monaco (Sanitary cities and localities), 27 July 1934 (ICRC) ihl-databases.icrc.org/applic/ihl/ihl.nsf/Treaty.xsp?action=openDocument&documentId=206E646653AB8F30C12563CD002D69E3 (Monaco Draft), pt IV art 2; Draft International Convention on the Condition and Protection of Civilians of Enemy Nationality Who Are on Territory Belonging to or Occupied by a Belligerent (Tokyo, 29 October 1934) reprinted in D Schindler and J Toman (eds), *Laws of Armed Conflict: A Collection of Conventions, Resolutions, and Other Documents*, 4th edn (Leiden, Nijhoff, 2004), art 1(a); Draft Convention for the Protection of Civilian Popula-

from the civilian population individuals who directly or indirectly participated in hostilities.[22] In its commentary accompanying the 1956 Draft Rules for the Limitation of the Dangers Incurred by the Civilian Population in Time of War, the ICRC noted that 'there are several schools of thought as regards the meaning of "civilian population"'.[23] It, therefore, examined the relationship between civilian status and participation in hostilities, for example, by unorganised partisans, 'workers in war industries', but also 'scientists' given recent developments in weaponry, in more detail in its consultation with experts.[24] The IDI drew a distinction between 'persons participating in the hostilities and members of the civilian population' in its Resolution on the Distinction Between Military Objectives and Non-military Objectives in General and Particularly the Problems Associated with Weapons of Mass Destruction.[25] The deliberations and reports behind the Resolution notably engaged with the meaning of civilians in the context of nuclear warfare, contributions of the civilian population to the war efforts, and so-called quasi-combatants.[26] Yet the Resolution deliberately refrained from defining the 'civilian population' in light of the difficulties this would involve. Overall, the post-1949 processes reveal discrepancies in the understanding of civilians, and the consequences that the changing nature of warfare has had on their protection among the epistemic community of international lawyers, as well as military experts and strategists, and public opinion leaders[27] involved in the discussions.

In preparation of the Additional Protocols, the ICRC accordingly noted that one 'takes a point of departure from the premise that there is such a notion of the civilian population, when in fact there is not'.[28] Drawing on its earlier work,

tions against New Engines of War (Amsterdam, 3 September 1938) (1938 ILA Draft Convention) reprinted in Schindler and Toman (ibid), art 1, which further excluded persons employed in military establishments.

[22] ICRC, Draft Rules for the Limitation of the Dangers Incurred by the Civilian Population in Time of War (1956) (1956 Draft Rules) reprinted in Schindler and Toman (n 21), art 4; ICRC, Resolution XXVIII on the Protection of Civilian Populations Against the Dangers of Indiscriminate Warfare (Vienna, 9 October 1965) (1965 ICRC Resolution) reprinted in Schindler and Toman (n 21); see also UNGA, 'Report of the Secretary-General: Respect for Human Rights in Armed Conflicts' (1970) UN Doc A/8052, 16.

[23] ICRC, *Draft Rules for the Limitation of the Dangers Incurred by the Civilian Population in Time of War* (Geneva, ICRC, 1956) 46.

[24] ibid 46–50; see also *Documents and Summary Records [of the] Commission of Experts for the Legal Protection of Civilian Populations and Victims of War from the Dangers of Aerial Warfare and Blind Weapons, Geneva, from 6 to 13 April 1954* (ICRC Library, CEG_1954_DOCUMENTS_PV_04_ENG).

[25] (Edinburgh, 9 September 1969) (1969 IDI Resolution) reprinted in Schindler and Toman (n 21), art 1.

[26] IDI, 'Reconsidération' (1957) (n 5) 340–43, 515 and 531–32; IDI, 'Le problème' (n 5) 170–71.

[27] Mantilla notes the 'interesting mix' of experts consulted by the ICRC, G Mantilla, *Lawmaking under Pressure: International Humanitarian Law and Internal Armed Conflict* (Ithaca, Cornell University Press, 2020) 113.

[28] *Conference of Government Experts on the Reaffirmation and Development of International Humanitarian Law Applicable in Armed Conflicts, vol III – Protection of the Civilian Population Against Dangers of Hostilities* (Geneva, ICRC, 1971) 17.

as well as IDI and United Nations (UN) resolutions, it continued to exclude individuals involved in direct participation in hostilities (DPH) from the definition of civilians throughout the preliminary Conferences of Government Experts (1971 Conference and 1972 Conference).[29] In his review of the 1971 Conference, Frits Kalshoven observed that 'there might be agreement that the civil population includes those who do not take part in the hostilities, no such agreement could be achieved about what constitutes participation in the hostilities'.[30] Opinions differed whether the degree of participation required for exclusion should be 'direct', 'immediate' or could also be 'indirect', and whether it should be related to military operations or the military effort.[31] At the 1972 Conference, the concern was voiced, however, that this approach may create a 'new category of persons, somewhere between combatants and civilians' who are not protected by the law.[32] Six Western states consequently submitted a joint proposal[33] that the ICRC seems to have endorsed in Draft Protocol I which it submitted to the Diplomatic Conference.[34] Like the eventually adopted Article 50 AP I, it defined civilians negatively only with respect to combatants recognised under GC III and AP I.

Although AP I 'went against the tide of history' in its definition of civilians,[35] the delegations at the Diplomatic Conference did not resume the more general debate whether individuals who directly or indirectly participate in hostilities should qualify as civilians. Instead, the disagreement in the responsible Committee III largely centred on the wording of the provision, whether it should refer to 'combatants' or 'armed forces'.[36] Some delegates still seemed to believe that DPH entailed the loss of civilian status,[37] suggesting that the ostensible agreement on the definition of civilians may not have reflected a shared understanding among the drafters. Yet their insinuations went unaddressed in the negotiations. The ICRC delegate Jean Mirimanoff-Chilikine declared in his introduction to the draft provision that the '*a contrario* definition of the civilian

[29] *Conference of Government Experts on the Reaffirmation and Development of International Humanitarian Law Applicable in Armed Conflicts – Report on the Work of the Conference* (Geneva, ICRC, 1971) (hereafter *1971 Report*) 76; *Conference of Government Experts on the Reaffirmation and Development of International Humanitarian Law Applicable in Armed Conflicts – Report on the Work of the Conference*, vol I (Geneva, ICRC 1972) (hereafter *1972 Report*) 143–44.

[30] F Kalshoven, 'Reaffirmation and Development of International Humanitarian Law Applicable in Armed Conflicts: The Conference of Government Experts, 24 May – 12 June, 1971' (1971) 2 *NYIL* 68, 84.

[31] *1971 Report* (n 29) 75–77.

[32] *1972 Report* (n 29) 143.

[33] Australia, Belgium, Canada, the Federal Republic of Germany, the UK and the USA, ibid.

[34] Reprinted in *Official Records of the Diplomatic Conference on the Reaffirmation and Development of International Humanitarian Law Applicable in Armed Conflicts: Geneva (1974–1977)* (hereafter *CDDH*), vol I (Bern, Federal Political Department, 1978) art 45.

[35] E Camins, 'The Past as Prologue: The Development of the "Direct Participation" Exception to Civilian Immunity' (2008) 90:872 *IRRC* 853, 880.

[36] *CDDH*, vol XIV (Bern, Federal Political Department, 1978) 39–47.

[37] Ukraine, Brazil, China, ibid 39, 54, 57, 71–72 and 80.

population ... had been almost unanimously approved at various governmental and Red Cross meetings'[38] giving it an air of legitimacy. While this may have been true for the preference of a negative as opposed to a positive definition, it drew attention away from the persisting differences in opinion regarding the personal scope of the civilian status. This may have contributed to the uncontested acceptance of the definition despite some of the delegates having participated in earlier processes which excluded persons involved in DPH from the civilian population.[39] Other reasons for the adoption of the definition may be deduced from the drafting process and, in particular, the manner in which the protection of civilians was framed in the ideational context.

Committee III deliberated the definition and protection of the civilian population before it turned to the more controversial question of the 'new category' of POWs. The negative definition of civilians in relation to combatants, therefore, does not reflect the construction of the civilian concept. Indeed, the adopted formalistic approach did not require an engagement with the meaning of civilians at the Diplomatic Conference. Rather, the apparent dichotomy in the definition derived from a shift in the perceived purpose and scope of IHL, which was then seen as in need of providing every person with a status under the law. In response to the concern mentioned above, the more comprehensive definition of civilians in AP I abstains from creating a category of individuals unregulated by law, who would neither qualify as combatants nor as civilians. Louise Doswald-Beck proclaims that the value of this definition is 'enormous, as it puts to rest all arguments in favour of "quasi-combatants"'.[40] As a humanitarian actor, the ICRC may have seized the definition proposed at the 1972 Conference to create a protection regime that is purposefully inclusive, despite the resultant loss of nuance. Its commentary on the Draft Protocol is revealing in this regard. It not only emphasised that DPH deprives individuals of civilian immunity, but also remarked that its consequences for civilians falling into the power of the adversary need to be considered as well. Their non-qualification for protection under GC III, and the wish that these individuals would benefit from the Geneva Convention Relative to the Protection of Civilian Persons in Time of War (GC IV)[41] may have informed the decision to divorce DPH from the civilian status, and to limit it to the loss of civilian immunity instead.

The abstract definition in Article 50 AP I demarcates civilians within a general understanding of regulated and organised warfare, where they themselves

[38] ibid 36.

[39] Only Erik Castrén was involved in the drafting of the 1969 IDI Resolution as well as AP I. Yet several experts consulted at the 1971 and 1972 Conferences later participated as delegates in Committee III of the Diplomatic Conference. The absence of minutes and non-identification of individual experts in the reports of the preparatory conferences, unfortunately, preclude inferences on the influence of individual actors.

[40] Doswald-Beck (n 3) 155.

[41] ICRC, *Draft Additional Protocols to the Geneva Conventions of August 12, 1949 – Commentary* (Geneva, ICRC, 1973) 58.

constitute the presumed peaceful component of the state. They comprise individuals who do not have the right to directly participate in hostilities, regardless of their possible participation in practice. Indeed, AP I expressly recognises the possibility of civilians taking a direct part in hostilities, suspending protection for the time of their participation.[42] It thus still echoes the belief enshrined in earlier proposed definitions that not everyone who is not enrolled in the armed forces has the same claim to protection, probably rendering the definition of civilians more acceptable for all the delegations involved. Although a definition of DPH in relation to this provision was called for in the Working Group at the Diplomatic Conference,[43] the issue was not broached in the Committee's debate and the term remains undefined in the treaty.[44] The conditionality of civilian immunity on peaceful conduct was only indirectly constructed and confirmed in the deliberation of the new category of POWs,[45] rather than the protection of civilians. The discussion of DPH appears to have been again displaced to the negotiation of the combatant status.

The conceptualisation of civilians originated in experience and discourses outside of the diplomatic law-making process. It derived from the notion of civilian immunity as a seemingly firmly established shared understanding among the actors involved in the drafting process, rather than the personal scope of the concept of civilians. The presumption of civilian status in cases of doubt under Article 50(1) AP I further indicates that civilian immunity had become the starting point for the conception of civilians. It was believed that civilians should not be the object of direct attacks, even though no agreement existed as to who these civilians were. Indeed, civilian immunity was occasionally suggested to belong to the civilian population as a collective rather than individual civilians. In his report to the IDI, Baron von der Heydte, for example, observed that the immunity of the civilian population as such can be proclaimed even without resolving the difficult question of the distinction between the civilian population and the armed forces.[46] The position of the individual is here obscured in the normative belief that the civilian population as a whole should be spared from suffering the consequences of warfare.

Civilian immunity was commonly regarded as a social or moral norm, and often even portrayed as a principle of customary international law (CIL). The ICRC emphasised this generally agreed norm in its commentary on the 1956 Draft Rules and a memorandum providing a 'Summary review of the international law rules concerning the protection of civilian populations against the dangers of indiscriminate warfare' following its 1965 Resolution on the subject. It declared that it was 'widely accepted in the teachings of qualified writers,

[42] AP I, art 51(3).
[43] *CDDH*, vol XV (Bern, Federal Political Department, 1978) 274 and 330.
[44] See also chapter 6, section III.C.
[45] *CDDH*, vol XIV (n 36) 349 and 492.
[46] IDI, 'Le problème' (n 5) 181.

in attempts at codification and in judicial decisions'.[47] Despite the lack of a clear expression of civilian immunity in conventional law and 'blatant disregard' for it in recent experiences of armed conflicts, the ICRC considered it as 'one of the main pillars of the law of war'.[48] Other international lawyers and states approached the matter more critically. Georg Schwarzenberger, for example, seemed somewhat dismissive of civilian immunity in his report to the ILA in 1962 on 'The Protection of the Civilian Population and the Trend towards Total War'. He portrayed it as having been undermined by the experience of the Second World War and subsequent treaties, and claimed that the principle of distinction was no more than an idea or argument of its proponents rather than *lex lata*.[49] Giovanni Mantilla notes that the United States responded to the 1956 Draft Rules declaring that 'in their view, to presume that civilians could be rendered immune from the direct effects of modern warfare was "fanciful"'.[50] Nonetheless, AP I has been described as reaffirming or restoring an established principle of civilian immunity which had lost its effectiveness or validity.[51] During the Diplomatic Conference itself, the central prohibition of direct attacks on civilians was repeatedly emphasised as being no more than the codification of existing international law.[52] Hans-Peter Gasser, who argues that the provisions in Part IV Section I are based on customary civilian immunity, believes that controversies in the negotiation derived from 'the mere fact of translating general principles into specific rules'.[53] For example, different opinions existed on how to measure excessive harm to civilians and thus to delineate proportionality in attacks despite the general belief in civilian immunity.

Besides civilian immunity, the principle of distinction was also said, noticeably by participating international lawyers, to reaffirm the 1868 St Petersburg Declaration or CIL.[54] Kalshoven, who was a special advisor for the Dutch delegation in the first three sessions, remarked that, at the Diplomatic Conference itself, the delegates did not 'at any time throw into doubt the continued validity of this customary principle of distinction, which indeed constitutes a basic tenet of the existing law of warfare'.[55] The fundamental nature of the principle of

[47] ICRC, 'Protection of Civilian Populations Against the Dangers of Indiscriminate Warfare (Circular No. 468)' (1967) 7:75 *IRRC* 300, 307; see also ICRC, *Draft Rules* (n 23) 57.

[48] ICRC, 'Circular' (n 47) 307.

[49] ILA, 'Committee' (n 5) 212–18; other members of the ILA, however, seemed to disagree with his evaluation.

[50] Mantilla, *Lawmaking* (n 27) 109–10.

[51] See, eg, C Greenwood, 'A Critique of the Additional Protocols to the Geneva Conventions of 1949' in H Durham and TLH McCormack (eds), *The Changing Face of Conflict and the Efficacy of International Humanitarian Law* (The Hague, Martinus Nijhoff, 1999) 6; F Bugnion, 'Adoption of the Additional Protocols of 8 June 1977: A Milestone in the Development of International Humanitarian Law' (2017) 99:905 *IRRC* 785, 793.

[52] *CDDH*, vol VI (Bern, Federal Political Department, 1978) 164 and 169; *CDDH*, vol XIV (n 36) 36.

[53] Gasser (n 2) 86.

[54] *CDDH*, vol XIV (n 36) 14, 17 and 25.

[55] F Kalshoven, 'Reaffirmation and Development of International Humanitarian Law Applicable in Armed Conflicts: The Diplomatic Conference, Geneva, 1974–77 – Part I: Combatants and Civilians' (1977) 8 *NYIL* 107, 116.

distinction for IHL was also asserted in scholarship parallel to the drafting of AP I.[56] However, it had been a slow progress to this stage and not all international lawyers shared this view. As the analysis of the early written laws of war has shown,[57] the principle of distinction and dichotomous conceptualisations of combatants and civilians are not an inherent feature of the legal framework. While various non-binding instruments in the inter-war years prohibited direct attacks on the civilian population and indiscriminate warfare, an explicit formulation of the principle of distinction was absent.[58] After the Second World War, Hersch Lauterpacht argued that civilian immunity remained an 'unchallenged principle' and a 'dictate both of law and of humanity'; yet he suggested that the distinction between combatants and civilians was obsolete.[59] Even when the distinction was recognised as positive law, its meaning may have been unclear. This was due to the uncertainty about where the dividing line between combatants and civilians should be drawn.[60]

The 1956 Draft Rules, resulting from the ICRC's first attempts at protecting the civilian population post-1949, did also not institutionalise the principle of distinction. Only when it abridged the detailed Draft Rules to a resolution comprising four principles applicable to armed conflicts, did the ICRC include the principle of distinction as one of them.[61] Affirming the 1965 ICRC Resolution, the 1968 United Nations General Assembly (UNGA) Resolution 2444(XXIII) verbatim reproduced the provision on this principle[62] and the 1970 UNGA Resolution 2675(XXV) slightly modified it.[63] The 1969 IDI Resolution on the distinction between military and non-military objectives also enshrined the principle and declared that it '*remains* a fundamental principle of the international law in force'.[64] The ICRC later acknowledged their nature as 'only resolutions', yet argued that 'the unanimous support which they have received shows that it is an expression of *opinio juris* of the international community'.[65]

[56] See, eg, E Rosenblad, 'Area Bombing and International Law' (1976) 15 *Military Law and the Law of War Review* 53, 72; Rosenblad participated in the Diplomatic Conference, but the records show no apparent involvement in the drafting of the civilian protection regime.

[57] See chapter 3.

[58] Hague Draft Rules concerning the Control of Wireless Telegraphy in Time of War and Air Warfare (1923) reprinted in Schindler and Toman (n 21); 1934 Monaco Draft; 1938 ILA Draft Convention; League of Nations, 'Resolution for the Protection of Civilian Populations Against Bombing from the Air in Case of War' (30 September 1938) reprinted in Schindler and Toman (n 21); see also chapter 4, section II.B.i.

[59] H Lauterpacht, 'The Problem of the Revision of the Law of War' (1952) 29 *BYIL* 360, 364–65.

[60] IDI, 'Le problème' (n 5) 238–39.

[61] 1965 ICRC Resolution.

[62] UNGA, 'Respect for Human Rights in Armed Conflicts' (1968) UN Doc A/RES/2444(XXIII), para 1(c).

[63] UNGA, 'Basic Principles for the Protection of Civilian Populations in Armed Conflicts' (1970) UN Doc A/Res/2675(XXV), para 2.

[64] 1969 IDI Resolution, art 1 (emphasis added).

[65] *1971 Conference*, vol III (n 28) 14; One of the US delegates to the Diplomatic Conference also noted in a separate publication that 'The United States has expressly declared that it regards this resolution [UNGA Resolution 2444(XXIII)] as an accurate declaration of existing customary law',

Indeed, Mirimanoff-Chilikine remarked at the Diplomatic Conference that the principle of distinction stipulated in Article 48 AP I built on the work of the IDI and the UNGA Resolutions.[66] Doswald-Beck observes that by the time of the Conference 'a certain consensus of State opinion in favour of the principle of distinction' existed and '[a]cademic opinion had also begun to recognise the change, albeit somewhat cautiously'.[67] The belief in codifying the principle of distinction thus seems to have reached a momentum in the latter half of the 1960s.

Indeed, the delegates at the Diplomatic Conference generally portrayed AP I's set of regulations for the protection of civilians as a combination of reaffirming and improving existing laws, as well as progressively developing new ones.[68] These claims of reaffirmation were made despite the fact that, before the adoption of the Additional Protocols, conventional 'international law provided very little protection for civilians' and arguably insufficient state practice existed in support of customary norms, as Amanda Alexander remarks.[69] As noted above, the epistemic community of international lawyers also raised questions regarding the effects that new technologies, economic warfare, and especially the two World Wars might have had on the legal framework and the position of civilians.[70] In relation to air warfare, it seems to have been a widely-held belief by scholars that 'no positive rules' existed.[71] The ICRC itself believed that 'the law can no longer fulfil its protective function' considering the disagreement in scholarship and differences in the practice of states who no longer regarded themselves bound.[72] While non-state actors deliberated the continued importance, applicability and suitability of the laws of war for the protection of civilians, these uncertainties were seemingly overlooked or brushed aside in the alleged codification process at the Diplomatic Conference.

Some provisions for the protection of civilians in AP I were, in fact, inspired by and partly resemble legal rules and drafts by non-state actors, namely the Hague Regulations, safety and security zones, and regulations of means and methods of warfare, some of which have been discussed in the previous chapters.[73] These existing and proposed rules were reinterpreted in light of the perceived common

W Reed, 'Laws of War: The Developing Law of Armed Conflict – Some Current Problems' (1977) 9 *Case Western Reserve Journal of International Law* 17, 23.

[66] *CDDH*, vol XIV (n 36) 14.

[67] Doswald-Beck (n 3) 152; see also A Alexander, 'Revolutionary War and the Development of International Humanitarian Law' in B Cuddy and V Kattan (eds), *Making Endless War: The Vietnam and Arab-Israeli Conflicts in the History of International Law* (Ann Arbor, University of Michigan Press, 2023) 126.

[68] *CDDH*, vol VI (n 52) 193, 199, 200–02 and 241.

[69] Alexander, 'Postcolonialism' (n 20) 27–28.

[70] See, eg, IDI, 'Reconsidération' (1957) (n 5); JL Kunz, 'The Chaotic Status of the Laws of War and the Urgent Necessity for Their Revision' (1951) 45 *AJIL* 37.

[71] H DeSaussure, 'The Laws of Air Warfare: Are There Any?' (1971) 5 *The International Lawyer* 527, 529.

[72] ICRC, *Draft Rules* (n 23) 53.

[73] See chapter 3, section II.A and chapter 4, section II.B.

value of safeguarding civilians from suffering the consequences of hostilities. The treaty thus consolidates a range of norms from binding and non-binding instruments which not only had diverse histories, but were also rooted in different understandings of warfare. Collectively, their new formulations indirectly shape the concept of civilians as comprising individuals who are presumed to be innocent and vulnerable, and who should be shielded from effects of warfare by the law.

The earliest proposed form of protection for individuals who are today known as civilians was the spatial demarcation of the battlefield, and later zones immune from attack. Article 59 AP I regulates 'non-defended localities', which the *Additional Protocols Commentary* considers a reiteration of Article 25 of the Hague Regulations on undefended towns as well as a codification of CIL.[74] The relation was also acknowledged by a few delegations during the negotiations,[75] suggesting that the fit with the existing framework may have provided the provision with a greater degree of persuasiveness. Article 59 AP I, however, more closely resembles the more complex and detailed regimes on safety zones and localities under GC IV[76] and 'open towns' under the 1956 Draft Rules,[77] than the one-sentence provision in the Hague Regulations. Article 60 AP I additionally provides for the establishment of 'demilitarized zones', which are more clearly reminiscent of the 'lieux de Genève' that acquired increasing support during the inter-war years.[78] It should be noted that 'localities and zones under special protection' in AP I are not intended for any particularly vulnerable group of persons, but for the civilian population as a whole which is located therein. Although only few territorial safety zones in accordance with GC IV had been created in practice, various actors advocated them and some even argued that physically excluding civilians from the danger zones would be the most or only effective safeguard.[79]

Yet a territorial understanding of hostilities seems to have already lost part of its compelling character by the time the 1956 Draft Rules were deliberated.[80] The ICRC noted that '[n]owadays, a belligerent's whole territory may be considered a theatre of hostilities' in aerial warfare.[81] Modern technology as well as changing forms of warfare had eradicated the significance of location in front of or behind the battle lines. While AP I continues the idea of territorial regulations, they only supplement the general rule of the principle of distinction. The status of persons and objectives became more relevant than specifically designated zones. It was recognised from an early stage in the law-making process

[74] *Additional Protocols Commentary* (n 10) para 2263.
[75] *CDDH*, vol XIV (n 36) 201–15 and 304.
[76] GC IV, arts 14–15.
[77] 1956 Draft Rules, art 16.
[78] See chapter 4, section II.B.ii.
[79] See, eg, IDI, 'Reconsidération' (1957) (n 5) 343–45; UN Doc A/8052, 15 and 82.
[80] ICRC, *Draft Rules* (n 23) 119.
[81] ICRC, 'Circular' (n 47) 308.

of the Additional Protocols that IHL itself would 'place certain categories of persons legally "hors combat" as it were',[82] not leaving it to the de facto scope of the hostilities. The conceptualisation of the nature of international armed conflicts (IACs) and the rules regulating it *de lege lata* and *de lege ferenda* thus shifted from a spatial to a person-centred approach. This development correlated with the above-mentioned increasing prevalence of civilian immunity as a norm.

The general protection of civilians also comprises precautionary measures, both 'in attack' and 'against the effects of attacks'.[83] Moreover, Article 51(7) proscribes the employment of civilians and the civilian population as human shields. AP I thus invokes the responsibility of both the attacking and the attacked state. Precautions were already implied to a very limited extent in earlier binding and non-binding instruments.[84] However, the regulation of the relationship between the state and its own population leading to the *mandatory* protection of civilians can be seen as a new development in conventional IHL. The drafters of GC IV had only adopted recommendations rather than binding obligations for states protecting their own population.[85] Indeed, it should be noted that the creation of localities and zones under special protection is still not obligatory.[86]

The introduction of precautionary measures faced opposition at the 1972 Conference where it was argued that they might infringe state sovereignty.[87] While they were largely supported at the Diplomatic Conference, the French delegation most notably,[88] but also some small and developing states, objected to the draft provisions on precaution[89] as well as the detailed regulations under now Article 51, including the prohibition of indiscriminate attacks.[90] They maintained that provisions on means and methods of warfare 'should not be such as to prevent a State from defending its territory against an invader, even if this were to entail losses in its own population'.[91] The French delegation's arguments raised the question whether the same rules should apply to

[82] *1971 Report* (n 29) 5.

[83] AP I, arts 57–58.

[84] 1907 Hague Regulations, art 27; 1938 League of Nations Resolution, para 1(3); ICRC, *Draft Rules* (n 23) 75 and 93.

[85] GC IV, arts 14–15.

[86] AP I, arts 59–60.

[87] Bothe, Partsch and Solf (n 15) 413–414.

[88] *CDDH*, vol VII (Bern, Federal Political Department, 1978) 192–94.

[89] Including Switzerland, Austria and Italy, *CDDH*, vol VI (n 52) 213–14; *CDDH*, vol VII (n 88) 222.

[90] *CDDH*, vol VI (n 52) 161–63 and 165.

[91] *Additional Protocols Commentary* (n 10) para 1925; cf chapter 3 where the right to national defence was in tension with the regulation of organised warfare, rather than the protection of the civilian population. Indeed, among the objecting states in the 1970s were notably those which had promoted the recognition of the *levée en masse* as an additional means of defending the nation in the early written laws of war.

an aggressor and a victim state. Reference to the prohibition of aggression had still been rebuffed in 1949; however, other actors had added it to their agenda in relation to the development of IHL.[92] The UNGA's adoption of a definition of aggression in 1974[93] shows the currency of the issue at the time of the Diplomatic Conference, suggesting that it was likely on the minds of some delegates. Reference to Article 51 of the UN Charter and states' right to self-defence was not only made in the discourse on the protection of civilians. Yet differences existed among the actors with newly independent and Soviet bloc states considering colonial powers as the aggressors, whereas Western European states, such as France, Switzerland and Austria, were seemingly informed by their historical experience of the Second World War and previous wars.[94] Ultimately, however, the principle of equality between belligerent parties again prevailed with some participants emphasising the difference between *jus ad bellum* and *jus in bello*. The Protocol's preamble consequently declares that the treaty 'must be fully applied in all circumstances … without any adverse distinction based on the nature or origin of the armed conflict or on the causes espoused by or attributed to the Parties to the conflict'.

Although the French delegation proclaimed its support for the humanitarian objective to protect the civilian population,[95] its opposition to Article 51 AP I and precautionary measures suggests an inclination towards states' self-interest at the expense of the individual civilian. However, concerns rooted in states' national self-interests were rather exceptional in the discourse surrounding the protection of civilians, which took the shape of a predominantly technical discussion. Indeed, the successful adoption of a protection regime for civilians at the Diplomatic Conference may have been facilitated by the (in all likelihood deliberately) decontextualised and depoliticised quality of the negotiations which instead emphasised the codification of allegedly existing principles and rules, and ostensibly universal and objective humanitarian aims.

Set against the background of the novel threat of nuclear weapons and weapons of mass destruction more widely, earlier post-1949 attempts at developing the law on the means and methods of warfare had been less successful. The 1956 Draft Rules by the ICRC were considered a bold proposal in this field. The Committee itself was self-conscious about intruding into the rules of warfare, or 'Hague Law',[96] which had been largely left outside of its realm of competence

[92] See, eg, ILA, 'Committee' (n 5); FR Coudert, JPA François and H Lauterpacht, 'La Revision du Droit de la Guerre' (1954) 45:1 *AIDI* 555; IDI, 'Reconsidération' (1957) (n 5); IDI, 'Reconsidération des principes du droit de la guerre' (1959) 48:2 *AIDI* 178; IDI, 'L'égalité d'application des règles du droit de la guerre aux parties à un conflit armé' (1963) 50:1 *AIDI* 5.

[93] UNGA, 'Definition of Aggression' (1974) UN Doc A/RES/3314(XXIX).

[94] See, eg, *CDDH*, vol VI (n 52) 161–658, 177, 197, 232–36; *CDDH*, vol XIV (36) 121–22 and 130–35.

[95] *CDDH*, vol VI (n 52) 161–62, 186 and 213.

[96] ICRC, *Draft Rules* (n 23) 18; the sentiment was also expressed by the former ICRC President Paul Ruegger in the discussion of the laws of war at the IDI, see IDI, 'Reconsidération' (1959) (n 92) 190.

during the inter-war years. According to Alexander, the enlargement of its work was achieved 'by a broad interpretation of the word "humanitarian"'.[97] Yet the ICRC's 1956 Draft Rules failed to receive the required response from governments that may have led to the adoption of binding law. It has often been argued that the reason the instrument did not acquire the necessary support was the inclusion of the controversial question of nuclear weapons and the implications of the rules for their status and employment,[98] rather than the protective value of the rules for the civilian population generally. It was the provision concerning atomic and other weapons with uncontrollable effects which provoked the most objections during the discussion of the instrument at the 1957 International Conference of the Red Cross in New Delhi.[99] The ICRC subsequently changed its approach a few years later, and proposed 'elementary humanitarian principles to be applied in all cases to the treatment of the civilian population in the conduct of military operations' instead.[100]

The ICRC's preliminary study for the 1971 Conference again included a chapter on the dangers posed by certain weapons, emphasising that the context of technological developments needed to be taken into account for achieving the protection of civilians.[101] However, the question of nuclear weapons was excluded from the Diplomatic Conference. According to François Bugnion, 'certain States had made their participation in the proceedings conditional on the understanding that it would not be raised'.[102] The discussion of the prohibition and restriction of certain conventional weapons was conferred on an *ad hoc* committee which only led to a resolution recommending a separate diplomatic conference on the issue.[103] It is also noticeable that the negotiation of the protection regime for civilians did not meaningfully engage with the issue of guerrilla warfare, which proved to be problematic in the discussion of the combatant and POW status.[104] The removal of the politically contentious context of certain weapons, and avoidance of the guerrilla question may have contributed to the apparent ease and straightforwardness of achieving agreement on protecting civilians from the consequences of hostilities at the Diplomatic Conference.

Furthermore, as Alexander remarks and as was noted above, the 'shared belief that civilians were protected by customary international law allowed

[97] Alexander, 'Short History' (n 1) 122.

[98] See, eg, *Additional Protocols Commentary* (n 10) xxix; Bugnion, 'Additional Protocols' (n 51) 787; Mantilla, *Lawmaking* (n 27) 114; E Benvenisti, 'The Birth and Life of the Definition of Military Objectives' (2022) 71 *ICLQ* 269, 277–78.

[99] JL Kunz, 'The 1956 Draft Rules of the International Committee of the Red Cross at the New Delhi Conference' (1959) 53 *AJIL* 132, 136.

[100] J Pictet, 'The XXth International Conference of the Red Cross: Results in the Legal Field' (1966) 7 *Journal of the International Commission of Jurists* 3, 12–13.

[101] *1971 Conference*, vol III (n 28) 110.

[102] F Bugnion, 'The International Committee of the Red Cross and Nuclear Weapons: From Hiroshima to the Dawn of the 21st Century' (2005) 87:859 *IRRC* 511, 519–20.

[103] CDDH, vol I (n 34) 215.

[104] See sections II.A–II.B.

delegates to agree easily on the *Protocol's* broader, foundational, statements about the protection of civilians and the nature of civilians'.[105] The drafters' arguably anachronistic reading of the existing law facilitated the law-making process as it drew on an ideational framework of shared beliefs between the actors, with significant persuasiveness. In particular, it was primarily the insistence on the fundamental nature of civilian immunity and the principle of distinction as a long-standing, yet diminishing, principle which led to the reaffirmation of 'established' law.

B. The Changing Conceptualisation of Civilians and its Limits

The predisposition of the actors towards the protection of civilians may have been related to the changing understanding of IACs themselves, which were increasingly perceived as reprehensible, with the parallel development of the *jus ad bellum*.[106] The actors involved also acknowledged that silences in IHL would not function as a constraint for military conduct beyond the explicit permissions in the law. The scope of the regulation and protection became determined by the law and not the de facto or desired nature of IACs. The evolution of the laws of war into IHL, further discussed below,[107] also suggests a more restraining and protective role for the law.[108] In his report to the IDI on the distinction between military and non-military objectives, von der Heydte argued that the law was based on the idea of protection rather than the principle of the freedom of destruction.[109] A similar statement was made by a delegate of the German Democratic Republic at the 1970s Diplomatic Conference.[110] Although the majority of new rules on the civilian population regulates means and methods of warfare, including the establishment of targeting rules, the underlying rationale had changed. The ideal of organised and orderly warfare was joined, if not surpassed, by the perceived ultimate value of IHL in protecting the individual and sparing the innocent.

In an empirical study of the treaty's drafting history, Mantilla argues that the US and the UK were more reluctant to adopt a stringent regulation of the conduct of hostilities and thus 'strict rules and prohibitions to protect civilians from the dangers of warfare'.[111] According to him, the protection of civilians

[105] Alexander, 'Postcolonialism' (n 20) 28.
[106] JG Gardam, *Non-Combatant Immunity as a Norm of International Humanitarian Law* (London, Martinus Nijhoff, 1993) 37–38.
[107] See section III.C.
[108] SC Neff, *War and the Law of Nations: A General History* (Cambridge, Cambridge University Press, 2005) 340–41.
[109] IDI, 'Le problème' (n 5) 80–81.
[110] *CDDH*, vol XIV (n 36) 130.
[111] G Mantilla, 'Social Pressure and the Making of Wartime Civilian Protection Rules' (2020) 26 *European Journal of International Relations* 443, 444.

under AP I was the outcome of social pressure by Third World and Socialist states and a strategy of 'leadership capture'. The isolated position of these Western states, and what he elsewhere calls 'growing humanitarian pressure'[112] show the importance attached to the protection of civilians by a majority of states. It was concern for civilians, individually and collectively, that informed the law-making process and, consequently, the limits imposed upon the conduct of hostilities in AP I. The humanitarian focus of the law transformed the well-being of the civilian population into a standard for appropriate warfare. While this might seem trite to contemporary lawyers, it constituted a significant shift compared to earlier periods.

Although the beginnings of this development were already seen in GC IV, concern for civilians became predominant in the time immediately leading up to the adoption of the Additional Protocols. The UNGA declared in the preambular paragraphs of its 1970 resolution on the 'Basic Principles for the Protection of Civilian Populations in Armed Conflicts' that 'in the present century the international community has accepted an increased role and new responsibilities for the alleviation of human suffering in any form and in particular during armed conflicts'.[113] It is notable that this is the only one of five successive resolutions that year on 'human rights in armed conflicts' that received a special title indicating its purpose.

Alexander argues that by the time the Additional Protocols were drafted, the language and value system had changed with respect to the civilian population. According to her, by the end of the Vietnam War, '[i]t had become impossible to say that civilians were being killed in the course of the war without appearing to be a perpetrator of a war crime'.[114] Civilians were thus increasingly portrayed as 'victims of war', and it was believed to be the duty of states to protect them. Civilians were no longer expected to be in charge of their own well-being by ensuring that they remained outside of the scope of hostilities on their own account, or to be spared on grounds of military necessity. Instead, an obligation to safeguard civilians was imposed on the attacking state and the state to which they belonged. The US delegate Walter Reed emphasised in this respect that '[t]he Conference's task was to ensure maximum protection for the civilian population and civilian objects, whether the latter were in the hands of the aggressor or in those of the party defending its own territory'.[115] Emerging international human rights law (IHRL) probably facilitated the constraining power of international law on state conduct towards individuals in their own jurisdiction, as well as states' responsibility regarding these individuals' well-being. Writing at the time of the Diplomatic Conference, Burrus Carnahan considers

[112] G Mantilla, 'The Protagonism of the USSR and Socialist States in the Revision of International Humanitarian Law' (2019) 21 *Journal of the History of International Law* 181, 198.

[113] UN Doc A/Res/2675(XXV).

[114] Alexander, 'Postcolonialism' (n 20) 48; see also Alexander, 'Revolutionary War' (n 67) 133.

[115] *CDDH*, vol XIV (n 36) 193; see also Reed (n 65) 21.

this development with respect to aerial attacks as a 'tendency to regard the law of war and armed conflict more and more as an aspect of international humanitarian and human rights law'.[116]

The prime concern for the civilian population in IACs can also be seen in the introduction into conventional law of provisions regulating and enabling civil defence. This comprises 'humanitarian tasks intended to protect the civilian population against the dangers, and to help it to recover from the immediate effects, of hostilities or disasters and also to provide the conditions necessary for its survival'.[117] The 1956 Draft Rules already contained a single provision asking parties to the conflict to 'facilitate the work of the civilian bodies exclusively engaged in protecting and assisting the civilian population in case of attack', calling for guarantees similar to those provided for medical personnel in the Geneva Conventions.[118] While this would have been rejected as undue interference of private persons and associations on the battlefield a hundred years before,[119] the idea was largely unchallenged at the Diplomatic Conference. Indeed, it was the involvement of military personnel that proved the subject of controversy.[120] This entailed the structural distinction between combatants and civilians as two concepts with distinct privileges, obligations and protections. AP I, therefore, provides different guarantees for civilian civil defence, and military personnel or units engaged in civil defence.[121] Although it had already been part of the objective of the first 1864 Geneva Convention to protect not only war victims but also the personnel and organisations helping them,[122] the notion of civil defence owed its existence to the changing conception of 'victims' of armed conflicts. It was the overarching aim to protect civilians from the consequences of hostilities which justified the participation of civilians in the context of IACs, albeit not in the conduct of hostilities. This concern for the wellbeing of the civilian population also appears to underlie the additional, innovative creation of indirect protections. These can be found, for example, in the 'protection of objects indispensable to the survival of the civilian population', 'protection of works and installations containing dangerous forces' and 'protection of the natural environment'.[123]

Indeed, the justification of the respect for 'harmless civilians' as having the same basis as the safeguards for soldiers *hors de combat* in the *Additional Protocols Commentary*,[124] disregards the complexity and idiosyncrasy of the

[116] BM Carnahan, 'The Law of Air Bombardment in Its Historical Context' (1975) 17 *Air Force Law Review* 39, 59.
[117] AP I, art 61.
[118] 1956 Draft Rules, art 12.
[119] See chapter 3, section II.B.
[120] Bothe, Partsch and Solf (n 15) 468.
[121] AP I, arts 62–67.
[122] *Additional Protocols Commentary* (n 10) para 2321.
[123] AP I, arts 54–56.
[124] *Additional Protocols Commentary* (n 10) para 1605.

protection regime for the civilian population in AP I. The analogy to the protection of combatants in particular vulnerable circumstances played an important part in the making of GC IV.[125] Yet the immunity of individuals protected under Part IV of AP I was apparently perceived as inherent to being civilians, and not the particular situation in which they found themselves. Several of the provisions have in common that civilian immunity was seemingly both the foundation and objective of the proposed rules. Civilians had thus gained a protective status in their own right.

In light of these important developments in the law and the surrounding ideational context, a few silences in the negotiations at the Diplomatic Conference stand out. First, although the qualification of national liberation wars (NLWs) as either IACs or NIACs, and the relation between guerrilla fighters and POW status were significant points of debate at the Conference,[126] these issues do not seem to have informed the construction of civilians and their protection. Guerrilla warfare was discussed as a separate item which encompassed both the combatant status and the civilian population in such situations in the documents submitted to the 1971 Conference and at the expert event itself.[127] At the 1972 Conference, experts still voiced their concern regarding the protection of civilians in guerrilla warfare.[128] The experts thus engaged with the greater difficulty of distinguishing between combatants and civilians in guerrilla warfare compared to traditional wars and IACs. In contrast, only a few state delegations at the Diplomatic Conference mentioned the issue in relation to rules protecting civilians.[129] Two of the delegates had notably also participated in the 1971 and 1972 Conferences.[130] The particularities of such conflict situations, as well as the question of DPH more generally, as noted above, do not seem to have been taken into account in the definition of civilians. This may have been partly due to the discussion taking place before Committee I concluded the negotiation of AP I's material scope of application. The analysis above suggests that it may have also been a result of the decontextualised approach to the protection of civilians, and the reliance on a pre-existing vague notion of civilian immunity without discussing the personal scope of civilians in more detail.

Second, it is important to note that the notion of 'enemy civilians' or 'enemy nationals', prevalent in GC IV,[131] was no longer used. Indeed, the *Additional Protocols Commentary* emphasises that nationality no longer serves as the

[125] See chapter 4, section II.
[126] See sections II.B–II.C.
[127] *Conference of Government Experts on the Reaffirmation and Development of International Humanitarian Law Applicable in Armed Conflicts, vol VI – Rules Applicable in Guerrilla Warfare* (Geneva, ICRC, 1971) 24–32; *1971 Report* (n 29) 69–70.
[128] *1972 Report* (n 29) 29 and 143.
[129] *CDDH*, vol XIV (n 36) 51, 57, 69 and 80.
[130] China also made reference to the context of guerrilla warfare, but had abstained from sending a delegation to the preliminary conferences.
[131] See chapter 4, section II.A.iii.

basis for the protection or lack thereof for an individual.[132] The individual is not constructed along the lines of belligerency in the AP I protection regime for civilians. Thus, it is not the vertical relationship between a belligerent state and the individual, but the horizontal relationship between the armed forces and the presumed peaceful population which determines civilian status. By removing the requirement of a link to a state, individuals are classified as civilians with respect to both the enemy state and their own government. This provides the foundation for the regulation of protective measures both by the attacking and the attacked state, as discussed above.

Third, at the same time as AP I introduced into conventional law a detailed set of rules shielding civilians from the consequences of hostilities, it left the main protection regime for 'protected persons' in GC IV largely untouched. GC IV institutionalised in conventional law a disparity in protection for civilians in different situations, and AP I arguably continues it by failing to extend the consolidated concept of civilians to those in the power of a party to the conflict. At the Diplomatic Conference, the ICRC delegate Mirimanoff-Chilikine described the proposed AP I provisions on civilians as the reverse of GC IV, strengthening the protections in the less developed Part II of the 1949 instrument, and advancing to a lesser degree its more developed regime.[133] Yet the shortcomings of the GC IV protection regime were known,[134] as were the difficulties arising from expanding the treaty's scope of application *ratione materiae* to NLWs through Article 1(4) AP I.[135] The concept of 'protected persons' as defined in Article 4 could not operate in such wars since the resistance movements and the opposing party would be of the same nationality. This issue, which had been raised as a reason for not applying the regime to NIACs in 1949,[136] thus re-emerged. During a meeting of an informal working group in Lucerne in 1974, it was suggested that the problem could be resolved by expanding 'the definition of "protected persons" beyond its present scope by substituting some other criterion for that of nationality'.[137] However, this proposal still relied on the understanding of the individual as belonging to the opposing belligerent party. This indicates and reinforces the adversarial relations in which the protection regime for civilians in the power of a party to the conflict is embedded. The individual would benefit from protection as a potential enemy rather than a civilian. Even so, this issue was seemingly ignored by the drafters at the 1970s Diplomatic Conference, who

[132] *Additional Protocols Commentary* (n 10) para 1909.

[133] *CDDH*, vol XIV (n 36) 14–15.

[134] DG Burwell, 'Civilian Protection in Modern Warfare: A Critical Analysis of the Geneva Civilian Convention of 1949' (1973) 14 *Virginia Journal of International Law* 123.

[135] UN Doc A/8052, 73; JF DePue, 'The Amended First Article to the First Draft Protocol Additional to the Geneva Conventions of 1949 – Its Impact Upon Humanitarian Constraints Governing Armed Conflict' (1977) 75 *Military Law Review* 71, 125–26.

[136] See chapter 4, section III.B.

[137] DePue (n 135) 126.

failed to engage with the difference in the conceptualisation of civilians under the respective protection regimes of GC IV and AP I. Ultimately, the new treaty extended the so-called 'Geneva Law' not to protect civilians as defined in AP I, but vulnerable human beings, as will be shown in section III.

C. Civilians in Non-international Armed Conflicts

In the first instance, the provisions concerning the safeguards for civilians in IACs and NIACs were discussed jointly in the responsible Committee III. Once it became apparent that states were reluctant to adopt detailed regulations for NIACs under Draft Protocol II, a simplified draft was submitted *ad hoc* to the plenary level.[138] Several delegations voiced their concern regarding the subsequent gradual removal of provisions intended for the protection of civilians during NIACs. Some even questioned the humanitarian nature of the second additional protocol as the truncated version of the protection system emerged.[139] Colonel Draper, who had been a delegate himself, later described the content of AP II as being in a 'debilitated form' and only 'a pale shadow of Protocol I'.[140]

One of the provisions notably omitted is the definition of civilians. The ICRC's Draft Proposal II submitted to the Diplomatic Conference included one which stipulated that '[a]ny person who is not a member of armed forces is considered to be a civilian'.[141] Australia preferred a definition that would exclude individuals participating in the hostilities, whereas other delegations sought to bring the wording into line with Draft Article 1 on the material scope of NIACs referring to armed forces as well as organised armed groups under responsible command.[142] Yet a general reluctance to properly engage with the scope of application *ratione personae* so long as the scope *ratione materiae* of NIACs had not been determined by Committee I prevented a more substantial discussion.[143] The sequence of the agenda items, placing the protection of the civilian population at the beginning of the First Session, thus proved problematic. The definition of civilians was not revisited at the Second Session after a decision had been made on the type of situations regulated under the Protocol.[144] Instead, the clause was deleted by consensus at the plenary level

[138] *Additional Protocols Commentary* (n 10) paras 4411–18; for more detail on the drafting history see Mantilla, *Lawmaking* (n 27) 165–66.

[139] *CDDH*, vol VII (n 88) 125–26, 129, 135–37, 163 and 206.

[140] GIAD Draper, 'Humanitarian Law and Human Rights' [1979] *Acta Juridica* 193, 203 and 205.

[141] Reprinted in *CDDH*, vol I (n 34) art 25(1).

[142] *CDDH*, vol IV (Bern, Federal Political Department, 1978) 73–74; *CDDH*, vol XIV (n 36) 41–42 and 71–72; The Brazilian delegate Teixeira Starling, similar to his comments in relation to IACs, again implied that civilians would temporarily lose their status due to DPH even though this was not reflected in the amendment proposed by the Brazilian delegation.

[143] *CDDH*, vol XIV (n 36) 41–48.

[144] ibid 387–88.

without discussion.[145] As Michael Bothe, Karl Josef Partsch and Waldemar Solf remark in their commentary on the Additional Protocols, '[t]he elimination of this Article does not however eliminate the problem as to who the persons are who are entitled to the protection' under Part IV AP II.[146]

In the absence of a definition, the question arises whether individuals who directly participate in hostilities would merely temporarily lose their civilian immunity under Article 13(3), or fail to qualify as civilians. The Rapporteur of the Working Group, Richard Baxter, informed the responsible Committee III that the issue of various forms of participation in or contributions to the armed conflict had emerged in its discussions.[147] Unfortunately, the official records of the Diplomatic Conference do not contain minutes of the Working Group discussions. Despite these apparent differences in opinion regarding the civilian status and loss of protection, the Committee itself again abstained from sustained deliberations. The issue was set aside without a trace of having been picked up again later on. While the *travaux préparatoires*, as a result, do not give much insight into how civilians in NIACs were perceived by the drafters, the relevant rules in AP II still indicate the existence of a distinct concept of civilians, the personal scope of which remained unsettled. The safeguards by their nature, like their AP I equivalents, derive from the notion of civilian immunity. Prior to the commencement of the Diplomatic Conference, James E Bond argued that, notwithstanding the difficulty of '[d]rafting a uniform set of rules for the conduct of military operations in internal conflicts', it was generally agreed that 'the civilian population should be spared the sufferings of war' and that civilians should not be targeted.[148]

Nevertheless, the prohibition of indiscriminate attacks and the use of civilians as human shields are also missing from the set of rules. More significantly, the principle of distinction is not formulated in the text of AP II. In introducing the draft 'basic rules', including this principle, to Committee III, Mirimanoff-Chilikine stated that it had been recognised as an obligation of belligerents even in NIACs in 'the relevant international resolutions', referring to UNGA Resolutions 2444(XXIII) and 2675(XXV) as examples.[149] At the Diplomatic Conference, however, the opinions on the inclusion of the principle of distinction in a treaty regulating NIACs were divided. The Indian delegation strongly opposed it claiming that it would be 'out of context and have no place in an internal armed conflict'.[150] In his study on *Negotiating Civil War*, Henry Lovat notes that the Indian delegation 'played the role of antagonistic

[145] *CDDH*, vol VII (n 88) 135.

[146] Bothe, Partsch and Solf (n 15) 773.

[147] *CDDH*, vol XIV (n 36) 82–83; see also *CDDH*, vol XV (n 43) 243.

[148] JE Bond, 'Proposed Revisions in the Law of War Applicable to Internal Conflict' (1972) 12 *Santa Clara Lawyer* 223, 226.

[149] *CDDH*, vol XIV (n 36) 15.

[150] *CDDH*, vol VII (n 88) 139.

developing world, post-colonial state par excellence' and was 'consistently opposed to Protocol II, its delegates querying the desirability of and need for this protocol'.[151] The New Zealand delegation, on the other hand, believed that it would be sufficient to incorporate a provision declaring that civilians and the civilian population should not be made the object of attack.[152] Emanuela-Chiara Gillard suggests that the avoidance of any reference to 'combatants' or 'parties to the armed conflict' in AP II, as further discussed below, meant that the principle of distinction was impossible to formulate.[153] The proposed article on the principle of distinction failed to attain the required two-thirds majority of votes on the plenary level in 1977. Some commentators, including Kalshoven, who was a delegate for the Netherlands at the Diplomatic Conference, nevertheless, perceive it as implicit in the provision on civilian immunity in Article 13 AP II.[154]

The history of efforts for protecting civilians in NIACs may shed some light on the similarity of the related rules in the two Additional Protocols. Various post-1949 proposals for the protection of the civilian population from the consequences of warfare abstained from qualifying the nature of the conflict to which they would apply[155] or explicitly extended the scope of application *ratione materiae* to IACs and NIACs alike.[156] As Draper remarked, these instruments gave the impression that the distinction between the two types of conflict, favoured by states, should be removed.[157] Indeed, during the discussion of the 1965 Resolution at the International Conference of the Red Cross, the chairman acknowledged that the drafting committee had only IACs in mind; yet the ICRC delegate Frédéric Siordet as well as some national Red Cross and governmental delegates promoted the deletion of an explicit exclusive focus on such conflicts.[158] The ICRC's preference for equal protection of the civilian population in all armed conflicts regardless of their nature was supported by the experts it had consulted in 1970.[159] The 1971 Conference still considered the possibility of creating 'a single protocol relating to the protection of the civilian population in all types of conflict'.[160] While the idea was especially

[151] H Lovat, *Negotiating Civil War: The Politics of International Regime Design* (Cambridge, Cambridge University Press, 2020) 176.

[152] *CDDH*, vol VII (n 88) 140.

[153] E-C Gillard, 'Protection of Civilians in the Conduct of Hostilities' in R Liivoja and T McCormack (eds), *Routledge Handbook of the Law of Armed Conflict* (London, Routledge, 2016) 159.

[154] F Kalshoven, '1974–1977, Part I' (n 55) 118–19; see also Y Dinstein, *Non-International Armed Conflicts in International Law* (Cambridge, Cambridge University Press, 2014) para 793.

[155] 1965 ICRC Resolution; UN Doc A/Res/2444(XXIII) and A/Res/2675(XXV).

[156] 1956 Draft Rules, art 2.

[157] GIAD Draper, 'The Status of Combatants and the Question of Guerilla Warfare' (1971) 45 *BYIL* 173, 184.

[158] ICRC, *XXth International Conference of the Red Cross* (Geneva, ICRC, 1965) 85–86.

[159] *1971 Conference*, vol III (n 28) 8; ICRC, *XXIInd International Conference of the Red Cross* (Geneva, ICRC, 1973) 80.

[160] *Additional Protocols Commentary* (n 10) para 4387.

advocated by the Norwegian delegation,[161] the proposal was faced with mixed views from the other delegates.[162] A general discussion at the plenary level of the 1972 Conference showed that '[t]he vast majority of the experts were in favour of retaining the distinction between the two types of conflict' and thus the 'preparation of two Draft Additional Protocols'.[163] The Norwegian delegation attempted again to persuade the delegates at the Diplomatic Conference to 'establish identical legislation for all victims of all armed conflicts'.[164] Hans Wilhelm Longva, who had participated in both the 1971 and 1972 Conference, argued that the adoption of two separate protocols 'with different levels of protection for victims' would lead to discrimination and 'what had been called "selective humanitarianism"',[165] yet without success. The neighbouring country Sweden also pleaded that '[a]ll armed conflicts, whatever their magnitude should be subject to the same humanitarian rules', although accepting their existence in separate Protocols.[166]

Despite being regulated in two regimes with different amount of detail, the protection of civilians in NIACs thus owes its existence and formulation to the regulation of IACs. The provisions in the ICRC's Draft Protocol II relating to the civilian population were 'derived directly' from proposals for Draft Protocol I with some omissions.[167] More importantly, the concept of civilians was not constructed in any sustained manner in relation to NIACs and with the particularities of such conflicts in mind. Instead, it is the result of adopting rules analogous to IACs.

II. THE CONCEPT OF COMBATANTS

AP I seems to reaffirm the established, long-standing concept of combatants with only a limited relaxation of the conditions for certain lawful participants in IACs. Article 43 provides as a simple general rule that every member of the armed forces, with the exception of medical and religious personnel, qualifies as a combatant. As a prerequisite for combatant status, paragraph 1 endorses the existence of organised armed forces characterised by a system of command and discipline to which the individual belongs. The intended consequent 'compliance with the rules of international law applicable in armed conflicts' further emphasises the underlying ideational framework of regulated warfare.

[161] *1971 Report* (n 29) 61.
[162] ibid 74.
[163] *1972 Report* (n 29) 27.
[164] *CDDH*, vol VIII (Bern, Federal Political Department, 1978) 217; see also *CDDH*, vol V (Bern, Federal Political Department, 1978) 91; *CDDH*, Vol XIV (n 36) 72.
[165] *CDDH*, vol VIII (n 164) 217.
[166] *CDDH*, vol V (n 164) 142.
[167] Bothe, Partsch and Solf (n 15) 769.

Moreover, Article 43(2) makes explicit the previously implicit privileged belligerency of combatants, declaring that 'they have the right to participate directly in hostilities'. It abstains from distinguishing between regular and irregular armed forces, and thus avoids 'such terms as "irregular", "guerrilla", "lawful combatant", or "privileged combatant"' following a proposal by the Norwegian delegation.[168] The ICRC draft had still 'contemplated perpetuating the dichotomy' between regular and irregular forces.[169]

The *Additional Protocols Commentary* interprets Article 43 as meaning that '*only* members of the armed forces are combatants'.[170] However, it admits that the drafters did not seemingly intend to exclude from the combatant status individuals who took part in a *levée en masse*.[171] It declares that the Diplomatic Conference 'took full account of the new forces which have appeared on the modern battlefield in the course of the last few decades'.[172] Compared to GC III, AP I seems to expand the combatant status to comprise members of irregular armed forces in more diverse, yet still narrowly defined, situations of IACs. However, three exceptions to the combatant status have been identified, namely guerrillas in occupied territory who fail to distinguish themselves from civilians, spies and mercenaries.[173]

The negotiation of the combatant and related POW status at the 1970s Diplomatic Conference differed significantly from the 1949 process. While the evolution of the concept of combatants was stifled by a restrictive, predominantly legal discourse after the Second World War,[174] a prolonged and explicit discussion of its criteria emerged 25 years later. The rights and duties attached to combatant status were directly addressed as part of the debate. Moreover, it was deliberated whether the delineation of the status should function as yet another safeguard for civilians, or provide guarantees for individuals who are fighting for particular reasons. The negotiation was characterised by a confrontation of two groups of actors, which has been described as a 'North-South split', although not in a narrow geographic sense.[175] The two emerging discourses, both of which resonated with the ideational contexts of the time, intersected without aligning. Articles 43 and 44 AP I, as a result, constitute only a veneer of a shared understanding of the meaning of combatants.

[168] ibid 270.
[169] ibid 269.
[170] *Additional Protocols Commentary* (n 10) para 1677 (emphasis added).
[171] ibid para 1722.
[172] ibid para 1672.
[173] GH Aldrich, 'New Life for the Laws of War' (1981) 75 *AJIL* 764, 770. While the explicit exclusion of mercenaries from the concept of combatants in Article 47 AP I is an important development, its political rather than legal origins and drafting history exceed the scope of this book. For an analysis of the evolution of the norm against mercenaries see S Percy, *Mercenaries: The History of a Norm in International Relations* (Oxford, Oxford University Press, 2007).
[174] See chapter 4, section I.
[175] Bothe, Partsch and Solf (n 15) 9; see also Alexander, 'Postcolonialism' (n 20) 27.

A. The Influence of the Principle of Distinction and Civilian Immunity

While the 1970s Diplomatic Conference was convened for the reaffirmation and development of IHL, Draft Protocol I did not envisage a reconsideration of the combatant status *per se*. It only provided a supplementary clause to Article 4 GC III defining a 'new category of prisoners of war' regarding 'members of organised resistance movements'.[176] Indeed, not much attention had been paid to the concept of combatants in the preceding years. The protection of civilians dominated the agenda of the ICRC and its endeavours to shape IHL post-1949, whereas combatants in the context of IACs were largely absent from the discourse.[177] The Committee, as well as the epistemic community of international lawyers only revisited the issue at the end of the 1960s following an increase in activity in the United Nations.[178] The experts at the 1971 and 1972 Conferences were still only preoccupied with the POW status in relation to guerrilla fighters and members of national liberation movements (NLMs), rather than the concept of combatants generally.[179] The then President of the ICRC, Eric Martin, emphasised that the Draft Conventions for the Diplomatic Conference were dealing 'mainly with the protection of the civilian population against the effects of war, and the safeguarding of victims of non-international conflicts',[180] leaving the question of the combatant status unmentioned.

At the Diplomatic Conference itself, the Hague Regulations' criteria served once again as the starting point for discussing the narrow expansion of the status. Western states and the ICRC, in particular, continued the earlier conceptualisation of combatants and showed an unwillingness to relax the qualifying conditions. These actors had notably participated in diplomatic conferences on the written laws of war before, some even for the past century. However, despite their stated belief and appearance of acting in the tradition of existing law, a change in their discourse had occurred. While seemingly defending the

[176] Draft Protocol I, art 42.

[177] ICRC, *XVIIIth International Red Cross Conference* (Geneva, ICRC, 1952); ICRC, *XIXth International Conference of the Red Cross* (Geneva, ICRC, 1957); ICRC, *XXth International Conference* (n 158); ICRC, *XXIst International Conference of the Red Cross* (Geneva, ICRC, 1969); ICRC, *XXIInd Conference* (n 159).

[178] See also Bindschedler-Robert (n 5); (1971) 10 *Military Law and Law of War Review* 15 providing a special issue on the fifth Congress held by the International Society for Military Law and the Law of War in Dublin in 1970.

[179] *1971 Report* (n 29) 68–69; *Conference of Government Experts on the Reaffirmation and Development of International Humanitarian Law Applicable in Armed Conflicts: Introduction*, vol I (Geneva, ICRC, 1971) Annex I; *1972 Report* (n 29) 133; the focus on guerrilla warfare was also reflected in contemporaneous scholarship, see, eg, Draper, 'Status of Combatants' (n 157); F Kalshoven, 'The Position of Guerrilla Fighters under the Law of War' (1972) 11 *Military Law and the Law of War Review* 55; E Rosenblad, 'Guerrilla Warfare and International Law' (1973) 12 *Military Law and the Law of War Review* 91; M Veuthey, *Guérilla et Droit Humanitaire* (Geneva, ICRC, 1983); K Suter, *An International Law of Guerrilla Warfare – The Global Politics of Law-Making* (London, Frances Pinter, 1984).

[180] ICRC, *XXIInd Conference* (n 159) 55.

status quo, these actors also engaged in a debate on the form and purpose of the regulation and protection of combatants and POWs. It is here that the main difference to the construction of combatants in the past transpired by interlinking the concept with the principle of distinction and civilian immunity.

The conditions for the new category of POWs proposed by Draft Protocol I differed slightly, but significantly, from those laid out in the Hague Regulations. It replaced the requirements 'to have a fixed distinctive emblem recognizable at a distance' and 'to carry arms openly'[181] with the obligation to 'distinguish themselves from the civilian population in military operations'.[182] In introducing the provision to the responsible Committee III at the Diplomatic Conference, the ICRC delegate Michel Veuthey justified the change by arguing that the conditions had the same *ratio legis*.[183] Article 44(3) itself clarifies that the obligation of combatants to distinguish themselves 'while they are engaged in an attack or in a military operation preparatory to an attack' serves 'to promote the protection of the civilian population from the effects of hostilities'. Because of this fundamental objective, some delegations believed that the failure to distinguish oneself was the only exception which would justify the deprivation of POW status.[184] It was briefly debated whether the obligation should be a basic rule regarding the methods and means of warfare rather than a constitutive condition for combatant status.[185] Ultimately, however, the established criteria for lawful combatants were reinterpreted through the lens of the principle of distinction, and the new condition acquired a predominant position in the regulation of combatant status. Although the definition appears to exist independently of the 'civilian', it is qualified by the relationship between combatants and the civilian population.

Kalshoven described the inclusion of the principle of distinction in the reformulated conditions of POW status as 'a most noteworthy innovation'.[186] Some experts who were consulted for the 1970 United Nations Secretary-General (UNSG) Report on 'Respect for Human Rights in Armed Conflicts', or who participated in the 1971 Conference in preparation of AP I, had already considered the requirements of wearing a fixed distinctive sign and carrying arms openly as means of distinguishing combatants from civilians.[187] At the Diplomatic Conference, the actors promoting the principle of distinction as a criterion for POW status portrayed it as established law,[188] and seem to have again occasionally resorted to anachronism. The US delegate Reed, for instance, declared that

[181] 1907 Hague Regulations, art 1.
[182] Draft Protocol I, art 42.
[183] *CDDH*, vol XIV (n 36) 319 and 450.
[184] ibid 328, 331, 473 and 477.
[185] ibid 333, 481 and 491–92; *CDDH*, vol XV (n 43) 158.
[186] Kalshoven, '1974–1977, Part I' (n 55) 122.
[187] UN Doc A/8052, 55–56; *1971 Report* (n 29) 69; some of these experts also participated in the negotiation of the POW status at the Diplomatic Conference.
[188] See, eg, *CDDH*, vol VI (n 52) 123; *CDDH*, vol XIV (n 36) 457 and 508.

'[t]he desire and urgency to protect the civilians is no different today than it was in 1907 – or 1949 – and the lives of civilians are no less important today than they were then'.[189] The importance of the principle of distinction for the well-being of civilians was thus not only stressed in the drafting of AP I's protection regime for the civilian population, but also permeated the discussion of the conditions for combatant status, where it was sometimes even framed as underlying the purpose of AP I as a whole.[190]

In contrast, when the combatant status was first regulated in an international instrument a century before, 'civilians', in the sense of innocent, vulnerable individuals who need to be protected, were seemingly not on the minds of the drafters.[191] At that time, it was implied that the recognisability of combatants through a visible sign and carrying arms openly was for the purpose of distinguishing members of different armed forces, as well as lawful combatants from irregular fighters. Anyone other than an identifiable combatant was left to the grey zone of the unwritten laws of war and largely responsible for their own fate. Indeed, the duty to distinguish themselves was arguably de facto required from individuals who are now called 'civilians', since they were expected to abstain from participating and thus intruding in hostilities. The objective was the conduct of organised warfare which enabled a fair tournament between lawful combatants, rather than the protection of peaceful 'civilians'. Admittedly, the requirement of distinction was still partially rooted in the idea of fair and honourable warfare in the drafting of AP I.[192] The ICRC preparatory study on guerrilla warfare explains the duty to 'clearly display their combatant status by openly bearing their arms' as preventing combatants from disguising their military status.[193] Alexander describes this approach as entailing 'a Western aesthetic, much shaken but not completely shattered, of decent military behaviour'.[194]

Inherent in the newly introduced principle of distinction as a requirement for POW status was also the understanding that an individual could not simultaneously benefit from combatant and civilian status.[195] With the recognition that each individual should have a status under IHL, the difficulty of drawing a line between combatants and civilians became increasingly apparent. This was already hinted at in the POW Committee in 1949,[196] yet neither GC III nor GC IV conceptualise the interrelation between the beneficiaries of the respective treaties. Unlike in 1949, the same Committee was responsible for the regulation

[189] *CDDH*, vol XIV (n 36) 477.
[190] See, eg, ibid 330, 349–72 and 451–536.
[191] See chapter 3.
[192] *1971 Conference*, vol VI (n 127) 13.
[193] ibid 52 and 11.
[194] Alexander, 'Postcolonialism' (n 20) 27.
[195] *1971 Conference*, vol VI (n 127) 11; MHF Clarke, T Glynn and APV Rogers, 'Combatant and Prisoner of War Status' in Meyer (n 2) 117.
[196] See chapter 4, section I.

and protection of combatants and civilians at the 1970s Diplomatic Conference. More importantly, the status and protection of civilians had already been agreed upon when it commenced the arduous negotiation of the combatant status. While it was generally believed that the POW status needed to be adapted to contemporary armed conflicts, this aim was balanced against the well-being of civilians.[197] Bothe, Partsch and Solf observe that this 'proved to be one of the most difficult dilemmas of the Conference'.[198]

The regulation of POW status was thus perceived as being framed by the protection of the (peaceful) civilian population, which seemingly held a more fundamental position. The principle of distinction was invoked as a standard for possible changes to the combatant criteria and acquired a restraining force which limited their evolution.[199] In the explanation of votes following the adoption of Article 44, delegations justified their abstention or rejection of the provision arguing that it undermined the principle of distinction or failed to respect the protection of civilians. Conversely, other Western delegations apparently felt the need to defend their vote in favour by stating their belief that the provision did not erode the principle of distinction.[200] Nevertheless, some commentators maintain that the new combatant status risks weakening or obscuring the distinction.[201] In a piercing critique, Guy Roberts declares that AP I has turned the distinction between combatants and civilians from a 'triumph' into a 'disaster'.[202]

As has been shown in relation to the concept of civilians, the predominance of the principle of distinction was part of a shifting normative framework which, in this context, seemed to inform at least the understandings and beliefs of Western delegations and the ICRC, and provided them with a new language for the negotiations. As a result, the 'combatant' was constructed at the intersection between lawful participation in hostilities and the protection of the civilian population. Bugnion, for example, describes the definition of combatants as seemingly 'the other side of the same coin' of civilian immunity.[203] It is conceivable that the principle of distinction was also introduced into the POW status as an explicit criterion to counteract its perceived diminishing standing in the practice of warfare. Its proponents argued that the reformulated POW status would provide 'an incentive for the irregular combatant to comply with the law,

[197] *CDDH*, vol VI (n 52) 132.
[198] Bothe, Partsch and Solf (n 15) 213.
[199] *CDDH*, vol XV (n 43) 156–87.
[200] *CDDH*, vol VI (n 52) 121–55.
[201] DE Hacker, 'The Application of Prisoner-of-War Status to Guerrillas under the First Protocol Additional to the Geneva Conventions of 1949' (1978) 2 *Boston College International and Comparative Law Journal* 131, 160; Kinsella (n 4) 144; Alexander, 'Postcolonialism' (n 20) 27.
[202] GB Roberts, 'New Rules of Waging War: The Case Against Ratification of Additional Protocol I' (1985) 26 *Virginia Journal of International Law* 109, 129–30.
[203] Bugnion, 'Additional Protocols' (n 51) 793.

thereby increasing the protection of both civilians and regular soldiers'.[204] In this respect, it should be remembered that the Additional Protocols were adopted in the context of an increase in civilian casualties even since the Second World War; a development which Doswald-Beck attributes to the predominance of internal conflicts and guerrilla warfare at the time.[205] While AP I created an extensive protection regime for civilians, it was the regulation of the POW status which was seemingly intended as a safeguard for the civilian population against the effects of guerrilla warfare.

An apparent merger between Hague and Geneva Law under AP I[206] may also partly explain the growing influence of the principle of distinction on the definition of POW status. Although the Hague Regulations contained both a definition of combatant status and a (rudimentary) protection regime for POWs, lawful conduct in warfare was a requirement for the former, but not the latter. It was only introduced in the regulations of POWs in 1929 and 1949.[207] AP I suggests a more complete overlap between combatant and POW status.[208] This conflation of the concepts poses difficulties since they fulfil different functions in dissimilar situations. While the regulation of combatant status concerns the conduct of hostilities, the POW system safeguards combatants *hors de combat* in the power of the enemy. This distinction was clearly drawn by Draper who emphasised that the qualification as combatant is a question of 'military nature', whereas the entitlement to POW treatment 'is a humanitarian problem'.[209] Yet the requirements for POW status in AP I blend the two. The obligation of combatants to distinguish themselves from the civilian population links a rule on the conduct of warfare, regulating the relationship between combatants and civilians, to the system of protection for war victims.

Moreover, the discourse of the group of Western states and the ICRC was likely a response to the discourse of new actors. By conceptualising combatants and formulating the status requirements in relation to the principle of distinction and civilian immunity, the delegations seemingly adhered to the Diplomatic Conference's objective to reaffirm and develop the law rather than to revise it. They embedded their argumentation in the framework of IHL, even though the requirement of the principle of distinction for combatant status can be seen as a reinterpretation. By grounding their defence of the *status quo* in the existing qualification of combatants and the new 'established' law for protecting

[204] GH Aldrich, 'Progressive Development of the Laws of War: A Reply to Criticisms of the 1977 Geneva Protocol I' (1986) 26 *Virginia Journal of International Law* 693, 704.

[205] Doswald-Beck (n 3) 149; see also D Schindler, 'International Humanitarian Law: Its Remarkable Development and Persistent Violations' (2003) 5 *Journal of the History of International Law* 165, 171–72.

[206] RJ Erickson, 'Protocol I: A Merging of the Hague and Geneva Law of Armed Conflict' (1979) 19 *Virginia Journal of International Law* 557, 592; Bothe, Partsch and Solf (n 15) 212.

[207] See chapter 4, section I.

[208] AP I, art 44(1).

[209] Bindschedler-Robert (n 5) 82–83.

civilians, discussed above, their argumentation achieved a degree of persuasiveness in the law-making process in this period. As Alexander emphasises, it also upheld the perception of international law as 'neutral – blind to causes or values or politics'.[210] In contrast, the discourse of the other group of states, considered next, was criticised as 'political' rather than legal, and thus outside of the scope of ostensibly permissible arguments for the development of international law.

B. 'Freedom Fighters' and the Principle of Self-determination

The second prevalent discourse on the combatant status at the Diplomatic Conference was mainly driven by newly independent or 'Third World' states, many of which were attending a diplomatic conference on IHL for the first time. They were supported by NLMs, which had been admitted to the event as observers, and Socialist states, which, according to Mantilla, not only sympathised with the agenda of the decolonised states, but also utilised it to embarrass the West.[211] Unlike the first discourse, which placed the interrelation between combatants and civilians at the centre, the second one focused more on legitimate participation in hostilities and the situation of combatants themselves. It sought the expansion of POW status through the relaxation or even removal of the existing criteria for individuals who would likely not qualify under the strict conditions. As Sibylle Scheipers observes, '[o]ne of the most pressing issues on the agenda of the decolonized states was protections for irregular fighters'.[212]

The characterisation of armed conflicts and individuals participating therein was central to their argumentation. The majority of experts consulted before the Diplomatic Conference deemed NLWs as being of a non-international character.[213] Yet '[a] bloc of developing countries, carrying over the voting strength and solidarity of the so-called "Group of 77" in the United Nations' demanded that NLWs would be recognised as IACs.[214] The scope *ratione materiae* of wars and IACs, as defined in Article 2 common to all 1949 Geneva Conventions, was expanded under Article 1(4) AP I to situations of 'armed conflicts in which peoples are fighting against colonial domination and alien occupation and against racist régimes in the exercise of their right of self-determination'. This made the combatant status ripe for its adaptation to

[210] A Alexander, 'Filling the Gaps: The Expansion of International Humanitarian Law and the Juridification of the Free-Fighter' (2023) 14 *Journal of International Humanitarian Legal Studies* 274, 290.

[211] Mantilla, *Lawmaking* (n 27) 137.

[212] S Scheipers, *Unlawful Combatants: A Genealogy of the Irregular Fighter* (Oxford, Oxford University Press, 2015) 185.

[213] *Additional Protocols Commentary* (n 10) para 89.

[214] RR Baxter, 'Humanitarian Law or Humanitarian Politics? – The 1974 Diplomatic Conference on Humanitarian Law' (1975) 16 *Harvard International Law Journal* 1, 11.

armed conflicts which had not been envisaged in the inter-state framework of the existing law. As a logical consequence of recognising NLWs as IACs,[215] the perceived lawfulness of combatants was due to the nature of the armed conflict as a whole.

In the deliberation of the combatant criteria, actors in this group exposed a different understanding of the principle of distinction compared to the Western states and the ICRC. Frédéric Mégret highlights the Western-centric nature of the conditions for combatant status, noting that the requirements of distinguishability were, in particular, 'unduly privileging the regular armies of the West'.[216] According to Scheipers, the Diplomatic Conference and its outcomes constituted 'a deliberate attempt at de-westernizing the law of armed conflict'.[217] Indeed, some delegations and observers rejected the newly proposed condition most vehemently and asserted that members of NLMs 'should *never* have to distinguish themselves'.[218] This position was sometimes justified as a question of fairness with regard to 'ill-armed, repressed groups, fighting against imperialist aggression'.[219] A member of the Zimbabwe African National Union, for example, declared in a passionate speech that the requirement was 'totally unrealistic' and revealed 'a failure to understand the positive nature of wars of national liberation'.[220] Other delegations considered the balance between the interests and protection of the guerrillas and civilian population to be adequately met.[221] Quach Tong Duc, a delegate of the Republic of Vietnam and lawyer, provided an exception by emphasising the importance of distinction for the protection of civilians.[222]

Underlying the dissimilar approaches were divergent perceptions of the civilian population by the regular armed forces in Western states, on the one hand, and guerrilla or resistance fighters, on the other. While the former were conscious of and sought the distance and difference between themselves and civilians, the latter 'was more likely to feel closeness and affinity; he was, perhaps literally, "one of them"'.[223] NLWs were 'premised on securing the loyalty and complicity, if not participation, of the civilian population'.[224] They were portrayed as the people's war in which the lives of combatants were 'inseparable from the

[215] *CDDH*, vol XIV (n 36) 358 and 378; *CDDH*, vol VI (n 52) 124–29, 150–51 and 183; a delegate of the Socialist Republic of Viet Nam even claimed that Article 1(4) AP I had changed the combatant status already, 153.

[216] F Mégret, 'From "Savages" to "Unlawful Combatants": A Postcolonial Look at International Humanitarian Law's "Other"' in A Orford (ed), *International Law and Its Others* (Cambridge, Cambridge University Press, 2006) 306.

[217] Scheipers (n 212) 185.

[218] Alexander, 'Postcolonialism' (n 20) 25; see also *CDDH*, vol XIV (n 36) 324, 344–45 and 531.

[219] Alexander, 'Postcolonialism' (n 20) 25; see also *CDDH*, vol XIV (n 36) 522.

[220] *CDDH*, vol XIV (n 36) 384.

[221] See, eg, *CDDH*, vol VI (n 52) 143 and 145.

[222] *CDDH*, vol XIV (n 36) 319 and 346.

[223] G Best, *War and Law Since 1945* (Oxford, Clarendon Press, 1994) 335–36.

[224] Kinsella (n 4) 136.

civilian population'.[225] In arguing for the expansion of combatant status, newly independent states repeatedly invoked their own experience of hostilities for the persuasiveness of their arguments at the Diplomatic Conference. However, Western delegations arguably failed to engage in a constructive conversation across the divide. As Lovat observes, 'delegates appeared on many occasions to be speaking past one another' having different 'assumptions regarding appropriate frames of reference within which principled arguments could be made'.[226]

Despite being novices in the negotiation of IHL treaties, the newly independent states partly employed the language of the normative framework which had emerged in a European context in form of the written laws of war. Eleanor Davey argues that '[a]nti-colonial actors sought admission to the ranks of civilization even as they contested the way those ranks had been constituted and defined in the past'.[227] By demanding the recognition of 'freedom fighters' as combatants and POWs under international law, instead of 'criminals' subject to domestic legislation,[228] they reaffirmed the significance of these concepts and their respective protection regimes. Nevertheless, some delegations lacked relevant substantive legal expertise, as admitted by a delegate of a developing country at the 1972 Conference.[229] David Forsythe, an observer to the first session of the Diplomatic Conference, recounted similar observations from the diplomatic event. He suggested that the newly independent states' approach was informed by their previous experience in political UN forums where less attention was paid to legal technicalities. According to him, their 'statements were as devoid of legal formulation as the West's tended toward legalism', trying to preserve 'traditional definitions and the traditional structure of the law'.[230] Lovat submits that, indeed, 'technical arguments mattered little to the majority of developing world delegations' believing that 'these arguments effectively served as a fig leaf for a politically driven preference to accord preferential treatment to anticolonial conflicts'.[231] Conversely, while the UNSG and UNGA strategically employed the label 'freedom fighters',[232] the US delegate and law professor Baxter rejected the

[225] *CDDH*, vol XIV (n 36) 466, see also 384; *CDDH*, vol VI (n 52) 149.

[226] Lovat (n 151) 192–93.

[227] E Davey, 'Decolonizing the Geneva Conventions: National Liberation and the Development of Humanitarian Law' in AD Moses, M Duranti and R Burke (eds), *Decolonization, Self-Determination, and the Rise of Global Human Rights Politics* (Cambridge, Cambridge University Press, 2020) 390–91.

[228] Kinsella (n 4) 134.

[229] RR Baxter, 'The Evolving Laws of Armed Conflicts' (1973) 60 *Military Law Review* 99, 103.

[230] DP Forsythe, 'The 1974 Diplomatic Conference on Humanitarian Law' (1975) 69 *AJIL* 77, 81–82.

[231] Lovat (n 151) 190–91; see also J Whyte, 'The "Dangerous Concept of the Just War": Decolonization, Wars of National Liberation, and the Additional Protocols to the Geneva Conventions' (2018) 9 *Humanity* 313, 322–23.

[232] See, eg, UN Doc A/8052; UNGA, 'Respect for Human Rights in Armed Conflicts' (1970) UN Doc A/Res/2674(XXV); UNGA, 'Respect for Human Rights in Armed Conflicts' (1971) UN Doc A/Res/2852(XXVI).

term as 'political rhetoric that passes for legal terminology in these days' at the Diplomatic Conference.[233]

However, the political environment of the UN had provided the first platform for the deliberation of NLWs and the uncertain status of guerrilla fighters after the adoption of the 1949 Geneva Conventions. Its various efforts may have provided the impetus for the objectives and claims of the newly independent states during the negotiation of the Additional Protocols.[234] For instance, the 1968 International Conference on Human Rights (Teheran Conference) declared that individuals struggling against minority racist or colonial regimes should be treated as POWs, or 'political prisoners under international law'.[235] The UNGA also called for the treatment of members of NLMs as POWs both in resolutions directly related to decolonisation and self-determination, as well as on 'human rights in armed conflicts'.[236] In 1973 it adopted a resolution specifically on the 'Basic Principles of the Legal Status of the Combatants Struggling against Colonial and Alien Domination and Racist Regimes'.[237] It promoted the recognition of such conflicts as IACs and the application of the 1949 Geneva Conventions, in particular POW status and treatment.[238] Yet Christina Murray points out that this Resolution 'was adopted without the support of many Western States'.[239] Moreover, Keith Suter argues that some UNGA resolutions on the topic 'were adopted simply to give political support to certain guerrilla movements'.[240] Overall, Kalshoven believed that the extension of POW status to members of NLMs in UNGA resolutions had not reached the status of CIL prior to the Diplomatic Conference.[241]

Emily Crawford still views the UNGA resolutions regarding colonial wars in the 1960s and 1970s as having 'directly contributed to the adoption of the Additional Protocols' and, in particular, the recognition of NLWs as IACs.[242] More generally, developments in the UN regarding the principle of self-determination contributed to 'new legal arguments, ideas and principles', which may not have been universally accepted; however, 'they were still there as an alternative and a reference point that was making it harder to simply insist on

[233] Baxter, 'Humanitarian Law' (n 214) 15; see further Alexander, 'Filling the Gaps' (n 210) 290–91.

[234] Several of the newly independent states' delegates who participated in the negotiation of the POW status at the Diplomatic Conference were notably permanent representatives of their respective states to the Office of the United Nations in Geneva.

[235] 'Final Act of the International Conference on Human Rights' (1968) UN Doc A/Conf.32/41, 18.

[236] See, eg, UNGA, 'Question of Southern Rhodesia' (1968) UN Doc A/Res/2383(XXIII); UN Doc A/Res/2674(XXV); UN Doc A/Res/2852(XXVI), para 2; see also Schindler and Toman (n 21) 695.

[237] (1973) UN Doc A/Res/3103(XXVIII).

[238] ibid paras 3–4.

[239] C Murray, 'The 1977 Geneva Protocols and Conflict in Southern Africa' (1984) 33 *ICLQ* 462, 465.

[240] Suter, *Guerrilla Warfare* (n 179) 58.

[241] Kalshoven, '1974–1977, Part I' (n 55) 133.

[242] E Crawford, 'Regulating the Irregular – International Humanitarian Law and the Question of Civilian Participation in Armed Conflicts' (2011) 18 *U.C.Davis Journal of International Law & Policy* 163, 174–75.

the traditional application of law'.[243] Both Scheipers and, in a more detailed analysis, Alexander argue that changes in the belief system post-Second World War informed and facilitated the development of the law at the Diplomatic Conference to regulate NLWs, as well as belligerents and civilians involved in and affected by such situations.[244] While the issue of irregular warfare had also been debated in earlier efforts of law-making, the ideational and normative context in which it was discussed had evolved.

Accordingly, newly independent and Socialist states argued for the inherent legitimacy of NLWs at the Diplomatic Conference, and discussed not only the expansion of IACs but also the combatant status with reference to the principle of self-determination.[245] They believed that combatants in NLWs 'should have *more* protection, not less, to assist them in their struggle for "sovereignty, political independence and freedom"'.[246] Conversely, Western delegates and commentators rejected the argumentation partly for reintroducing the just war doctrine, which they ascribed to former times.[247] For instance, the French delegate Christian Girard discarded the UN approach as unsuitable for the development of IHL since it pursued 'political solutions to specific problems of the moment' considering 'elements such as motivation, justice and legitimacy' which contradict IHL's objective to 'provide protection for all war victims at all times' without 'subjective considerations of any sort'.[248] While the Conference was ongoing, Baxter also lamented that the question of NLWs was dominating the proceedings and hindered 'hard, concentrated work on the substance of international humanitarian law'.[249] The provisions on NLWs in AP I have been criticised as 'very much a product of the decolonisation era' and 'an example of how international agreements on international humanitarian law always focus upon the last conflict rather than the next one'.[250]

The new ideational context and language may, however, obscure the resemblance to discourses of the earlier periods. The status of irregular participants in hostilities had been a subject of debate in the law-making processes since the 1874 Brussels Conference, and had not been fully resolved with the adoption of GC III, as even pointed out by the Norwegian delegate Longva, a legally trained diplomat, at the Diplomatic Conference.[251] A hundred years later, the

[243] Alexander, 'Postcolonialism' (n 20) 44.

[244] See generally ibid; Scheipers (n 212) 147.

[245] See, eg, *CDDH*, vol VI (n 52) 130; *CDDH*, vol XIV (n 36) 320 and 371; occasionally in relation to the UN Charter and the Declaration on Principles of International Law concerning Friendly Relations and Co-operation, 342.

[246] Alexander, 'Postcolonialism' (n 20) 24.

[247] See, eg, *CDDH*, vol XIV (n 36) 350 and 380; DE Graham, 'The 1974 Diplomatic Conference on the Law of War: A Victory for Political Causes and A Return to the "Just War" Concept of the Eleventh Century' (1975) 32 *Washington & Lee Law Review* 25, 55; Whyte (n 231).

[248] *CDDH*, vol VIII (n 164) 14; see also Draper, 'Humanitarian Law' (n 140) 203.

[249] Baxter, 'Humanitarian Law' (n 214) 11.

[250] Greenwood (n 51) 16.

[251] *CDDH*, vol XIV (n 36) 332.

military concerns of major military powers and states without large standing armies which rely upon civilian resistance and militia were unchanged.[252] Belgium, Norway, Finland and France still promoted a more inclusive approach to POW status, drawing on their shared history of resistance movements in their argumentation.[253] The French delegation in particular emphasised once again a state's right to self-defence against invasion pointing to the experience of occupation by (European) states.[254] Yet the inequality between small and large, or occupied and occupying European and Western states was no longer at the centre of the debate. As mentioned before, the main division was in relation to NLWs between 'the poorly armed national liberation fighters' and their adversaries who were 'equipped with all modern military resources'.[255] Certain delegations again argued that participation in hostilities for a just cause should be legitimate, or indeed lawful, irrespective of the fulfilment of the technical conditions of combatant status.[256] This inherent tension in the drafting history of earlier conventional law was conveniently overlooked in the Western states' insistence on upholding the non-political nature of the law, and thus the *status quo*.

Helen Kinsella describes the negotiation of what has become Article 44 AP I as 'one of the most contentious article debates of the diplomatic conference'.[257] As at the Brussels and Hague Peace Conferences, the scope *ratione personae* of the combatant status was once again a breaking point for the law-making process. The outcome of the 1970s Diplomatic Conference, however, differed from the earlier events. AP I partly embraces the disparity between belligerent parties whereas it was suppressed by the formal equality of belligerents in the Brussels Declaration and the Hague Regulations. Although a distinction between regular and irregular armed forces is avoided under Article 43, Article 44(3) allows for some flexibility in the requirement of distinction in 'situations in armed conflicts where, owing to the nature of the hostilities an armed combatant cannot so distinguish himself'. The obligation to carry arms openly in these situations is temporally limited to 'each military engagement' or 'military deployment preceding the launching of an attack'. Whether these types of situations entailed NLWs or occupied territories was the subject of disagreement as the explanations of votes on the provision show.[258] Nevertheless, Alexander argues that the legal concept of combatants was reshaped, namely, '[i]nstead of the traditional, jealous guarding of the privileges of combatants, the category became inclusive'.[259]

[252] Baxter, 'Evolving Laws' (n 229) 106–07.
[253] See, eg, *CDDH*, vol XIV (n 36) 322, 375 and 379; while objecting to initiatives in the UN forums to extend the combatant status to so-called 'freedom fighters', Bothe, Partsch and Solf (n 15) 279–80.
[254] *CDDH*, vol XIV (n 36) 339–40, 374–75 and 379.
[255] *CDDH*, vol VI (n 52) 146.
[256] Kalshoven, '1974–1977, Part I' (n 55) 122.
[257] Kinsella (n 4) 143.
[258] *CDDH*, vol VI (n 52) 122–39.
[259] Alexander, 'Postcolonialism' (n 20) 27.

The disagreement between Western states and advocates of a more flexible approach was also partly resolved by ensuring treatment *equivalent* to POWs for individuals who fail to fulfil the formal requirements of the status.[260] A similar practice had already been followed in South Vietnam and Algeria.[261] In light of post-1949 jurisprudence, Draper suggested 'that the circle of persons entitled to prisoner-of-war treatment be enlarged, but that the rules concerning the attribution of combatant status remain limitative'.[262] After conceptually merging the two statuses, as mentioned above, the exception in Article 44(4) AP I effectively delinks the form of protection accorded to POWs from combatant status. When losing combatant and POW status, individuals may be prosecuted for acts falling under combatant privilege in war;[263] yet the report of Committee III elaborated that 'they shall benefit from procedural and substantive protections equivalent to those accorded' to POWs under GC III and AP I.[264] The lack of clarification of the nature of such guarantees, however, had already given rise to confusion and criticism at the Diplomatic Conference itself.[265]

Article 44 as a compromise clause was approved after a prolonged debate.[266] Diverging from the standard procedure of adoption by consensus, Article 44 as a whole was adopted by vote with 73 in favour, 21 abstentions and Israel voting against, indicating the considerable disagreement among the delegations.[267] The Article's vague language permits various, indeed incongruent, interpretations of the requirements for combatant status.[268] The rapporteur of the Committee, George Aldrich, later reflected on AP I noting, for example, that with regard to 'deployment' in Article 44(3)(b), 'there was no agreement on the meaning of that term' at the Diplomatic Conference; 'the word is ambiguous, and its ambiguity was probably essential to agreement at the conference to the text'.[269] In his critique of the Additional Protocols, Christopher Greenwood describes the second sentence of the controversial Article 44(3) as 'perhaps the best example in the international humanitarian law texts of the saying that a treaty is "a disagreement reduced to writing"'.[270] The Article was still contentious in the immediate aftermath of the Diplomatic Conference. Several states abstained from ratifying AP I, including some who voiced their support for the text during the Conference, or were at least actively involved in its negotiation. Moreover,

[260] AP I, art 44(4); see also Mantilla, 'Protagonism' (n 112) 194.
[261] Hacker (n 201) 153.
[262] Bindschedler-Robert (n 5) 83.
[263] Bothe, Partsch and Solf (n 15) 289–90.
[264] *CDDH*, vol XV (n 43) 403.
[265] Kalshoven '1974–1977, Part I' (n 55) 131–32.
[266] For more detail on the drafting history see Mantilla, *Lawmaking* (n 27) ch 5.
[267] *CDDH*, vol VI (n 52) 121.
[268] *CDDH*, vol VII (n 88) 221.
[269] Aldrich, 'New Life' (n 173) 774.
[270] Greenwood (n 51) 17.

state parties submitted numerous 'reservations', 'declarations' and 'interpretative statements' regarding the meaning of Article 44.[271]

Consequently, despite the lengthy discussion over the course of three sessions with almost all states and NLMs actively participating in the negotiation, a socially constructed shared understanding of the concept of combatants arguably cannot be discerned. Unfortunately, the deliberations within the Working Group of Committee III, responsible for the drafting of the eventually adopted provision, are excluded from the official records of the Diplomatic Conference and cannot shed more light on the issue. As with civilians, the definition of combatants was believed to be essential for their regulation and protection under the laws of war. However, whereas the concept of civilians was characterised by a naturalised position in the beliefs and values of the delegations, the concept of combatants was severely contested. Instead of enshrining a common conception of combatants under AP I, the notion has perhaps become more ambiguous.

C. Combatants and Non-international Armed Conflicts

In its note on the historical background of AP II, the *Additional Protocols Commentary* emphasises as one of the shortcomings of CA3 that it placed insurgents in a precarious position without procedural safeguards and combatant immunity.[272] Although AP II considerably expanded the law of NIACs, it abstained from establishing the combatant status in such conflicts. According to Bothe, Partsch and Solf, elements of Article 43 AP I are inferred in Article 1 AP II, namely, 'that the armed force be linked to one of the parties to the conflict; that they be organized, and that they be under responsible command'.[273] Yet they also stress that members of the armed forces on neither side of the conflict benefit from a special status under AP II.[274] The deliberate non-incorporation of combatant privilege was aimed, in all likelihood, at the armed opponent of the government, rather than the regular armed forces. As the *Additional Protocols Commentary* notes, the creation of combatant status in NIACs seems 'unrealistic' since it would violate the principle of state sovereignty and states' domestic legislations criminalising insurgency.[275] The closest the treaty comes to approximating combatant immunity, according to Crawford,[276] is Article 6(5), which recommends that 'the authorities in power shall endeavour to grant the broadest possible amnesty to persons who have participated in the armed conflict'.

[271] Best (n 223) 418.
[272] *Additional Protocols Commentary* (n 10) para 4363.
[273] Bothe, Partsch and Solf (n 15) 773–74.
[274] ibid 740.
[275] *Additional Protocols Commentary* (n 10) para 4397.
[276] E Crawford, *Non-Binding Norms in International Humanitarian Law: Efficacy, Legitimacy, and Legality* (Oxford, Oxford University Press, 2021) 80.

Article 5 AP II provides guarantees for 'persons whose liberty has been restricted', without distinguishing between military or civilian persons, and without employing the terms 'prisoners' or 'detainees'.[277] The provision abstains from conferring a special status similar to POWs. A clause on perfidy proposed by the ICRC was also deleted from the treaty text, not least due to the concern of several delegations that the prohibition of certain conduct might imply the legitimacy or lawfulness of the belligerent generally.[278] The drafting history of Article 2 on the scope of application *ratione personae* of AP II similarly indicates the avoidance of implying a combatant status in NIACs. Draft Protocol II provided for its application 'without any adverse distinction, to all persons, whether military or civilian, combatant or non-combatant, affected by an armed conflict within the meaning of Article 1'.[279] While it would have thus covered everyone, including insurgents without a defined status,[280] the qualifications were removed from Article 2 of the treaty. This shows the reluctance of states to confer explicitly – or even implicitly – combatant status, with all its rights and obligations, on insurgents under AP II. The use of the language of 'combatants' by the ICRC Draft Protocol and various delegations, as well as in the *Additional Protocols Commentary* which declares that '[*r*]*atione temporis* combatants are protected as soon as they are *hors de combat*',[281] seems merely to rely on the term as a descriptor rather than a legal qualification.

Prior to the Diplomatic Conference, some actors deliberated the extension of combatant and POW status to members of NLMs while NLWs were still conceived as being of a non-international character. At its 1969 International Conference, the ICRC adopted a resolution on the 'Status of Combatants in Non-International Armed Conflicts'. Although it did not shy away from using the term 'combatant' in the context of NIACs, the resolution fell short of extending combatant and POW status to members of resistance movements. Instead, it declared that such individuals should receive 'similar' treatment to POWs subject to conforming to the traditional conditions under Article 4 GC III.[282] The ICRC submitted a comparable proposal to the 1972 Conference, emphasising that it would not amount to conferring POW status nor belligerent immunity.[283] Yet, in 1969, the ICRC also recognised the need 'to make a thorough study of the legal status of such persons' and called for action in this regard.[284] The ICRC preparatory material for the 1971 Conference considered the question of guerrilla fighters in relation to IACs, but noted at the beginning that most of

[277] *Additional Protocols Commentary* (n 10) para 4564.
[278] *CDDH*, vol XV (n 43) 214–20.
[279] Draft Protocol II, art 2.
[280] *Additional Protocols Commentary* (n 10) para 4487.
[281] ibid para 4520.
[282] ICRC, *XXIst Conference* (n 177) 100.
[283] *1972 Report* (n 29) 77.
[284] ICRC, *XXIst Conference* (n 177) 100.

its conclusions were 'also valid and necessary' for NIACs.[285] Indeed, in addition to a relaxation of the POW criteria under Article 4(A)(2) GC III relating to irregular armed forces including organised resistance movements, it proposed 'standard minimum rules' for situations where the nature of the conflict is not agreed. Importantly, it envisaged a definition of combatants in such conflicts and their treatment as POWs.[286] However, at the 1971 Conference itself, several experts opposed conferring on 'rebels' the entitlement to POW treatment, which they considered to be 'equivalent to granting rebels the privilege of a right to participate in a civil war', and advocated humane treatment in general instead.[287] In light of these diverse approaches to individuals participating in NIACs, the silence at the Diplomatic Conference was likely not unintentional or an oversight.

By the time the 'fundamental guarantees' for NIACs were discussed at the Diplomatic Conference, the ICRC delegate Danièle Bujard admitted that 'the ICRC had given up the idea of assimilating combatants who were *hors de combat* and had fallen into the hands of the adverse Party, to prisoners of war' in such conflicts.[288] Lovat notes that the ICRC was 'in a weaker position in the 1970s than in 1949 in terms of both moral and expert authority' given 'the multiplicity of voices raised with respect to "human rights in armed conflict" in UN circles since 1968' and the failure 'to establish itself sufficiently as a source of technical expertise in the eyes of developing world governments and representatives'.[289] He suggests instead that Finland and the Scandinavian countries, out of humanitarian inclination, promoted a common set of standards for both IACs and NIACs.[290] At the Diplomatic Conference, only Sweden still advocated an improved protection for participants in hostilities when captured in NIACs 'on a more equal footing with prisoners of war in international conflicts'.[291]

The failure to adopt a more comprehensive Protocol for NIACs has been inter alia attributed to the recognition of NLWs as IACs and thus their regulation under AP I. As a result, the non-Western majority of states lacked interest in advancing the rules for other armed conflicts.[292] Mantilla suggests that newly independent states experiencing internal instability, and often repressive – in parts authoritarian – regimes of sympathising states were indeed against expanding IHL into the domestic realm.[293] Bothe, Partsch and Solf also note concerns from some newly independent states that the regulation of warfare,

[285] *1971 Conference*, vol VI (n 127) 9–10.
[286] ibid 50–52.
[287] *1971 Report* (n 29) 47 and 69; see also *1972 Report* (n 29) 79.
[288] *CDDH*, vol VIII (n 164) 323, see also 332.
[289] Lovat (n 151) 189–90.
[290] ibid 170–72.
[291] *CDDH*, vol VIII (n 164) 359.
[292] Draper, 'Humanitarian Law' (n 140) 203; Greenwood (n 51) 7.
[293] Mantilla, *Lawmaking* (n 27) 137–38; see also Best (n 223) 346.

and even the protection of the civilian population, in NIACs would likely encourage rebellion.[294] Several provisions were consequently removed from the final text. It is also notable that individuals involved in insurrection movements were mentioned and considered in the discussion of combatants in IACs. Some delegations who advocated the expansion of POW status to so-called 'freedom fighters' distinguished them from 'minority movements rebelling against a lawful authority and threatening the territorial integrity of a State'.[295] The exclusion of combatant status from AP II can thus be seen as a deliberate step in response to sovereign concerns over insurrection movements.

The absence of the combatant status in AP II may be a reflection of an agreement, rather than disagreement, between the states participating at the Diplomatic Conference. The delegations collectively stayed silent on the issue in negotiating the regulation of NIACs, while they were explicit on their perception of the combatant status *de lege ferenda* in IACs, sometimes even in contradistinction to insurgents in NIACs. The concept of combatants was indirectly reconstructed as entailing lawful and legitimate participation in hostilities, and the entitlement to POW status when in the power of the enemy. It was confirmed as an element of the sovereign right to engage in war and IACs, since even NLMs were seen as belonging to a nation with the right to self-determination under international law. The privileges, obligations and protections belonging to the combatant status were thus reaffirmed for IACs to which it was limited in its scope of application *ratione materiae*. The concept was not reconstructed for the purpose of NIACs. Indeed, the position of participants in such conflicts remained ambiguous as the drafters refrained from engaging with their meaning, and failed to develop a status with privileges or obligations for them.

III. A HUMANITARIAN CONCEPTUALISATION OF INDIVIDUALS

A. The Human Person Protected by the 1977 Additional Protocols

While the concepts of civilians and combatants were strengthened and developed post-1949, a more humanitarian approach to protection emerged as well. Both Additional Protocols comprise provisions which guarantee the well-being of individuals regardless of their status under the law. These cover a variety of persons who may or may not have participated in hostilities, lawfully or unlawfully. They are not designed for a distinct category of individuals, but are based on the person's human dignity and value as human being.

Article 75 AP I stipulates a set of humanitarian standards which apply to all 'persons who are in the power of a Party to the conflict and who do not benefit

[294] Bothe, Partsch and Solf (n 15) 771.
[295] *CDDH*, vol XIV (n 36) 320, see also 499.

from more favourable treatment under the Conventions or under this Protocol'. Paragraph 8 of this provision further clarifies that any other more favourable rules applicable under conventional or customary international law more widely would also not be limited or infringed by the provision. It thus indicates a deference towards the greatest protection of individuals under international law, rather than inter-state relations.[296] During the drafting process, Article 75 was described as a 'mini-convention' similar to CA3.[297] Indeed, it has a 'unique history' since 'it was drafted only after and on the model of the corresponding articles of Protocol II – Arts. 4 to 6 – but not by the same Committee'.[298] It is thus noteworthy that the fundamental guarantees in AP I followed the humanitarian approach to regulating NIACs, whereas the general protection regime for civilians is rooted in inter-state hostilities and only adopted by analogy to NIACs.

The creation of Article 75 demonstrates the perceived need at the time to provide a safety net for individuals who do not fit within the specified categories of protected persons under the 1949 Geneva Conventions.[299] The *Additional Protocols Commentary* acknowledges, in this respect, the (technical) difficulties in applying the main protection regimes of GC III and GC IV.[300] While IHL traditionally regulated the treatment of 'many categories of persons in a certain number of clearly defined situations', armed conflicts at the time of the drafting of AP I made it necessary 'to protect without exception all the constituent elements of the population of a geographical area affected by a conflict situation'.[301] Article 75 is thus the result of the recognition that status-based protection was insufficient and even potentially detrimental to the well-being of individuals who might fall in between the gaps.

Although Article 75 is situated within Part IV on the civilian population, the title of the relevant Section III provides for the 'treatment of *persons* in the power of a Party to the conflict'.[302] According to the *Additional Protocols Commentary*, its location and Article 72 on the field of application of the section 'do not leave any room for doubt' that Article 75 pertains to civilians.[303] Nonetheless, it may protect individuals who committed hostile acts, but who do not qualify as combatants or POWs.[304] Article 75 is also believed to apply to mercenaries, even though this is not expressly provided for in the treaty

[296] cf chapter 4, section II.A.iii; see further S Landefeld, 'The Changing Significance of Nationality for the Protection of Civilians in the Hands of a Party to an International Armed Conflict' (2023) 28 *Journal of Conflict & Security Law* 501.
[297] *CDDH*, vol XV (n 43) 31.
[298] Bothe, Partsch and Solf (n 15) 513; see also *Additional Protocols Commentary* (n 10) para 3005.
[299] *CDDH*, vol XV (n 43) 25–26.
[300] *Additional Protocols Commentary* (n 10) para 1761.
[301] *CDDH*, vol XV (n 43) 9.
[302] AP I, pt IV s III (emphasis added).
[303] *Additional Protocols Commentary* (n 10) para 2909.
[304] ibid; *CDDH*, vol XV (n 43) 25; AP I, art 45(3).

text itself.[305] During the negotiations, some delegations called for an explicit reference to this effect in the provision, or declared that the absence of such would not prejudice its application.[306] Refraining from a status-based approach, Article 75 protects individuals deemed vulnerable to adverse treatment on the basis of their conduct. The provision thus requires a more individualised appraisal than is inherent in the concepts of combatants and civilians.

A related conceptualisation of individuals in IACs can be seen in the provision of humane treatment for individuals who are involved in DPH, yet who are deprived of their combatant or POW status. The guarantee of protection equivalent to POWs for such individuals under Article 44(4) AP I bears similarities to the approach to enemy civilians in the inter-war years and in GC IV.[307] However, it also shows the preference for humanitarian safeguards for all individuals in the power of a party to the conflict regardless of their legal status. At the Diplomatic Conference, the Dutch delegate and lawyer Julian Schutte emphatically argued for the non-deprivation of humanitarian treatment for individuals who lose their status as POWs, asserting their 'right to recognition of their inalienable human rights'.[308] Similarly, the additionally introduced provision for individuals whose POW status was uncertain 'was based on a concern for the protection of human beings, in whatever capacity they played a part in the conflict'.[309]

The focus on the individual human being rather than categories of persons is even more apparent in AP II. Its preamble recalls 'international instruments relating to human rights [which] offer a basic protection to the human person', as well as CA3 as constituting 'the foundation of respect for the human person' in NIACs. It thus differs from the preamble of AP I, which is framed within prevailing inter-state relations, in particular states' obligations under the UN Charter, and which only uses the traditional language of IHL calling for 'protecting the victims of armed conflicts'. In introducing the material field of application of Draft Protocol II, the ICRC delegate Bujard declared that '[t]he entire Protocol was centred on the protection of the human being'.[310]

The text of AP II itself also promotes this humanitarian approach. Article 2(1) implies the non-distinction between individuals who participate in hostilities and those who do not in stipulating the general 'personal field of application' as 'all persons affected by an armed conflict as defined in Article 1'. Part II on humane treatment is not limited in its scope of application *ratione personae*, unlike Part IV which only pertains to the civilian population. The 'fundamental

[305] *Additional Protocols Commentary* (n 10) paras 1798 and 3029–30; Bothe, Partsch and Solf (n 15) 514–15.
[306] *CDDH*, vol VI (n 52) 158–61, 175–98 and 249; *CDDH*, vol XV (n 43) 191–202.
[307] See chapter 4, section II.A.
[308] *CDDH*, vol XIV (n 36) 328.
[309] ibid 336.
[310] *CDDH*, vol VIII (n 164) 201.

guarantees' provision in Article 4 resembles CA3 in ensuring minimum protection for '[a]ll persons who do not take a direct part or who have ceased to take a part in hostilities'. The *Additional Protocols Commentary* not only describes the provision as developing and supplementing the rules in CA3 but also as containing 'inalienable and fundamental rights, inherent in the respect due to the human person'.[311] As noted above, Article 5 on 'persons whose liberty has been restricted' was also framed as a humanitarian safeguard, rather than a status-based protection regime. The underlying preconception in the negotiation of the provisions in Committee I seems to have been the entitlement of individuals to humane treatment as human beings.

Another development regarding humanitarian standards of treatment can be seen in the elimination of the distinction between military and civilian persons who are 'wounded', 'sick' or 'shipwrecked'. The definition of those terms in AP I relates to 'persons, whether military or civilian',[312] whereas AP II refers to '[a]ll the wounded, sick and shipwrecked, whether or not they have taken part in the armed conflict'.[313] The binary distinction is thus mentioned in relation to IACs, however, without a discriminating effect on the treatment and care provided. Whereas the respective protection regimes were still fragmented across the four 1949 Geneva Conventions, the Additional Protocols adopt a more egalitarian approach.

B. A Conceptual Shift in Geneva Law?

The emphasis on the protection of the human person as the rationale behind the reaffirmation and development of IHL was apparent throughout the process leading to the adoption of the Additional Protocols.[314] Even so, the concern for the individual *qua* human being cannot be seen in the newly adopted law as a whole. At the Diplomatic Conference, 'Hague Law' was structured and developed around the concepts of combatants and civilians. The above-described protection mechanisms for persons irrespective of status fall under 'Geneva Law', guaranteeing humane treatment and care for war victims in the power of a party to the conflict. The humanitarian safeguards of the Geneva Conventions had included the doctrine of non-discrimination since the first treaty in 1864. Yet they were constrained by the ideational framework of regulating belligerent relations, and thus provided protection for individuals belonging to parties to the conflict.[315] AP I and AP II dispose of this layer of conceptualising the

[311] *Additional Protocols Commentary* (n 10) para 4508.
[312] AP I, art 8(a)–(b).
[313] AP II, art 7(1).
[314] See, eg, ICRC, *XXIst Conference* (n 177) 71; *1971 Report* (n 29) 5; *CDDH*, vol VII (n 88) 281–329.
[315] See chapters 3–4.

human person in certain provisions. The construction of individuals protected by these clauses is stripped back to their bare humanity and to human dignity, thus moving away from the state-centric foundations of the laws of war. This shift from a 'sovereign dignity paradigm', concerned with the protection of state interests, to a 'human dignity paradigm' has been described as part of the 'humanisation' of IHL.[316]

'Geneva Law' may have thus partly undergone a conceptual shift. The provisions for the treatment of the wounded, sick and shipwrecked constitute a particularly illustrative example. Following decades of neglect or the deliberate exclusion of civilians from the safeguards for individuals in such vulnerable situations, GC IV indicates the professed necessity of providing protection for civilians analogous to soldiers. Yet the attempt to establish guarantees under the same instrument failed.[317] In contrast, the vulnerability and needs of the individual human being are the starting point for conceptualising wounded, sick and shipwrecked persons under the Additional Protocols. The *Additional Protocols Commentary* emphasises in this respect that 'this criterion – being in need of medical care – is the only valid one for determining whether a person is "wounded" or "sick" in the sense of the Protocol' and thus entitles civilians and combatants to identical protection.[318] Only if the person is in the power of the adverse party does the POW status establish a difference.[319] By comprising both military and civilian individuals under the same provision and protection regime, the article removes the structuring and distinguishing effect of these classifications.

The humanitarian provisions for everyone do not, however, replace, but only supplement the more detailed status-based protection regimes. Indeed, the drafters of AP I sought to expand the status of 'protected persons' under GC IV by filling gaps and resolving ambiguities. For instance, Article 73 specifically designates stateless persons and refugees as 'protected persons' under GC IV. The Office of the UN High Commissioner for Refugees resumed the advocacy on behalf of refugees that the International Refugee Organisation had pursued in the drafting of the 1949 Geneva Conventions. It advocated the expansion of their protection under GC IV[320] with the support of the ICRC.[321] Although Article 73 takes a more humanitarian and individualised approach than GC IV, it is still embedded in its framework. It does not dispose of the exclusionary category of 'protected persons', but only slightly amends the scope of application *ratione personae* of GC IV. It thus reaffirms and develops the regime rather

[316] G Le Moli, *Human Dignity in International Law* (Cambridge, Cambridge University Press, 2022) 210–11; see also T Meron, 'The Humanization of Humanitarian Law' (2000) 94 *AJIL* 239.
[317] See chapter 4, section II.
[318] *Additional Protocols Commentary* (n 10) para 304.
[319] ibid.
[320] UNGA, 'Report of the Secretary-General: Respect for Human Rights in Armed Conflicts' (1969) UN Doc A/7720, 93; *1972 Report* (n 29) 144.
[321] *CDDH*, vol XV (n 43) 13.

than replacing it with more humanitarian standards. Since AP I was created as a supplementary instrument, and not a stand-alone treaty, it is explicitly bound by the existing normative framework. The specialised regulations and safeguards for specific categories of persons under the 1949 Geneva Conventions still constitute the primary system of protection.

Nevertheless, by adding supplementary safeguards, the purpose of the law is reconceptualised. Instead of regulating clearly defined situations in IACs and NIACs from which various individuals are excluded into the grey zone of silence or unwritten IHL, it is accepted that every individual might be affected. For the most part, individuals are perceived as either combatants or civilians subject to distinct codes of conduct and protection regimes. However, when this dichotomy breaks down or is inapplicable, the individual is still protected as a human being under the Additional Protocols. More importantly, IHL is recognised as part of a wider system of international law with the objective of ensuring the well-being of the individual human person.

C. The Influence of Human Rights

By this time, the ideational and normative context of the law-making process had changed since the period of the early written laws of war. Draper observed that in the Hague Regulations the 'position of the individual … was still that of an object of the Law and not that of a legal *persona* endowed with rights under the Law of Nations'.[322] Writing in the early 1970s, he noted that it was subject to debate whether individuals had by then acquired legal rights under IHL.[323] Some scholars believe that the (direct) endowment of rights on individuals can also be found in earlier treaties on the laws of war,[324] and the 1949 Geneva Conventions themselves provide for the non-renunciation of rights by protected persons.[325] Regardless of whether individuals were already recognised as subjects of international law in these earlier treaties, the post-1949 period saw an increase in attention on the protection of human beings. The emerging movement promoting IHRL after the Second World War listed and defined 'those fundamental human rights which ought to be accorded to all by reason of the dignity and worth of all human beings'.[326] This changing position of the human person

[322] GIAD Draper, 'Human Rights and the Law of War' (1972) 1 *Virginia Journal of International Law* 326, 328.

[323] ibid 328–29.

[324] A Peters, *Beyond Human Rights: The Legal Status of the Individual in International Law* (Cambridge, Cambridge University Press, 2016) 195–99; L Hill-Cawthorne, 'Rights under International Humanitarian Law' (2017) 28 *EJIL* 1187, 1196–200; *cf* R Provost, *International Human Rights and Humanitarian Law* (Cambridge, Cambridge University Press, 2002) 27–32; K Parlett, *The Individual in the International Legal System: Continuity and Change in International Law* (Cambridge, Cambridge University Press, 2011) 178–89.

[325] See, eg, GC III, art 7; GC IV, art 8.

[326] Draper, 'Law of War' (n 322) 336.

was also remarked upon at the Diplomatic Conference.[327] The humanitarian provisions in the Additional Protocols suggest that individuals were gradually placed at the centre of the regulations as human beings. The following analysis examines whether this development may have been influenced by human rights.

It is a common belief that IHL and IHRL developed as two separate fields which were linked at the 1968 Teheran Conference, adopting a resolution entitled 'Human Rights in Armed Conflicts',[328] and by the UN's subsequent work on the issue. Only once IHL was thus brought into correlation with human rights did the UN accord it the necessary attention.[329] The UNGA framed its concern therein as part of the UN's 'faith in the dignity and worth of the human person' and its objective to achieve 'international co-operation in solving international problems of a humanitarian character and the promotion of respect for human rights'.[330] It adopted a series of resolutions under the title 'Respect for Human Rights in Armed Conflicts'.[331] However, the influence of human rights on IHL was at first promoted outside the UN. Seán MacBride, Secretary-General of the International Commission of Jurists, chaired a Human Rights Conference for non-governmental organisations in 1968 and successfully lobbied for the inclusion of 'human rights in armed conflict' on the agenda of the subsequent Teheran Conference.[332] In 1970, he published a memorandum which was intended to 'draw attention to the important nexus which exists between some of the Humanitarian Conventions, and some of the Human Rights Conventions and to urge that both codes should be brought into conformity with each other and reinforced'.[333]

Nevertheless, a close reading of the UN documents shows that human rights may have only played a minor role in the conceptualisation of individuals for the development of IHL. Firstly, the 1968 Teheran Resolution itself only mentions the term 'human rights' in its title and twice in the preambular paragraphs, but not in the operative body. UNGA Resolution 2444(XXIII) also employs the term only in reference to the title of the Teheran Resolution. Suter, tracing 'the development of the phrase "human rights in armed conflicts"',[334] argues that it

[327] *CDDH*, vol VII (n 88) 291; *CDDH*, vol VIII (n 164) 220.

[328] *Additional Protocols Commentary* (n 10) para 4371; Alexander, 'Short History' (n 1) 119; *cf* K Fortin, 'Complementarity between the ICRC and the United Nations and International Humanitarian Law and International Human Rights Law, 1948–1968' (2012) 94:888 *IRRC* 1433.

[329] D Schindler, 'L'évolution du droit de la guerre des Conventions de la Haye aux Protocoles Additionnels aux Conventions de Genève' (1982) 21 *Military Law and the Law of War Review* 23, 29.

[330] UNGA, 'Respect for Human Rights in Armed Conflicts' (1970) UN Doc A/RES/2676(XXV), Preamble.

[331] UN Doc A/Res/2444(XXIII), A/RES/2674(XXV), A/Res/2852(XXVI).

[332] Alexander, 'Short History' (n 1) 118–19.

[333] S MacBride, 'Human Rights in Armed Conflicts' (1970) 9 *Military Law and the Law of War Review* 373, 380.

[334] KD Suter, 'An Enquiry into the Meaning of the Phrase "Human Rights in Armed Conflicts"' (1976) 15 *Military Law and the Law of War Review* 393, 395.

involves 'clumsy wording' born out of political motivations without taking into account its legal implications.[335] He notes the absence of an explanation of it in the UNGA Resolutions and deliberations, and even MacBride, 'the person most responsible for the phrase's popularity', failed to establish its meaning, yet seemed to broadly equate it with 'the humanitarian international law of armed conflicts'.[336] Mantilla suggests that '[a]lthough he was a lawyer, MacBride was not encumbered by the legal subtleties and doctrinal differences between' international humanitarian, human rights and criminal law.[337]

The Teheran Resolution itself does not refer to IHRL instruments, 'except for the obligatory passing reference' to the non-binding Universal Declaration of Human Rights (UDHR), while it pays attention to 'nearly all the components' of IHL.[338] Upon the UNGA's invitation, the UNSG published a preliminary report in 1969 which acknowledged that the development of the law should be founded on the existing IHL conventions, and called for the reaffirmation of their validity and their better application.[339] The UNGA itself consistently called for better protection of civilians, and combatants or 'freedom fighters'.[340] Consequently, it is notable that these various instruments endorsed the traditional framework of IHL rather than the rights of individual human beings. Suter criticises this approach arguing that the UN, unlike the ICRC, would not have been wed to the 1949 Geneva Conventions; even so, it refrained from 'any radical change to the framework of the law of armed conflicts'.[341]

For its 1970 Report, the UNSG consulted the ICRC and experts in the field, including international lawyers who had participated in other efforts aimed at developing IHL.[342] It went further than the 1969 Report, advocating that civilians who may participate in NLWs should enjoy rights under UN human rights instruments, the Hague Regulations, GC IV and CA3,[343] without specifying which 'rights' in the laws of war it was referring to. It also included in its annex extracts of a report by the UN Commission on Human Rights which proposed the study of 'a set of standard minimum rules for the protection of human rights in armed conflicts'.[344] More generally, it promoted the application of IHRL to ensure minimum standards of treatment for civilians and detainees.

Nevertheless, at a more conceptual level, neither report engaged with the fundamentally dissimilar nature of human rights and the traditional laws of war. Scholars emphasise as a crucial difference the relationship that is governed

[335] ibid 421.
[336] ibid 397.
[337] Mantilla, *Lawmaking* (n 27) 120.
[338] Suter, 'An Enquiry' (n 334) 422.
[339] UN Doc A/7720, 39.
[340] See, eg, UN Doc A/Res/2444(XXIII), A/RES/2674(XXV), A/RES/2676(XXV).
[341] Suter, *Guerrilla Warfare* (n 179) 59–60.
[342] UN Doc A/8052, 8.
[343] ibid 73–74.
[344] ibid 115.

by the respective laws, namely, that between the government and its citizens or individuals in its jurisdiction, compared to the hostile relations between states.[345] The 1969 UNSG Report compared the 1949 Geneva Conventions with human rights instruments. While it noted certain similarities in specific provisions, the comparison was pursued on the basis of substantive rules rather than in relation to the conceptualisation of individuals, or the duty bearers of the obligations. Even the outline of categories of individuals qualifying for GC III and GC IV protection was only descriptive, without regard to the conceptual underpinnings.[346] In the subsequent report in 1970, the UNSG remarked upon the difference in the scope of application *ratione personae* between the International Covenant on Civil and Political Rights and the conventional laws of war. The report identified only Part II GC IV, which applies to the whole population without any adverse distinction, as being comparable to the International Covenant.[347] Ultimately, however, the UNSG Report again called for the application and improvement of IHL along its traditional lines and advocated the expansion of the concepts of combatants and civilians. It mentioned that all individuals should be treated humanely, but the humanitarian treatment was perceived as embedded in the protections for combatants and civilians. The existing classifications were not challenged and the individual was not reconceptualised in accordance with IHRL.

The ICRC's efforts to develop the law were initially conducted separately from the field of IHRL. Indeed, at the 1957 International Conference of the Red Cross, the erroneous translation from French to English of the Commission for International Humanitarian Law as 'Human Rights Commission' was forcefully rejected by the chairman and president of the ICRC at the time, Leopold Boissier. He declared that the ICRC 'has never made any pronouncement concerning the rights of man; that is a matter for the national legislation of States and, to a certain extent, for the United Nations, but is of no concern to us for the present'.[348] Even so, the ICRC seems to have been encouraged by the Teheran Conference to further pursue the reaffirmation and development of IHL.[349] In a resolution adopted in 1969, it emphasised 'the necessity and urgency' to reaffirm and develop IHL 'in order to strengthen the effective protection of the fundamental rights of human beings, in keeping with the Geneva Conventions of 1949'.[350] Considering the relationship between the two fields of law in preparation of the Additional Protocols, however, the ICRC pointed out that IHRL was not designed (for the most part) with armed conflict situations in mind. It believed that IHL would 'contribute to the protection of the

[345] See, eg, Suter, 'An Enquiry' (n 334) 402; Draper, 'Humanitarian Law' (n 140) 204.
[346] UN Doc A/7720, 29–36.
[347] UN Doc A/8052, 13 and 101–02.
[348] ICRC, *XIXth Conference* (n 177) 24.
[349] ICRC, *XXIst Conference* (n 177) 71.
[350] ibid 98.

fundamental right of the human person' in times of armed conflicts instead.[351] Bothe, Partsch and Solf argue that the ICRC and UN divided the labour between themselves, the former 'taking on the task of drafting concrete proposals', while the latter 'submitted a series of reports which shed further light on the issues'.[352] It is, therefore, not surprising that the conceptualisation of individuals in armed conflicts was somewhat constrained by the existing ideational framework in which the ICRC was deeply immersed. The main objective of the Diplomatic Conference seems to have been the reaffirmation and development of the established notions, structures and rules of the laws of war with only supplementary humanitarian provisions.

Parallel to these developments, the International Institute of Humanitarian Law, founded in 1970, focused its first Congress on 'Human Rights as the Basis for International Humanitarian Law'.[353] Yet this meeting of experts also failed to extensively discuss and resolve the relationship between these two areas of law and their conceptual discrepancies. Some participants, including Paul de Lapradelle and Adolfo Maresca, who had been delegates at the 1949 Diplomatic Conference, even criticised the chosen title highlighting the continued differences between the legal regimes.[354] Jovica Patrnogic, who was involved in various post-1949 efforts and later attended the 1970s Diplomatic Conference, noted the increasingly central status of the human person for IHL, but also acknowledged the different intentions and foundations of the legal systems.[355] Others believed that, while not yet its basis at the time, human rights might inform the development of IHL in the future when new conventions might guarantee human rights for all respecting their humanity and dignity.[356] This may be seen in some of the Additional Protocols' new humanitarian provisions which apply irrespective of the individual's status.

The Teheran Conference and the subsequent UN work on 'human rights in armed conflicts' may have been necessary to focus the international community's attention and gather its support around the reaffirmation and development of IHL.[357] Moreover, they brought IHL into closer proximity with a changing ideational framework. References to human rights and the concern for the vulnerable individual human being were more prevalent at the 1970s Diplomatic Conference than in the immediate aftermath of the Second World War. In its opening session, the UN representative Vittorio Winspeare Guicciardi declared that the UN and ICRC efforts were informed by 'the same ideal: a mutual belief

[351] *1971 Conference*, vol I (n 179) 30.
[352] Bothe, Partsch and Solf (n 15) 3.
[353] *Proceedings of the International Conference on Humanitarian Law, Sanremo 24/27.IX.1970* (Lugano-Bellinzona, Grassi Istituto Editoriale Ticinese, 1970).
[354] ibid 133–35 and 196–98.
[355] ibid 156–66.
[356] ibid 66–72.
[357] Meron (n 316) 247.

in human dignity'.[358] Yet whereas he saw the abolished distinction between IACs and NIACs in the UNGA resolutions as reaffirming 'the existence and primacy of the inalienable rights of the human person by dissociating them from political, military or other considerations',[359] the Diplomatic Conference adopted two separate protocols. Indeed, the human rights approach was not shared by all delegations. Several newly independent states seemed to rely on the UN Charter's preamble, reproduced in the preamble of the UDHR, when invoking fundamental or basic human rights and the dignity and value of the human person at the plenary level.[360] Western delegations, on the other hand, were less prone to using a human rights discourse and instead argued within the more traditional IHL framework. This may have been due to their long-standing involvement in the written laws of war before IHRL emerged and gained traction after the Second World War.

Nevertheless, the more general shift at the Diplomatic Conference from military necessity to humanitarian concerns has been attributed to human rights.[361] IHRL may have influenced the changing perception of the role and power of international law compared to the previous periods. It was no longer regarded as only regulating inter-state relations; instead, it acquired a more protective function for individuals. This can *inter alia* be seen in the changing terminology from laws of war to IHL, 'which owes its inspiration to a feeling for humanity and which is centred on the protection of the individual'.[362] Draper believed that it showed a human rights approach to the revision of the laws of war[363] and argued that 'the humanitarian law of armed conflict has been the portal through which the human-rights regimes have been admitted' into the laws of war.[364] He and other IHL scholars viewed the blurring and confusion of the two distinct, and to some extent incompatible, legal regimes critically.[365] Yet IHL found its way into the title of the Diplomatic Conference, although the ICRC first recorded the endeavour as 'Reaffirmation and Development of the Laws and Customs applicable in Armed Conflicts' even in the resolution underlying the formal law-making process.[366] According to Alexander, '[c]ommentators and states, therefore, considered the Additional Protocols to be the framework and embodiment of a new approach to the *ius in bello* – international humanitarian law'.[367]

[358] *CDDH*, vol V (n 164) 11.
[359] ibid 10.
[360] See, eg, ibid 359; *CDDH*, vol VII (n 88) 83, 218, 244 and 301.
[361] Alexander, 'Short History' (n 1) 126.
[362] J Pictet, 'The Principles of International Humanitarian Law' (1966) 6:66 *IRRC* 455, 455.
[363] Draper, 'Law of War' (n 322) 339–40.
[364] Draper, 'Humanitarian Law' (n 140) 195.
[365] ibid 206; see also, eg, Schindler, 'International Humanitarian Law' (n 205) 696.
[366] ICRC, *XXIst Conference* (n 177) 5 and 98.
[367] Alexander, 'Short History' (n 1) 126.

Placing the well-being of the individual into the foreground may have motivated the elimination of certain *lacunae* in the existing protection regimes. In particular, unlike the traditional laws of war, the new understanding of international law enabled the protection of states' own nationals by international rules and regulations. Whereas such alleged interference into domestic affairs had been forcefully rejected before, AP I provides for certain guarantees for all individuals regardless of their nationality.[368] The Austrian delegation welcomed the adoption of Article 75, for example, as a safeguard of 'the absolute minimum of rights that a human being should have in all circumstances in relation to whatever Party, including the Party of which such persons are nationals'.[369] Continuing their opposition from the 1949 Diplomatic Conference, the delegations of Australia, Canada, the UK and the US still regarded the relationship between individuals and the state to whom they belong as the *domaine réservé* of sovereign states.[370] Indeed, the Canadian delegate John Wolfe stressed that the state's jurisdiction over domestic matters should be respected and that '[t]he purpose of the Conference was not to draft a Convention on Human Rights'.[371] Nonetheless, Article 75 stands out as being discussed and adopted within a human rights discourse. It was believed to set out human rights for situations of armed conflicts.[372]

The development of the rules on NIACs was also strategically framed within the normative context of IHRL which regulates the relationship between states and their nationals. As mentioned above, the concern for state sovereignty resulted in an abridged convention for NIACs and the absence of the concept of combatants therein. The German delegate, international law professor and human rights advocate Partsch held against this that the international legal order had changed and that '[o]ne of the most important limitations on State sovereignty was respect for human rights'.[373] The influential Egyptian delegate and international law professor Georges Abi-Saab argued that 'a human-rights approach rather than one of the law of war' would be strategically advisable for developing the law of NIACs. He believed that this would be more acceptable in light of newly independent states' opposition to the 'projection into the internal sphere of the legal regulations developed for international armed conflicts'.[374] It was already emphasised during the 1971 Conference that CA3 did not constitute a contractual agreement between parties to the conflict but instead comprised '*individual* rights' which were 'in the interest of the intended

[368] AP I, pt IV s III; *Additional Protocols Commentary* (n 10) para 2915; Bothe, Partsch and Solf (n 15) 444–45; see also Landefeld (n 296).

[369] *CDDH*, vol VI (n 52) 264.

[370] *CDDH*, vol XV (n 43) 35–36, 40–42 and 49.

[371] ibid 49.

[372] See, eg, *CDDH*, vol VI (n 52) 264–65; *CDDH*, vol XV (n 43) 28–29 and 41; Doswald-Beck (n 3) 163.

[373] *CDDH*, vol VIII (n 164) 220.

[374] ibid 234.

beneficiaries'.[375] It was believed that the additional protocol should also draw on IHRL and not only 'Geneva Law'.[376] During the negotiation process at the Diplomatic Conference, Draft Protocol II was described as falling generally within the context of human rights.[377] The development of the law governing NIACs was thus part of 'a growing awareness that even the archetypal "internal affair" of the State, viz., the treatment of its own subjects, may under certain conditions become a legitimate concern of the international community'.[378]

Indeed, the changing perception of the purpose of the law and the strengthening of humanitarian protection for the individual may have also been related to a shift in the value system of the international community more generally. In the concluding observations of the 1970 Report, the UNSG remarked that the normative context of the law-making process had changed compared to the adoption of the 1899 and 1907 Hague Regulations. Seven decades later, these treaties as well as the Geneva Conventions co-existed with 'a system of concrete and detailed norms of positive international law' consisting of various IHRL treaties, and the 'principles of the law of nations to which the Martens clause referred' had been developed and expanded by state practice and jurisprudence.[379] The text of AP I itself suggests the recognition of the simultaneous application of its provisions and IHRL,[380] thus seemingly overcoming the traditional distinction between the laws of war and laws of peace. More importantly, it incorporates the humanitarian safeguards specifically designed for situations of armed conflicts into a larger normative framework with the objective to protect individual human beings.

IV. CONCLUSION

During this period, IHL evolved from a system that primarily regulates the relationship between states to one that also governs the relationship between states and individuals. The interests and well-being of individuals, and not only states, were thus increasingly taken into consideration. More importantly, the reaffirmation and development of the law in the Additional Protocols has arguably been characterised by a two-tier evolution. Humanitarian considerations underlying IHL in a changing ideational context shaped the concepts of combatants and civilians but also informed, to a lesser extent, the protection of human beings in the post-1949 period. The regulations primarily (re)produced and strengthened

[375] *1971 Report* (n 29) 45.
[376] ibid.
[377] See, eg, *CDDH*, vol VIII (n 164) 223 and 232–33.
[378] Kalshoven, '1974–1977, Part I' (n 55) 109.
[379] UN Doc A/8052, 111–12.
[380] See, eg, AP I, art 72.

the distinction between combatants and civilians. Even in relation to NIACs, both concepts were reaffirmed in their importance; the concept of combatants by being reserved as a fundamental status with distinct privileges and obligations in IACs. The evolution of both concepts was partly influenced by the principle of distinction which had achieved an essential position in the discourse and the perception of the objective of the law itself. Nevertheless, although the concepts were formulated in AP I as operating in an interplay, they did not evolve in unison. They developed separately in processes which were driven by diverse actors in dissimilar contexts and forums, and at different moments in time.

The construction of the concept of civilians was realised independently of the combatant status, indeed, prior to the negotiation of the latter's reformulation. The law mainly advanced to shield the civilian population from the consequences of hostilities since this area of law was perceived as in the greatest need of improvement. While critical *lacunae* were thus filled, the Diplomatic Conference did not overcome the disparate system of protection regarding civilians once they have fallen into the hands of a party to the conflict. The exclusionary GC IV regime for 'protected persons' was expanded, yet not to the extent that it would comprise all civilians as defined in Article 50 AP I. Instead, minimum guarantees for all human beings affected by IACs and NIACs had to be established. Nonetheless, the concept of civilians was systematised and institutionalised in the Additional Protocols by building upon progress achieved prior to the meeting of state representatives, and the *belief* in existing law. Not the meaning of 'civilians', but rather the technicalities of the forms of protection were negotiated at the diplomatic event. Indeed, the concept itself appears to have been rooted in the seemingly hegemonic belief that innocent and vulnerable civilians should be protected from direct attack, without the personal scope of the civilian status being settled. The Additional Protocols seem to codify a concept that may have existed in CIL before, or that, at least as a social construct, derived from vague intersubjective understandings of various actors in diverse forums.

This raises questions about the possibility of socially constructing a concept at a law-making assembly of states. The social process of construction need not begin at the inter-state level, but may be driven by norm entrepreneurs and epistemic communities, as can be seen in the transformation of the social construct of civilians into a legal concept. However, translating a vague social, or possibly even customary norm into conventional law proved to be difficult. The nuances of the complex, and in parts conflicting understandings are lost in the definition of civilians in AP I, which obscures the disagreement among the actors. Furthermore, efforts to rally support and agreement between states around a concept may also politicise an issue and move it away from the presumed objectivity of the law, as may have been the case with the concept of combatants in UN forums. In this regard, the Diplomatic Conference shows that an agreement between *states* is necessary, at least regarding the minimum outlines of a concept, in order to create or change it in treaty provisions. The Conference was not only 'an unwieldy gathering, consisting of around 700 delegates',[381] it was also a 'highly politicised, contentious and drawn out' process.[382] It is debatable whether AP I as the outcome of this process indeed developed a shared understanding of the concept of combatants among states, or instead made it more ambiguous.

The second important evolution was the shift towards a more humanitarian approach to protecting individuals who do not benefit from the established regimes. The drafters of the Additional Protocols recognised the limits of status-based protection regimes and, consequently, provided humanitarian guarantees for everyone affected by armed conflicts. Thus, a third fundamental conceptualisation of individuals seems to take shape in IHL besides combatants and civilians, namely the human person. The framing of the development of IHL under the phrase 'human rights in armed conflicts' does not seem to have led to a significant reconceptualisation of individuals generally. Yet the changing attitude in the international community which increasingly placed individuals at the centre of international law, and advances in IHRL which protects everyone by virtue of being human – even against their own government – probably facilitated the quintessentially humanitarian safeguards in the Additional Protocols. Ultimately, however, this 'humanisation' of IHL does not extend to the law as a whole. Instead, IHL continues to rely on the structural difference between IACs and NIACs, and strengthens the conceptual distinction between combatants and civilians. The principle of distinction itself appears to have achieved a fundamental position in the newly developed IHL.

[381] Alexander, 'Short History' (n 1) 124.
[382] Alexander, 'Postcolonialism' (n 20) 18.

6

The Post-1977 Era

OVER THE PAST three decades concerns have arisen over the applicability of international humanitarian law (IHL) to 'twenty-first century' warfare and 'contemporary challenges' in armed conflicts.[1] This language implies a break with the 'old wars' and injects urgency into addressing the seemingly changing nature of warfare especially since the end of the Cold War. Yet, notwithstanding apparent new challenges or unforeseen dimensions of old phenomena, no comprehensive attempt to reaffirm and develop the conventional law has been pursued since the adoption of the Additional Protocols to the 1949 Geneva Conventions in 1977. Various specialised treaties have been adopted in the meantime, each focusing on particular issues such as certain types of weapons.[2] Moreover, progress has been pursued through channels other than formal diplomatic conferences between states,[3] including customary international humanitarian law (CIHL), international criminal jurisprudence, and 'soft law', comprising 'non-legally binding but normatively worded instruments'.[4] States, on the other hand, have generally remained noticeably and significantly silent and inactive. This chapter examines whether the developments in IHL in the post-1977 years have extended to the legal construction of individuals in

[1] See, eg, D Wippman and M Evangelista (eds), *New Wars, New Laws? Applying Laws of War in 21st Century Conflicts* (Leiden, Brill, 2005); MN Schmitt, '21st Century Conflict: Can the Law Survive' (2007) 8 *Melbourne Journal of International Law* 443; K Watkin, '21st Century Conflict and International Humanitarian Law: Status Quo or Change?' in MN Schmitt and J Pejic (eds), *International Law and Armed Conflict: Exploring the Faultlines – Essays in Honour of Yoram Dinstein* (Leiden, Martinus Nijhoff, 2007); C Harvey, J Summers and ND White (eds), *Contemporary Challenges to the Laws of War: Essays in Honour of Professor Peter Rowe* (Cambridge, Cambridge University Press, 2014); International Law Association Study Group, 'The Conduct of Hostilities and International Humanitarian Law: Challenges of 21st Century Warfare' (2017) 93 *International Law Studies* 322.

[2] See, eg, Protocol on Prohibitions or Restrictions on the Use of Incendiary Weapons (Geneva, 10 October 1980) (CCW Protocol III); Protocol on Prohibitions or Restrictions on the Use of Mines, Booby-Traps and Other Devices as amended on 3 May 1996 (Geneva, 3 May 1996) (CCW Amended Protocol II); Convention on the Prohibition of the Use, Stockpiling, Production and Transfer of Anti-Personnel Mines and on their Destruction (Oslo, 18 September 1997) (Ottawa Convention).

[3] See, eg, H Krieger and J Püschmann (eds), *Law-Making and Legitimacy in International Humanitarian Law* (Cheltenham, Elgar, 2021); G Mantilla, 'From Treaty to Custom: Shifting Paths in the Recent Development of International Humanitarian Law' (2024) 37 *LJIL* 359.

[4] A Boyle, 'Soft Law in International Law-Making' in MD Evans (ed), *International Law*, 5th edn (Oxford, Oxford University Press, 2018) 121.

armed conflicts. It argues that the legal framework for combatants and civilians appears to remain static despite the ongoing struggle over the conceptualisation of individuals within and outside of the law.

Section I provides a brief overview of the main processes shaping IHL in this period. These diverge from earlier developments, and their analysis thus requires a different approach than that adopted in chapters three to five. In the absence of a principal diplomatic conference which denotes the overarching progress in the law, the influence of efforts by states and non-state actors prior to a formal law-making event cannot be traced. Nor can the proceedings be analysed in any great detail. However, it is not only the absence of a diplomatic conference and the inaction of states which may have stalled the evolution of the concepts of 'combatants' and 'civilians'. The relevant discourses seem to have been characterised by a reaffirmation of the law, and thus stability rather than change. Consequently, the second part of this chapter shows that the legal framework for combatants and civilians may have reached its pinnacle in 1977, especially in the text of the Protocol Additional to the Geneva Conventions of 12 August 1949, and relating to the Protection of Victims of International Armed Conflicts[5] (AP I). At the same time, the meaning and scope of the concepts remain contested, possibly even more so than before.

Section III examines certain ambiguities and *lacunae* in the legal framework which may have provided opportunities and space for further developments in conceptualising individuals for the purpose of IHL. It addresses shortcomings of the law which have been highlighted in the previous chapters, namely the exclusionary nature of the civilian 'protected person' status under the Geneva Convention Relative to the Protection of Civilian Persons in Time of War[6] (GC IV) and the uncertainty regarding the status of individuals in non-international armed conflicts (NIACs). Moreover, it engages with contemporary debates about different participants in armed conflicts that are associated with the so-called 'civilianisation' of warfare, such as 'civilian contractors working with the military, or terrorists, or certain part-time participants in a civil war'.[7] Yet this chapter emphasises that the terms of the existing law have been reiterated in the midst of discourses on the changing nature of warfare. As a result, the legal concepts of combatants and civilians have not been significantly modified. Section IV then considers how individuals continue to be constructed not only in legal terms but also as social understandings in these processes.

[5] (Geneva, 8 June 1977).

[6] (Geneva, 12 August 1949).

[7] A Roberts, 'The Civilian in Modern War' (2009) 12 *YIHL* 13, 20; see also A Wenger and SJA Mason, 'The Civilianization of Armed Conflict: Trends and Implications' (2008) 90:872 *IRRC* 835; C Garraway, 'Changing Character of the Participants in War: Civilianization of Warfighting and the Concept of "Direct Participation in Hostilities"' (2011) 87 *International Law Studies* 177.

I. POST-1977 PROCESSES DEVELOPING INTERNATIONAL HUMANITARIAN LAW

Shortly after the adoption of the 1977 Additional Protocols, it was suggested that they 'will purport to regulate the conduct of international conflicts until the twenty-first century'.[8] Indeed, the conventional law on war and international armed conflicts (IACs) used to be updated in relatively regular intervals of approximately 25 to 30 years. Nevertheless, no attempt at a revision has been made during the first quarter of the twenty-first century, and seems unlikely in the future. The Additional Protocols have been identified as being 'still at the core of international humanitarian law today', both by binding state parties to the instruments and through some of its provisions being reflected in CIHL.[9] Although various aspects of the law may appear in need of clarification and adaptation to contemporary warfare, several scholars have cautioned against a reopening of the conventions in light of the possibility of undermining the legitimacy of the existing law and the risk of regression in humanitarian standards.[10] Especially the increasing number of actors possibly involved in such a process would pose difficulties, as was already seen in the drafting of the Additional Protocols compared to the 1949 Geneva Conventions.[11] According to Yves Sandoz, the time for developing IHL at global conferences may have come to an end and, instead, 'possible progress in this field must be achieved step by step, through dialog, expert meetings and doctrinal works, in order to clarify different subject matters and to create a better understanding'.[12]

The International Committee of the Red Cross (ICRC) functioned as a norm entrepreneur in the past by influencing the evolution of IHL.[13] As its guardian and promoter, it was entrusted with the mandate to prepare a report on CIHL applicable in international and non-international armed conflicts by

[8] K Suter, *An International Law of Guerrilla Warfare – The Global Politics of Law-Making* (London, Frances Pinter, 1984) 158.

[9] Y Sandoz, 'Preface to the New Edition of "New Rules for Victims of Armed Conflicts"' in M Bothe, KJ Partsch and WA Solf, *New Rules for Victims of Armed Conflicts: Commentary on the Two 1977 Protocols Additional to the Geneva Conventions of 1949*, 2nd edn (Leiden, Martinus Nijhoff, 2013) xx–xxi.

[10] See, eg, ibid xxii; F Bugnion, 'The International Committee of the Red Cross and the Development of International Humanitarian Law' (2004) 5 *Chicago Journal of International Law* 191, 211–12; M MacLaren and F Schwendimann, 'An Exercise in the Development of International Law: The New ICRC Study on Customary International Humanitarian Law' (2005) 6 *German Law Journal* 1217, 1222.

[11] E Crawford, *Identifying the Enemy: Civilian Participation in Armed Conflict* (Oxford, Oxford University Press, 2015) 208–10.

[12] Sandoz (n 9) xxiii; this appears to reflect a more general trend of stagnation in multi-lateral treaty-making in international law, which is turning to 'informal international lawmaking' instead, J Pauwelyn, R Wessel and J Wouters (eds), *Informal International Lawmaking* (Oxford, Oxford University Press, 2012).

[13] See chapters 3–5; see also Bugnion (n 10).

the 1995 International Conference of the Red Cross and Red Crescent.[14] This *ICRC Study* was, in particular, intended to address 'the uneven ratification record of humanitarian law treaties and the rudimentary nature of treaty law governing [NIACs]' and to examine whether 'gaps in treaty law were filled by customary international law'.[15] The ICRC itself cannot create law, especially CIHL constituted by state practice and *opinio juris*, and was thus limited to the identification of customary rules. Jakob Kellenberger, the then President of the ICRC, described the *Study* in his foreword as an attempt 'to capture the clearest possible "photograph" of customary international humanitarian law as it stands today'.[16] Since its publication, the *Study* has been 'increasingly seen as a highly authoritative instrument'.[17] Given the distance in time between the adoption of the 1977 Additional Protocols and the preparation of the *Study*, certain developments in the law seem to have occurred, especially with regard to NIACs. However, since the *Study* was undertaken to resolve the problem of the non-universality of the Additional Protocols, '[i]t is, subject to a few nuances, inspired by the content of the two Protocols, or more precisely Protocol I'.[18] As a result, general concepts and principles of IHL are reaffirmed rather than developed through CIHL. Furthermore, in 2011, the ICRC concluded after an internal study on 'strengthening legal protection for victims of armed conflicts' that the current legal framework was appropriate.[19] The Committee itself and several other actors who share this belief have, therefore, prioritised the clarification and enforcement of the law rather than its further development.[20]

It has been suggested that, given the difficulties of international treaty-making today, 'international tribunals will in the future fulfil, inconspicuously but efficiently, a large part of the task of developing international law'.[21] In his study on the formative role of international judicial bodies, Shane Darcy argues that the traditional doctrine of international law sources, which considers jurisprudence as subsidiary means of determining international law, 'understates

[14] J-M Henckaerts and L Doswald-Beck, *Customary International Humanitarian Law, Volume I: Rules* (Cambridge, Cambridge University Press, 2009) (hereafter *CIHL*, vol I) xxxiii.

[15] J-M Henckaerts, 'The International Committee of the Red Cross and Customary International Humanitarian Law' in R Geiß, A Zimmermann and S Haumer (eds), *Humanizing the Laws of War: The Red Cross and the Development of International Humanitarian Law* (Cambridge, Cambridge University Press, 2017) 89.

[16] *CIHL*, vol I (n 14) xvii.

[17] M Milanovic and S Sivakumaran, 'Assessing the Authority of the ICRC Customary IHL Study: How does IHL Develop?' (2022) 104:920/921 *IRRC* 1856, 1857.

[18] M Bothe, 'Customary International Humanitarian Law: Some Reflections on the ICRC Study' (2005) 8 *YIHL* 143, 146.

[19] ICRC, *31st International Conference of the Red Cross and Red Crescent: Strengthening Legal Protection of Victims of Armed Conflicts – Draft Resolution & Report* (Geneva, ICRC, 2011) 4.

[20] See, eg, ibid 4–5; M Meyer, 'The International Committee of the Red Cross and the Initiative to Strengthen Legal Protection for Victims of Armed Conflicts' in Harvey, Summers and White (n 1) 269.

[21] RY Jennings and A Watts (eds), *Oppenheim's International Law: Volume I: Peace*, 9th edn (Oxford, Oxford University Press, 2008) para 13.

the significant contribution that judicial bodies can make to the development of international law'.[22] He notes as examples the clarification of 'the meaning and scope of humanitarian law rules and principles, their application to specific armed conflicts, [and] the customary international law status of treaties or particular provisions'.[23] Similarly, while the International Court of Justice (ICJ) emphasises that it 'states the existing law and does not legislate', members of the Court themselves 'have acknowledged that judicial interpretation involves a creative element that may fill existing gaps'.[24] Indirectly, the jurisprudence of courts and tribunals may also inform discourses on the law and thus potentially function as a catalyst for its development outside of the courtroom.[25] Since adjudicating war crimes, and thus certain serious violations of IHL, is part of the mandate of international criminal tribunals, it is widely believed that especially the International Criminal Tribunal for the Former Yugoslavia (ICTY) and the International Criminal Tribunal for Rwanda (ICTR) have considerably influenced IHL.[26] Nevertheless, as Robert Heinsch cautions 'the "hidden" law-creation by originally law-determining agencies can only receive its legitimacy through either express consent or silent acquiescence from other law-creating subjects',[27] namely states.

Others have argued that 'most legal development is achieved through "soft law" measures, with changes made through shifting legal interpretations rather than by altering the word of the law'.[28] In his study of so-called expert manuals in IHL, Anton Petrov observes that '[e]xpert processes have in many respects replaced diplomatic state conferences'.[29] Non-state actors, such as epistemic communities involving international legal and military experts, provide collections of norms for areas where conventional IHL seems underdeveloped or inapt to address the challenges of contemporary warfare. Although these soft law instruments are intended to fill gaps and to remove ambiguities, they are derived from established law and reaffirm the existing concepts of combatants

[22] S Darcy, *Judges, Law and War: The Judicial Development of International Humanitarian Law* (Cambridge, Cambridge University Press, 2014) 80.

[23] ibid 11, see also 314.

[24] ibid 318.

[25] ibid 11.

[26] ibid 65; R Heinsch, 'Judicial "Law-Making" in the Jurisprudence of the ICTY and ICTR in Relation to Protecting Civilians from Mass Violence: How Can Judge-Made Law Be Brought into Coherence with the Doctrine of the Formal Sources of International Law?' in P Ambach et al (eds), *The Protection of Non-Combatants during Armed Conflict and Safeguarding the Rights of Victims in Post-Conflict Society – Essays in Honour of the Life and Work of Joakim Dungel* (Leiden, Brill, 2015); see also Mantilla (n 3).

[27] Heinsch (n 26) 312; see also WJ Fenrick, 'The Development of the Law of Armed Conflict Through the Jurisprudence of the International Criminal Tribunal for the Former Yugoslavia' (1998) 3 *Journal of Conflict & Security Law* 197, 197.

[28] OM Stern, *Gender, Conflict and International Humanitarian Law: A Critique of the 'Principle of Distinction'* (London, Routledge, 2018) 227.

[29] AO Petrov, *Expert Laws of War: Restating and Making Law in Expert Processes* (Cheltenham, Elgar, 2020) 4.

and civilians. These are apparently invoked as taken-for-granted notions without definition, not least in the declaration of the principle of distinction in the 1994 *San Remo Manual on International Law Applicable to Armed Conflicts at Sea*, adopted by the International Institute of Humanitarian Law (IIHL),[30] and in the 2009 *Manual on International Law Applicable to Air and Missile Warfare*, published by the Harvard Program on Humanitarian Policy and Conflict Research.[31] In his review of the 2009 *Manual*, Ian Henderson criticises this omission, stressing the importance of 'combatant' as a legal term of art.[32] Only the commentary on the 2009 *Manual*, which was not drafted by the responsible group of experts as a whole but by a smaller number of scholars, defines the terms in accordance with existing law.[33] The 2013 *Tallinn Manual on the International Law Applicable to Cyber Warfare*, on the other hand, explicitly delineates the concepts of combatants and civilians, relying primarily on the 1949 Geneva Convention on Prisoners of War (GC III) and AP I for the former, and on AP I and CIHL for the latter.[34] It also declares that the principle of distinction and protection regime for civilians apply to cyber warfare.[35] These instruments have in common that they neither expand nor challenge the concepts of combatants and civilians. Instead, they try to fit individuals in particular situations within the legal framework that was developed in earlier periods for different contexts, indeed, other dimensions of armed conflicts.

Another soft law instrument that will be considered in more detail in section III.C below is the *Interpretive Guidance on the Notion of Direct Participation in Hostilities under International Humanitarian Law* (*Interpretive Guidance*).[36] It resulted from an expert process which had been jointly organised by the ICRC and TMC Asser Institute; yet the instrument was published only by the former. The President of the ICRC acknowledged the instrument's limits in the state-centric international legal system: while it reflects the ICRC's perspective, it 'is not and cannot be a text of a legally binding nature'.[37] Moreover, it is not intended to change the law but to interpret the notion of 'direct participation in hostilities' (DPH) within the established legal framework and thus adapt it to modern armed conflicts.[38] Orly Stern believes that the instrument was still an

[30] L Doswald-Beck (ed), *San Remo Manual on International Law Applicable to Armed Conflicts at Sea* (Cambridge, Cambridge University Press, 1995) para 39.

[31] See rules 5(a) and 10 in *HPCR Manual on International Law Applicable to Air and Missile Warfare* (Cambridge, Cambridge University Press, 2013) 60 and 85.

[32] I Henderson, 'Manual on International Law Applicable to Air and Missile Warfare: A Review' (2010) 49 *Military Law and the Law of War Review* 169, 174.

[33] HPCR (n 31) 86–88 and 90.

[34] MN Schmitt (ed), *Tallinn Manual on the International Law Applicable to Cyber Warfare* (Cambridge, Cambridge University Press, 2013) (hereafter *Tallinn Manual*), rules 25–27 and 29 and their commentary, 95–103 and 104–05.

[35] ibid rules 31–36.

[36] N Melzer, *Interpretive Guidance on the Notion of Direct Participation in Hostilities under International Humanitarian Law* (Geneva, ICRC, 2009) (hereafter *Interpretive Guidance*).

[37] ibid 6.

[38] ibid 9.

attempt to amend the law without the difficulties of the formal process by 'filling in gaps and opening the way to new interpretations and new potential avenues of development'.[39] Eight years after the publication of the *Interpretive Guidance*, Robin Geiß and Andreas Zimmermann noted that 'many of its suggestions have gained increasing relevance and acceptance not only among academics, but notably also in State practice'.[40] The acceptance and subsequent use of soft law instruments by states may lead to the development of the law itself.

II. REAFFIRMATION OF THE 1977 LEGAL FRAMEWORK

A. Reaffirmation and Elevation of the Principle of Distinction

AP I established the principle of distinction as the apparent underlying logic and guiding principle of IHL.[41] Since then it has not only been reaffirmed but even seemingly elevated in the hierarchy of international law sources. In its Advisory Opinion on the *Legality of the Threat or Use of Nuclear Weapons*, the ICJ identified two 'cardinal principles … constituting the fabric of humanitarian law', namely the principle of distinction and the prohibition of unnecessary suffering of combatants.[42] The Court elaborated the first principle as entailing the protection of civilians and civilian objects by prohibiting direct attacks against them as well as indiscriminate weapons. It held that 'these fundamental rules are to be observed by all States whether or not they have ratified the conventions that contain them, because they constitute intransgressible principles of international customary law'.[43] While the ICJ itself intentionally abstained from describing them as *jus cogens*,[44] its statement has been read as implying this status. For example, in its Commentary on the Draft Articles on Responsibility of States for Internationally Wrongful Acts, the International Law Commission states that since the ICJ identifies certain IHL norms as 'intransgressible' in character 'it would also seem justified to treat these as peremptory'.[45]

[39] Stern (n 28) 28.

[40] R Geiß and A Zimmermann, 'The International Committee of the Red Cross: A Unique Actor in the Field of the International Humanitarian Law Creation and Progressive Development' in Geiß, Zimmermann and Haumer (n 15) 240.

[41] See chapter 5.

[42] *Legality of the Threat or Use of Nuclear Weapons*, Advisory Opinion [1996] ICJ Rep 226, para 78.

[43] ibid para 79; the ICJ's finding has been repeatedly invoked and reaffirmed by a variety of actors, see, eg, *Prosecutor v Galić*, Judgment (5 December 2003) IT-98-29-T, para 45; *Prosecutor v Kordić and Čerkez*, Judgment (17 December 2004) IT-95-14/2-A, para 54; *Public Committee against Torture in Israel and Palestinian Society for the Protection of Human Rights and the Environment v Government of Israel* (2006) HCJ 769/02 (*Targeted Killings* case) para 23; *CIHL*, vol I (n 14) 5; *Tallinn Manual* (n 34) rule 31.1; N Melzer, 'The Principle of Distinction between Civilians and Combatants' in A Clapham and P Gaeta (eds), *The Oxford Handbook of International Law in Armed Conflict* (Oxford, Oxford University Press, 2014) 297.

[44] *Nuclear Weapons* (n 42) para 83.

[45] ILC, *Yearbook of the International Law Commission 2001, vol II Part Two* (Geneva, UN, 2007) 113; see also V Chetail, 'The Contribution of the International Court of Justice to International

The customary nature of the principle of distinction, at least, has also been recognised by the *ICRC Study* which formulates it in similar terms to Article 48 AP I.[46] It declares that the principle also applies to NIACs, which is only implied in the Protocol Additional to the Geneva Conventions of 12 August 1949, and Relating to the Protection of Victims of Non-International Armed Conflicts (AP II) in the absence of an explicit provision.[47] It is notable that the stipulated customary rule refers to 'civilians' only, and not the civilian population, thus emphasising the protection of the individual rather than the collective. The *ICRC Study* arguably renders the principle of distinction more central even than AP I. The 1977 treaty formulates the principle as a 'basic rule' for the 'General protection against effects of hostilities' for the civilian population, rather than as a 'basic rule' under the 'Methods and means of warfare'.[48] In contrast, the *ICRC Study* combines rules enshrined under the sections on 'combatant and prisoner-of-war status' and the protection of the civilian population in AP I[49] in its first part entitled 'The Principle of Distinction'.[50] The organisation of Part I into distinct chapters reflect what have been identified as the 'basic elements' of the principle of distinction.[51] Accordingly, the six chapters and 24 rules not only define civilians and combatants as well as civilian objects and military objectives but also regulate the conduct of hostilities for the protection of civilians. The *Study* frames the principle of distinction implicitly as underlying the general rules on warfare, compared to 'specific methods of warfare' in Part III and the use of weapons in Part IV. Moreover, Chapter 1 on the 'Distinction between Civilians and Combatants' reinforces the dichotomous categorisation of individuals under IHL, with the exception of 'specifically protected persons' in Part II, some of which also qualify as civilians.

It seems to be a common approach of commentators to reaffirm the importance of the principle of distinction in IHL while noting practical problems in its application today.[52] For instance, Jann Kleffner argues that the principle of

Humanitarian Law' (2003) 85:850 *IRRC* 235, 251; J-F Quéguiner, 'The Principle of Distinction: Beyond an Obligation of Customary International Humanitarian Law' in HM Hensel (ed), *The Legitimate Use of Military Force: The Just War Tradition and the Customary Law of Armed Conflict* (Aldershot, Ashgate, 2008) 171.

[46] *CIHL*, vol I (n 14) rule 1; it is said that the customary nature of the principle is 'beyond doubt', A Bellal and S Casey-Maslen, *The Additional Protocols to the Geneva Conventions in Context* (Oxford, Oxford University Press, 2022) 144.

[47] See also MN Schmitt, CHB Garraway and Y Dinstein (eds), *The Manual on the Law of Non-International Armed Conflict – With Commentary* (Sanremo, IIHL, 2006) (hereafter *San Remo Manual*) 11.

[48] AP I, art 48, cf art 35.

[49] ibid, pts III and IV.

[50] *CIHL*, vol I (n 14) pt 1.

[51] Bothe, 'CIHL' (n 18) 166.

[52] See, eg, S Oeter, 'Comment: Is the Principle of Distinction Outdated?' in W Heintschel von Heinegg and V Epping (eds), *International Humanitarian Law Facing New Challenges: Symposium in Honour of Knut Ipsen* (Berlin, Springer, 2007); A van Engeland, *Civilian or Combatant? A Challenge for the 21st Century* (Oxford, Oxford University Press, 2015) 16–17 and 161–62;

distinction 'is as pertinent as ever'; yet 'the actual operationalisation of the principle faces a number of challenges in contemporary armed conflicts'.[53] Using a more specific example, Mark David Maxwell declares that '[e]ven though the principle of distinction is a bedrock principle of the law of war, the number of civilians accompanying the force has steadily increased'.[54] Moreover, the actors asserting the fundamental status of the principle of distinction often rely on a discourse of tradition, as has been seen in earlier periods. The *ICRC Study* seems to follow the approach of AP I and its drafters in defining and historicising the principle of distinction as a matter of course.[55] Besides regarding the principle as taken for granted in the commentary to the rule, it, for example, anachronistically proclaims that it 'was first set forth in the St. Petersburg Declaration' and that it underlies the limited protection from attack for individuals, who would be now considered civilians, in Article 25 of the Hague Regulations.[56] In the *San Remo Manual on the Law of Non-International Armed Conflict* (*San Remo Manual*), the IIHL similarly traces the roots of the principle of distinction to the Lieber Code and notes that it was subsequently 'confirmed in numerous legal instruments, including the Hague Regulations'.[57] Also arguing the 'long-standing history' of the 'principles of distinction and protection' which 'form the basic foundation of international humanitarian law', the ICTY Appeals Chamber in the *Galić* case not only referred to Article 51 AP I and Article 13 AP II but also Hugo Grotius and the Lieber Code.[58] The constructed history seems to endow the principle with import and eminence.

B. Reaffirmation of the Concept of Civilians

The protection of civilians has moved to the centre of attention of the international community as diverse actors have adopted it on their agendas in a variety of fields.[59] Karma Nabulsi observes that '[l]awyers, members of humanitarian relief organizations and international agencies, policymakers, and the

Crawford, *Identifying the Enemy* (n 11) 232–33; cf Marco Sassòli argues that the principle of distinction has lost some of its relevance, M Sassòli, *International Humanitarian Law: Rules, Controversies, and Solutions to Problems Arising in Warfare* (Cheltenham, Elgar, 2019) paras 3.23–3.27.

[53] JK Kleffner, 'From "Belligerents" to "Fighters" and Civilians Directly Participating in Hostilities – On the Principle of Distinction in Non-International Armed Conflicts One Hundred Years After the Second Hague Peace Conference' (2007) 54 *Netherlands International Law Review* 315, 336.

[54] MD Maxwell, 'The Law of War and Civilians on the Battlefield: Are We Undermining Civilian Protection?' (2004) 84:5 *Military Review* 17, 19.

[55] See, eg, J-M Henckaerts and L Doswald-Beck, *Customary International Humanitarian Law, Volume II: Practice* (Cambridge, Cambridge University Press, 2005) (hereafter *CIHL*, vol II) 4.

[56] *CIHL*, vol I (n 14) 3; cf chapter 3.

[57] *San Remo Manual* (n 47) 11.

[58] *Prosecutor v Galić*, Judgment (30 November 2006) IT-98-29-A, para 87.

[59] eg, since 1999 it has been on the agenda of the United Nations Security Council, 'Thematic Items' (UN, 2018) www.un.org/securitycouncil/content/repertoire/thematic-items.

public broadly agree that the protection of noncombatants is the most pressing concern'.[60] Many actors are engaged in discussing the implementation and enforcement of the applicable law for this purpose,[61] rather than its development. The protection of civilians has, however, also featured in more traditional law-making processes leading to the adoption of specialised treaties which regulate or ban certain means and methods of warfare. A number of these instruments declare the prohibition of direct attacks against civilians and the principle of distinction as preambular principles or operative rules.[62] They are built upon a naturalised understanding of civilians and civilian immunity. Indeed, an ideal of innocent civilians who are not involved in DPH and are in need of protection seems to be the guiding value. Since these specialised treaties implicitly reaffirm the concept of civilians without meaningfully engaging with it, they are not examined here in detail.

IHL is generally framed as having the protection of civilians as its principal objective. While not considering the principle of distinction or the notion of civilian immunity, the ICJ, for example, declared in its Advisory Opinion on the *Construction of a Wall in the Occupied Palestinian Territories* that 'one of the paramount purposes' of IHL is 'to protect civilian life'.[63] The ICTY also endorsed its significance proclaiming that '[t]he protection of civilians in time of armed conflict, whether international or internal, is the bedrock of modern humanitarian law'.[64] In the words of Frits Kalshoven, it maintained 'the sacrosanct character of the obligation to respect and protect civilians'.[65] The 'protection of civilians' itself is identified as a customary 'principle', sometimes alongside the principle of distinction.[66] Accordingly, the ICTY read into the ICJ jurisprudence that 'the principle of distinction, along with the principle of protection of the civilian population' are 'cardinal principles'.[67] The Trial Chamber in the *Milošević* case invoked a tripart set of principles underlying

[60] K Nabulsi, 'Evolving Conceptions of Civilians and Belligerents: One Hundred Years After the Hague Peace Conferences' in S Chesterman (ed), *Civilians in War* (London, Lynne Rienner, 2001) 9.

[61] The symposium held by the International Peace Academy/Carnegie Corporation of New York in 1999 is one such example which led to the edited volume by Simon Chesterman on *Civilians in War*; BD Jones and CK Cater, 'From Chaos to Coherence? Toward a Regime for Protecting Civilians in War' in Chesterman (n 60) 237–38.

[62] See, eg, Protocol on Prohibitions or Restrictions on the Use of Mines, Booby-Traps and Other Devices (Geneva, 10 October 1980), art 3(2)–(4); CCW Protocol III, art 2; CCW Amended Protocol II, art 3(7)–(11); Ottawa Convention, Preamble; Convention on Cluster Munitions (Dublin, 30 May 2008), Preamble; Treaty on the Prohibition of Nuclear Weapons (New York, 7 July 2017), Preamble.

[63] *Legal Consequences of the Construction of a Wall in the Occupied Palestinian Territories*, Advisory Opinion [2004] ICJ Rep 136, para 162.

[64] *Prosecutor v Kupreškić et al*, Judgment (14 January 2000) IT-95-16-T, para 521.

[65] F Kalshoven, 'Reprisals and the Protection of Civilians: Two Recent Decisions of the Yugoslavia Tribunal' in F Kalshoven (ed), *Reflections on the Law of War: Collected Essays* (Leiden, Martinus Nijhoff, 2007) 822.

[66] *Galić* (2003) (n 43) para 19; *Kordić and Čerkez* (2004) (n 43) para 59; *Galić* (2006) (n 58) para 87.

[67] *Galić* (2003) (n 43) para 45; *Kordić and Čerkez* (2004) (n 43) para 54; see also *Galić* (2006) (n 58) para 190.

the 'well-established' CIHL rule prohibiting unlawful attacks against civilians as consisting of 'the principles of distinction, precaution and protection'.[68] The Trial Chamber in the *Galić* case even declared that 'the general prohibition [of attacks against civilians] is a peremptory norm of customary international law'.[69] The protection of civilians has seemingly acquired an independent existence among the principles of IHL, although it could be seen as entailing civilian immunity which is already the objective of the principle of distinction according to the conventional narrative today.

In light of the apparent fundamental importance of the protection of civilians under contemporary IHL, the question arises whether the meaning of the concept and scope of its protection are clear. The negative definition of civilians in Article 50 AP I has been repeatedly reaffirmed in similar terms. The *ICRC Study*[70] and the *Interpretive Guidance* on DPH[71] define civilians in IACs as everyone who is not a member of the armed forces, and the latter instrument also excludes participants in a *levée en masse*. The *ICRC Study* only acknowledges this exception in its commentary rather than the definition itself.[72] Both definitions only differ from AP I in stipulating explicitly the categories of persons which form the counterpart to civilians, rather than referring to treaty provisions, since they are detached from the 1949 Geneva Conventions. Nevertheless, the practice invoked in support of the definition of civilians in the *Study* is less consistent. Similar to various definitions preceding AP I,[73] certain military manuals and state documents define civilians on the basis of their conduct rather than status.[74] The commentary acknowledges that some practice adds a conduct-based requirement, yet it reaffirms that such individuals would not qualify as combatants or prisoners of war (POWs).[75] While it leaves it open whether DPH would result in the loss of protection from direct attacks or civilian status, a minority of state practice suggests the latter.[76] Although a general understanding of civilians as defined in AP I arguably generally exists, it seems not to be the only one among states.

The ICTY has usually refrained from examining the definition of civilians when laying out the law on the prohibition of direct attacks against civilians. It has only occasionally explicitly declared its meaning negatively as 'persons who are not, or no longer, members of the armed forces',[77] or cited Article 50 AP I directly. It reformulated the latter definition without reference to treaty

[68] *Prosecutor v Milošević*, Judgment (12 December 2007) IT-98-29/1-T, para 941.
[69] *Galić* (2003) (n 43) para 98.
[70] *CIHL*, vol I (n 14) rule 5.
[71] *Interpretive Guidance* (n 36) 16.
[72] *CIHL*, vol I (n 14) 18.
[73] See chapter 5, section I.A.
[74] *CIHL*, vol II (n 55) 102–04.
[75] *CIHL*, vol I (n 14) 18.
[76] *CIHL*, vol II (n 55) 111–12.
[77] See, eg, *Prosecutor v Blaškić*, Judgment (3 March 2000) IT-95-14-T, para 180.

provisions as meaning 'anyone who is not a member of the armed forces or of an organized military group belonging to a party to the conflict'.[78] The definition of civilians and the civilian population has been a more prominent and contested issue in the ICTY jurisprudence on crimes against humanity[79] than war crimes. As Theodor Meron remarks, 'protection of civilians is not a unitary field of law in the jurisprudence of the Tribunals, but instead constitutes distinct strands of protections emerging from the separate legal settings of crimes against humanity and war crimes'.[80] The discussions of the notion of the 'civilian population' for the purpose of crimes against humanity are arguably immaterial for the development of IHL. Not only has its evolving interpretation occurred in international criminal law, rather than IHL, but also it relates to another distinct international crime.

The ICTY has, however, repeatedly reaffirmed the immunity of civilians in the context of armed conflicts in its jurisprudence. This is noteworthy since the ICTY Statute itself does not mention the prohibition of direct attacks against civilians. The United Nations Security Council created the ICTY purportedly as a response to the widespread attacks against civilians during the conflicts.[81] Nevertheless, the jurisdiction of the *ad hoc* tribunal was limited to grave breaches of the 1949 Geneva Conventions,[82] which concern 'protected persons' as defined in the four treaties, and 'violations of the laws or customs of war'.[83] The illustrative, non-exhaustive list of such latter violations resembles the law on the conduct of hostilities as enshrined in the 1907 Hague Regulations, more so than the 1977 Additional Protocols. While the drafters of the Statute thus intended to carefully avoid a breach of the *nullum crimen sine lege* principle by including only rules which 'are beyond any doubt part of customary law',[84] a firm belief in the customary nature of the principle of distinction and civilian immunity seemed to already prevail at the time the Additional Protocols were drafted.[85] After a direct attack against civilians and the civilian population had

[78] *Galić* (2003) (n 43) para 47; reaffirmed in *Prosecutor v Karadžić*, Judgment (24 March 2016) IT-95-5/18-T, para 452.

[79] For an overview see R Kolb, 'The Jurisprudence of the Yugoslav and Rwandan Criminal Tribunals on their Jurisdiction and on International Crimes (2000–2004)' (2004) 75 *BYIL* 269, 323–24; R Kolb, 'The Jurisprudence of the Yugoslav and Rwandan Criminal Tribunals on their Jurisdiction and on International Crimes (2004–2013)' (2014) 84 *BYIL* 131, 141–48.

[80] T Meron, 'The Protection of Civilians in the Jurisprudence of the ICTY and ICTR' in T Meron (ed), *The Making of International Criminal Justice: The View from the Bench – Selected Speeches* (Oxford, Oxford University Press, 2011) 209.

[81] D Luban, 'Human Rights Thinking and the Laws of War' in JD Ohlin (ed), *Theoretical Boundaries of Armed Conflict and Human Rights* (Cambridge, Cambridge University Press, 2016) 61.

[82] Statute of the International Tribunal for the Prosecution of Persons Responsible for Serious Violations of International Humanitarian Law Committed in the Territory of the Former Yugoslavia since 1991 in UNSC, 'Report to the Secretary-General Pursuant to Paragraph 2 of Security Council Resolution 808' (1993) UN Doc S/25704, Annex art 2.

[83] ibid art 3.

[84] UN Doc S/25704, 9.

[85] See chapter 5, section I.A.

been accorded the standing of a grave breach under AP I,[86] it was also enshrined as a war crime under the Rome Statute of the International Criminal Court.[87] It may thus seem a peculiar consequence of the absence of an explicit provision in the ICTY Statute that the Trial and Appeals Chamber had to prove in their judgments that the prohibition of direct attacks against civilians constitutes a rule in CIHL.[88]

The ICTY jurisprudence on the conduct of hostilities, however, occasionally misinterpreted the existing law with regard to the protection of civilians. In its early case-law, the Trial Chamber inaccurately framed the prohibition of direct attacks against civilians as being qualified when 'justified by military necessity',[89] thus erring in favour of military interests. Intending to 'rectify' the judgment, the Appeals Chamber in the *Blaškić* case was rather categorical in declaring an absolute prohibition,[90] thus overstating the protection of civilians. Although it also asserted a complete prohibition in the *Galić* case, it recognised 'the possibility of legitimate civilian casualties incidental to the conduct of military operations'.[91] The *Kupreškić* case noted that the protection of civilians 'may cease entirely or be reduced or suspended in three exceptional circumstances', namely 'when civilians abuse their rights', in the case of 'collateral damage', and 'at least according to some authorities, when civilians may legitimately be the object of reprisals'.[92] The first point is elaborated to include the loss of civilian immunity for DPH.[93] Some judgments acknowledged the different standing of civilians who directly participate in hostilities, but failed to mention it as an exception to the asserted absolute prohibition of attacks.[94] The difficulties arising from the uncertainty surrounding DPH generally will be further discussed below.[95]

Given its mandate under the Statute, the ICTY has emphasised the customary nature of the general protection regime for civilians; yet it consistently refers to Article 51 AP I and, less frequently, to Article 13 AP II as standards which reflect CIHL.[96] The ICTY jurisprudence should, therefore, be seen as a

[86] AP I, art 85(3).

[87] (Rome, 17 July 1998) (Rome Statute), arts 8(2)(b)(i) and 8(2)(e)(i).

[88] *Galić* (2003) (n 43) paras 45 and 57–62; reaffirmed by eg *Kordić and Čerkez* (2004) (n 43) para 48; see also D Kravetz, 'The Protection of Civilians in War: The ICTY's *Galić* Case' (2004) 17 *LJIL* 521, 528–33.

[89] *Blaškić* (2000) (n 77) para 180; *Prosecutor v Kordić and Čerkez*, Judgment (26 February 2001) IT-95-14/2-T, para 328.

[90] *Prosecutor v Blaškić*, Judgment (29 July 2004) IT-95-14-A, para 109; see also *Galić* (2003) (n 43) para 44; *Prosecutor v Milošević*, Judgment (12 November 2009) IT-98-29/1-A, para 53; *Karadžić* (n 78) para 449.

[91] *Galić* (2006) (n 58) para 190.

[92] *Kupreškić* (n 64) para 522.

[93] ibid para 523.

[94] *Galić* (2003) (n 43) para 48; *Blaškić* (2004) (n 90) para 157; *Milošević* (2009) (n 90) para 57; *Karadžić* (n 78) para 450.

[95] See section III.C.

[96] *Kordić and Čerkez* (2004) (n 43) para 59; *Milošević* (2009) (n 90) para 57.

reaffirmation of the concept of civilians. Its interpretations of the 1977 legal framework, albeit occasionally diverging from the text, do not amount to new developments. It arguably only indicates a general trend in which the established law is read through the prism of shielding innocent civilians from the consequences of warfare. It reflects the prevailing social conception of civilians as vulnerable war victims who are not participating themselves in the hostilities. The need for protecting civilians under IHL seems to be fervently pursued, sometimes without paying attention to the nuances of the legal rules and regulations.

C. Reaffirmation of the Concept of Combatants

The previous chapters have shown the contested origin of the concept of combatants and the absence of a shared understanding between states. Indeed, AP I may have further undermined the legal concept by providing a different definition than the Hague Regulations. AP I enshrined in its terms the disagreement prevalent at the Diplomatic Conference, and it has still not been ratified by some states.[97] Christopher Greenwood argues that '[t]he highly unsatisfactory result is that there are currently two different standards of what constitutes lawful combatancy'.[98] Nonetheless, states have abstained from renegotiating the criteria for combatant status. Although discontent with the definition of 'combatants' and 'armed forces' has been voiced in the evaluation of AP I,[99] pragmatic concerns over the likelihood of not achieving a better provision have militated against a revision.[100] Greenwood notes that '[t]he controversy over Article 44(3) shows that what was an intractable problem in 1899 remains difficult a century later'.[101]

The *ICRC Study* follows the simplified definition of combatants as provided in AP I. Accordingly, '[a]ll members of the armed forces of a party to the conflict are combatants, except medical and religious personnel',[102] referring to both regular and irregular armed forces fulfilling conditions equivalent to those under Article 43 AP I.[103] This may have been an attempt to overcome the inconsistency and disagreement with respect to conventional law by finding a common understanding in CIHL. The *Study* refers to military manuals, official statements and

[97] See chapter 5, sections II.A–II.B.

[98] C Greenwood, 'The Law of War (International Humanitarian Law)' in MD Evans (ed), *International Law*, 2nd edn (Oxford, Oxford University Press, 2006) 790.

[99] P Benevenuti, 'General Introduction' in IIHL, *Current Problems of International Humanitarian Law – The Two Additional Protocols to the Geneva Conventions: 25 Years Later* (IIHL, 2002) iihl.org/wp-content/uploads/2022/07/The-two-Additional-Protocols-to-the-Geneva-Conventions-25-years-later.pdf, 29.

[100] C Greenwood, 'International Humanitarian Law (Laws of War)' in F Kalshoven (ed), *The Centennial of the First International Peace Conference – Reports & Conclusions* (The Hague, Kluwer Law International, 2000) 206.

[101] ibid.

[102] *CIHL*, vol I (n 14) rule 3.

[103] ibid rule 4.

reported state practice in support of this definition.[104] Yet Volume II, which outlines practice as additional support of the customary nature of the identified rules, lists various definitions. Most states seem to define combatants as members of the armed forces. Some refer specifically to Article 43 AP I, while others additionally provide for irregular armed forces or acknowledge that the armed forces consist of combatant and non-combatant members. Other documents still define combatants with reference to Article 4(A) GC III.[105] Maxwell and Meyer also observe that a number of states continue to insist on the fulfilment of the four-fold criteria of the Hague Regulations for combatant status.[106] On the other hand, seemingly as a more functional definition, the Military Manual of the Dominican Republic states that '[a]ll persons participating in military operations or activities are considered combatants'.[107] Without going into the debate whether the 'practice' referred to by the *Study* is adequate for the constitution of CIHL,[108] no uniform understanding of the personal scope of the concept of combatants seems to exist.

Under the *ICRC Study*, combatants lose their entitlement to POW status when failing to distinguish themselves from civilians. It thus identifies the obligation that AP I introduced into conventional law as a norm of customary nature. However, it omits the exception to the rule in Article 44(3) AP I and instead provides for an absolute obligation within the time-frame of their engagement 'in an attack or in a military operation preparatory to an attack',[109] regardless of circumstances.[110] It acknowledges the controversy over the treaty provision; yet it points out that '[a]ll but two of the abstaining States have in the meantime ratified Additional Protocol I without any reservation in this respect'.[111] Similar to the drafters of AP I, the *Study* frames the principle of distinction requirement for combatants as a 'long-standing rule of customary international law already recognised in the Brussels Declaration, the Oxford Manual and the Hague Regulations. It was subsequently codified in the Third Geneva Convention and Additional Protocol I'.[112] While this is arguably an anachronistic statement,[113] the majority of state practice regarding POW status referred to by the *Study*

[104] ibid 12.

[105] *CIHL*, vol II (n 55) 80–84.

[106] MD Maxwell and RV Meyer, 'The Principle of Distinction: Probing the Limits of Its Customariness' [2007] 3 *Army Lawyer* 1, 4.

[107] *CIHL*, vol II (n 55) 80.

[108] See, eg, JB Bellinger and WJ Haynes, 'A US Government Response to the International Committee of the Red Cross Study *Customary International Humanitarian Law*' (2007) 89:866 *IRRC* 443; J-M Henckaerts, '*Customary International Humanitarian Law*: A Response to US Comments' (2007) 89:866 *IRRC* 473.

[109] *CIHL*, vol I (n 14) rule 106.

[110] Bothe criticises the Study for failing to explain the rationale behind this diversion from AP I, Bothe, 'CIHL' (n 18) 165.

[111] *CIHL*, vol I (n 14) 387–88.

[112] ibid 384.

[113] See chapter 5, section II.A.

indicates that states have now adopted the obligation in their military manuals and other national practice.[114] The semblance of a long-standing rule and contemporary support by states may have strengthened the understanding of the distinguishability from civilians as part of the regulation of the combatant status.

An element of the traditional concept of combatants that has been questioned by some scholars in recent years is the *levée en masse*. Emily Crawford argues that the normative and practical environment regarding the law of armed conflict has rendered a *levée en masse* impossible.[115] Knut Ipsen likewise declares the diminished significance of this type of combatants in light of 'modern-day armed conflicts'.[116] The *Tallinn Manual* includes it as a rule, yet notes the uncertainty of its existence and implications in the specific context of cyber warfare.[117] Others believe that it may still occur, pointing to incidences in the twenty-first century which could potentially be considered as examples.[118] The ICTY also recognised that a *levée en masse* may have existed for a limited duration in Srebrenica, although not at the time under consideration in the *Orić* case itself.[119] While the changing nature of warfare may seem inconsistent with the historic notion of the *levée en masse*, supporters of its continuing relevance tend to rely on its long-established legal framework. Crawford herself observes that 'despite the practice of *levée en masse* seemingly falling into desuetude, it continues to have a place in modern international law' being, for example, still included in states' military manuals.[120] While the *ICRC Study* does not mention it in its definition of combatants, the commentary on the rules suggests that it forms part of CIHL.[121] The combatant status of the *levée en masse* has thus been recognised as a continuing part of the legal framework.

Overall, the significance of the combatant status has been reaffirmed. The *ICRC Study* emphasises, albeit in an additional note at the beginning of the chapter on combatant and POW status, that 'only combatants have the right to participate directly in hostilities' without being tried for such participation or

[114] *CIHL*, vol II (n 55) 2538–44.

[115] E Crawford, 'Tracing the Historical and Legal Development of the *Levée en Masse* in the Law of Armed Conflict' (2017) 19 *Journal of the History of International Law* 329, 359–60.

[116] K Ipsen, 'Combatants and Non-Combatants' in D Fleck (ed), *The Handbook of International Humanitarian Law*, 4th edn (Oxford, Oxford University Press, 2021) 108.

[117] *Tallinn Manual* (n 34) rule 27; cf David Wallace and Shane Reeves declare that '[a] cyber *levée en masse* is simply an unworkable notion', D Wallace and SR Reeves, 'The Law of Armed Conflict's "Wicked" Problem: *Levée en Masse* in Cyber Warfare' (2013) 89 *International Law Studies* 646, 661.

[118] A Rogers, 'Combatant Status' in E Wilmshurst and S Breau (eds), *Perspectives on the ICRC Study on Customary International Humanitarian Law* (Cambridge, Cambridge University Press, 2007) 111; GD Solis, *The Law of Armed Conflict: International Humanitarian Law in War*, 3rd edn (Cambridge, Cambridge University Press, 2022) 183–84.

[119] *Prosecutor v Orić*, Judgment (30 June 2006) IT-03-68-T, para 136.

[120] Crawford, '*Levée en Masse*' (n 115) 353.

[121] *CIHL*, vol I (n 14) 18 and 386–87.

for 'acts that do not violate international humanitarian law', and are entitled to POW status.[122] Michael Bothe questions why these essential implications of the combatant status, also often referred to as combatant privilege, are 'formulated in an explanatory text and not as a formal rule'.[123] Anthony Rogers suggests as a possible reason the intended applicability of the definition of armed forces and combatants to both IACs and NIACs.[124] Indeed, it is mainly in discussions regarding NIACs that the implications and exclusionary nature of the concept of combatants are apparent.[125]

The non-extension of combatant status to the law on NIACs raises questions in relation to so-called 'internationalised' armed conflicts, namely NIACs which transform or have been transformed into IACs. The law of IACs becomes applicable as a result; however, due to their origin in NIACs, certain elements which do not fit into the inter-state belligerent framework upon which the law is conceptually built remain, such as the involvement of non-state organised armed groups. In his recent study of the legal framework applicable to internationalised armed conflicts, Kubo Mačák argues that the principle of equal application of the law between the belligerent parties 'appears to support the extension of combatant status to members of non-state actors in internationalized conflicts'.[126] Yet, in practice, 'the territorial states in these conflicts have been reluctant to accord combatant status to their non-state opponents'.[127] While Mačák examines whether fighters of organised armed groups are eligible in principle for the qualification as combatants under the existing law of IACs, and whether it is practically feasible,[128] no conventional developments to reinforce this understanding have occurred.

As section III will show, discourses in the post-1977 period have often revolved around the participation of irregular fighters and non-state actors in armed conflicts. Nevertheless, the concept of combatants has been reaffirmed in the terms of the established legal framework, and as being rooted in inter-state belligerent relations. Its importance in IACs is undeniable even though it appears to have diverse meanings for different actors in a legal system that is fragmented into a range of treaties and CIHL. Notwithstanding its status as an essential, yet contested, element of IHL, the concept of combatants is commonly treated as settled. Questions *de lege ferenda* of who should be a combatant are thus avoided in discourses in which states are often critically not involved.

[122] ibid 384.
[123] Bothe, 'CIHL' (n 18) 164.
[124] Rogers (n 118) 109.
[125] See further section III.D.
[126] K Mačák, *Internationalized Armed Conflicts in International Law* (Oxford, Oxford University Press, 2018) 148.
[127] ibid 152.
[128] ibid 180.

III. AMBIGUITIES AND *LACUNAE* – DEVELOPMENT OR CONTINUATION OF THE LAW?

While the concepts of civilians and combatants have been generally reaffirmed, debates concerning individuals in contemporary armed conflicts suggest that IHL may not always be clear or complete. The underlying questions regarding the status and treatment of participants in hostilities, as well as who should be protected as victims of armed conflicts, precede the post-1977 period. However, they have acquired prominence in IHL discourses in the past three decades. The following sections examine whether changes in the legal framework in accordance with the ostensible practical developments in armed conflicts have occurred.

A. The Civilian 'Protected Person' under the Fourth Geneva Convention

As chapter five has shown, AP I did not remove the exclusionary scope of application *ratione personae* of GC IV's main protection regime and only supplemented it with minimum guarantees for all persons regardless of their status. The *ICRC Study* does not provide for a separate protection regime for civilians in the power of a party to the conflict. Instead, it pursues a humanitarian approach in the form of standards of treatment which apply equally to all civilians and persons *hors de combat*,[129] similar to AP II. Sixty years after the adoption of the 1949 Geneva Conventions, the ICRC conducted an internal study, which was followed by consultations with states, on the strengthening of legal protection for victims of armed conflicts.[130] One of the key areas which emerged as in need of action was the protection of persons deprived of their liberty. The ICRC itself believed that 'the negotiation and adoption of a binding international treaty – or an amendment to an existing one – would be the most effective way to strengthen IHL in this area', but political support for this approach was lacking.[131] Yet it needs to be noted that the ICRC deemed the humanitarian needs of individuals deprived of their liberty in IACs sufficiently addressed by conventional and customary law, while it considered the legal framework for NIACs inadequate.[132] Not only was parity between the protection regimes applicable in IACs and NIACs not achieved, but also the study's conclusion may have generally prevented an extension of safeguards to all civilians in IACs. GC IV in its exclusionary form remains the dominant legal framework.

[129] *CIHL*, vol I (n 14) chs 32 and 37.
[130] ICRC, *31st International Conference* (n 19) 4.
[131] ICRC, *Strengthening International Humanitarian Law Protecting Persons Deprived of their Liberty – Concluding Report* (Geneva, ICRC, 2015) 3.
[132] ibid 10–11.

The limits of GC IV's main protection regime, which is contingent on the so-called nationality requirement,[133] have become apparent in the post-1977 period. The nature of the armed conflicts in the former Yugoslavia, for example, diverged from the conceptualisation of IACs and individuals as enshrined in the treaty, not least because of the internationalisation of NIACs and the ethnic dimension of the hostilities. The ICTY was faced with these issues in the prosecution of grave breaches in relation to GC IV. Initially, the Trial Chamber in the *Tadić* case in 1997 still applied the nationality requirement in its literal sense, excluding states' own nationals from protection.[134] Recognising that ethnicity, and not the formal legal bond of nationality, was more central to the IACs under consideration, the ICTY subsequently turned to different grounds for allegiance in its determination of 'protected persons'.[135] By exploring the substantial relations between states and individuals, including their own nationals, in the relevant conflict situations,[136] it moved beyond the consideration of individuals as subjects of states. In its attempt to construct the meaning and form of allegiance, it entered discourses on identity, including ethnic relations,[137] and thus resorted to other ideational frameworks for making sense of the situations on the ground. Although individuals continue to be perceived as victims or in need of protection on the basis of their affiliation with one side of the armed conflict, it is recognised that belligerent lines in IACs do not necessarily follow inter-state relations. The changing conceptualisation of civilian 'protected persons' is thus related to a shift in the understanding of IACs themselves.

The broad approach to the 'protected persons' status under GC IV also seems to be informed by the evolving perception of IHL generally. The ICTY grounded its interpretation in its understanding of the object and purpose of GC IV as being 'directed to the protection of civilians to the maximum extent possible'.[138] Calling for a 'more flexible' approach, the Trial Chamber in the *Čelebići Camp* case held that the protections of the Geneva Conventions 'should be applied to as broad a category of persons as possible'.[139] Citing the ICRC's

[133] See chapter 4, section II.A.iii; see also S Landefeld, 'The Changing Significance of Nationality for the Protection of Civilians in the Hands of a Party to an International Armed Conflict' (2023) 28 *Journal of Conflict & Security Law* 501.

[134] *Prosecutor v Tadić*, Judgment (7 May 1997) IT-94-1-T, para 608.

[135] *Prosecutor v Delalić et al*, Judgment (16 November 1998) IT-96-21-T (*Čelebići Camp*), para 263; *Prosecutor v Tadić*, Judgment (15 July 1999) IT-94-1-A, para 164–68; *Prosecutor v Aleksovski*, Judgment (24 March 2000) IT-95-14/1-A, para 152; *Kordić and Čerkez* (2001) (n 89) paras 152–53; *Prosecutor v Naletilić and Martinović*, Judgment (31 March 2003) IT-98-34-T, para 207; *Blaškić* (2004) (n 90) para 172; *Prosecutor v Prlić et al*, Judgment, Vol I (29 May 2013) IT-04-74-T, para 100.

[136] See, eg, *Tadić* (1999) (n 135) para 166; *Blaškić* (2000) (n 77) para 146; *Prosecutor v Delalić et al*, Judgment (20 February 2001) IT-96-21-A (*Čelebići Camp*), para 83.

[137] C Garbett, *The Concept of the Civilian: Legal Recognition, Adjudication and the Trials of International Criminal Justice* (Abingdon, Routledge, 2015) 69.

[138] See, eg, *Tadić* (1999) (n 135) para 168; reaffirmed in *Aleksovski* (n 135) para 152; *Blaškić* (2004) (n 90) para 172; see also K Mačak and E Policinski, 'In Pursuit of a Treaty's Soul: A Study of the Object and Purpose of the Fourth Geneva Convention' (2024) 73 ICLQ 385.

[139] *Čelebići Camp* (1998) (n 135) para 263.

GC IV Commentary, it portrayed the drafting history as showing that 'the Conventions have been drawn up first and foremost to protect individuals, and not to serve State interests'.[140] As argued in chapter four, the understanding of the drafters in 1949 was more complex. Nevertheless, the ICTY's approach has also been endorsed by some academics. Meron, for example, implores that '[i]n interpreting the law, our goal should be to avoid paralyzing the legal process as much as possible and, in the case of humanitarian conventions, to enable them to serve their protective goals'.[141] While the laws of war used to be confined to specific categories of persons, no person today is deemed beyond the protective scope of IHL.

The ICTY has argued that no gap exists between the protection regimes of GC III and GC IV, and thus that individuals not qualifying as POWs automatically fall under the latter.[142] This interpretation sometimes relied on the *GC IV Commentary* for authority,[143] which, however, was adopted in the post-1949 period. Moreover, as Boyd van Dijk points out, the *Commentary* 'represents just one account, written by just one former drafter, with its own particular aims'.[144] Although the binary distinction between combatants and civilians emerged and is prevalent in the so-called 'Hague Law', regulating the conduct of hostilities, a similar understanding of individuals in the power of a party to an IAC seems now apparent in the jurisprudence. Indeed, the ICTY appears to have occasionally even confused 'protected persons' under GC IV and 'civilians' as having the same meaning. The Trial Chamber in the *Prlić* case, for instance, referred in this context to the negative definition of civilians as persons who are not combatants,[145] before citing Article 4 GC IV as defining 'protected persons'.[146] Moreover, the ICTY has identified 'individuals who took no active part in hostilities and yet found themselves engulfed in the horror and violence of war' as beneficiaries of the GC IV protection regime.[147] Its language resembles the general discourse on the protection of innocent civilians, even though not all civilians are protected under GC IV, and DPH is not a ground for their exclusion.

Nevertheless, the ICTY was ultimately not able to equate 'protected persons' under Article 4 GC IV to 'civilians' as defined in Article 50 AP I. Its intention to

[140] ibid.

[141] T Meron, 'Classification of Armed Conflict in the Former Yugoslavia: Nicaragua's Fallout' (1998) 98 *AJIL* 236, 239; cited in *Čelebići Camp* (1998) (n 135) para 266.

[142] See, eg, *Čelebići Camp* (1998) (n 135) para 271; *Prlić* (n 135) para 98.

[143] JS Pictet (ed), *The Geneva Conventions of 12 August 1949, Commentary IV: Geneva Convention Relative to the Protection of Civilian Persons in Time of War* (Geneva, ICRC, 1958) (hereafter *GC IV Commentary*) 51.

[144] B van Dijk, *Preparing for War: The Making of the Geneva Conventions* (Oxford, Oxford University Press, 2022) 4.

[145] *Prlić* (n 135) para 99, although probably erroneously declaring that 'Civilian persons under the *Third Geneva Convention* are defined by their exclusion with respect to the armed forces' (emphasis added).

[146] ibid para 100.

[147] *Čelebići Camp* (1998) (n 135) para 275.

adapt the law to the changing nature of warfare was restricted by its mandate to enforce the law, rather than to create it. The extension of the GC IV main protection regime to all civilians would require state action in the form of adopting a protocol to the treaty or a new convention. Instead, the ICTY sought to resolve the practical difficulties of applying the formalistic definition of 'protected persons' under GC IV to the complex conflict situations before it by using an expansive, evolutionary interpretation of Article 4. While its approach was challenged during the judicial proceedings for allegedly going beyond the realm of accepted treaty interpretations and creating judge-made law instead,[148] the Tribunal defended its methods vehemently arguing that it 'does not constitute a rewriting of Geneva Convention IV or a "re-creation" of the law'.[149] Its progressive expansion of the 'protected person' status has been subsequently endorsed by other international judicial bodies.[150] Under this approach the meaning of 'protected persons' continues to be informed by the notion of allegiance to a belligerent party rather than the distinction between combatants and civilians.

The construction of individuals in ICTY jurisprudence, bound by the rules of treaty interpretation, differs from the law-making processes analysed in the previous chapters. It is limited by the possible meanings of the nationality requirement, which is an essential part of the definition of 'protected persons' under GC IV and cannot be removed. Nevertheless, the ICTY was also engaged in the social construction of meaning, arguably even more so than some participants in the diplomatic conferences of earlier periods. It often seems to have deliberated who may be vulnerable in a specific situation, grafting the law upon this understanding of the individual by expanding the scope of the category of 'protected persons'. Accordingly, rather than establishing the status of individuals in light of the legal regime, the case-law indicates a development of the law itself to reflect the ICTY's understanding of the nature and dynamics of the armed conflicts before it. Furthermore, its teleological approach reinterprets the object and purpose of the treaty in accordance with the contemporary view of GC IV: it is seen as protecting civilians, who are generally perceived as innocent victims of armed conflicts, rather than protecting persons narrowly conceived within inter-state armed conflicts and the international legal system as in 1949.

[148] See, eg, *Čelebići Camp* (2001) (n 136) para 65, where the appellants called for a diplomatic conference to revise GC IV if it was considered to be obsolete.

[149] ibid para 73; see also *Blaškić* (2004) (n 90) para 180–81.

[150] *Kaing Guek Eav alias Duch*, Judgment (16 August 2010) 001/18-07-2007-ECCC/TC, paras 419; *Prosecutor v Thomas Lubanga Dyilo*, Decision on the Confirmation of Charges (Pre-Trial Chamber I) (29 January 2007) ICC-01/04-01/06, paras 277–80; *Prosecutor v Germain Katanga and Mathieu Ngudjolo Chui*, Decision on the Confirmation of Charges (Pre-Trial Chamber I) (30 September 2008) ICC-01/04-01/07, paras 290–91; *Nuon Chea et al*, Closing Order (15 September 2010) 002/19-09-2007-ECCC-OCIJ, para 1482 (noting the application of the 'allegiance test' in 'internecine armed conflicts occurring pursuant to the dissolution of a pre-existing state and in the context of the formulation of new states', while questioning its general applicability to IACs); see also Darcy (n 22) 121–22; Mačák (n 126) 232–33.

B. 'Unlawful Combatants'

In the aftermath of the terrorist attacks of 11 September 2001, a debate over so-called 'unlawful combatants', 'unprivileged combatants' or 'enemy combatants' emerged.[151] Academics have not failed to point out that these terms are not part of conventional IHL.[152] While the terminology is not used in the 1949 Geneva Conventions and 1977 Additional Protocols, Crawford believes that only spies and mercenaries are identified as 'unlawful combatants' in the treaties.[153] In past decades, the notion of 'unlawful combatants' seems to have been commonly used to refer to 'all persons taking a direct part in hostilities without being entitled to do so (ie without having a combatant's privilege) and who therefore cannot be classified as prisoners of war when falling into the power of the enemy'.[154] It has been emphasised that the term as such 'serves a descriptive function only'.[155] The generic term 'combatants' is apparently invoked based on the individuals' conduct rather than status. In contrast, Charles Garraway understands the term 'unlawful combatant' to mean a person entitled to combatant status, who is, however, deprived of the privileges belonging to this status for failing to act within the rules that govern it.[156] The discussion has led to the question whether a third category besides (lawful) combatants and civilians exists under IHL. This section examines whether a new conceptualisation of individuals for the purpose of the legal regulation of armed conflicts has appeared in this period.

Kenneth Watkin believes that a 'rich history and customary legal basis of "unlawful combatancy"' exists.[157] The scholarship and case-law that is commonly referred to in support of this claim precedes the adoption of the 1977 Additional Protocols, and some even the 1949 Geneva Conventions.[158] Yet following the reference to 'unlawful combatants' in the *Quirin* judgment in 1942,[159] states abstained from including such a third category in conventional law. More recent state practice invoking the notion of 'unlawful combatants' seems varied. The *ICRC Study* on CIHL shows that some states mention 'unlawful combatants' in their military manuals.[160] Although the extracts provided are insufficient to draw

[151] E Crawford, *The Treatment of Combatants and Insurgents under the Law of Armed Conflict* (Oxford, Oxford University Press, 2010) 56–60.

[152] See, eg, K Dörmann, 'Unlawful Combatants' in Clapham and Gaeta (n 43) 606; N Melzer, *International Humanitarian Law: A Comprehensive Introduction* (Geneva, ICRC, 2019) 84.

[153] Crawford, *Combatants and Insurgents* (n 151) 54.

[154] Dörmann, 'Unlawful Combatants' (n 152) 607.

[155] Crawford, *Combatants and Insurgents* (n 151) 60; see also *Targeted Killings* case (n 43) para 31.

[156] CHB Garraway, '"Combatants" – Substance or Semantics?' in Schmitt and Pejic (n 1) 327.

[157] Watkin, '21st Century Conflict' (n 1) 287; see also M Newton, 'Unlawful Belligerency after September 11: History Revisited and Law Revised' in Wippman and Evangelista (n 1).

[158] Notably RR Baxter, 'So-Called Unprivileged Belligerency: Spies, Guerrillas, and Saboteurs' (1951) 28 *BYIL* 323; GIAD Draper, 'The Status of Combatants and the Question of Guerilla Warfare' (1971) 45 *BYIL* 173; *Ex parte Quirin* (1942) 317 US 1.

[159] *Ex parte Quirin* (n 158).

[160] *CIHL*, vol II (n 55) 108–10, 2012, 2582–83 and 3894.

conclusions, the term appears to be largely employed as a descriptor in various contexts. Neither a distinct legal status nor a discrete scope *ratione personae* for the term can be discerned. While Israel has passed legislation specifically on the detention of 'unlawful combatants',[161] the Israeli Supreme Court negated the existence of 'unlawful combatants' as a third category having found no support for it in conventional and customary IHL.[162] The understanding of the United States' administration and judiciary of the meaning of 'unlawful combatants' and their entitlement to protection has also been inconsistent since its infamous memorandum in 2002.[163] The discourse on 'unlawful combatants' within states, therefore, does not suggest a shared understanding of such a legal concept as a third category besides combatants and civilians.

The notion of 'unlawful combatants' has met with wider opposition;[164] yet a difference can be drawn in relation to the so-called 'Hague Law' and 'Geneva Law'. With respect to the rules on the conduct of hostilities, the binary distinction between combatants and civilians has been emphasised, allowing for no gap in between.[165] Since civilians are defined as anyone who is not a member of the armed forces, 'unlawful combatants' fall within this category. This is the approach taken by the Israeli Supreme Court in the *Targeted Killings* case, which then continued to examine the meaning of DPH by civilians who thus perform 'the function of a combatant'.[166] A more complex picture emerges regarding detention. A minority of commentators has argued that 'unlawful combatants' fall outside of the protective scope of IHL.[167] Given the contested nature of the so-called 'war on terror', the term 'unlawful combatants' has been rejected on the basis that the combatant status is exclusive to the law of IACs.[168] If an IAC, however, is established, irregular fighters may be seen as not fulfilling the requirements of the POW protection regime, including belonging to a state party to the conflict or compliance with IHL.[169] Other scholars accord 'unlawful combatants' protection under the minimum humanitarian standards of Article 75 AP I, Article 3 common to all 1949 Geneva Conventions (CA3) and CIHL, or even 'protected person' status under GC IV provided the nationality requirement is met.[170] Along the lines of the ICRC's

[161] Dörmann, 'Unlawful Combatants' (n 152) 619.

[162] *Targeted Killings* case (n 43) para 28.

[163] I Venzke, 'Legal Contestation about "Enemy Combatants": On the Exercise of Power in Legal Interpretation' (2009) 5 *Journal of International Law and International Relations* 155, 170–73; Dörmann, 'Unlawful Combatants' (n 152) 620–21.

[164] See, eg, R Kolb, *Advanced Introduction to International Humanitarian Law* (Cheltenham, Elgar, 2014) 126–27.

[165] Dörmann, 'Unlawful Combatants' (n 152) 618.

[166] *Targeted Killings* case (n 43) paras 28 and 31.

[167] J Pejic, '"Unlawful/Enemy Combatants": Interpretations and Consequences' in Schmitt and Pejic (n 1) 338–39; see also Dörmann, 'Unlawful Combatants' (n 152) 607.

[168] See Venzke (n 163) 176.

[169] M Sassòli, 'The Status of Persons Held in Guantánamo under International Humanitarian Law' (2004) 2 *JICJ* 96, 102–03; see also Sassòli, *International Humanitarian Law* (n 52) para 8.115.

[170] Pejic (n 167) 338–39; see also Dörmann, 'Unlawful Combatants' (n 152) 607–08.

GC IV Commentary,[171] it has been frequently argued that the 1949 Geneva Conventions protection regimes allow no intermediate status and that individuals are thus protected under either GC III or GC IV.[172]

Accordingly, similar to the ICTY's jurisprudence on civilian 'protected persons', a binary distinction between combatants and civilians has been apparently retrospectively read into the protection regimes of the 1949 Geneva Conventions. For example, Marco Sassòli asserts that

> there are two categories of 'protected persons', who are subject to two very different legal regimes: combatants, who become prisoners of war protected by the Third Geneva Convention if they fall into the power of the enemy; and civilians protected by the Fourth Geneva Convention when in enemy hands.[173]

As shown in chapter four, however, neither the concept of combatants nor civilians is decisive for protection under the 1949 Geneva Conventions. The POW status in GC III is often mistakenly equated to combatant status although certain 'civilians' also qualify under the regime.[174] In contrast, GC IV, with the exception of Part II, does not protect civilians generally but only a narrowly defined category of individuals. The common understanding of these treaties today as protection regimes for combatants and civilians in vulnerable situations may be influenced by the belief that the normative framework of IHL generally is built on this dichotomy. Moreover, it stems from the perception of IHL as an all-encompassing protection system leaving no one outside of the scope of law.

Opponents of the notion of 'unlawful combatants' indirectly reaffirm the existing legal framework by trying to give meaning to individuals through the prism of legal categories in IHL. Yet a discrepancy between the legal and the social understanding of the situations seems to exist. The discourse on 'unlawful combatants', both in relation to targeting and detention, is driven by the belief that the law does not reflect the changing nature of warfare.[175] For example, Sassòli points out that 'heavily armed Taliban fighters' would be 'civilians' under GC IV if they do not fall under GC III, although '[t]his may not correspond to the use of that term as it is commonly employed'.[176] However, the drafters' understanding of individuals protected under GC IV was a different one than is now assumed in the modern social conception of innocent civilians. As explained in chapter four, GC IV was primarily designed for 'enemy

[171] *GC IV Commentary* (n 143) 51.

[172] Sassòli, 'Status of Persons' (n 169) 101; Pejic (n 167) 342; Dörmann, 'Unlawful Combatants' (n 152) 608.

[173] Sassòli, 'Status of Persons' (n 169) 100.

[174] Geneva Convention Relative to the Treatment of Prisoners of War (Geneva, 12 August 1949), art 4(A)(4)–(5).

[175] See, eg, *Targeted Killings* case (n 43) para 28; S Scheipers, *Unlawful Combatants: A Genealogy of the Irregular Fighter* (Oxford, Oxford University Press, 2015) 207.

[176] M Sassòli, '"Unlawful Combatants": The Law and Whether it Needs to be Revised' (2003) 97 *Proceedings of the Annual Meeting (American Society of International Law)* 196, 197–98.

civilians' who were deemed potential threats to the state in whose power they were, and who were vulnerable to adverse treatment because of their belonging to the opposing belligerent party. Moreover, (unprivileged) DPH is not a criterion for exclusion from the GC IV protection regime.[177] Both GC IV and AP I 'reject divesting civilian status in favour of permitting temporary derogation of the protections associated with the civilian class'.[178]

A different dynamic in attaching meaning to individuals can be found in arguments in favour of the notion of 'unlawful combatants'. Here, the understanding of individuals participating in hostilities seems to be constructed first, and the law is then bent accordingly; or, if this seems impossible, a third category outside of the law is declared. While the lead judgment in the *Targeted Killings* case examined 'unlawful combatants' under the law regulating civilian DPH, Judge Rivlin appears to suggest in his concurring statement that the same conceptual result could have been achieved by an approach to 'unlawful combatants' derived from combatancy. According to him, the former would entail 'uncivilized civilians' forming 'a group of international-law-breaking civilians', whereas the latter considers 'international-law-breaking combatants'.[179] Either way, he seems to perceive these individuals as being distinct from 'legal combatants' and 'innocent civilians'. He even raises the question 'whether *reality* has not created, *de facto*, an additional group, with a special legal status'.[180]

Various writings by Yoram Dinstein, one of the most prominent advocates of a 'third category', also consider 'unlawful combatants' using combatancy as his starting point.[181] Emphasising that an individual cannot be a combatant and a civilian at the same time, he includes 'unlawful combatants' among the former.[182] In particular, he states that 'civilians are assimilated to combatants for such time as they engage in the hostilities'.[183] Under this approach civilians involved in DPH would not only lose their protection but also their status as civilians.[184] Dinstein seems to derive his understanding from a conceptualisation of civilians as individuals who are not directly participating in and are thus outside of hostilities. This is also supported by his occasional added emphasis that civilians are 'non-combatants'.[185] He appears to distinguish, primarily based on conduct, between participants in IACs and peaceful or innocent individuals, or in other words between functional combatants and literal non-combatants. Significantly,

[177] Dörmann, 'Unlawful Combatants' (n 152) 610.

[178] MD Maxwell and SM Watts, '"Unlawful Enemy Combatant": Status, Theory of Culpability, or Neither?' (2007) 5 *JICJ* 19, 22.

[179] *Targeted Killings case* (n 43) Judge Rivlin paras 2–3.

[180] ibid para 2.

[181] See, eg, Y Dinstein, 'Unlawful Combatancy' (2003) 79 *International Law Studies* 151; Y Dinstein, *The Conduct of Hostilities under the Law of International Armed Conflict*, 3rd edn (Cambridge, Cambridge University Press, 2016) ch 2.

[182] Dinstein, *Conduct of Hostilities* (n 181) para 122.

[183] ibid para 115.

[184] ibid para 471.

[185] See, eg, ibid para 370.

he further differentiates between 'lawful' and 'unlawful' combatants, 'to ensure in every feasible manner that inter-state armed conflicts be waged solely among the combatants of the belligerent parties'.[186] He believes that this distinction complements and preserves the principle of distinction, and that it is necessary for the effective protection of 'non-combatants'.[187] The understanding of individuals in this approach is detached from the contemporary conventional and customary legal framework.

The foregoing chapters have shown how the criteria for combatant status have been repeatedly negotiated against the background of irregular fighters' participation in wars and IACs. Incentives and occasions to continue this discourse have not been missing since the adoption of the 1977 Additional Protocols. Watkin, therefore, advocates to 'critically analyze the historically-based criteria for distinction', among others 'because contemporary conflict involves "insurgents" and "terrorists"'.[188] Although the discourse analysed here revolves around 'unlawful *combatants*' in a normative environment where 'the term "combatants" denotes the right to participate directly in hostilities',[189] a renegotiation of lawful or legitimate participation in armed conflicts has not been attempted in this context. Instead, the debate is characterised by a struggle over the interpretation of the law and state compliance with it. More specifically, the discussion seems to centre on the protection of individuals under IHL with proponents of an 'unlawful combatant' category trying to remove them from its shield. Different approaches have been taken with respect to detention and targeted killings. On the one side, the case has been made to exclude 'unlawful combatants' from the protective scope of conventional law; on the other side, 'the justification for targeted killings operates on the basis of widening the category of combatants so as to include, on a prolonged basis, civilians who are directly participating in the hostilities'.[190] While the notion of 'unlawful combatants' has been framed as a response to new developments in warfare, the law itself cannot be said to have changed in the process.

C. 'Direct Participation in Hostilities'

The apparent trend of increasing civilian involvement in armed conflicts 'underlines the importance of distinguishing not only between civilians and the armed forces, but also between civilians who do and, respectively, do not take a direct part in hostilities'.[191] AP I acknowledges the possibility of civilian DPH, and

[186] Dinstein, 'Unlawful Combatancy' (n 181) 151.
[187] ibid 153.
[188] Watkin, '21st Century Conflict' (n 1) 279–80.
[189] Dörmann, 'Unlawful Combatants' (n 152) 606.
[190] Scheipers (n 175) 190.
[191] *Interpretive Guidance* (n 36) 12.

provides for the temporary loss of civilian immunity as a result.[192] However, no sustained deliberation of such irregular participation took place at the Diplomatic Conference, leaving the clause undefined and vague.[193] State practice on the matter has not been 'clear and uniform',[194] and is often examined on a case-by-case basis, for example, in ICTY jurisprudence.[195] Andreas Wenger and Simon Mason argue that clarifying the legal meaning of DPH is 'a necessary part of the process of adapting to the changing nature of armed conflict'.[196]

In the period following the adoption of the 1977 Additional Protocols, and mainly in the last two decades, DPH has become 'subject to serious, sustained scrutiny from courts and tribunals, and from non-governmental, inter-governmental, and academic sources'.[197] After the ICTY had previously only defined DPH as 'acts of war which by nature or purpose are likely to cause actual harm to the personnel or equipment of the enemy's armed forces', in accordance with the ICRC's *Commentary on the Additional Protocols*,[198] the Appeals Chamber in the *Strugar* case considered the meaning of DPH in more detail.[199] According to Crawford, the *Targeted Killings* case was the first and most influential attempt to define DPH.[200] However, the most prominent effort at clarification is probably the *Interpretive Guidance* under the auspices of the ICRC, and initially the TMC Asser Institute. A year before its publication in 2009, the *International Review of the Red Cross* also dedicated a special issue to the topic.[201]

Nonetheless, a shared understanding has arguably still not been achieved. The *Interpretive Guidance*, although endorsed by the ICRC, seems overshadowed by the disagreement among the participants which led to the withdrawal of experts from the process prior to its publication.[202] Yet, as Sandesh Sivakumaran

[192] AP I, art 51(3).
[193] See chapter 5, section I.A.
[194] *CIHL*, vol I (n 14) 23; see also Crawford, *Identifying the Enemy* (n 11) 211.
[195] S Sivakumaran, *The Law of Non-International Armed Conflict* (Oxford, Oxford University Press, 2012) 364.
[196] Wenger and Mason (n 7) 851.
[197] Crawford, *Identifying the Enemy* (n 11) 206.
[198] *Galić* (2003) (n 43) para 48; *Kordić and Čerkez* (2004) (n 43) para 51.
[199] *Prosecutor v Strugar*, Judgment (17 July 2008) IT-01-42-A, paras 174–77.
[200] Crawford, *Identifying the Enemy* (n 11) 60.
[201] (2008) 90:872 *IRRC* 1.
[202] Some of the experts involved subsequently published their positions, including disagreements, in a forum on 'Direct Participation in Hostilities: Perspectives on the ICRC Interpretive Guidance', see B Boothby, '"And for Such Time As": The Time Dimension to Direct Participation in Hostilities' (2010) 42 *New York University Journal of International Law & Politics* 741; WH Parks, 'Part IX of the ICRC "Direct Participation in Hostilities" Study: No Mandate, No Expertise, and Legally Incorrect' (2010) 42 *New York University Journal of International Law & Politics* 769; MN Schmitt, 'Deconstruction of Direct Participation in Hostilities: The Constitutive Elements' (2010) 42 *New York University Journal of International Law & Politics* 697; K Watkin, 'Opportunity Lost: Organized Armed Groups and the ICRC "Direct Participation in Hostilities Interpretive Guidance' (2010) 42 *New York University Journal of International Law & Politics* 641; N Melzer, 'Keeping the Balance Between Military Necessity and Humanity: A Response to Four Critique s of the ICRC's Interpretive Guidance on the Notion of Direct Participation in Hostilities' (2010) 42 *New York University Journal of International Law & Politics* 831.

cautions, this 'must be balanced against the instances in which it has been used'.[203] Others have emphasised the usefulness of the process 'in enabling matters of controversy to be aired and elaborated', albeit leaving behind uncertainties.[204] Helen Durham and Eve Massingham also maintain that, despite the criticism the *Interpretive Guidance* has received, 'the fact the ICRC has started the conversation on this topic is commendable and necessary to ensure IHL remains relevant and vibrant'.[205]

First, it needs to be noted that the expert process and the resultant *Interpretive Guidance* deliberately distanced the discussion of DPH from the concept of combatants and the contemporaneous discourse on 'unlawful combatants'. In a summary report of the first expert meeting, the ICRC observed that civilians involved in DPH are 'generically labelled "unlawful combatants" or "unprivileged belligerents"';[206] however, the *Interpretive Guidance* has been read as rejecting a '"third status" between combatant and civilian'.[207] One expert in the negotiations seemed to believe that a third category could be avoided by defining and employing the notion of DPH as to address the problematic position of, for example, mercenaries, terrorists and transnational armed groups.[208] Several participants recommended to abstain from even using 'the adjective "combatant" … as it was important to avoid giving the impression that a civilian, by taking a direct part in hostilities, could somehow acquire combatant status' and thus combatant privilege.[209] Instead, the term 'continuous combat function' was created in the deliberations.[210] The *Interpretive Guidance* seems to detach the discussion of DPH from its legitimacy and lawfulness focusing rather on its consequences.

With respect to IACs, the *Interpretive Guidance* relies on the established legal framework and binary distinction between combatants and civilians, and only clarifies the parameters for the loss of protection of the latter. Nevertheless,

[203] S Sivakumaran, 'Making and Shaping the Law of Armed Conflict' (2018) 71 *Current Legal Problems* 119, 152.

[204] D Turns, 'Cyber Warfare and the Notion of Direct Participation in Hostilities' (2012) 17 *Journal of Conflict & Security Law* 279, 285.

[205] H Durham and E Massingham, 'Who Is Protected Under International Humanitarian Law? Finding a Definition for "Direct Participation in Hostilities"' in DW Lovell and I Primoratz (eds), *Protecting Civilians During Violent Conflict: Theoretical and Practical Issues for the 21st Century* (London, Routledge, 2012) 115.

[206] ICRC, 'Direct Participation in Hostilities under International Humanitarian Law – Summary Report' (ICRC, 2003) www.icrc.org/en/doc/assets/files/other/2003-03-report-dph-2003-icrc.pdf, 6.

[207] R Cryer, 'The International Committee of the Red Cross' "Interpretive Guidance on the Notion of Direct Participation in Hostilities": See a Little Light' in Geiß, Zimmermann and Haumer (n 15) 121.

[208] ICRC, 'Fourth Expert Meeting on the Notion of Direct Participation in Hostilities – Summary Report' (ICRC, 2006) www.icrc.org/en/doc/assets/files/other/2006-03-report-dph-2006-icrc.pdf, 14.

[209] ibid 10 and 23; see also ICRC, 'Fifth Expert Meeting on the Notion of Direct Participation in Hostilities – Summary Report' (ICRC, 2008) www.icrc.org/en/doc/assets/files/other/2008-05-report-dph-2008-icrc.pdf, 51–52.

[210] Watkin, 'Opportunity Lost' (n 202) 656.

a reconceptualisation seems to have occurred regarding civilians generally. Rebecca Sutton suggests that the concept of DPH introduces temporal fluidity, and 'challenges the notion that the civilian and combatant categories are alternative and exhaustive'.[211] Underlying contemporary IHL is 'the assumption that civilians do not take a direct part in hostilities';[212] yet the discourse surrounding DPH undermines this. Rather than drawing a conceptual line between combatants and civilians as innocent bystanders, the discourse implicitly focuses on the distinction between combatants and civilians involved in DPH.[213] The negotiation of interpretive standards for the DPH criterion constitutes an attempt at constructing civilians as participants and not only as victims. It can be argued that the *Interpretive Guidance* attaches meaning to individuals in terms of belligerent relations and individual participation, and intends to shape the law accordingly.

Different approaches to the meaning of DPH exist which are either more informed by humanitarian considerations or the principle of military necessity. The *Interpretive Guidance* seems to reflect an understanding of IHL that regards it as a system designed to protect civilians, a position commonly taken by the ICRC today. For instance, it declares that the so-called 'revolving door' of civilian protection, meaning that protection is lost and gained 'in parallel with the intervals of their engagement in direct participation in hostilities', 'is an integral part, not a malfunction, of IHL. It prevents attacks on civilians who do not, at the time, represent a military threat'.[214] It admits the resulting difficulty for military actors, but argues that 'it remains necessary to protect the civilian population from erroneous or arbitrary attack'.[215] Watkin criticises the approach noting that the 'revolving door' was 'first used as a pejorative term', whereas the *Interpretive Guidance* seems to utilise it 'as a form of shield to allow civilians to repeatedly claim the protection associated with that status'.[216] The *Targeted Killings* case also held that 'the "revolving door" phenomenon … is to be avoided'.[217] Another disagreement can be found in the interpretation of 'borderline situations' and whether these could be considered as DPH. Stern distinguishes two different approaches belonging to the 'human rights school' and the 'military perspective' which are respectively against or in favour of a broad interpretation of the notion of DPH.[218] Wenger and Mason observe this

[211] R Sutton, *The Humanitarian Civilian: How the Idea of Distinction Circulates Within and Beyond International Humanitarian Law* (Oxford, Oxford University Press, 2021) 178.

[212] K Dörmann, 'Protection of Civilians' in Fleck, *Handbook* (n 116) 273.

[213] J-F Quéguiner, 'Direct Participation in Hostilities under International Humanitarian Law – Background Paper' (ICRC, 2003) www.icrc.org/en/doc/assets/files/other/2003-02-background-document-icrc.pdf; ICRC, 'Summary Report' (2003) (n 206) 6–10.

[214] *Interpretive Guidance* (n 36) 70.

[215] ibid 71.

[216] Watkin, 'Opportunity Lost' (n 202) 682.

[217] *Targeted Killings* case (n 43) para 40.

[218] Stern (n 28) 28.

in the varying standards applied at the policy level of different actors who thus exploit for their own interests the absence of a clear definition of DPH and the grey zone of what constitutes hostile conduct.[219] According to Sivakumaran, the difference in adopting a broad or narrow understanding of DPH 'stems from the tension within the rule as to the identity of the principal beneficiary, namely whether it is the general civilian population or the individual civilian in question'.[220]

Ultimately, the question of the influence of the *Interpretive Guidance* on the development of the law arises. Geiß and Zimmermann note in this respect that it 'clearly pushed the limits of what is typically understood as "norm clarification"', not least because it relies on the notion of 'continuous combat function' in the application of the principle of distinction in NIACs.[221] This notion in particular has been highlighted as 'both complex and, to some extent, novel'.[222] It appears to introduce a 'conduct-based status determination' in NIACs,[223] which is further discussed below.[224] Garraway[225] and Watkin[226] believe that an apparent third status of individuals who are not considered civilians under the *Interpretive Guidance* is thus created, which casts doubt upon its assertion that it did not intend to change the law, but only interpret it. Nevertheless, the *Interpretive Guidance*, including its notion of 'continuous combat function', has been invoked by other subsequent instruments such as the *Tallinn Manual*.[227] As Petrov points out, '[d]espite allegations that this concept was *lex ferenda*, critics generally accepted the category and debate was channeled, for instance, into a nuanced discussion on the temporal element of when a function qualifies as *continuous*'.[228] Gary Solis, on the other hand, maintains that the concept 'does not enjoy either universal state practice or universal acceptance'.[229]

The notion of DPH under IHL has been part of various more specialised debates in the post-1977 period. It is particularly prevalent in contemporary concerns over the involvement of private military and security companies (PMSCs) in situations of armed conflicts. PMSC personnel may be contracted

[219] Wenger and Mason (n 7) 850–51.
[220] Sivakumaran, *Law of NIAC* (n 195) 365.
[221] Geiß and Zimmermann (n 40) 239–40.
[222] C Garraway, 'Direct Participation and the Principle of Distinction: Squaring the Circle' in Harvey, Summers and White (n 1) 176; see also Cryer (n 207) 124–25.
[223] G Corn, 'Two Sides of the Combatant Coin – Untangling Direct Participation in Hostilities from Belligerent Status in Noninternational Armed Conflicts' in W Banks (ed), *Counterinsurgency Law: New Directions in Asymmetric Warfare* (Oxford, Oxford University Press, 2013) 69.
[224] See section III.D.
[225] Garraway, 'Participants in War' (n 7) 180.
[226] Watkin, 'Opportunity Lost' (n 202) 643.
[227] *Tallinn Manual* (n 34) rules 34.4 and 35.4.
[228] Petrov (n 29) 193.
[229] Solis (n 118) 439; see also Bellal and Casey-Maslen (n 46) 137–39.

to fulfil a range of functions, not all of which would qualify as DPH,[230] whereas others amount to combat roles.[231] The surrounding academic discourse is characterised by a doctrinal analysis of the individuals' position under the established legal framework.[232] This has served as a rebuttal to claims and fears that PMSCs might 'operate in a legal vacuum'.[233] Lindsey Cameron, for example, asserts that IHL 'provides a coherent framework to cover all persons who find themselves in a situation of armed conflict'.[234] Accordingly, it has been noted that PMSC personnel may qualify as combatants if the traditional Hague Regulations or Article 43 AP I criteria are fulfilled. Since only a very limited basis for their combatant status exists, the binary logic of IHL would entail that most are civilians.[235] With respect to PMSC personnel who qualify as civilians but directly participate in hostilities, Cameron and Chetail notably take the *Interpretive Guidance* as their 'starting point as a means of outlining the key elements of the concept' of DPH.[236] Some PMSC personnel may also constitute mercenaries under AP I.[237] Yet due to the complexity of the definition they are unlikely to be regulated as such,[238] 'although their activities have characteristics in common with mercenarism'.[239]

A similar approach to identifying the PMSC personnel's status under existing IHL is adopted in the 2008 Montreux Document on PMSCs.[240] While it derived from intergovernmental consultations instigated by a joint initiative of Switzerland and the ICRC, it was deliberately not adopted as a treaty but only as a soft law instrument. It has been argued that the 'conservative approach to restating the law sought to depoliticise the process, reducing the possibility that the Initiative could be criticised for attempting to develop the law in a way that

[230] For categorisations of the types of services see, eg, L Cameron, 'Private Military Companies: Their Status under International Humanitarian Law and Its Impact on Their Regulation' (2006) 88:863 *IRRC* 573, 576.

[231] ibid 591.

[232] See, eg, ibid generally; E-C Gillard, 'Business Goes to War: Private Military/Security Companies and International Humanitarian Law' (2006) 88:863 *IRRC* 525; M Sossai, 'Status of Private Military and Security Company Personnel in the Law of International Armed Conflict' in F Francioni and N Ronzitti (eds), *War by Contract: Human Rights, Humanitarian Law, and Private Contractors* (Oxford, Oxford University Press, 2011); L Cameron and V Chetail, *Privatizing War: Private Military and Security Companies under Public International Law* (Cambridge, Cambridge University Press, 2013) 385–423; Crawford, *Identifying the Enemy* (n 11) 156–65.

[233] Sossai (n 232) 197; see also Cameron (n 230) 574; Gillard (n 232) 527–28.

[234] Cameron (n 230) 593.

[235] ibid 582–87.

[236] Cameron and Chetail (n 232) 432.

[237] AP I, art 47.

[238] Cameron (n 230) 583; M Mancini, FZ Ntoubandi and T Marauhn, 'Old Concepts and New Challenges: Are Private Contractors the Mercenaries of the Twenty-first Century?' in Francioni and Ronzitti (n 232).

[239] UN Working Group on the Use of Mercenaries cited in Mancini, Ntoubandi and Marauhn (n 238) 339.

[240] The Montreux Document on Pertinent International Legal Obligations and Good Practices for States Related to Operations of Private Military and Security Companies During Armed Conflict (Geneva, ICRC, 2009) pt I para 26(b).

aimed to legitimize PMSC activity'.[241] Sarah Percy also describes the Montreux Document as 'a very low-cost solution for states' since '[t]hey are not required to agree to anything that they have not previously agreed to; they are just required to consider it in a new context'.[242]

As a result, PMSCs as such are not conceptualised for the purpose of IHL. Instead, a case-by-case analysis is required to determine the status of particular PMSC personnel, 'according to the nature and circumstances of the functions in which they are involved'.[243] In practice, different actors tend to prefer the assertion of one status over another in accordance with their political interests.[244] Political exigencies have also likely restrained a discussion, and indeed action, on the regulation of PMSCs in hostilities with some powerful states trying to avoid the restriction of their future use.[245] It has been pointed out that 'it is predominantly states that rely heavily on PMSCs that are also proponents of the concept of "unlawful combatants"', for which some not even recognise a minimum of protection.[246] According to Cameron and Chetail, 'voluntarily creating a pool of "good" but potentially "unlawful combatants" while simultaneously condemning other (non-private sector) civilian participants in hostilities verges on hypocrisy'.[247]

The discourse on PMSCs differs from the more general debate on DPH by considering combatant status and even interrogating the legitimacy and lawfulness of participation in armed conflicts. It has been, at least partly, characterised by the 'fundamental question concerning the legitimacy of outsourcing activities which are inherently governmental'.[248] The concern over the states' monopoly on the use of force in the international political and legal system is, for example, prevalent in the draft convention on PMSCs proposed by the United Nations Working Group on the Use of Mercenaries in 2010.[249] Although the question of

[241] J Cockayne, 'Regulating Private Military and Security Companies: The Content, Negotiation, Weaknesses and Promise of the Montreux Document' (2009) 13 *Journal of Conflict & Security Law* 401, 419.

[242] S Percy, 'Regulating the Private Security Industry: A Story of Regulating the Last War' (2012) 94:887 *IRRC* 941, 954.

[243] Montreux Document, pt I para 24; see also Gillard (n 232) 530; E Crawford, *Non-Binding Norms in International Humanitarian Law: Efficacy, Legitimacy and Legality* (Oxford, Oxford University Press, 2021) 103–04.

[244] Cameron (n 230) 575.

[245] Percy (n 242) 954.

[246] Cameron and Chetail (n 232) 425–26.

[247] ibid 426.

[248] Sossai (n 232) 216; see also Cameron (n 230) 583.

[249] Human Rights Council, 'Report of the Working Group on the Use of Mercenaries as a Means of Violating Human Rights and Impending the Exercise of the Right of Peoples to Self-Determination' (2010) UN Doc A/HRC/15/25 Annex 'Draft of a Possible Convention on Private Military and Security Companies (PMSCs) for Consideration and Action by the Human Rights Council', Preamble and arts 1(1)(a)–(b) and 8–9; see also ND White, 'The Privatisation of Military and Security Functions and Human Rights: Comments on the UN Working Group's Draft Convention' (2011) 11 *Human Rights Law Review* 133, 137.

the status of PMSC personnel under IHL has been repeatedly raised in the ongoing consideration of an international framework for the regulation, monitoring and oversight of the activities of PMSCs,[250] it is not addressed in the text of the initial or updated draft convention.[251] This may be explained by its discursive setting in a United Nations forum where 'mercenary-related matters' have been traditionally discussed in the context of the right to self-determination and human rights,[252] rather than IHL. In comparison, the ICRC's concern over DPH by PMSC personnel is related to the blurring of the distinction between combatants and civilians, and the difficulty 'to ensure compliance with IHL when contractors act outside the military chain of command'.[253] Cameron and Chetail also argue that without being integrated in state armed forces, PMSC personnel should not directly participate in hostilities given the risk of jeopardising the principle of distinction. Their examination centres on civilians' loss of protection due to DPH, and the requirement for combatants to distinguish themselves from civilians in AP I.[254]

Some commentators seem to be concerned about the doctrinal categorisation of PMSC personnel under IHL given its divergence with the social understanding of civilians. José Gómez del Prado, for example, finds it 'very hard to believe that in some situations, these individuals can be considered civilians, given that they carry and use weapons, interrogate prisoners, load bombs, drive military trucks, and fulfill other essential military functions'.[255] He, instead, argues that 'they are neither civilians nor combatants. Rather, these "private soldiers"

[250] UN Doc A/HRC/15/25, para 72; Human Rights Council, 'Progress Report of the Open-Ended Intergovernmental Working Group to Elaborate the Content of an International Regulatory Framework, Without Prejudicing the Nature Thereof, to Protect Human Rights and Ensure Accountability for Violations and Abuses Relating to the Activities of Private Military and Security Companies on its First Session' (2019) UN Doc A/HRC/42/36, paras 22, 36 and 64; Human Rights Council, 'Progress Report on the Third Session of the Open-Ended Intergovernmental Working Group to Elaborate the Content of an International Regulatory Framework, Without Prejudicing the Nature Thereof, to Protect Human Rights and Ensure Accountability for Violations and Abuses Relating to the Activities of Private Military and Security Companies' (2022) UN Doc A/HRC/51/40, paras 11 and 57.

[251] UN Doc A/HRC/15/25; Second Draft Instrument on an International Regulatory Framework on the Regulation, Monitoring of and Oversight over the Activities of Private Military and Security Companies adopted in 2022 (UN Human Rights Council, 2022) www.ohchr.org/sites/default/files/documents/hrbodies/hrcouncil/wgmilitary/2022-11-03/PMSCs-Second-Draft%20-Instrument-Clean.pdf.

[252] JL Gómez del Prado, 'Private Military and Security Companies and the UN Working Group on the Use of Mercenaries' (2009) 13 *Journal of Conflict & Security Law* 429, 431.

[253] ICRC, *32nd International Conference of the Red Cross and Red Crescent: International Humanitarian Law and the Challenges of Contemporary Armed Conflicts – Report* (Geneva, ICRC, 2015) 60.

[254] Cameron and Chetail (n 232) 103–04; see also Crawford, *Identifying the Enemy* (n 11) 165–70.

[255] JL Gómez del Prado, 'A United Nations Instrument to Regulate and Monitor Private Military and Security Contractors' (2011) 1 *Notre Dame Journal of International, Comparative & Human Rights Law* 1, 8.

may be considered "unlawful combatants," similar in legitimacy to paramilitaries and terrorists'.[256] Joseph Hansen also believes that PMSCs 'strain the combatant-civilian dichotomy' under IHL.[257] In their analysis of PMSCs under international law, Cameron and Chetail admit that they constitute 'hard cases', which in law 'often push at the boundaries of existing legal definitions and lead to strange results'.[258] The hegemonic discourse portraying civilians as innocent and vulnerable individuals thus causes tensions in the context of their DPH, especially in relation to PMSCs.

D. Civilians and Combatants in Non-international Armed Conflicts?

Since most armed conflicts today are of a non-international character, the law applicable to NIACs and especially its shortcomings have moved increasingly to the centre of attention. While AP II provides a similar, albeit truncated, civilian protection regime to AP I, a definition of 'civilians' is missing.[259] Various treaties adopted post-1977 that apply to NIACs refer to civilians; yet also without defining the term.[260] At the same time, non-state actors have espoused dissimilar understandings of 'civilians' in NIACs mainly relying on either the individuals' status as members in a collective entity or their conduct.[261] The *ICRC Study* defines civilians in both IACs and NIACs as 'persons who are not members of the armed forces',[262] and thus follows the drafting history of AP II.[263] However, it notes that 'practice is ambiguous as to whether members of armed opposition groups are considered members of armed forces or civilians'.[264] The International Criminal Court's definition of civilians refers more specifically to 'any person who is not a member of either State or non-State armed forces'.[265] The IIHL's *San Remo Manual*, on the other hand, identifies as civilians 'all those who are not fighters', comprising both members of the governmental and dissident armed forces and organised armed groups, as well as individuals involved in DPH.[266] Drawing on the ICTR's definition of the civilian population for

[256] ibid 12.

[257] JC Hansen, 'Rethinking the Regulation of Private Military and Security Companies under International Humanitarian Law' (2012) 35 *Fordham International Law Journal* 698, 735.

[258] Cameron and Chetail (n 232) 421–22.

[259] See chapter 5, section I.C.

[260] CCW Amended Protocol II, art 3(7)–(11); CCW Protocol III, art 2; Ottawa Convention, Preamble; Rome Statute, art 8(2)(e).

[261] For an overview of the inconsistent jurisprudence of international criminal tribunals, albeit including the definition of 'civilians' for the purpose of crimes against humanity, see Kleffner (n 53) 326–28.

[262] *CIHL*, vol I (n 14) rule 5; see also *Blaškić* (2000) (n 77) para 180.

[263] *CIHL*, vol I (n 14) 19.

[264] ibid 17.

[265] *Prosecutor v Katanga*, Judgment (7 March 2014) ICC-01/04-01/07, para 801, see also para 788; reaffirmed in *Prosecutor v Ntaganda*, Judgment (8 July 2019) ICC-01/04-02/06, para 921 and 883.

[266] *San Remo Manual* (n 47) 4–5.

crimes against humanity in the *Akayesu* case, the ICTY Trial Chamber in the *Strugar* case

> notes that members of the civilian population are people who are not taking any active part in the hostilities, including members of the armed forces who laid down their arms and those persons placed *hors de combat* by sickness, wounds, detention or any other cause.[267]

The ICTR Trial Chamber itself occasionally disregarded the absence of the combatant status in NIACs when it drew on Article 50 AP I and declared that, 'in accordance with this definition, for the purpose of protection of victims of armed conflict, all persons who are not combatants might be considered civilians'.[268] Having analysed commitments by organised armed groups with respect to their different approaches to DPH and the loss of civilian immunity, Camille Marquis-Bissonnette concludes that no consensus on a definition of civilians in NIACs exists.[269]

Scholarship deduces from the *ICRC Study* and international jurisprudence a variety of approaches to delineating persons as part of the principle of distinction in NIACs. These can be described as membership approach, specific acts approach, and 'direct participation on a gliding scale'.[270] Marquis-Bissonnette suggests a fourth approach which hinges on DPH 'with extended temporal scope'.[271] Yet the *Interpretive Guidance* notes that identifying the recurrent nature of a civilian's DPH for this purpose would be impractical for targeting decisions on the ground due to 'insurmountable evidentiary problems'.[272] As a result, 'the conceptual integrity of the categories of persons underlying the principle of distinction' and thus the protection of civilians may be undermined.[273] However, the instrument does distinguish between civilians who would temporarily lose their protection due to sporadic DPH and individuals who assume a 'continuous combat function', and thus lose not only their immunity from direct attack but also their civilian status in NIACs. This suggests a different concept

[267] *Prosecutor v Strugar*, Judgment (31 January 2005) IT-01-42-T, para 282.

[268] *Prosecutor v Kayishema and Ruzindana*, Judgment (21 May 1999) ICTR-95-1-T, para 179; in a subsequent decision it stated: 'There is no concise definition of "civilian" in the Protocols. As such, a definition has evolved through a process of elimination, whereby the civilian population is made up of persons who are not combatants or persons placed hors de combat, in other words, who are not members of the armed forces. … However, if civilians take a direct part in the hostilities, they then lose their right to protection as civilians *per se* and could fall within the class of combatant', *Prosecutor v Rutaganda*, Judgment (6 December 1999) ICTR-96-3-T, para 100; it then further limited the category of civilians excluding persons who qualify as 'perpetrator' under its previously stipulated definition, para 101.

[269] C Marquis-Bissonnette, 'The Definition of Civilians in Non-International Armed Conflicts: The Perspective of Armed Groups' (2016) 7 *Journal of International Humanitarian Legal Studies* 129, 153.

[270] Kleffner (n 53) 330–35.

[271] Marquis-Bissonnette (n 269) 151.

[272] *Interpretive Guidance* (n 36) 45.

[273] ibid.

of civilians for IACs and NIACs for the purpose of the principle of distinction. The *Interpretive Guidance*'s definition of civilians in IACs follows AP I, whereas in NIACs it distinguishes them from members of both the state armed forces and organised armed groups that are parties to the conflict, limiting members of organised armed groups to individuals with 'continuous combat function'.[274] Nils Melzer, who authored the *Interpretive Guidance*, admits that the instrument's different understandings of civilians who become members of organised armed groups in NIACs and IACs may create confusion, especially if both types of conflicts 'occur simultaneously within the same geographical and political context and involve the same actors'.[275]

The notion of 'armed forces' itself has also become the subject of debate in the context of NIACs.[276] The meaning of the term in CA3 is considered either to apply to state armed forces exclusively, or to also include non-state organised armed groups.[277] It is often stated that members of the governmental armed forces in NIACs are not civilians.[278] However, in the absence of the concept of combatants, their status is arguably unclear. Under the membership approach, civilians would lose their civilian status for being a member of the state armed forces or an organised armed group. It thus provides for a balance in standards for state armed forces and organised armed groups.[279] The targetability of their members at any time stems from the underlying idea that the threat to the enemy emanating from them is continuous and not limited to the time of their DPH.[280] Kleffner praises the approach for 'accommodating most clearly the notion that an armed conflict involves at least two *parties* with their own armed forces, which are equal before the laws of armed conflict'.[281] It understands the individual 'as part of a structured collective' with the objective of participating in hostilities.[282] The approach constructs these members of armed forces in analogy to IACs, but without entitlement to combatant privilege. It has been argued

[274] ibid 16 and 33.

[275] N Melzer, '"Direct Participation in Hostilities" and Membership in Organized Armed Groups – Background Paper' (ICRC, 2005) www.icrc.org/en/doc/assets/files/other/2005-04-background-doc-ws-iv-v-icrc.pdf, 4; see also Watkin, 'Opportunity Lost' (n 202) 651.

[276] *CIHL*, vol I (n 14) 12.

[277] Melzer, 'Principle of Distinction' (n 43) 310–14; the updated ICRC Commentary on GC III declares that the term 'refers to the armed forces of both the State and non-State Parties' to a NIAC, yet it notes that members of organised armed groups do not benefit from combatant immunity, ICRC, *Commentary on the Third Geneva Convention* (ICRC, 2020) ihl-databases.icrc.org/ihl/full/GCIII-commentary, paras 564–65 and 568.

[278] See, eg, Kleffner (n 53) 326; P Spoerri, 'The Contemporary Challenges to the Law on the Conduct of Hostilities' in GL Beruto (ed), *The Conduct of Hostilities – Revisiting the Law of Armed Conflict 100 Years after the Hague Conventions and 30 Years after the 1977 Additional Protocols* (IIHL, 2007) iihl.org/wp-content/uploads/2022/07/The-conduct-of-hostilities_2007.pdf, 148.

[279] Melzer, 'Background Paper' (n 275) 4.

[280] ICRC, 'Third Expert Meeting on the Notion of Direct Participation in Hostilities – Summary Report' (ICRC, 2005) www.icrc.org/en/doc/assets/files/other/2005-09-report-dph-2005-icrc.pdf, 64; Corn (n 223) 71; Marquis-Bissonnette (n 269) 144.

[281] Kleffner (n 53) 332.

[282] ibid.

to be in accordance with the legal framework, including CA3 and its application to 'each Party to the conflict'. The 'existence of collective entities that face each other, at least one of which is a non-state actor',[283] was thus already recognised in 1949. Yet the more recent discussions engage with the implications of this understanding for conceptualising the individuals involved.

Others have questioned whether the membership approach reflects the nature and dynamics of NIACs, including the 'ad hoc character of most armed groups', temporary membership of individuals in such groups, and changing coalitions.[284] Highlighting the *Interpretive Guidance*'s dissimilar approaches to determining membership in dissident armed forces and organised armed groups, Watkin criticises the absence of an explanation 'at what point, or on what basis, dissident armed forces would no longer fall under the same structures as State armed forces'.[285] The importance of conceptualising individuals within organised armed groups has also been stressed. Garraway deliberates their 'amorphous nature', including their 'political wings and also social wings, responsible for matters like education and welfare'.[286] As he notes, 'the issue became where to draw the dividing line'.[287] The *Interpretive Guidance* seems to have adopted the notion of the 'continuous combat function' for this purpose. Sivakumaran believes that this 'unreasonably narrows the notion of membership in the military wing of an armed group', and suggests instead that membership could be established both de facto based on ongoing DPH as well as de jure under 'the law of the non-state armed groups'.[288] The 'continuous combat function' criterion is reminiscent of, yet not equivalent to, the (former) distinction between combatants and non-combatants in the armed forces, which has been reduced to excluding medical and religious personnel from the universal combatant status of members of the armed forces in IACs.

Overall, the expert discussions[289] and resultant *Interpretive Guidance*, as well as the wider discourse in the surrounding literature, show an interest and need to engage with NIACs not only in the abstract. Unlike the cursory references by analogy and in contrast to IACs in the drafting process of the 1977 Additional Protocols, the actors construct entities and individuals involved in these conflict situations. Compared to its approach to IACs, which is firmly embedded in the legal framework, the *Interpretive Guidance* takes a more grounded approach in attaching meaning to individuals in NIACs. It could be argued that this is justified by the continuing shortage of (conventional) law on NIACs, thus requiring an almost *ab initio* discussion. However, it should be kept in mind that the

[283] ibid 324.
[284] Wenger and Mason (n 7) 850.
[285] Watkin, 'Opportunity Lost' (n 202) 654.
[286] Garraway, 'Direct Participation' (n 222) 176.
[287] ibid.
[288] Sivakumaran, *Law of NIAC* (n 195) 360.
[289] See, eg, ICRC, 'Third Expert Meeting' (n 280) 47–48.

involvement of organised armed groups in IACs was also not sufficiently deliberated in earlier law-making processes and is thus not adequately reflected in the state-centric rules and regulations.

Moreover, it needs to be emphasised that the concept of combatants continues to be absent from the law of NIACs. Various actors have attempted to advance the legal framework, often by applying 'the established rules for governing international armed conflict to its non-international counterpart',[290] not least in international criminal jurisprudence[291] and the *ICRC Study*.[292] The combatant status is a notable and significant exception to this trend.[293] It stems from a continuing unwillingness of states to extend combatant privilege to their non-state adversaries in NIACs, and their wish to retain the option of prosecuting members of non-state armed groups under domestic law.[294] In her analysis of the abstention from general prosecution of all persons who had participated in hostilities, Crawford perceives a trend which has 'gone some way to creating an *ex post facto* combat status' for non-state fighters in NIACs.[295] Yet Sivakumaran rightly emphasises that, although they can be functionally equivalent, 'amnesties are by no means the same as combatant immunity'.[296] Mačák also stresses that 'it cannot be inferred that a novel type of combatant status with independent legal valance has emerged in the law of NIAC'.[297]

Scholarship has focused on the question whether individuals who fight in NIACs *should* be granted a combatant privilege similar to IACs.[298] However, proposals such as Crawford's 'qualified combatants' privilege [which] *could* be granted to non-State combatants, so that they enjoy the benefits of the POW/combatant privilege', without granting international personality and legitimacy,[299] have been criticised by other academics. Frédéric Mégret emphasises

[290] Watkin, '21st Century Conflict' (n 1) 273.

[291] See especially *Prosecutor v Tadić*, Jurisdiction (2 October 1995) IT-9-1-AR72, para 97.

[292] *CIHL*, vol I (n 14) xxxv.

[293] See, eg, Bothe, 'CIHL' (n 18) 174–75; Kleffner (n 53) 321–22; S Watts, 'Present and Future Conceptions of the Status of Government Forces in Non-International Armed Conflict' (2012) 88 *International Law Studies* 145, 163–64; Corn (n 223) 64.

[294] Sivakumaran, *Law of NIAC* (n 195) 71; for an assessment of domestic criminal prosecutions of members of armed groups for their participation in hostilities see R Bartels, '"The Right to Participate in Hostilities": Combatant Privilege vs Criminal Responsibility for Members of Organised Armed Groups During International and Domestic Criminal Trials' in K Fortin and E Heffes (eds), *Armed Groups and International Law: In the Shadowland of Legality and Illegality* (Cheltenham, Elgar, 2023).

[295] Crawford, *Combatants and Insurgents* (n 151) 79.

[296] Sivakumaran, *Law of NIAC* (n 195) 520; see also A Bellal, '"Equals, But Not Equals': The Paradox of Amnesties and Armed Groups in Non-International Armed Conflict' in Fortin and Heffes (n 294).

[297] Mačák (n 126) 155.

[298] C Kreß and F Mégret, 'Debate – The Regulation of Non-International Armed Conflicts: Can a Privilege of Belligerency Be Envisioned in the Law of Non-International Armed Conflicts?' (2014) 96:893 *IRRC* 29, 38; R Geiß, 'The Possibility and the Challenges Raised by the Importation in NIAC of the IAC Conduct of Hostilities Rules' in C Marchand (ed), *The Distinction between International and Non-International Armed Conflicts: Challenges for IHL* (Milano, FrancoAngeli, 2016) 129; Bartels (n 294) 66–70.

[299] Crawford, *Combatants and Insurgents* (n 151) 162.

that combatant privilege is not inherently a humanitarian concept, but originally derived from the state-centric understanding of the legitimate use of force.[300] Similarly, Knut Ipsen remarks that:

> [t]he fundamental and, therefore, indispensable structure both of customary and treaty law with regard to combatant status, that is the legitimizing chain between a state or at least a partial subject of international law, the armed forces as an organ of this legal entity, and the combatant as the constituent part of this organ is diametrically opposed to a universal combatant status for international and non-international armed conflicts.[301]

Non-state actors engaged in clarifying and applying the law have adopted different strategies to avoid the discussion of combatant status in the context of NIACs. As the most categorical step, the *Manual on International Law Applicable to Air and Missile Warfare* excluded NIACs from its scope pointing to 'terminological difficulties', including the term 'combatants', as its reason.[302] The *ICRC Study* emphasises that it employs the term 'combatant' in its generic meaning rather than as a legal term of art.[303] It explains that it comprises 'persons who do not enjoy the protection against attack accorded to civilians',[304] which, according to Melzer, means members of the armed forces and organised armed groups as well as civilians involved in DPH.[305] The *Study* seems to invert the formal relationship between combatants and civilians in AP I by defining (functional) combatants for the purpose of the principle of distinction as everyone who does not benefit from civilian immunity. Kleffner observes that this wording 'shifts the attention away from the question who is the object of legitimate attack, to the question who is a "civilian" and thus enjoys protection', and relatedly the conditions under which this protection is lost due to DPH.[306]

This approach has attracted some disapproval. Rogers notes that the *ICRC Study* draws a difference 'between "combatant", which denotes somebody taking an active part in hostilities and "combatant status", which implies more but does not apply in [NIACs]'.[307] While the *Study* may have avoided broaching the controversial question of legitimate and lawful participation in armed conflicts,[308] it has been criticised for negatively influencing the targeting of civilians engaged in DPH, referred to as generic 'combatants'.[309] Nevertheless, the *Study* is not alone in adopting this approach. The Inter-American Commission

[300] Kreß and Mégret (n 298) 51–52 and 57–59.
[301] Ipsen (n 116) 95.
[302] HPCR (n 31) xvii; see also Crawford, *Non-Binding Norms* (n 243) 109.
[303] *CIHL*, vol I (n 14) 3 and 12–13.
[304] ibid 3.
[305] Melzer, 'Principle of Distinction' (n 43) 321.
[306] Kleffner (n 53) 325–26.
[307] Rogers (n 118) 109.
[308] K Watkin, 'The Notions of Combatant, Armed Group, Civilians, and Civilian Population in International Armed Conflicts' in Beruto (n 278) 57.
[309] Melzer, 'Principle of Distinction' (n 43) 321.

on Human Rights, for example, seems to employ the functional term 'combatant' in laying out the standards for the principle of distinction.[310] Emphasising that no person may be considered as both at the same time,[311] it declares that a civilian involved in DPH 'assumes the role of a combatant'; yet without the privileges and without losing the civilian status.[312]

Others, such as the IIHL in the *San Remo Manual*, resort to the term 'fighters' to denote generally individuals who directly participate in hostilities in NIACs.[313] It has been emphasised that these 'fighters' do not enjoy combatant privilege or POW status when captured.[314] Bothe commends this approach for adopting 'a terminology which correctly reflects the remaining difference between international and non-international conflicts'.[315] The ICTY Trial Chamber also remarked in the *Mrkšić* case that 'the term "fighter" now seems to be the appropriate term to be used as the equivalent for "combatants" in [NIACs]'.[316] The *ICRC Study* acknowledges the possibility of using this term, but declares that it 'would be translated as "combatant" in a number of languages and is therefore not wholly satisfactory either'.[317] Indeed, according to Petrov, the *San Remo Manual*'s introduction of the term 'fighters' 'did not echo in subsequent debates'.[318]

The Commentary on the *San Remo Manual* itself observes that the term 'fighters' does not form part of conventional IHL.[319] In light of the undetermined status of participants in NIACs, it is interesting to note that none of the background papers to the study, published collectively in the *Israel Yearbook on Human Rights* in 2000, examined this issue.[320] At the opening panel for the project, Dietrich Schindler mentioned the absent language of 'combatants' in the law of NIACs, which distinguishes between individuals on the basis of DPH instead.[321] However, as far as can be discerned from these records, the term 'fighter' was employed in a naturalised manner by Dieter Fleck, who directed the IIHL project, in his introductory remarks to the collection.[322] This approach, seemingly taken for granted, stands in contrast to another IIHL project a decade prior to the initiation of the *San Remo Manual*. In 1990, it compiled

[310] Inter-American Commission on Human Rights, 'Third Report on the Human Rights Situation in Colombia' (26 February 1999) OAE/Ser.L/V/II.102, paras 43–46.

[311] ibid para 61.

[312] ibid paras 54–55.

[313] *San Remo Manual* (n 47) 4; see also Kleffner (n 53) 315.

[314] Watts (n 293) 148; Crawford, *Non-Binding Norms* (n 243) 97–98.

[315] M Bothe, 'Direct Participation in Hostilities in Non-International Armed Conflict – Expert Paper' (ICRC, 2004) www.icrc.org/en/doc/assets/files/other/2004-05-expert-paper-dph-icrc.pdf, 9.

[316] *Prosecutor v Mrkšić et al*, Judgment (27 September 2007) IT-95-13/1-T, para 457.

[317] *CIHL*, vol I (n 14) 13.

[318] Petrov (n 29) 69.

[319] *San Remo Manual* (n 47) 4.

[320] (2000) 30 *Israel Yearbook on Human Rights* 1.

[321] D Fleck, 'Humanitarian Protection in Non-International Armed Conflicts: The New Research Project of the International Institute of Humanitarian Law' (2000) 30 *Israel Yearbook on Human Rights* 1, 11.

[322] ibid generally.

'principles and norms as crystallized or as emergent rules of international law' in its Declaration on the Rules of International Humanitarian Law Governing the Conduct of Hostilities in Non-International Armed Conflicts.[323] The first rule declared the principle of distinction as '[t]he obligation to distinguish between *combatants* and civilians'.[324] Since it fails to define these two terms for the purpose of the Declaration, it is uncertain whether the term 'combatant' is used as a descriptor or as a legal concept.

These inconsistencies may have been partly influenced by different approaches to NIACs. While the absence of a definition in the 1990 IIHL Declaration is a significant oversight, it seems to have been a continuation of the approach in earlier periods.[325] It amounts to a seemingly analogous adoption of the rules on IACs to NIACs without a consideration of the particularities of such conflicts including the individuals involved in hostilities. The preamble of the Declaration itself states that 'the 14th [IIHL] Round Table examined the application of certain rules to [NIACs] independently of the existence of treaty rules expressly adopted for such conflicts', and that it took into account rules which inspired the early written laws of war.[326] This indicates the law of IACs as the starting point. Other post-1977 instruments providing rules for NIACs seem more disengaged from the law of IACs. The mention and regulation of 'fighters' show at least that the actors involved acknowledge and, in some form, construct the situations without being entrapped in the traditional understandings of the law of IACs and the legitimacy of combatants.

IV. CONCLUSION – THE CONSTRUCTION OF INDIVIDUALS UNDER OR FOR INTERNATIONAL HUMANITARIAN LAW?

The existing legal framework as established by 1977 has been repeatedly reaffirmed; yet the meaning and scope of the concepts of combatants and civilians still seem unclear. Vague and taken-for-granted notions are endorsed in principle and not developed further. The apparent stability of the law stands in contrast to the discourse on the changing nature of warfare, including its 'civilianisation'. The law arguably fails to capture the complexity of (modern) armed conflicts, and may seem inadequate in determining the status of a person and form of protection. Nevertheless, the most notable difference between the post-1977 era and the earlier periods examined in this book is the absence of a momentous

[323] (7 April 1990) (hereafter 1990 IIHL Declaration) reprinted in D Schindler and J Toman (eds), *Laws of Armed Conflict: A Collection of Conventions, Resolutions, and Other Documents*, 4th edn (Leiden, Martinus Nijhoff, 2004), Preamble.

[324] ibid s A para 1 (emphasis added).

[325] On modelling the law of NIACs on the law of IACs and its critique see also S Sivakumaran, 'Re-envisaging the International Law of Internal Armed Conflict' (2011) 22 *EJIL* 219, 225–28 and 237–38.

[326] 1990 IIHL Declaration, Preamble.

diplomatic conference attempting to reaffirm and develop the law more or less comprehensively. Non-state actors, especially, have instead resorted to dissimilar processes of interpreting and clarifying the law, thus tweaking it for its adaptation to particular situations.

This chapter has shown that the construction of individuals is pursued in two different ways in the post-1977 period. First, the consistent reaffirmation of the existing legal framework, even in response to 'hard cases', has led to the construction of individuals in accordance with the law. Through treaty interpretation, individuals are identified as falling under a legal category of persons. Implicitly, the legitimacy of IHL is strengthened in the process as the concepts of combatants and civilians are endorsed as the primary, if not only, means of understanding individuals involved in and affected by such hostilities. This approach seems to be informed by a belief that the contemporary conventional and customary legal framework regulates IACs and NIACs sufficiently, if not comprehensively. It is repeatedly insisted that no person falls outside of the scope of IHL, and either benefits from a designated status or at least fundamental minimum guarantees. This has, for example, served as a rebuttal to claims that certain new developments in warfare, such as PMSCs, are unregulated under IHL. The resilience of IHL, and its constraining force on the understanding of individuals in armed conflict may be welcome for ensuring their protection under existing law, and preventing attempts to find legal *lacunae* which would permit unregulated and self-interested state conduct. However, it strains the understanding and application of the law when modern armed conflicts are moulded to fit into the patterns of established distinctions in IHL. Moreover, contemporary issues are depoliticised through the reliance on the legal framework since the meaning of individuals and situations is identified under the ostensibly neutral and objective law.

Second, within the realm of interpreting and clarifying the law, social constructions of individuals are still taking place. At times, the understanding of individuals participating in or affected by armed conflicts is not (only) determined by the legal regulation of combatants and civilians. This approach has been adopted in areas where the existing legal framework seems unclear or obsolete, or where the legal understanding differs from social conceptions. In particular, actors have tried to make sense of individuals in light of the wider normative and ideational environment as well as practical concerns. Indirectly, the discourse has involved questions of who *should* be protected how under the law, rather than who *is*. The meaning of an individual is thus constructed first and foremost in order to adjust the rules and concepts to accommodate them. The exclusionary nature of the legal concepts may be ameliorated in the process; for instance, some of the judicial bodies have 'softened their harder edges'.[327] This social construction may not always be obvious since the discourse

[327] Darcy (n 22) 138.

still tends to be embedded in the existing law. Drawing attention to the ongoing social construction of individuals in the various discourses shows that the process is not neutral.

While various actors are now deliberating the meaning of individuals in armed conflicts, often in light of the changing nature of warfare, shared understandings have still not been achieved. The discourses are commonly situated in more particularised settings where the discussion of the rules seems more contextualised in their application in practice and rooted in experience compared to most diplomatic conferences in the earlier periods. With respect to some actors, their mandate and institutional identity indeed requires the focus on specific cases before them, for instance, in the criminal prosecution of individuals in courts and tribunals. Even so, despite its unique normative setting and discursive environment, the ICTY in particular has been inclined to make more general and progressive declarations in its decisions. Other expert processes are focusing on certain types of conflicts or forms of warfare. While this may allow for more detailed and individualised contemplations which inform the meaning then attached to individuals, it is unlikely to influence the general understanding of such broad concepts as 'combatants' and 'civilians'.

Furthermore, the relevant discourses transcend various environments and involve a range of different actors. As in earlier periods, some individuals have participated in multiple expert processes.[328] However, the manuals adopted by such processes do not always reflect the divergent views of the experts behind them.[329] Certain composite actors, such as the ICTY, also do not speak with one voice, as shown above. The exploration of the debates in this chapter has generally revealed different approaches and the absence of shared understandings regarding individuals in armed conflicts. In their study on *Law-Making and Legitimacy in International Humanitarian Law*, Heike Krieger and Jonas Püschmann remark that the diversity of actors and their agendas in a decentralised legal order 'might contribute to legal insecurities and ambiguities, instead of clearing them up'.[330] Yet an examination of the identity and interests of each of these actors and how these impact their understanding of combatants and civilians is beyond the scope of this book.

Moreover, the influence of specific actors on potentially more general understandings is diffuse. In earlier periods, discussions were concentrated at key diplomatic conferences. These provided opportunities for conceptualisations and discourses to be brought into focus and to meet, even if not all actors formerly involved may have been present at the time. In contrast, the post-1977 discourses seem rather disconnected lacking the necessary interaction which

[328] eg Michael Schmitt, William Boothby, Kenneth Watkin and Wolff Heintschel von Heinegg, see further Petrov (n 29) 79–80.

[329] ibid 78–79.

[330] H Krieger and J Püschmann, 'Law-Making and Legitimacy in International Humanitarian Law' in Krieger and Püschmann (n 3) 7.

may lead to the construction of a shared understanding. They sometimes overlap and intersect, especially in the consideration of participation in hostilities which is not regulated under the concept of combatants. Yet, although they are related, they remain separate as the efforts are concerned with different aspects of the law. Consequently, they provide diverse responses regarding the individuals' treatment in the power of a party to a conflict, targetability, or legitimacy when participating in hostilities. The multitude of attempts at interpreting, clarifying and developing IHL today through fragmented, dissimilar processes may indeed inhibit a coherent social construction of individuals in armed conflicts.

Additionally, the involvement of mainly non-state actors arguably also diminishes the influence of the discourses on the development of the law. Sivakumaran observes that IHL is developed in an interactive process by 'the community of international humanitarian lawyers' which 'includes, but is not limited to, states. It also includes international courts and tribunals, the ICRC, academics, and others'.[331] In particular, '[t]he day to day making and shaping of international law, in the form of interpretation of treaties, the identification of custom, and the clarification of the law tends to be done by state-empowered entities and non-state actors'.[332] Nevertheless, these actors themselves have no immediate law-making power and their conceptualisations, therefore, require state endorsement for the effectiveness of normative standards. This was reaffirmed in a resolution adopted at the International Conference of the Red Cross and Red Crescent in 2011.[333] International jurisprudence, the *ICRC Study*, the *Interpretive Guidance* on DPH, as well as other soft law instruments derive their legal value from their acceptance by states in their responses and interactions. Crawford further notes that state involvement in the creation of non-binding instruments increases the perception of their legitimacy.[334] The traditional state-centric nature of the international legal system thus continues to restrain non-state actors with varying authority and discursive power in an admittedly more complex process of shaping legal concepts. Yet the main conversations in this period remain distant from the formal international law-making level.

The approach and influence of non-states actors differs in this respect from their role in the wider law-making process in the earlier periods. The previous chapters examined numerous examples where non-state actors adopted draft conventions which they intended or hoped to be institutionalised by states as legally binding texts at diplomatic conferences. In terms of the regulation and

[331] Sivakumaran, 'Law of Armed Conflict' (n 203) 120.

[332] ibid 159–60; see also S Sivakumaran, 'Beyond States and Non-State Actors: The Role of State-Empowered Entities in the Making and Shaping of International Law' (2017) 55 *Columbia Journal of Transnational Law* 343.

[333] ICRC, *31st International Conference* (n 19) 1; see also G Nolte, 'Interpretation and Identification of International Humanitarian Law: Responses of the International Law Commission' in Krieger and Püschmann (n 3) 247; H Krieger and J Püschmann, 'A Legitimacy Crisis of International Humanitarian Law?' in Krieger and Püschmann (n 3) 433.

[334] Crawford, *Non-Binding Norms* (n 243) 233–34.

protection of individuals, this allowed the actors to proclaim *lex ferenda*. Even expert manuals such as the IDI's Oxford Manual on the Laws of War on Land in 1880 bore this characteristic. In contrast, expert manuals of the past decades are intended to reflect binding law in a non-binding document.[335] As Petrov observes, '[f]rom engines in the codification era expert manuals have turned into ends in themselves as a reaction to a halt in treaty-making'.[336] Consequently, while they may adapt the law to apply to different, possibly novel contexts, underlying elements of IHL are only reaffirmed,[337] including the concepts of combatants and civilians and the principle of distinction. Robin Geiß and Anni Pues also suggest that these manuals may indeed contribute to the stagnation or blockade of 'established, state-driven law-making processes' since 'they may help to conceal genuine gaps in the existing body of law and obfuscate normative demands for further development of the law'.[338]

The post-1977 discourses not only differ from those surrounding the reaffirmation and development of the law in earlier periods in terms of the processes of which they form part, but also to some degree in their content. While the language may have changed from '*franc-tireurs*' and 'partisans' to 'unlawful combatants' and civilians who are directly participating in hostilities, the underlying questions of who may engage in such conduct and who is protected remain ultimately the same. In particular, participation in hostilities by individuals without entitlement has been debated since the early written laws of war. Yet the protection of individuals, especially civilians, has taken centre-stage over the regulation of organised warfare today. Indeed, the question of combatant privilege seems to have been largely set aside as the concept of combatants has not been renegotiated or extended. This may be due to the lack of state involvement and non-state actors not broaching this highly political issue.

As in the post-1949 period,[339] the perceived objective of IHL is the protection of peaceful civilians and the civilian population. Despite this predominant concern for civilians, their presumed innocence does not always overshadow their potential role as fighting agents. Unlike during the negotiation at the 1970s Diplomatic Conference, they are constructed as both victims and participants in armed conflicts. Some actors today are attempting to align the existing law and its conceptualisation of civilians with concrete situations which include the possibility of their DPH. Shielding civilians is thus pursued not only by restricting the lawful participation of combatants, but also by clarifying and refining the limitations to the general protection of civilians themselves. At the same

[335] Petrov (n 29) 6; R Geiß and A Pues, 'International Manuals in International Humanitarian Law: A Rejoinder to Wouter G. Werner' in Krieger and Püschmann (n 3) 234.

[336] Petrov (n 29) 9.

[337] Wouter Werner describes this as the Janus-face character of these manuals, WG Werner, 'The Law at Hand: Paratext in Manuals on International Humanitarian Law' in Krieger and Püschmann (n 3) 221–22.

[338] Geiß and Pues (n 335) 239.

[339] See chapter 5.

time, the actors' apparent shared belief in the need for clear rules in a comprehensive, universal legal framework stands in contrast to the exclusionary, specific nature and scope of the laws of war in the early periods.[340] Leaving individuals, especially civilians involved in DPH, to the ambiguity of the unwritten laws of war seems no longer to be an option. Indeed, the *ICRC Study* indicates a desire for clarity and certainty even as regards CIHL, which is an inherently opaque form of law.

However, this construction of civilians as potential participants in hostilities appears to contradict the prevalent social understanding of civilians as innocent bystanders which is embedded in the 1977 legal framework itself. The negative definition of civilians as individuals who are not members of the armed forces or who do not qualify for combatant status[341] may have contributed to their perception as vulnerable non-belligerents. The principle of distinction also glosses over the potential DPH of civilians. Although the principle was designed and is perceived as a fundamental part of the protection regime for civilians, its codified form in Article 48 AP I does not in fact invoke a category of individuals which is immune from attack in absolute terms. It only establishes the presumption of their immunity.

In comparison to the early periods of the written laws of war, qualifiers such as 'inoffensive' or 'peaceful' no longer precede the word 'civilian'. Instead, the supposed exceptional 'offensiveness' or diversion from the naturalised peaceful existence of civilians is indicated with the notion of 'civilian DPH'. In her recent study on *The Humanitarian Civilian: How the Idea of Distinction Circulates Within and Beyond International Humanitarian Law*, Sutton highlights the qualities of 'civilianness' and 'combatantness' as signifiers where 'civilianness is connected to innocence, harmlessness, and non-participation, [whereas] combatantness is linked to danger, complicity, and participation in conflict'.[342] According to her, contemporary protection is based on these characteristics, which 'float in the air, potentially affixing to any individual at any given moment',[343] rather than the legal bright-line distinction between combatants and civilians. As seen above, in the post-1977 discourses, the concern for civilians takes shape as the professed need to provide protection for everyone who is not engaged in fighting. This assumption of civilian non-participation in hostilities also underlies the uneasiness with classifying, for example, 'unlawful combatants' and PMSC personnel as civilians. The social understanding of 'civilians' thus differs from the legal concept.

In the past years, emerging critical scholarship has demonstrated the (problematic) relationship between legal and social conceptualisations of civilians in the application and effectiveness of the law. Focusing on different aspects,

[340] See chapters 3–4.
[341] AP I, art 50.
[342] Sutton (n 211) 110.
[343] ibid 15.

these studies reveal the non-neutral nature and application of the concept of civilians, as well as understandings of innocence and vulnerability. In a detailed case-study of the ICTY, Claire Garbett shows how the meaning of civilians has been produced and shaped in the judicial process. In the absence of a positive definition of civilians in the law, she highlights the importance of national and ethnic group membership and social characteristics, such as gender and age, in constructing civilian identities.[344] Charli Carpenter argues that the principle of distinction and especially the notion of civilians have been gendered. She demonstrates how 'gender beliefs "piggy-backed" on or "stowed away" within the idea of civilian immunity'[345] affect the implementation and promotion of the legal norms by a variety of international actors.[346] Sutton examines the complexity and fluidity of the 'civilian' in IHL, arguing that civilianness in practice exists along a continuum comprising the 'civilian plus', 'mere civilian' and 'civilian minus'.[347] She suggests that 'civilianness' is a relative concept that has been pushed in different directions.[348] This development is not only driven by state practice but a variety of actors who 'avoid, ignore, adopt, apply, develop and promulgate IHL norms and rules', sometimes self-conceptualising their own status in the process in everyday life.[349] These studies have in common that they emphasise the influence of beliefs, ideas and biases on the functioning of IHL, and in particular the protection of civilians. In a significantly briefer form, this chapter has drawn attention to the importance of social understandings of individuals for the development of the law in the same period.

The ambiguity of the concept of civilians is at least partly due to the limited engagement with the notion during the drafting of AP I.[350] Another issue arising from the failure to construct individuals in the formal law-making process can be seen in the debate relating to NIACs. No shared social or legal understanding of participants in these types of conflicts existed by the time AP II was adopted. Out of fear of conferring or implying legitimacy contrary to the state-centric understanding of armed conflicts, the actors largely remained silent on this point.[351] The resultant implantation of concepts derived from a different context and legal body, namely relating to IACs, has caused uncertainties in the context of NIACs. Consequently, the post-1977 period has been characterised by a constant construction of meaning outside of the legal framework, albeit disguised as a form of interpretation and clarification. Melzer argues that conventional IHL applicable to IACs and NIACs 'builds on the same cardinal distinction between

[344] Garbett (n 137).
[345] C Carpenter, *Innocent Women and Children: Gender, Norms and the Protection of Civilians* (Aldershot, Ashgate, 2006) 19.
[346] ibid generally.
[347] Sutton (n 211) see especially 144–48.
[348] ibid 138–43.
[349] ibid 12–13.
[350] See chapter 5, section I.A.
[351] See chapter 5, sections I.C and II.C.

fighters and civilians'.[352] However, the term 'civilian' appears to have different meanings with respect to these two types of conflicts. The 'civilian' in the generally more conduct-based approach to the principle of distinction in NIACs seems to be exclusively of a peaceful character. Those participating in hostilities are no exception under the civilian side of the principle of distinction, as in IACs, since they are implicitly included in the notion of fighters. Referring to participants in NIACs as 'combatants', on the other hand, reveals the importance of social constructs instead of legal concepts. This is similarly noticeable in the discussion regarding 'unlawful combatants'. Problems may arise when differing understandings of 'civilians' and 'combatants' are confused in practice.[353] The generic use of terms today may risk the interpretation of the law of IACs through the prism of an understanding of the terms in NIACs.

The principle of distinction itself has also shaped the understanding of individuals in armed conflicts. Although the principle 'is premised on the dyad of military and civilian, targetable and non-targetable',[354] and thus constitutes a principle of the 'Hague Law', it structures the discourse in IHL generally, and seems to have been superimposed on all aspects of the law through a contemporary reading of its rules and regulations. The examination of the debates in relation to 'twenty-first century' warfare has shown that some uncertainties and ambiguities not only, or not at all, arise from an outdated legal framework. They sometimes emerge when the history inscribed in the law itself is inconsistent with present-day ideas, assumptions and values. Yet modifying the exclusionary protection regime of GC IV, for example, in accordance with contemporary understandings of civilians and victims of armed conflicts, or the prevalent belief in IHL's comprehensive protecting function, is restrained by the nature of international legal processes. Furthermore, some of the contested contemporary issues examined in this chapter suggest that certain participants in armed conflicts do not neatly fit into the concepts of combatants and civilians. Apparent 'categories' of individuals, such as 'unlawful combatants' or PMSC personnel, seem to transcend the boundaries and may fall into both depending on the circumstances and perspective. The more particularised discussions of situations of armed conflicts and the individuals implicated therein may evidence the inappropriateness of the binary distinction itself.

Indeed, while the principle of distinction has generally been reaffirmed and even elevated in its importance, it has also become the subject of critique among some scholars and commentators. Garbett notes various difficulties in its relation to contemporary armed conflicts. Most notably, she argues that, founded on an obsolete understanding of inter-state wars, the principle of distinction

[352] Melzer, *Comprehensive Introduction* (n 152) 125.

[353] The debate on the meaning of 'civilian population' in the context of crimes against humanity, and the conflation of the notion of 'civilian' in relation to this crime with IHL may further muddy the concept of civilians.

[354] Crawford, *Identifying the Enemy* (n 11) 16.

and notion of 'civilians' do 'not capture the complexities of the different "types" of persons present within internal conflicts'.[355] Moreover, no clear-cut distinction can be drawn between civilian and military functions of individuals and objects.[356] Stern also observes that the principle of distinction does not match reality where '[e]vents, people and actions rarely break down into the neat categories proposed by law. As such, applications of IHL require manipulating facts to fit within rigid legal categories'.[357] She believes that the laws 'are premised on inaccurate, outdated or unworkable categorisations' and stresses in particular its gendered problems.[358] Watkin criticises the binary understanding of individuals as either combatants or civilians, since it 'could erode the sanctity of "civilian" status if insurgent and other armed groups, who have no chance of attaining combatant status, are permitted to hide behind its protective cover'.[359] Also criticising the formalism of the principle of distinction, Martijn Keeman submits that difficulties in its interpretation and application could be avoided through a functional approach which relies on the concept of military objectives rather than formal categories of combatants and civilians.[360] Sutton suggests that the intensive debate on the notion of DPH in more recent years has drawn 'attention to the fact that the principle of distinction was widely viewed as a "disputed concept, one that was open to multiple reasonable interpretations"'.[361] She believes that 'the distinction between the civilian and the combatant is more a matter of degree than category'.[362]

A final word should be said about the humanitarian conceptualisation of individuals identified as a third approach in the post-1949 period.[363] A humanitarian protection of individuals irrespective of their status can be seen, for example, in the asserted extension of CA3, as comprising 'elementary considerations of humanity', to all armed conflicts regardless of their categorisation in the ICJ's decision in the *Nicaragua* case.[364] The ICTY's interlocutory decision in the *Tadić* case, often cited as an indication for the merging of the laws on IACs and NIACs, also declared that 'international law, while of course duly safeguarding the legitimate interests of States, must gradually turn to the protection of *human beings*'.[365] In 1983, Meron, one of the most prominent advocates of the idea of the 'humanisation' of IHL, called for a new instrument laying

[355] Garbett (n 137) 154.
[356] ibid.
[357] Stern (n 28) 176.
[358] ibid 219.
[359] Watkin, '21st Century Conflict' (n 1) 285.
[360] MJ Keeman, 'Is Formalism a Friend or Foe? Saving the Principle of Distinction by Applying Function over Form' (2013) 4 *Journal of International Humanitarian Legal Studies* 354.
[361] Sutton (n 211) 179.
[362] ibid 206.
[363] See chapter 5, section III.
[364] *Case Concerning Military and Paramilitary Activities in and against Nicaragua (Nicaragua v USA)*, Merits [1986] ICJ Rep 14, para 218.
[365] *Tadić* (1995) (n 291) para 97 (emphasis added).

out fundamental humanitarian standards in all situations which would consist of 'an irreducible and nonderogable core of human rights' in light of the 'inadequate reach of humanitarian and human rights law'.[366] Indeed, during the 1980s 'several, partly parallel and overlapping processes, mainly representing the work of academic or other experts', engaged with the issue.[367] In 1990, the Declaration of Minimum Humanitarian Standards[368] (Turku Declaration) was adopted at an expert meeting convened by the Institute for Human Rights of the Åbo Akademi University. It notes in its preamble the inadequacy of existing law in protecting 'human beings', and provides for the protection of 'all persons ... *irrespective of their legal status* and without any adverse discrimination'.[369] The terms 'combatants' and 'civilians' are not mentioned, nor is 'civilian' as a qualifier in the prohibition of spreading 'terror among the population' and the 'displacement of the population'.[370] Since the 1990 non-binding declaration was lacking official character and authority, the issue of 'Fundamental Standards of Humanity' was then adopted on the United Nations agenda. Yet Crawford notes that this 'instrument was considered by the United Nations in several forums, but did not eventuate into a UN declaration'.[371]

Nevertheless, it is not only because of the non-achievement of an influential international instrument providing safeguards for all human beings in conflict situations that the approach is not considered here in more detail. The Turku Declaration and related drafts proposed by academics,[372] as well as the wider discussions on the interplay between IHL and international human rights law, have not displaced the dominant conceptual structures of IHL which distinguish between IACs and NIACs, and categorise individuals as either combatants or civilians. More importantly, the idea of minimum humanitarian standards was not driven by concerns over deficiencies and gaps in the scope of application *ratione personae* of IHL rules. Instead, these standards were intended to apply regardless of the characterisation of conflict situations as IACs, NIACs or 'the gray zone between war and peace'.[373]

The principle of distinction and conceptualisation of individuals as either combatants or civilians informs and constrains the regulation of armed conflicts

[366] T Meron, 'On the Inadequate Reach of Humanitarian and Human Rights Law and the Need for a New Instrument' (1983) 77 *AJIL* 589, 604.

[367] M Scheinin, 'Turku/Åbo Declaration of Minimum Humanitarian Standards (1990)' (ICHPR 2005) ichrp.org/files/papers/91/120B_-_Turku-Abo_Declaration_of_Minimum_Humanitarian_Standards_Scheinin__Martin__2005.pdf, para 2.

[368] (2 December 1990) reprinted in Schindler and Toman (n 323).

[369] ibid, Preamble and art 2 (emphasis added), see also art 4.

[370] ibid arts 6–7.

[371] Crawford, *Non-Binding Norms* (n 243) 55.

[372] See also T Meron, 'Draft Model Declaration in Internal Strife' (1988) 28:262 *IRRC* 59; H-P Gasser, 'A Measure of Humanity in Internal Disturbances and Tensions: Proposal for a Code of Conduct' (1988) 28:262 *IRRC* 38.

[373] A Eide, A Rosas and T Meron, 'Combating Lawlessness in Gray Zone Conflicts through Minimum Humanitarian Standards' (1995) 89 *AJIL* 215, 216–17.

today. Persisting uncertainties and perceived gaps may theoretically function as starting points for developments in the law through the adoption of new regulations or the evolutionary interpretation of existing ones. However, no overarching change can be observed with respect to the concepts of combatants and civilians in the post-1977 era. The incoherent construction of individuals in constant struggles between understandings *de lege ferenda* and *de lege lata* fails to influence the development of the law. Yet a caveat seems to be in order. As Robert Kolb remarks in his attempt to periodise modern IHL, '[i]t is always difficult to encapsulate current developments within a clear-cut set of theoretical explanations'.[374]

[374] R Kolb, 'The Main Epochs of Modern International Humanitarian Law since 1864 and Their Related Dominant Legal Constructions' in KM Larsen, CG Cooper and G Nystuen (eds), *Searching for a "Principle of Humanity" in International Humanitarian Law* (Cambridge, Cambridge University Press, 2013) 52.

7

Conclusion

THE REGULATION AND protection of individuals in armed conflicts under international humanitarian law (IHL) are fundamentally linked to understandings of legitimate and lawful participants in hostilities, and war victims. As this book has shown, the conceptualisation of individuals in this respect has changed over time since the adoption of the first multilateral treaty on the laws of war on land in 1864. Contrary to the dominant understanding of the law and its history today, the rules and regulations have generally *not* been formed based on a binary distinction between combatants and civilians. While this book is not the first historical account to challenge the conventional narrative, it contributes to the existing critical studies by providing a detailed analysis of how individuals have been perceived and negotiated in the social processes leading to the adoption of conventional law. It emphasises the contestations over meanings attached to individuals for the purpose of IHL at various moments in time, by diverse actors and in different settings. This struggle has impacted the writing of the book itself, which strains to convey unsettled ideas in a coherent narrative. Moreover, each period in the history of conventional IHL has been characterised by significantly different factors and dynamics which render generalisations about the evolution of the law difficult. Nevertheless, some overarching developments can be deduced.

I. THE SEPARATE HISTORIES OF THE CONCEPTS OF COMBATANTS AND CIVILIANS

The enquiry in this book has emphasised that the principle of distinction is not a timeless, foundational element of IHL. The law has not been characterised by a shifting dividing line between the concepts of 'combatants' and 'civilians' which may suggest their interrelated nature. The relationship between combatants and civilians was occasionally hinted at in the negotiations of treaties, yet without constructing them as counterparts of a clear binary system in the discourses. For practical reasons, the formation of interdependent conceptualisations of combatants and civilians was partly prevented by the negotiation of the prisoners of war and civilian convention in different committees in 1949, and the sequencing of agenda items of the same committee at the 1970s Diplomatic Conference. More generally, however, the concepts were introduced into conventional IHL at different moments in time, through dissimilar dynamics and actors. Although the structure of the forgoing chapters may suggest the parallel regulation and protection of two primary categories of persons, each concept has its own unique history with divergent trajectories.

The concept of combatants was principally constructed by states at diplomatic conferences. Some elements of the concept appear to have been uncontroversial throughout its history, including the conferral of belligerent immunity and prisoner of war status on lawful participants in hostilities. It was introduced into conventional law at the 1899 Hague Peace Conference, but the meaning and personal scope of the concept had mainly been shaped a quarter of a century earlier at the 1874 Brussels Conference. Although the well-known criteria for the scope *ratione personae* of the combatant status thus originated from the first attempts at developing the written laws of war, they were the institutionalisation of a disagreement. It was commonly believed at the time that the provisions in the Hague Regulations were not a comprehensive delineation of who may count as a combatant. Even so, this nineteenth-century concept, which derived from the context of European warfare and was negotiated by only a small number of states, became naturalised and was subsequently reaffirmed in several law-making processes. Indeed, states which were reluctant to revise its personal scope often deliberately relied on the established legal framework to maintain the status quo. The contested origin of the concept, as well as values and ideas ingrained in it, were thus disguised under the ostensibly neutral and universal language of the law. The Hague Regulations' conditions were, nonetheless, reinterpreted and slightly modified under the 1977 First Additional Protocol to the 1949 Geneva Conventions (AP I), which brought the combatant status for the first time into interrelation with civilians. Moreover, a more flexible design was adopted under the pressure of the vocal movement in support of freedom fighters and self-determination. As a result, two divergent definitions of combatants coexist today in conventional law in form of the Hague Regulations and AP I. This may arguably even further undermine a shared understanding of the concept's personal scope under IHL.

Throughout the negotiations of the combatant status, different assumptions and biases regarding legitimate participation in hostilities were voiced. They were informed by varying perceptions of the value of regular and organised warfare as the presumed ideal way of conducting hostilities, on the one hand, and the importance of fighting for a just cause, on the other. The normative basis and argumentation for the latter claims have evolved in accordance with a changing ideational framework from patriotism, leading to the rise of the population in defence of the nation, to the notion of self-determination in the context of the decolonisation process. Overall, however, the concept of combatants has been fairly static in the history of conventional IHL. Its significance in designating lawful participation in hostilities has been consistently reaffirmed. It continues to be associated with states, and their sovereign right to use force. For example, in the development of the early written laws of war, the *levée en masse* was associated with the state's sovereign self-defence. AP I, meanwhile, stipulates that the armed forces must belong to a party to the conflict, normally a state. This connection persisted even when the ideational and normative context had sufficiently evolved to facilitate the regulation of guerrilla warfare under the law. The state-centric nature of the concept can also be seen in the non-incorporation of the combatant status into the law of non-international armed conflicts (NIACs). Lastly, its discussion has been largely confined to the inter-state level as non-state actors appear to have refrained from broaching this highly sensitive and political question. Nevertheless, the combatant status remains a contested concept in which the perception of legitimate participation in hostilities and its lawful regulation do not always clearly align.

The concept of civilians has a significantly shorter history since it was arguably only established in conventional IHL in 1977. The path towards its formalisation in law has been shaped by intermittent developments along different routes. While other scholars have noted that the concept was absent in the early written laws of war,[1] this book has highlighted the complexity of how individuals who do not belong to the armed forces have been considered in the law-making processes and how they have been incorporated into the rules and regulations. The dissimilar approaches to these individuals throughout the early periods suggest that a clear understanding of a status of persons who would today be termed civilians, with distinct privileges and protections, did not exist. They were initially considered as intruders in the organised conduct of warfare and as potential threats to regular combatants, for example, due to their engagement in unregulated combat and in the treatment of wounded soldiers. Only since the First World War were they increasingly seen as vulnerable victims of armed conflicts. The perceived role of the law in relation to these individuals has consequently shifted from restraining their involvement in the hostilities, to shielding them from the consequences of warfare. The objective of protecting civilians and the civilian population rose in significance over time and even became the seemingly primary aim of IHL.

The changing assumptions about individuals who do not belong to the armed forces and their relation to and involvement in hostilities is also reflected in the varying terminology that has been employed to describe them, ranging from 'inhabitants' and the 'population' to 'non-combatants' and 'civilians'. Their presumed or desired character has been emphasised differently throughout the periods as 'peaceful' and 'non-offensive', as 'enemy civilians', or as merely 'civilians' whose 'direct participation in hostilities' needs to be stressed for its deviation from the supposed norm. In deliberating the law, the participating actors did not have the opposite of combatants in mind; instead, they were regulating and protecting, for example, inhabitants of undefended towns or occupied territory, enemy nationals, women and children, wounded and sick persons, or

[1] See, eg, A Alexander, 'The Genesis of the Civilian' (2007) 20 *LJIL* 359; S Scheipers, *Unlawful Combatants: A Genealogy of the Irregular Fighter* (Oxford, Oxford University Press, 2015) 101.

human beings. Indeed, some of the first safeguards were informed by similarities, rather than differences, between the situations of combatants and civilians. The otherwise *unprotected* 'civilian' was seen to benefit from the provision of safeguards analogous to the rules and regulations on combatants. Moreover, a conceptual change occurred from considering individuals as members of a collective, especially as belonging to a party to the armed conflict, to protecting them in their own right. The various rules and protection regimes in the early periods were designed for individuals in specific circumstances. In some ways, the provisions suggest a more intimate construction of individuals since they were not just built upon the theoretical interrelation between civilians and combatants and the principle of distinction. They provide more specialised guarantees compared to general protections associated with the abstract notion of civilians. This closer reading of the law-making processes reveals a variety of conceptualisations of individuals in armed conflicts that are commonly not mentioned, or conflated with the overarching concept of civilians in the dominant narrative.

Nevertheless, the diplomatic conferences have been characterised by the absence of a sustained engagement with individuals who do not belong to the armed forces, each for different reasons. During the period of the early written laws of war, these individuals were normally deemed to be outside of the battlefield or involved as unregulated and unprotected intruders, and thus a general legal status was seemingly not believed to be required. The value of protecting innocent and vulnerable individuals who do not belong to the armed forces had yet to be embraced in a legal framework that was biased towards inter-state relations. The 1949 Geneva Convention Relative to the Protection of Civilian Persons in Time of War (GC IV) expanded the protective scope of the laws of war. However, its drafters were still only concerned with a narrowly defined category of 'protected persons' in the hands of the enemy. The treaty arguably sheds no light on the meaning of 'civilians', most of whom were still not regarded as requiring protection under the conventional laws of war. In 1977, AP I established a general concept of civilians and a related comprehensive protection regime in conventional IHL. It transformed the notion of civilian immunity, which merged diverse normative frameworks and efforts of non-state actors, into a legal concept. The moral belief in the virtue of protecting civilians from the consequences of war began to shape the directedness of the development of the law and became the yardstick against which new proposals, including the reformulation of the combatant status, were judged. The same normative underpinnings informed a similar protection regime in the second Additional Protocol on NIACs. Yet the negotiations at the 1970s Diplomatic Conference took for granted an understanding of innocent civilians which had been shaped outside of the formal law-making process.

Consequently, the question of who qualifies as civilians and why these persons should be protected were not sufficiently addressed at times when it was necessary to consider them. Differences in the perceived personal scope of the vague notion of civilians were left unsettled both during the inter-war years, when a social concept of civilians appears to have emerged, as well as at the 1970s Diplomatic Conference. Indeed, throughout a century of law-making up to that point, there had been no shared agreement that all individuals who do not belong to the armed forces are innocent and vulnerable persons who should be shielded by the law from suffering the consequences of war. AP I naturalised and depoliticised an abstract concept of civilians that diverged from definitions which non-state actors had proposed in their respective attempts to promote the protection of civilians under IHL. Although any legal status is necessarily a generalisation, the definition of civilians enshrined in Article 50 is deliberately wide enough to comprise anyone who would not qualify as a combatant, thus embedding the binary distinction that permeates the conventional narrative today. It was informed by the belief that every person should have a status under the law, rather than a common understanding of which persons would be considered civilians. Nevertheless, this negative definition seems to have closed the discussion of the scope *ratione personae* of civilians; as part of a binary, it is assumed to provide the desired clarity and effectiveness of the law.

Yet the concept of civilians established in AP I is intangible without taking into consideration the scope *ratione personae* of combatants. This blunt dichotomy fails to reflect the position, needs and vulnerabilities of everyone who qualifies as a civilian especially in complex conflict situations. Due to its inherent vagueness and indeterminateness, the definition of civilians in AP I is also open to being imbued with social understandings which are not substantiated in the law itself. Critical studies have shown how the concept of civilians has been imparted with certain ideas, assumptions and biases in the application of the law, and how it has been manipulated for the agendas of different actors.[2] The resultant shared understanding of civilians as a social construct seems to be at odds with the legal definition of its personal scope under Article 50 AP I. This can be seen, for example, in the debates regarding 'unlawful combatants' and private military and security companies. The apparent inconsistency is arguably enshrined in the convention itself given the difference between the scope of this definition and civilians who are immune from direct attack.

The struggle to conceptualise individuals who do not belong to the armed forces is ongoing, but it is now bound by the language of the law which itself is unquestioned in the dominant narrative. After the construction of civilians was insufficiently pursued in the inter-state law-making processes, various non-state actors have been constructing the meaning of the law in the post-1977 era, yet without developing the general concept of civilians. By interpreting and applying the law in practice, as well as trying to clarify it in expert processes, these

[2] See, eg, C Carpenter, *Innocent Women and Children: Gender, Norms and the Protection of Civilians* (Aldershot, Ashgate, 2006); C Garbett, *The Concept of the Civilian: Legal Recognition, Adjudication and the Trials of International Criminal Justice* (Abingdon, Routledge, 2015); R Sutton, *The Humanitarian Civilian: How the Idea of Distinction Circulates Within and Beyond International Humanitarian Law* (Oxford, Oxford University Press, 2021).

actors focus on certain elements of the concept of civilians, including 'direct participation in hostilities' (DPH) and the loss of civilian immunity. Their efforts constitute a move away again from the abstract, generic concept of civilians to considerations of particular forms of warfare or situations. Their attempts to make sense of civilians in armed conflicts suggest that in order to appreciate the experience of hostilities and the available protection under IHL, it may be necessary to step back and construct the individual, rather than the 'civilian'.

Overall, the historical development of the concept of civilians has been more complex than that of the concept of combatants. The protection of civilians has been constructed and reconstructed through the efforts of among others humanitarian actors and international lawyers acting as norm entrepreneurs and epistemic communities. Yet the role of non-state actors in shaping conceptualisations of individuals for the purpose of IHL has been constrained by their own self-understanding and their perception by states, as well as the nature of the international legal system. The law expanded incrementally to protect individuals who are today known as civilians, first as enemies who may be vulnerable to unnecessary suffering or arbitrary abuse, and later as the main victims of armed conflicts due to their presumed innocence. The development of the law has not been linear; instead, different conceptualisations of individuals who do not belong to the armed forces experienced continuities and breaks before the concept of civilians systematised many, but not all, proposals for their protection. For instance, the reliance on nationality as a criterion for protection illustrates a fluctuation in the humanitarian scope of the safeguards, which have not always been progressively expanded to shield an increasing number of individuals.[3] Rather than a history of a sustained effort to protect (innocent) civilians, this book has shown a varying degree of attention paid to individuals who neither belong to the armed forces nor take part in the hostilities. Although the overall growing focus on civilians and their protection may seem to be in line with the common theorisation of IHL's history as humanitarian progress,[4] the historical account offered in this book emphasises that this 'progress' was not inevitable or smooth. It was shaped by changing and continuing struggles over the conceptualisation of individuals, as well as inadvertent and strategic oversights.

II. THE IMPORTANCE OF A CRITICAL HISTORICAL APPROACH

With the adoption of AP I, the principle of distinction and a binary understanding of combatants and civilians appears to have gained momentum.

[3] See further S Landefeld, 'The Changing Significance of Nationality for the Protection of Civilians in the Hands of a Party to an International Armed Conflict' (2023) 28 *Journal of Conflict & Security Law* 501.

[4] F Mégret, 'Theorizing the Laws of War' in A Orford and F Hoffmann (eds), *The Oxford Handbook of the Theory of International Law* (Oxford, Oxford University Press, 2016) 769.

Contemporary international legal scholarship, expert proceedings and jurisprudence tend to interpret IHL and its history through the prism of the principle of distinction. The prima facie simplicity of the principle, with individuals being either combatants or civilians, implies certainty regarding the privileges, obligations and protections associated with each status. As Rebecca Sutton remarks, many international actors 'continue to reach for this bright-line binary vision' since it 'remains alluring for its promise of clarity'.[5] The superimposition of the concepts of combatants and civilians onto the fragmented system of IHL may be deemed to unify its constituent parts by injecting coherence and filling any gaps. However, approaching the law of former times with the contemporary desire to bring all situations and persons under the protective mantle of the law may falter due to inconsistencies in the conceptualisations which are embedded in the treaty texts. Moreover, even today, following the adoption of definitions, regulations and protections for combatants and civilians in conventional law and statements of the customary legal framework, the concepts appear to mean different things to different people. The dominant narrative hides the nuances, incoherence and gaps in the law, and overlooks that its history is riddled with tensions and disagreements. It not only disregards the long and continuing struggle of conceptualising individuals for the purpose of IHL, it also exaggerates the role of the principle of distinction in the legal framework.

This book has shown that the development of the regulations and protections of individuals in armed conflicts has been significantly more complicated than the established narrative suggests. It provides a critical historical account of the evolving understandings of individuals which have informed conventional IHL since the latter half of the nineteenth century. Its elucidation of the laws and their conceptual underpinnings, adopted at different stages in the history of IHL, also undermines the centrality of the principle of distinction in the contemporary legal framework since many of the conventions are still in force today. Much of the fragmented system of IHL, both with regard to the conduct of hostilities and the protection of victims, does not provide for a binary distinction between combatants and civilians. A closer reading of the law and its history reveals more nuances in the rules and regulations; yet the law inevitably still fails to reflect the messiness of wars and armed conflicts on the ground.

The various conceptualisations of individuals who fall under the definition of civilians today may suggest a more fine-grained system of regulations and safeguards than the binary distinction. However, each of these categories of individuals is still necessarily exclusionary, leading to a possible lack of protection for some and *lacunae* in situations which are not regulated by the law. Comprising clusters of protection for diverse categories of individuals, with overlaps and gaps in between, the system may not provide sufficient safeguards.

[5] Sutton (n 2) 206.

The implication of this study may seem to be an increase in uncertainty, rather than a contribution to the prevalent attempt in the discipline to clarify the law. There may be a concern that highlighted *lacunae* may be exploited, and civilians may be vilified, thus questioning their innocence and undermining their protection. Yet some of these problems already exist today, and may in fact be driven by the dominant narrative on the binary distinction between combatants and civilians. The notion of the 'innocent' civilian has raised questions about the applicability of the law, including GC IV, notwithstanding its protection regime being designed for individuals regardless of their participation in hostilities. It may lead to the non-application of a law that is not based on this understanding. Awareness therefore needs to be drawn to the discrepancy between the conceptual underpinnings of the law and contemporary dispositions towards viewing individuals in armed conflicts. An ostensibly overarching concept of civilians should not distract from the continuation of a more multifaceted understanding of individuals underneath.

The interpretation and application of the law in complex conflict situations is challenging; however, the challenge of attaching meaning to individuals has also shaped the creation and evolution of conventional IHL, which is the focus of this book. Instead of attempting to solve the commonly perceived issue that the distinction between combatants and civilians is increasingly becoming blurred, and as a result the law difficult to apply, this book queries whether the legal framework has been indeed crafted upon this binary distinction. The blinkered focus on the principle of distinction, and concepts of combatants and civilians, arguably stifles an engagement with the question of how and why certain categories, including the combatant and civilian status themselves, seem not to be fit for the purpose for which they were designed. This is not to suggest that the principle of distinction, or the concepts of combatants and civilians are unnecessary or obsolete. The principle has its place and role to play in the regulation of armed conflicts, notably with respect to targeting, including the evaluation of the prohibition of indiscriminate attacks and the principle of proportionality. The protection of vulnerable and innocent human beings under IHL has undeniably been a valuable and important development of the law over the past approximately 160 years. It could be argued that difficulties and problems arise from the general prevalence of the principle of distinction and the transferral of its concepts into regimes for which they have not been designed, such as the so-called 'Geneva Law'. However, the debates surrounding DPH also show that, even in the application of the principle of distinction to targeting, the contemporary notion of innocent civilians may be inadequate. Protection from direct attack is not synonymous with the concept of civilians, as civilians involved in DPH may be targeted, while combatants *hors de combat* may not. The conduct of the individual and the context need to be considered to determine whether civilian immunity applies.

Indeed, although the concepts of combatants and civilians are repeatedly reaffirmed in contemporary discourses, they are broken down again into their various layers in an engagement with specific (categories of) individuals in particular situations. Such grounded considerations as in specialised expert processes and jurisprudence may not naturally be achieved in formal law-making settings. Contextualised deliberations of individuals and how they are involved in or affected by armed conflicts were often eclipsed by technical debates over legal norms and rules at diplomatic conferences. While the negotiations were occasionally interspersed with states' particular concerns derived from their own experiences, participants with a history of law-making and existing normative obligations in the field tended to be engaged in abstract and detached legal discourses. Many actors deliberately invoked (allegedly) existing principles and regulations to achieve desired outcomes, to facilitate new developments, and sometimes to hide politically and historically motivated interests behind the ostensibly neutral language of the law. Yet the belief in and portrayal of the legal framework has also had a constraining effect on the conceptualisation of individuals and development of the law.

The plethora of compromise provisions, including the frequently disputed scope *ratione personae* of the concept of combatants, may give reason to doubt whether achieving shared understandings among states through treaty negotiations is in fact possible. Ambiguous clauses appear necessary for reaching required agreements among delegations. The nature of diplomatic conferences, especially since 1945, as unwieldy events with a multitude of diverse participating actors may also inherently prevent the construction of individuals to an extend that would reflect and do justice to the complexity and diversity of armed conflicts themselves, and amount to shared understandings. The question, therefore, arises whether the meaning of individuals in armed conflicts can be sufficiently constructed within the formal law-making process.

The enquiry into the different ways of constructing individuals in armed conflicts throughout the law-making processes is, nonetheless, relevant. The law guides our understanding of social phenomena and relations, in this case the position and role of individuals in armed conflicts; yet it is itself also based on a certain interpretation of the world. In other words, since the law is constitutive of the meaning of combatants and civilians, it is important to understand the ideas and assumptions upon which it has been grafted. The approach adopted in this book may expose the absence of a shared understanding that has been enshrined in the law. It highlights whether the law reflects the beliefs and perceptions of just a few, and not all, participating actors. By considering the social processes behind the law, it reveals why certain understandings of individuals are *not* adopted in treaties at specific points in time. It draws attention to the non-engagement with some meanings when actors instead rely on taken-for-granted notions which have their origins outside of the inter-state negotiations at diplomatic conferences. In such cases, it may emphasise the shortcomings of the entrenchment of vague ideas in legal rules and regulations. The enquiry's approach inspired by social constructivism thus sheds a new light on uncertainties in the law. In response to the conventional narrative, it shows that the law is not based on a clear distinction between combatants and civilians but an unresolved struggle over the meaning of individuals in armed conflicts. Moreover, while IHL masks social conceptualisations of individuals in armed conflicts and depoliticises the process of treaty interpretation, this book is intended to highlight the continuing social construction and thus serves as a tool for critique.

Nevertheless, the limits of the approach should not be overlooked. Despite drawing attention to the complexity of law-making, it still constitutes a simplification of the intricate processes at diplomatic conferences and their histories. Furthermore, the narrow focus of the enquiry on deliberate attempts at developing the law fails to provide a complete picture of how and where certain understandings are produced which are taken-for-granted at these events. Although the additional analysis of the efforts of non-state actors provides further insights into the social process of law-making, an even more nuanced understanding of individuals in armed conflicts could be attained through wider social, political and historical explorations of developments at the international level and within different regions, states and cultures. However, such an examination of the development of IHL over more than 160 years is beyond the scope of this book.

Ultimately, this study provides no more and no less than a historical account of how certain understandings of individuals have emerged, evolved, persisted or disappeared in the law-making processes of conventional IHL. In this respect, since 'descriptive beliefs deal with questions of *is* (as actors see it), they can be subjected to empirical scrutiny in a way that *ought* questions cannot'.[6] The book, therefore, does not consider who *should* fall under the combatant or civilian status, or what the respective concepts *should* entail, which would require a normative analysis. It does not propose a framework for legal reform. Even without the analytical constraints of the adopted approach, such an endeavour would be inconsequential in light of the requirement of shared understandings between states for effective international law. Under the current political international climate, a renegotiation of conventional IHL remains unlikely and would potentially be even dangerously regressive regarding the regulation and protection of individuals in armed conflicts. Nevertheless, because of the continuation of the existing legal framework, a critical understanding of its terms is essential. In his study of the 'entangled foundations' of the 1949 Geneva Conventions, Boyd van Dijk emphasises the historical, theoretical and conceptual importance of recovering the past. According to him, '[u]nearthing international law's history brings to life the original registers of key terms, thereby fracturing entrenched understandings of its principal ideas and norms'.[7]

[6] Carpenter (n 2) 28.

[7] B van Dijk, 'Human Rights in War: On the Entangled Foundations of the 1949 Geneva Conventions' (2018) 112 *AJIL* 553, 579; regarding the significance of engaging with the history of IHL see also B van Dijk, 'What Is IHL History Now?' (2022) 104:920–921 *IRRC* 1621.

This study reveals the historicity of the concepts of combatants and civilians as the history of constructing individuals in armed conflicts has become embedded in the conventional rules and regulations. It thus highlights the nuances and complexity which a reading of the law through the prism of the principle of distinction obscures. Moreover, it challenges the universality of the law and undermines any assumptions about its inevitability. Even though the law may not change, it still needs to be problematised and its neutrality and objectivity questioned.

Appendix: Chronology of Binding and Non-binding Instruments

1863 General Orders No 100: Instructions for the Government of Armies of the United States in the Field

Resolutions of the Geneva International Conference, International Committee for Relief to the Wounded

1864 Convention for the Amelioration of the Condition of the Wounded in Armies in the Field

1868 Additional Articles Relating to the Condition of the Wounded in War

Declaration Renouncing the Use, in Time of War, of Explosive Projectiles under 400 Grammes Weight

1874 Project of an International Declaration Concerning the Laws and Customs of War

1880 Manual on the Laws of War on Land, IDI

1899 Convention (II) with Respect to the Laws and Customs of War on Land and Its Annex: Regulations Respecting the Laws and Customs of War on Land

1906 Convention for the Amelioration of the Condition of the Wounded and Sick in Armies in the Field

1907 Convention (IV) Respecting the Laws and Customs of War on Land and Its Annex: Regulations Respecting the Laws and Customs of War on Land

Convention (V) Respecting the Rights and Duties of Neutral Powers and Persons in Case of War on Land

Convention (IX) concerning Bombardment by Naval Forces in Time of War

1917 Agreement between Great Britain and Germany Concerning Combatant and Civilian Prisoners of War

1918 Agreement between the British and German Governments Concerning Combatant Prisoners of War and Civilians

1921	Résolution XII: Limitation de la guerre, ICRC
	Résolution XIV: Guerre civile, ICRC
	Résolution XV: Code des prisonniers de guerre déportés, évacués et réfugiés, ICRC
1923	Hague Rules concerning the Control of Wireless Telegraphy in Time of War and Air Warfare
	Résolution VIII: Situation des civils tombés au pouvoir de l'ennemi, ICRC
1924	Draft Regulations for the Treatment of Civilian Prisoners of War, ILA
1925	Résolution XII: Situation des non-combattants sur territoire ennemi, ICRC
1929	Convention Relative to the Treatment of Prisoners of War
1934	First draft Convention adopted in Monaco (Sanitary cities and localities)
	Draft International Convention on the Condition and Protection of Civilians of Enemy Nationality Who Are on Territory Belonging to or Occupied by a Belligerent, ICRC
1938	Resolution XIV: Rôle and Activity of the Red Cross in Time of Civil War, ICRC
	Draft Convention for the Protection of Civilian Populations against New Engines of War, ILA
	Protection of Civilian Populations against Bombing from the Air in Case of War, League of Nations
1948	Draft Convention Relative to the Treatment of Prisoners of War, ICRC
	Draft Convention Relative for the Protection of Civilian Persons in Time of War, ICRC
1949	Geneva Convention for the Amelioration of the Condition of the Wounded and Sick in Armed Forces in the Field
	Geneva Convention for the Amelioration of the Condition of Wounded, Sick and Shipwrecked of Armed Forces at Sea
	Geneva Convention Relative to the Treatment of Prisoners of War
	Geneva Convention Relative to the Protection of Civilian Persons in Time of War
1956	Draft Rules for the Limitation of the Dangers Incurred by the Civilian Population in Time of War, ICRC

1965	Resolution XXVIII: Protection of Civilian Populations Against the Dangers of Indiscriminate Warfare, ICRC
1968	Resolution XXIII: Human Rights in Armed Conflicts, International Conference on Human Rights
	Respect for Human Rights in Armed Conflicts, UNGA Res 2444(XXIII)
1969	Resolution on the Distinction Between Military Objectives and Non-military Objectives in General and Particularly the Problems Associated with Weapons of Mass Destruction, IDI
	Resolution XVIII: Status of Combatants in Non-International Armed Conflicts, ICRC
1970	Respect for Human Rights in Armed Conflicts, UNGA Res 2674(XXV)
	Basic Principles for the Protection of Civilian Populations in Armed Conflicts, UNGA Res 2675(XXV)
	Respect for Human Rights in Armed Conflicts, UNGA Res 2676(XXV)
1971	Respect for Human Rights in Armed Conflicts, UNGA Res 2852(XXVI)
1973	Basic Principles of the Legal Status of the Combatants Struggling against Colonial and Alien Domination and Racist Regimes, UNGA Res 3103(XXVIII)
	Draft Protocol Additional to the Geneva Conventions of 12 August 1949, and Relating to the Protection of Victims of International Armed Conflicts
	Draft Protocol Additional to the Geneva Conventions of 12 August 1949, and Relating to the Protection of Victims of Non-International Armed Conflicts
1977	Protocol Additional to the Geneva Conventions of 12 August 1949, and Relating to the Protection of Victims of International Armed Conflicts
	Protocol Additional to the Geneva Conventions of 12 August 1949, and Relating to the Protection of Victims of Non-International Armed Conflicts
1980	Protocol on Prohibitions or Restrictions on the Use of Incendiary Weapons
	Protocol on Prohibitions or Restrictions on the Use of Mines, Booby-Traps and Other Devices

1990	Declaration on the Rules of International Humanitarian Law Governing the Conduct of Hostilities in Non-International Armed Conflicts, IIHL
	Declaration of Minimum Humanitarian Standards, Institute for Human Rights, Åbo Akademi University
1994	San Remo Manual on International Law Applicable to Armed Conflicts at Sea, IIHL
1996	Protocol on Prohibitions or Restrictions on the Use of Mines, Booby-Traps and Other Devices as amended on 3 May 1996
1997	Convention on the Prohibition of the Use, Stockpiling, Production, and Transfer of Anti-Personnel Mines and on their Destruction
1998	Rome Statute of the International Criminal Court
2005	Study into Customary International Humanitarian Law, ICRC
2006	The Manual on the Law of Non-International Armed Conflict, IIHL
2008	Convention on Cluster Munitions
	The Montreux Document on Pertinent International Legal Obligations and Good Practices for States Related to Operations of Private Military and Security Companies During Armed Conflict
2009	Interpretive Guidance on the Notion of Direct Participation in Hostilities under International Humanitarian Law, ICRC
	Manual on International Law Applicable to Air and Missile Warfare, Harvard Program on Humanitarian Policy and Conflict Research
2013	Tallinn Manual on the International Law Applicable to Cyber Warfare
2017	Treaty on the Prohibition of Nuclear Weapons

Bibliography

Abbenhuis, M, *The Hague Conferences and International Politics, 1898–1915* (London, Bloomsbury, 2019)

Adler, E, 'Seizing the Middle Ground: Constructivism in World Politics' (1997) 3 *European Journal of International Relations* 319

Adler, E, 'Constructivism and International Relations' in W Carlsnaes, T Risse and BA Simmons (eds), *A Handbook of International Relations*, 2nd edn (London, SAGE, 2013)

Ador, G, 'Egalité de traitement pour les prisonniers de guerre militaires ou civils' (1915) 46:181 *Bulletin International des Sociétes de la Croix-Rouge* 5

Aldrich, GH, 'New Life for the Laws of War' (1981) 75 *AJIL* 764

Aldrich, GH, 'Progressive Development of the Laws of War: A Reply to Criticisms of the 1977 Geneva Protocol I' (1986) 26 *Virginia Journal of International Law* 693

Alexander, A, 'The Genesis of the Civilian' (2007) 20 *LJIL* 359

Alexander, A, 'A Short History of International Humanitarian Law' (2015) 26 *EJIL* 109

Alexander, A, 'International Humanitarian Law, Postcolonialism and the 1977 *Geneva Protocol I*' (2016) 17 *Melbourne Journal of International Law* 15

Alexander, A, 'The "Good War": Preparations for a War against Civilians' (2019) 15 *Law, Culture and the Humanities* 227

Alexander, A, 'Filling the Gaps: The Expansion of International Humanitarian Law and the Juridification of the Free-Fighter' (2023) 14 *Journal of International Humanitarian Legal Studies* 274

Alexander, A, 'Revolutionary War and the Development of International Humanitarian Law' in B Cuddy and V Kattan (eds), *Making Endless War: The Vietnam and Arab-Israeli Conflicts in the History of International Law* (Ann Arbor, University of Michigan Press, 2023)

Allott, P, 'The Concept of International Law' (1999) 10 *EJIL* 31

Alschner, W, 'Locked in Language: Historical Sociology and the Path Dependency of Investment Treaty Design' in M Hirsch and A Lang (eds), *Research Handbook on the Sociology of International Law* (Cheltenham, Elgar, 2020)

Armstrong, D, Farrell, T and Lambert, H, *International Law and International Relations* (Cambridge, Cambridge University Press, 2007)

Barsalou, O, 'Preparing for War: The USA and the Making of the 1949 Geneva Conventions on the Laws of War' (2018) 23 *Journal of Conflict & Security Law* 49

Bartels, R, '"The Right to Participate in Hostilities": Combatant Privilege vs Criminal Responsibility for Members of Organised Armed Groups During International and Domestic Criminal Trials' in K Fortin and E Heffes (eds), *Armed Groups and International Law: In the Shadowland of Legality and Illegality* (Cheltenham, Elgar, 2023)

Baxter, RR, 'So-Called Unprivileged Belligerency: Spies, Guerrillas, and Saboteurs' (1951) 28 *BYIL* 323

Baxter, RR, 'The First Modern Codification of the Law of War: Francis Lieber and General Orders No. 100 (II)' (1963) 3:26 *IRRC* 234

Baxter, RR, 'The Evolving Laws of Armed Conflicts' (1973) 60 *Military Law Review* 99

Baxter, RR, 'Humanitarian Law or Humanitarian Politics? – The 1974 Diplomatic Conference on Humanitarian Law' (1975) 16 *Harvard International Law Journal* 1

Bellal, A, '"Equals, But Not Equals': The Paradox of Amnesties and Armed Groups in Non-International Armed Conflict' in K Fortin and E Heffes (eds), *Armed Groups and International Law: In the Shadowland of Legality and Illegality* (Cheltenham, Elgar, 2023)

Bellal, A and Casey-Maslen, S, *The Additional Protocols to the Geneva Conventions in Context* (Oxford, Oxford University Press, 2022)

Bellinger, JB and Haynes, WJ, 'A US Government Response to the International Committee of the Red Cross Study *Customary International Humanitarian Law*' (2007) 89:866 *IRRC* 443

Ben-Nun, G, *The Fourth Geneva Convention for Civilians: The History of International Humanitarian Law* (London, IB Tauris, 2020)

Benvenisti, E, 'The Birth and Life of the Definition of Military Objectives' (2022) 71 *ICLQ* 269

Benvenisti, E and Lustig, D, 'Monopolizing War: Codifying the Laws of War to Reassert Governmental Authority, 1856–1874' (2020) 31 *EJIL* 127

Benvenisti, E and Lustig, D, 'Revisiting the Memory of Solferino: Knowledge Production and the Laws of War' in A Bianchi and M Hirsch (eds), *International Law's Invisible Frames: Social Cognition and Knowledge Production in International Legal Processes* (Oxford, Oxford University Press, 2021)

Berman, N, 'Privileging Combat? Contemporary Conflict and the Legal Construction of War' (2004) 43 *Columbia Journal of Transnational Law* 1

Best, G, *Humanity in Warfare – The Modern History of the International Law of Armed Conflicts* (London, Methuen, 1983)

Best, G, *War and Law Since 1945* (Oxford, Clarendon Press, 1994)

Bianchi, A, 'Epistemic Communities' in J d'Aspremont and S Singh (eds), *Concepts for International Law: Contributions to Disciplinary Thought* (Cheltenham, Elgar, 2019)

Bindschedler-Robert, D (ed), *Report of the Conference on Contemporary Problems of the Law of Armed Conflicts* (New York, Carnegie Endowment for International Peace, 1971)

Bluntschli, JC, *Das Moderne Kriegsrecht der Civilisirten Staten: Als Rechtsbuch Dargestellt* (Nördlingen, Beck, 1866)

Bluntschli, JC, *Das Moderne Völkerrecht der Civilisirten Staten: Als Rechtsbuch Dargestellt* (Nördlingen, Beck, 1872)

Bluntschli, JC, *Denkwürdiges aus meinem Leben, III. Band* (R Seyerlen ed, Nördlingen, Beck, 1884)

Bond, JE, 'Proposed Revisions in the Law of War Applicable to Internal Conflict' (1972) 12 *Santa Clara Lawyer* 223

Boothby, B, '"And for Such Time As": The Time Dimension to Direct Participation in Hostilities' (2010) 42 *New York University Journal of International Law & Politics* 741

Bordwell, P, *The Law of War between Belligerents: A History and Commentary* (Chicago, Callaghan & Co, 1908)

Bothe, M, 'Customary International Humanitarian Law: Some Reflections on the ICRC Study' (2005) 8 *YIHL* 143

Bothe, M, Partsch, KJ and Solf, WA, *New Rules for Victims of Armed Conflicts: A Commentary on the Two 1977 Protocols Additional to the Geneva Conventions of 1949*, 2nd edn (Leiden, Martinus Nijhoff, 2013)

Boyle, A, 'Soft Law in International Law-Making' in MD Evans (ed), *International Law*, 5th edn (Oxford, Oxford University Press, 2018)

Boyle, A and Chinkin, C, *The Making of International Law* (Oxford, Oxford University Press, 2007)

de Breucker, J, 'La Déclaration de Bruxelles de 1874 concernant les lois et coutumes de la guerre' (1974) 28 *La chronique de politique étrangère* 3

Brunnée, J and Toope, SJ, *Legitimacy and Legality in International Law: An Interactional Account* (Cambridge, Cambridge University Press, 2010)

Bujard, D, 'The Geneva Convention of 1864 and the Brussels Conference of 1874' (1974) 14:163 *IRRC* 527

Bugnion, F, 'The International Committee of the Red Cross and the Development of International Humanitarian Law' (2004) 5 *Chicago Journal of International Law* 191

Bugnion, F, 'The International Committee of the Red Cross and Nuclear Weapons: From Hiroshima to the Dawn of the 21st Century' (2005) 87:859 *IRRC* 511

Bugnion, F, 'Birth of an Idea: The Founding of the International Committee of the Red Cross and of the International Red Cross and Red Crescent Movement: From Solferino to the Original Geneva Convention (1859–1864)' (2012) 94:888 *IRRC* 1299

Bugnion, F, 'Adoption of the Additional Protocols of 8 June 1977: A Milestone in the Development of International Humanitarian Law' (2017) 99:905 *IRRC* 785

Burwell DG, 'Civilian Protection in Modern Warfare: A Critical Analysis of the Geneva Civilian Convention of 1949' (1973) 14 *Virginia Journal of International Law* 123

Caglioti, DL, *War and Citizenship: Enemy Aliens and National Belonging from the French Revolution to the First World War* (Cambridge, Cambridge University Press, 2021)

Cameron, L, 'Private Military Companies: Their Status under International Humanitarian Law and Its Impact on Their Regulation' (2006) 88:863 *IRRC* 573

Cameron, L and Chetail, V, *Privatizing War: Private Military and Security Companies under Public International Law* (Cambridge, Cambridge University Press, 2013)

Camins, E, 'The Past as Prologue: The Development of the "Direct Participation" Exception to Civilian Immunity' (2008) 90:872 *IRRC* 853

Carnahan, BM, 'The Law of Air Bombardment in Its Historical Context' (1975) 17 *Air Force Law Review* 39

Carpenter, C, *Innocent Women and Children: Gender, Norms and the Protection of Civilians* (Aldershot, Ashgate, 2006)

Checkel, JT, 'The Constructivist Turn in International Relations Theory' (1998) 50 *World Politics* 324

Chetail, V, 'The Contribution of the International Court of Justice to International Humanitarian Law' (2003) 85:850 *IRRC* 235

Choate, JH, *The Two Hague Conferences* (New York, Kraus Reprint, 1969)

Clarke, MHF, Glynn, T and Rogers, APV, 'Combatant and Prisoner of War Status' in MA Meyer (ed), *Armed Conflict and the New Law: Aspects of the 1977 Geneva Protocols and the 1981 Weapons Convention* (London, British Institute of International and Comparative Studies, 1989)

Clémens, R, *Le projet de Monaco: le droit et la guerre, villes sanitaires et villes de sécurité, assistance sanitaire internationale* (Paris, Libraire du Recueil Sirey, 1937)

Cockayne, J, 'Regulating Private Military and Security Companies: The Content, Negotiation, Weaknesses and Promise of the Montreux Document' (2009) 13 *Journal of Conflict & Security Law* 401

Colby, E, 'Laws of Aerial Warfare' (1926) 10 *Minnesota Law Review* 207

Collin, F, *Social Reality* (London, Routledge, 1997)

Commission of Jurists, 'General Report' (1938) 32 *AJIL Supplement* 1

Corn, G, 'Two Sides of the Combatant Coin – Untangling Direct Participation in Hostilities from Belligerent Status in Noninternational Armed Conflicts' in W Banks (ed), *Counterinsurgency Law: New Directions in Asymmetric Warfare* (Oxford, Oxford University Press, 2013)

Coudert, FR, François, JPA and Lauterpacht, H, 'La Revision du Droit de la Guerre' (1954) 45:1 *AIDI* 555

Crawford, E, *The Treatment of Combatants and Insurgents under the Law of Armed Conflict* (Oxford, Oxford University Press, 2010)

Crawford, E, 'Regulating the Irregular – International Humanitarian Law and the Question of Civilian Participation in Armed Conflicts' (2011) 18 *U.C.Davis Journal of International Law & Policy* 163

Crawford, E, *Identifying the Enemy: Civilian Participation in Armed Conflict* (Oxford, Oxford University Press, 2015)

Crawford, E, 'Tracing the Historical and Legal Development of the *Levée en Masse* in the Law of Armed Conflict' (2017) 19 *Journal of the History of International Law* 329

Crawford, E, 'The Enduring Legacy of the St Petersburg Declaration: Distinction, Military Necessity, and the Prohibition of Causing Unnecessary Suffering and Superfluous Injury in IHL' (2018) 20 *Journal of the History of International Law* 544

Crawford, E, *Non-Binding Norms in International Humanitarian Law: Efficacy, Legitimacy, and Legality* (Oxford, Oxford University Press, 2021)

Crossland, J, *War, Law and Humanity: The Campaign to Control Warfare, 1853–1914* (London, Bloomsbury, 2018)

Crowe, J and Weston-Scheuber, K, *Principles of International Humanitarian Law* (Cheltenham, Elgar, 2013)

Cryer, R, 'The International Committee of the Red Cross' "Interpretive Guidance on the Notion of Direct Participation in Hostilities": See a Little Light' in R Geiß, A Zimmermann and S Haumer (eds), *Humanizing the Laws of War: The Red Cross and the Development of International Humanitarian Law* (Cambridge, Cambridge University Press, 2017)

Cryer, R, 'The Impact of Human Rights Advocacy: Between (mis)stating the Law and Pursuing Humanitarian Policies?' in H Krieger and J Püschmann (eds), *Law-Making and Legitimacy in International Humanitarian Law* (Cheltenham, Elgar, 2021)

Cullen, A, *The Concept of Non-International Armed Conflict in International Humanitarian Law* (Cambridge, Cambridge University Press, 2010)

Darcy, S, *Judges, Law and War: The Judicial Development of International Humanitarian Law* (Cambridge, Cambridge University Press, 2014)

Darcy, S, *To Serve the Enemy: Informers, Collaborators, and the Laws of Armed Conflict* (Oxford, Oxford University Press, 2019)

Davey, E, 'Decolonizing the Geneva Conventions: National Liberation and the Development of Humanitarian Law' in AD Moses, M Duranti and R Burke (eds), *Decolonization, Self-Determination, and the Rise of Global Human Rights Politics* (Cambridge, Cambridge University Press, 2020)

Davis, GB, 'Doctor Francis Lieber's Instructions for the Government of Armies in the Field' (1907) 1 *AJIL* 13

DePue, JF, 'The Amended First Article to the First Draft Protocol Additional to the Geneva Conventions of 1949 – Its Impact Upon Humanitarian Constraints Governing Armed Conflict' (1977) 75 *Military Law Review* 71

DeSaussure, H, 'The Laws of Air Warfare: Are There Any?' (1971) 5 *The International Lawyer* 527

Diggelmann, O, 'The Periodization of the History of International Law' in B Fassbender and A Peters (eds), *The Oxford Handbook of the History of International Law* (Oxford, Oxford University Press, 2012)

van Dijk, B, 'Human Rights in War: On the Entangled Foundations of the 1949 Geneva Conventions' (2018) 112 *AJIL* 553

van Dijk, B, '"The Great Humanitarian": The Soviet Union, the International Committee of the Red Cross, and the Geneva Conventions of 1949' (2019) 37 *Law and History Review* 209

van Dijk, B, 'What Is IHL History Now?' (2022) 104:920-921 *IRRC* 1621

van Dijk, B, *Preparing for War: The Making of the Geneva Conventions* (Oxford, Oxford University Press, 2022)

Dinstein, Y, 'Unlawful Combatancy' (2003) 79 *International Law Studies* 151

Dinstein Y, *Non-International Armed Conflicts in International Law* (Cambridge, Cambridge University Press, 2014)

Dinstein, Y, *The Conduct of Hostilities under the Law of International Armed Conflict*, 3rd edn (Cambridge, Cambridge University Press, 2016)

Dörmann, K, 'Unlawful Combatants' in A Clapham and P Gaeta (eds), *The Oxford Handbook of International Law in Armed Conflict* (Oxford, Oxford University Press, 2014)

Dörmann, K, 'Protection of Civilians' in D Fleck (ed), *The Handbook of International Humanitarian Law*, 4th edn (Oxford, Oxford University Press, 2021)

Doswald-Beck, L, 'The Value of the 1977 Geneva Protocols for the Protection of Civilians' in MA Meyer (ed), *Armed Conflict and the New Law: Aspects of the 1977 Geneva Protocols and the 1981 Weapons Convention* (London, British Institute for International and Comparative Law, 1989)

Doswald-Beck, L, (ed), *San Remo Manual on International Law Applicable to Armed Conflicts at Sea* (Cambridge, Cambridge University Press, 1995)
Dowdeswell, TL, 'The Brussels Peace Conference of 1874 and the Modern Laws of Belligerent Qualification' (2017) 54 *Osgoode Hall Law Journal* 805
Draper, GIAD, 'The "Protected Person" in Occupied Territory' (1965) 114 *Collected Courses of the Hague Academy of International Law* 119
Draper, GIAD, 'The Status of Combatants and the Question of Guerilla Warfare' (1971) 45 *BYIL* 173
Draper, GIAD, 'Human Rights and the Law of War' (1972) 1 *Virginia Journal of International Law* 326
Draper, GIAD, 'Humanitarian Law and Human Rights' [1979] *Acta Juridica* 193
Droop, HR, 'On the Relations between an Invading Army and the Inhabitants, and the Conditions under which Irregular Troops are Entitled to the Same Treatment as Regular Soldiers' in *Papers Read Before the Juridical Society: 1863–1870*, vol 3 (London, Wildy & Sons, 1871)
Durand, A, *History of the International Committee of the Red Cross: From Sarajevo to Hiroshima* (Geneva, Henry Dunant Institute, 1984)
Durham, H and Massingham, E, 'Who Is Protected Under International Humanitarian Law? Finding a Definition for "Direct Participation in Hostilities"' in DW Lovell and I Primoratz (eds), *Protecting Civilians During Violent Conflict: Theoretical and Practical Issues for the 21st Century* (London, Routledge, 2012)
Eide, A, Rosas, A and Meron, T, 'Combating Lawlessness in Gray Zone Conflicts through Minimum Humanitarian Standards' (1995) 89 *AJIL* 215
van Engeland, A, *Civilian or Combatant? A Challenge for the 21st Century* (Oxford, Oxford University Press, 2015)
Epstein, C, *The Power of Words in International Relations: Birth of an Anti-Whaling Discourse* (Cambridge, MIT Press, 2008)
Erickson, RJ, 'Protocol I: A Merging of the Hague and Geneva Law of Armed Conflict' (1979) 19 *Virginia Journal of International Law* 557
Eyffinger, A, *The 1899 Hague Peace Conference: 'The Parliament of Man, the Federation of the World'* (The Hague, Kluwer Law International, 1999)
Eyffinger, A, *The 1907 Hague Peace Conference: 'The Conscience of the Civilized World'* (The Hague, JudiCap, 2007)
Fazal, TM, *Wars of Law: Unintended Consequences in the Regulation of Armed Conflict* (Ithaca, Cornell University Press, 2018)
Fenrick, WJ, 'The Development of the Law of Armed Conflict Through the Jurisprudence of the International Criminal Tribunal for the Former Yugoslavia' (1998) 3 *Journal of Conflict & Security Law* 197
Ferrière, F, 'Projet d'une Convention internationale réglant la situation des civils tombés à la guerre au pouvoir de l'ennemi' (1923) 5:54 *IRRC* 560
Field, DD, *Draft Outlines of an International Code* (New York, Baker, Voorhis & Co, 1872)
Fierke, KM, 'Constructivism' in T Dunne, M Kurki and S Smith (eds), *International Relations Theories: Discipline and Diversity*, 4th edn (Oxford, Oxford University Press, 2016)
Finnemore, M, 'Rules of War and Wars of Rules: The International Red Cross and the Restraint of State Violence' in J Boli and GM Thomas (eds), *Constructing World Culture: International Nongovernmental Organizations Since 1875* (Stanford, Stanford University Press, 1999)
Finnemore, M, *The Purpose of Intervention: Changing Beliefs About the Use of Force* (Ithaca, Cornell University Press, 2003)
Finnemore, M and Sikkink, K, 'International Norm Dynamics and Political Change' (1998) 52 *International Organization* 887
Finnemore, M and Sikkink, K, 'Taking Stock: The Constructivist Research Program in International Relations and Comparative Politics' (2001) 4 *Annual Review of Political Science* 391
Fleck, D, 'Humanitarian Protection in Non-International Armed Conflicts: The New Research Project of the International Institute of Humanitarian Law' (2000) 30 *Israel Yearbook on Human Rights* 1

Fleck, D, 'The Law of Non-International Armed Conflict' in D Fleck (ed) *The Handbook of International Humanitarian Law*, 4th edn (Oxford, Oxford University Press, 2021)
Forsythe, DP, 'The 1974 Diplomatic Conference on Humanitarian Law' (1975) 69 *AJIL* 77
Fortin, K, 'Complementarity between the ICRC and the United Nations and International Humanitarian Law and International Human Rights Law, 1948–1968' (2012) 94:888 *IRRC* 1433
Frick-Cramer, RM, 'A propos des projets de conventions internationales réglant le sort des prisonniers' (1925) 7:74 *IRRC* 73
Frick-Cramer, R-M, 'Le Comité international de la Croix-Rouge et les Conventions internationals pour les prisonniers de guerre et les civils' (1943) 25:295 *IRRC* 567
Gade, EK, 'Defining the Non-Combatant: How Do We Determine Who is Worthy of Protection in Violent Conflict?' (2010) 9 *Journal of Military Ethics* 219
Gallopin, R, 'Action des Conférences internationales de la Croix-Rouge et du Comité international de la Croix-Rouge dans le domaine de la protection des civils en temps de guerre' (1939) 21:244 *IRRC* 287
Gallopin, R, 'La protection des civils en temps de guerre et la notion de l'objectif militaire' (1939) 21:247 *IRRC* 545
Garbett, C, *The Concept of the Civilian: Legal Recognition, Adjudication and the Trials of International Criminal Justice* (Abingdon, Routledge, 2015)
Gardam, JG, *Non-Combatant Immunity as a Norm of International Humanitarian Law* (London, Martinus Nijhoff, 1993)
Garner, JW, 'International Regulation of Air Warfare' (1932) 3 *Air Law Review* 103
Garraway, C, '"Combatants" – Substance or Semantics?' in MN Schmitt and J Pejic (eds), *International Law and Armed Conflict: Exploring the Faultlines – Essays in Honour of Yoram Dinstein* (Leiden, Martinus Nijhoff, 2007)
Garraway, C, 'Changing Character of the Participants in War: Civilianization of Warfighting and the Concept of "Direct Participation in Hostilities"' (2011) 87 *International Law Studies* 177
Garraway, C, 'Direct Participation and the Principle of Distinction: Squaring the Circle' in C Harvey, J Summers and ND White (eds), *Contemporary Challenges to the Laws of War – Essays in Honour of Professor Peter Rowe* (Cambridge, Cambridge University Press, 2014)
Gasser, H-P, 'A Measure of Humanity in Internal Disturbances and Tensions: Proposal for a Code of Conduct' (1988) 28:262 *IRRC* 38
Gasser, H-P, 'Some Legal Issues Concerning Ratification of the 1977 Geneva Protocols' in MA Meyer (ed), *Armed Conflict and the New Law: Aspects of the 1977 Geneva Protocols and the 1981 Weapons Convention* (London, British Institute for International and Comparative Law, 1989)
Geiß, R, 'The Possibility and the Challenges Raised by the Importation in NIAC of the IAC Conduct of Hostilities Rules' in C Marchand (ed), *The Distinction between International and Non-International Armed Conflicts: Challenges for IHL* (Milan, FrancoAngeli, 2016)
Geiß, R and Pues, A, 'International Manuals in International Humanitarian Law: A Rejoinder to Wouter G. Werner' in H Krieger and J Püschmann (eds), *Law-Making and Legitimacy in International Humanitarian Law* (Cheltenham, Elgar, 2021)
Geiß, R and Zimmermann, A, 'The International Committee of the Red Cross: A Unique Actor in the Field of the International Humanitarian Law Creation and Progressive Development' in R Geiß, A Zimmermann and S Haumer (eds), *Humanizing the Laws of War: The Red Cross and the Development of International Humanitarian Law* (Cambridge, Cambridge University Press, 2017)
Giladi, R, 'A Different Sense of Humanity: Occupation in Francis Lieber's Code' (2012) 94:885 *IRRC* 81
Giladi, R, 'The Enactment of Irony: Reflections on the Origins of the Martens Clause' (2014) 25 *EJIL* 847
Gill, R, 'The 1938 International Committee of the Red Cross Conference: Humanitarian Diplomacy and the Cultures of Appeasement in Britain' in N Wylie, M Oppenheimer and J Crossland (eds), *The Red Cross Movement: Myths, Practices and Turning Points* (Manchester, Manchester University Press, 2020)

Gillard, E-C, 'Business Goes to War: Private Military/Security Companies and International Humanitarian Law' (2006) 88:863 *IRRC* 525
Gillard, E-C, 'Protection of Civilians in the Conduct of Hostilities' in R Liivoja and T McCormack (eds), *Routledge Handbook of the Law of Armed Conflict* (London, Routledge, 2016)
Gómez del Prado, JL, 'Private Military and Security Companies and the UN Working Group on the Use of Mercenaries' (2009) 13 *Journal of Conflict & Security Law* 429
Gómez del Prado, JL, 'A United Nations Instrument to Regulate and Monitor Private Military and Security Contractors' (2011) 1 *Notre Dame Journal of International, Comparative & Human Rights Law* 1
Graf-Brugère, A-L, 'The Derogation Clause' in A Clapham, P Gaeta, and M Sassòli (eds), *The 1949 Geneva Conventions: A Commentary* (Oxford, Oxford University Press, 2015)
Graham, DE, 'The 1974 Diplomatic Conference on the Law of War: A Victory for Political Causes and A Return to the "Just War" Concept of the Eleventh Century' (1975) 32 *Washington & Lee Law Review* 25
Green, LC, *The Contemporary Law of Armed Conflict*, 3rd edn (Manchester, Manchester University Press, 2008)
Greenspan, M, *The Modern Law of Land Warfare* (Berkeley, University of California Press, 1959)
Greenwood, C, 'A Critique of the Additional Protocols to the Geneva Conventions of 1949' in H Durham and TLH McCormack (eds), *The Changing Face of Conflict and the Efficacy of International Humanitarian Law* (The Hague, Martinus Nijhoff, 1999)
Greenwood, C, 'International Humanitarian Law (Laws of War) – Revised Report for the Centennial Commemoration of the First Hague Peace Conference 1899' in F Kalshoven (ed), *The Centennial of the First International Peace Conference – Reports & Conclusions* (The Hague, Kluwer Law International, 2000)
Greenwood, C, 'The Law of War (International Humanitarian Law)' in MD Evans (ed), *International Law*, 2nd edn (Oxford, Oxford University Press, 2006)
Gutteridge, JAC, 'The Geneva Conventions of 1949' (1949) 26 *BYIL* 294
Haas, PM, 'Introduction: Epistemic Communities and International Policy Coordination' (1992) 46 *International Organization* 1
Hacker, DE, 'The Application of Prisoner-of-War Status to Guerrillas under the First Protocol Additional to the Geneva Conventions of 1949' (1978) 2 *Boston College International and Comparative Law Journal* 131
Hall, WE, *International Law* (Oxford, Clarendon Press, 1880)
Halleck, HY, *International Law; or Rules Regulating the Intercourse of States in Peace and War* (San Francisco, Bancroft & Co, 1861)
Hanke, HM, 'The 1923 Hague Rules of Air Warfare: A Contribution to the Development of International Law Protecting Civilians from Air Attack' (1993) 33:292 *IRRC* 12
Hansen, JC, 'Rethinking the Regulation of Private Military and Security Companies under International Humanitarian Law' (2012) 35 *Fordham International Law Journal* 698
Harvey, C, Summers, J and White, ND (eds), *Contemporary Challenges to the Laws of War – Essays in Honour of Professor Peter Rowe* (Cambridge, Cambridge University Press, 2014)
Hayashi, MN, 'The Principle of Civilian Protection and Contemporary Armed Conflict' in HM Hensel (ed), *The Law of Armed Conflict: Constraints on the Contemporary Use of Military Force* (Aldershot, Ashgate, 2006)
Heinsch, R, 'Judicial "Law-Making" in the Jurisprudence of the ICTY and ICTR in Relation to Protecting Civilians from Mass Violence: How Can Judge-Made Law Be Brought into Coherence with the Doctrine of the Formal Sources of International Law?' in P Ambach et al (eds), *The Protection of Non-Combatants during Armed Conflict and Safeguarding the Rights of Victims in Post-Conflict Society – Essays in Honour of the Life and Work of Joakim Dungel* (Leiden, Brill, 2015)
Heinsch, R, 'Distinction' in D Djukić and N Pons (eds), *The Companion to International Humanitarian Law* (Leiden, Brill, 2018)

Henckaerts, JM, '*Customary International Humanitarian Law*: A Response to US Comments' (2007) 89:866 *IRRC* 473
Henckaerts, J-M, 'The International Committee of the Red Cross and Customary International Humanitarian Law' in R Geiß, A Zimmermann and S Haumer (eds), *Humanizing the Laws of War: The Red Cross and the Development of International Humanitarian Law* (Cambridge, Cambridge University Press, 2017)
Henckaerts, J-M and Doswald-Beck, L, *Customary International Humanitarian Law, Volume II: Practice* (Cambridge, Cambridge University Press, 2005)
Henckaerts, J-M and Doswald-Beck, L, *Customary International Humanitarian Law, Volume I: Rules* (Cambridge, Cambridge University Press, 2009)
Henderson, I, 'Manual on International Law Applicable to Air and Missile Warfare: A Review' (2010) 49 *Military Law and the Law of War Review* 169
Higgins, A Pearce, *War and the Private Citizen* (London, PS King & Son, 1912)
Hill-Cawthorne, L, 'Rights under International Humanitarian Law' (2017) 28 *EJIL* 1187
Hill-Cawthorne, L, 'Persons Covered by International Humanitarian Law: Main Categories' in B Saul and D Akande (eds), *The Oxford Guide to International Humanitarian Law* (Oxford, Oxford University Press, 2020)
Hitchcock, WI, 'Human Rights and the Laws of War: The Geneva Conventions of 1949' in K Iriye, P Goedde and WI Hitchcock (eds), *The Human Rights Revolution: An International History* (Oxford, Oxford University Press, 2012)
Holland, TE, *A Lecture on the Brussels Conference of 1874, and other Diplomatic Attempts to Mitigate the Rigour of Warfare* (Oxford, Parker, 1876)
Holland, TE, *The Laws of War on Land (Written and Unwritten)* (Oxford, Clarendon Press, 1908)
Holmes, B, 'The *IRRC* and the Protection of Civilians, c. 1919–1939' (2018) 100:907/908/909 *IRRC* 115
Hopf, T, 'The Promise of Constructivism in International Relations Theory' (1998) 23 *International Security* 171
ILA Study Group, 'The Conduct of Hostilities and International Humanitarian Law: Challenges of 21st Century Warfare' (2017) 93 *International Law Studies* 322
Inal, T, *Looting and Rape in Wartime: Law and Change in International Relations* (Philadelphia, University of Pennsylvania Press, 2013)
Ipsen, K, 'Combatants and Non-Combatants' in D Fleck (ed), *The Handbook of International Humanitarian Law*, 4th edn (Oxford, Oxford University Press, 2021)
Ivanenko, V, 'The Origins, Causes and Enduring Significance of the Martens Clause: A View from Russia' (2022) 104:920–921 *IRRC* 1708
Jennings, RY and Watts, A (eds), *Oppenheim's International Law: Volume I, Peace*, 9th edn (Oxford, Oxford University Press, 2008)
Jochnick, C and Normand, R, 'The Legitimation of Violence: A Critical History of the Laws of War' (1994) 35 *Harvard International Law Journal* 49
Jones, BD and Cater, CK, 'From Chaos to Coherence? Toward a Regime for Protecting Civilians in War' in S Chesterman (ed), *Civilians in War* (London, Lynne Rienner, 2001)
Kalshoven, F, 'Reaffirmation and Development of International Humanitarian Law Applicable in Armed Conflicts: The Conference of Government Experts, 24 May – 12 June, 1971' (1971) 2 *NYIL* 68
Kalshoven, F, 'The Position of Guerrilla Fighters under the Law of War' (1972) 11 *Military Law and the Law of War Review* 55
Kalshoven, F, 'Reaffirmation and Development of International Humanitarian Law Applicable in Armed Conflicts: The Diplomatic Conference, Geneva, 1974–1977, Part I' (1977) 8 *NYIL* 107
Kalshoven, F, 'Reaffirmation and Development of International Humanitarian Law Applicable in Armed Conflicts: The Diplomatic Conference, Geneva, 1974–1977, Part II' (1978) 9 *NYIL* 107
Kalshoven, F, 'Reprisals and the Protection of Civilians: Two Recent Decisions of the Yugoslavia Tribunal' in F Kalshoven (ed), *Reflections on the Law of War: Collected Essays* (Leiden, Martinus Nijhoff, 2007)

Katzenstein, PJ, 'Introduction: Alternative Perspectives on National Security' in PJ Katzenstein (ed), *The Culture of National Security: Norms and Identity in World Politics* (New York, Columbia University Press, 1996)
Keck, ME and Sikkink, K, 'Transnational Advocacy Networks in International and Regional Politics' (1999) 51 *International Social Science Journal* 89
Keeman, MJ, 'Is Formalism a Friend or Foe? Saving the Principle of Distinction by Applying Function over Form' (2013) 4 *Journal of International Humanitarian Legal Studies* 354
Kinsella, H, *The Image Before the Weapon: A Critical History of the Distinction Between Combatant and Civilian* (Ithaca, Cornell University Press, 2011)
Kleffner, JK, 'From "Belligerents" to "Fighters" and Civilians Directly Participating in Hostilities – On the Principle of Distinction in Non-International Armed Conflicts One Hundred Years After the Second Hague Peace Conference' (2007) 54 *Netherlands International Law Review* 315
Kleffner, JK, 'The Beneficiaries of the Rights Stemming from Common Article 3' in A Clapham, P Gaeta and M Sassòli (eds), *The 1949 Geneva Conventions: A Commentary* (Oxford, Oxford University Press, 2015)
Kleinfeld, M, 'Too Difficult to Protect: A History of the 1934 Monaco Draft and the Problem of Territory for International Humanitarian Law' (2015) 33 *Environment and Planning D: Society and Space* 592
Klotz, A and Lynch, C, *Strategies for Research in Constructivist International Relations* (London, Routledge, 2015)
Kolb, R, 'The Jurisprudence of the Yugoslav and Rwandan Criminal Tribunals on their Jurisdiction and on International Crimes (2000–2004)' (2004) 75 *BYIL* 269
Kolb, R, 'The Protection of the Individual in Times of War and Peace' in B Fassbender and A Peters (eds), *The Oxford Handbook of the History of International Law* (Oxford, Oxford University Press, 2012)
Kolb, R, 'The Main Epochs of Modern International Humanitarian Law since 1864 and Their Related Dominant Legal Constructions' in KM Larsen, CG Cooper and G Nystuen (eds), *Searching for a "Principle of Humanity" in International Humanitarian Law* (Cambridge, Cambridge University Press, 2013)
Kolb, R, 'The Jurisprudence of the Yugoslav and Rwandan Criminal Tribunals on their Jurisdiction and on International Crimes (2004–2013)' (2014) 84 *BYIL* 131
Kolb, R, *Advanced Introduction to International Humanitarian Law* (Cheltenham, Elgar, 2014)
Kolb, R and del Mar, K, 'Treaties for Armed Conflict' in A Clapham and P Gaeta (eds), *The Oxford Handbook of International Law in Armed Conflict* (Oxford, Oxford University Press, 2014)
Kolb, R and Milanov, M, 'The 1868 St Petersburg Declaration on Explosive Projectiles: A Reappraisal' (2018) 20 *Journal of the History of International Law* 515
Koskenniemi, M, *The Gentle Civilizer of Nations: The Rise and Fall of International Law 1870–1960* (Cambridge, Cambridge University Press, 2004)
Kratochwil, F, *Rules, Norms and Decisions: On the Conditions of Practical and Legal Reasoning in International Relations and Domestic Affairs* (Cambridge, Cambridge University Press, 1989)
Kravetz, D, 'The Protection of Civilians in War: The ICTY's *Galić* Case' (2004) 17 *LJIL* 521
Kreß, C and Mégret, F, 'Debate – The Regulation of Non-International Armed Conflicts: Can a Privilege of Belligerency Be Envisioned in the Law of Non-International Armed Conflicts?' (2014) 96:893 *IRRC* 29
Krieger, H and Püschmann, J, 'A Legitimacy Crisis of International Humanitarian Law?' in H Krieger and J Püschmann (eds), *Law-Making and Legitimacy in International Humanitarian Law* (Cheltenham, Elgar, 2021)
Krieger, H and Püschmann, J, 'Law-Making and Legitimacy in International Humanitarian Law' in H Krieger and J Püschmann (eds), *Law-Making and Legitimacy in International Humanitarian Law* (Cheltenham, Elgar, 2021)
Kritsiotis, D, 'Intervention and the Problematisation of Consent' in D Kritsiotis, O Corten and GH Fox, *Armed Intervention and Consent* (Cambridge, Cambridge University Press, 2023)

Krook, ML and True, J, 'Rethinking the Life Cycles of International Norms: The United Nations and the Global Promotion of Gender Equality' (2012) 18 *European Journal of International Relations* 103

Kuhn, AK, 'Report of the Stockholm Conference of the International Law Association, 1925' (1925) *Proceedings of the American Branch of the International Law Association* 22

Kunz, JL, 'Plus de lois de la guerre?' (1934) 41 *Revue générale de droit international public* 22

Kunz, JL, 'The Chaotic Status of the Laws of War and the Urgent Necessity for Their Revision' (1951) 45 *AJIL* 37

Kunz, JL, 'The Geneva Conventions of August 12, 1949' in GA Lipsky (ed), *Law and Politics in the World Community: Essays on Hans Kelsen's Pure Theory and Related Problems in International Law* (Berkeley, University of California Press, 1953)

Kunz, JL, 'The 1956 Draft Rules of the International Committee of the Red Cross at the New Delhi Conference' (1959) 53 *AJIL* 132

Laffey, M and Weldes, J, 'Beyond Belief: Ideas and Symbolic Technologies in the Study of International Relations' (1997) 3 *European Journal of International Relations* 193

Landefeld, S, 'The Evolution of Norms and Concepts in International Law: A Social Constructivist Approach' in R Deplano (ed), *Pluralising International Legal Scholarship: The Promise and Perils of Non-Doctrinal Research Methods* (Cheltenham, Elgar, 2019)

Landefeld, S, 'The Changing Significance of Nationality for the Protection of Civilians in the Hands of a Party to an International Armed Conflict' (2023) 28 *Journal of Conflict & Security Law* 501

Lauterpacht, H, 'The Problem of the Revision of the Law of War' (1952) 29 *BYIL* 360

Lauterpacht, H (ed), *International Law: A Treatise by L Oppenheim, vol II: Disputes, War and Neutrality*, 7th edn (London, Longmans, Green and Co, 1952)

de Laveleye, É, *Les actes de la Conférence de Bruxelles et la participation de la Belgique à la Conférence de Saint-Pétersbourg* (Brussels, Muquardt, 1875)

Le Moli, G, *Human Dignity in International Law* (Cambridge, Cambridge University Press, 2022)

Levy, JS, 'Explaining Events and Developing Theories: History, Political Science, and the Analysis of International Relations' in C Elman and MF Elman (eds), *Bridges and Boundaries: Historians, Political Scientists, and the Study of International Relations* (Cambridge, MIT Press, 2001)

Lieber, F, *Guerrilla Parties: Considered with Reference to the Laws and Usages of War* (New York, D Van Nostrand 1862)

Lippman, M, 'Aerial Attacks on Civilians and the Humanitarian Law of War: Technology and Terror from World War I to Afghanistan' (2002) 33 *California Western International Law Journal* 1

Lovat, H, *Negotiating Civil War: The Politics of International Regime Design* (Cambridge, Cambridge University Press, 2020)

Low, S, 'The International Conference of Peace' (1899) 169 *The North American Review* 625

Luban, D, 'Military Necessity and the Cultures of Military Law' (2013) 26 *LJIL* 315

Luban, D, 'Human Rights Thinking and the Laws of War' in JD Ohlin (ed), *Theoretical Boundaries of Armed Conflict and Human Rights* (Cambridge, Cambridge University Press, 2016)

Lueder, C, *La Convention de Genève au point de vue historique, critique et dogmatique* (Erlangen, Édouard Besold, 1876)

Mačák, K, *Internationalized Armed Conflicts in International Law* (Oxford, Oxford University Press, 2018)

Mačak, K and Policinski, E, 'In Pursuit of a Treaty's Soul: A Study of the Object and Purpose of the Fourth Geneva Convention' (2024) 73 *ICLQ* 385

MacBride, S, 'Human Rights in Armed Conflicts' (1970) 9 *Military Law and the Law of War Review* 373

MacLaren, M and Schwendimann, F, 'An Exercise in the Development of International Law: The New ICRC Study on Customary International Humanitarian Law' (2005) 6 *German Law Journal* 1217

Maganza, B, 'Unveiling Common Article 3 to the Geneva Conventions: Contingency, Necessity, and Possibility in International Humanitarian Law' in I Venzke and KJ Heller (eds), *Contingency in International Law: On the Possibility of Different Legal Histories* (Oxford, Oxford University Press, 2021)

Mailler, A, *De la distinction des combattants et non combattants comme base du droit de guerre* (Paris, A Pedone, 1916)

Mälksoo, L, 'F.F. Martens and His Time: When Russia Was an Integral Part of the European Tradition of International Law' (2014) 25 *EJIL* 811

Mancini, M, Ntoubandi, FZ and Marauhn, T, 'Old Concepts and New Challenges: Are Private Contractors the Mercenaries of the Twenty-first Century?' in F Francioni and N Ronzitti (eds), *War by Contract: Human Rights, Humanitarian Law, and Private Contractors* (Oxford, Oxford University Press, 2011)

Mantilla, G, 'The Origins and Evolution of the 1949 Geneva Conventions and the 1977 Additional Protocols' in M Evangelista and N Tannenwald (eds), *Do the Geneva Conventions Matter?* (Oxford, Oxford University Press, 2017)

Mantilla, G, 'The Protagonism of the USSR and Socialist States in the Revision of International Humanitarian Law' (2019) 21 *Journal of the History of International Law* 181

Mantilla, G, 'Social Pressure and the Making of Wartime Civilian Protection Rules' (2020) 26 *European Journal of International Relations* 443

Mantilla, G, *Lawmaking under Pressure: International Humanitarian Law and Internal Armed Conflict* (Ithaca, Cornell University Press, 2020)

Mantilla, G, 'From Treaty to Custom: Shifting Paths in the Recent Development of International Humanitarian Law' (2024) 37 *LJIL* 359

Marquis-Bissonnette, C, 'The Definition of Civilians in Non-International Armed Conflicts: The Perspective of Armed Groups' (2016) 7 *Journal of International Humanitarian Legal Studies* 129

de Martens, F, *Traité de Droit International, tome III* (A Léo tr, Paris, Chevalier-Marescq, 1887)

de Martens, F, *La paix et la guerre: la Conférence de Bruxelles 1874, droits et devoirs des belligérants (leur application pendant la guerre d'Orient 1874–1878), la Conférence de La Haye 1899* (Paris, A Rousseau, 1901)

Maxwell, MD, 'The Law of War and Civilians on the Battlefield: Are We Undermining Civilian Protection?' (2004) 84:5 *Military Review* 17

Maxwell, MD and Meyer, RV, 'The Principle of Distinction: Probing the Limits of Its Customariness' (2007) 2007:3 *Army Lawyer* 1

Maxwell, MD and Watts, SM, '"Unlawful Enemy Combatant": Status, Theory of Culpability, or Neither?' (2007) 5 *JICJ* 19

McLaughlin, R, *Recognition of Belligerency and the Law of Armed Conflict* (Oxford, Oxford University Press, 2020)

Mégret, F, 'From "Savages" to "Unlawful Combatants": A Postcolonial Look at International Humanitarian Law's "Other"' in A Orford (ed), *International Law and Its Others* (Cambridge, Cambridge University Press, 2006)

Mégret, F, 'War and the Vanishing Battlefield' (2011) 9 *Loyola University Chicago International Law Review* 131

Mégret, F, 'Theorizing the Laws of War' in A Orford and F Hoffmann (eds), *The Oxford Handbook of the Theory of International Law* (Oxford, Oxford University Press, 2016)

Melillo, M, 'Labels as the *Visible* Part of International Law's *Invisible* Frames' in A Bianchi and M Hirsch (eds), *International Law's Invisible Frames* (Oxford, Oxford University Press, 2021)

Melzer, N, *Interpretive Guidance on the Notion of Direct Participation in Hostilities under International Humanitarian Law* (Geneva, ICRC, 2009)

Melzer, N, 'Keeping the Balance Between Military Necessity and Humanity: A Response to Four Critiques of the ICRC's Interpretive Guidance on the Notion of Direct Participation in Hostilities' (2010) 42 *New York University Journal of International Law & Politics* 831

Melzer, N, 'The Principle of Distinction between Civilians and Combatants' in A Clapham and P Gaeta (eds), *The Oxford Handbook of International Law in Armed Conflict* (Oxford, Oxford University Press, 2014)

Melzer, N, *International Humanitarian Law: A Comprehensive Introduction* (Geneva, ICRC, 2019)

Mérignhac, A, *Les lois et coutumes de la guerre sur terre d'après le droit international moderne et la codification de la Conférence de La Haye de 1899* (Paris, Chevalier-Marescq, 1903)

Meron, T, 'Classification of Armed Conflict in the Former Yugoslavia: Nicaragua's Fallout' (1998) 98 *AJIL* 236

Meron, T, 'Draft Model Declaration in Internal Strife' (1988) 28:262 *IRRC* 59

Meron, T, 'Francis Lieber's Code and Principles of Humanity' (1997) 36 *Columbia Journal of Transnational Law* 269

Meron, T, 'On the Inadequate Reach of Humanitarian and Human Rights Law and the Need for a New Instrument' (1983) 77 *AJIL* 589

Meron, T, 'The Humanization of Humanitarian Law' (2000) 94 *AJIL* 239

Meron, T, 'The Protection of Civilians in the Jurisprudence of the ICTY and ICTR' in T Meron (ed), *The Making of International Criminal Justice: The View from the Bench – Selected Speeches* (Oxford, Oxford University Press, 2011)

Meyer, M, 'The International Committee of the Red Cross and the Initiative to Strengthen Legal Protection for Victims of Armed Conflicts' in C Harvey, J Summers and ND White (eds), *Contemporary Challenges to the Laws of War – Essays in Honour of Professor Peter Rowe* (Cambridge, Cambridge University Press, 2014)

Milanovic, M and Sivakumaran, S, 'Assessing the Authority of the ICRC Customary IHL Study: How does IHL Develop?' (2022) 104:920/921 *IRRC* 1856

Moir, L, *The Law of Internal Armed Conflict* (Cambridge, Cambridge University Press, 2002)

Moore, JB, *International Law and Some Current Illusions and other Essays* (New York, The Macmillan Company, 1924)

Münzel, G, *Untersuchungen über die Genfer Konvention: eine Darstellung und Kritik des nach diesem Vertrage geltenden Landkriegsrechtes, mit einem geschichtlichen Überblick über die Bestrebungen bis zum Abschlusse des Vertrages und über die Versuche zu seiner Fortbildung* (Freiburg, G Ragoczy, 1901)

Murray, C, 'The 1977 Geneva Protocols and Conflict in Southern Africa' (1984) 33 *ICLQ* 462

Nabulsi, K, *Traditions of War: Occupation, Resistance and the Law* (Oxford, Oxford University Press, 1999)

Nabulsi, K, 'Evolving Conceptions of Civilians and Belligerents: One Hundred Years After the Hague Peace Conferences' in S Chesterman (ed), *Civilians in War* (London, Lynne Rienner, 2001)

Naundorff, J, *Unter dem rothen Kreuz – Fremde und eigene Erfahrungen auf Böhmischer Erde und den Schlachtfeldern der Neuzeit* (Leipzig, Veit, 1867)

Neff, SC, *War and the Law of Nations: A General History* (Cambridge, Cambridge University Press, 2005)

Newton, M, 'Unlawful Belligerency after September 11: History Revisited and Law Revised' in D Wippman and M Evangelista (eds), *New Wars, New Laws? Applying Laws of War in 21st Century Conflicts* (Leiden, Brill, 2005)

Nishat, N, 'The Structure of Geneva Convention IV and the Resulting Gaps in that Convention' in A Clapham, P Gaeta and M Sassòli (eds), *The 1949 Geneva Conventions: A Commentary* (Oxford, Oxford University Press, 2015)

Nolte, G, 'Interpretation and Identification of International Humanitarian Law: Responses of the International Law Commission' in H Krieger and J Püschmann (eds), *Law-Making and Legitimacy in International Humanitarian Law* (Cheltenham, Elgar, 2021)

Nurick, L, 'The Distinction Between Combatant and Noncombatant in the Law of War' (1945) 39 *AJIL* 680

Nys, E, 'Francis Lieber – His Life and His Works: Part I' (1911) 5 *AJIL* 84

O'Connell, ME, 'Historical Development and Legal Basis' in D Fleck (ed), *The Handbook of International Humanitarian Law*, 4th edn (Oxford, Oxford University Press, 2021)

Oeter, S, 'Comment: Is the Principle of Distinction Outdated?' in W Heintschel von Heinegg and V Epping (eds), *International Humanitarian Law Facing New Challenges: Symposium in Honour of Knut Ipsen* (Berlin, Springer, 2007)

Oppenheim, L, *International Law: A Treatise, vol II: War and Neutrality* (London, Longmans, Green, and Co, 1906)

Parks, WH, 'Air War and the Law of War' (1990) 32 *Air Force Law Review* 1

Parks, WH, 'Part IX of the ICRC "Direct Participation in Hostilities" Study: No Mandate, No Expertise, and Legally Incorrect' (2010) 42 *New York University Journal of International Law & Politics* 769

Parlett, K, *The Individual in the International Legal System: Continuity and Change in International Law* (Cambridge, Cambridge University Press, 2011)

Pauwelyn, J, Wessel, R and Wouters, J (eds), *Informal International Lawmaking* (Oxford, Oxford University Press, 2012)

Payne, RA, 'Persuasion, Frames and Norm Construction' (2001) 7 *European Journal of International Relations* 37

Pejic, J, '"Unlawful/Enemy Combatants": Interpretations and Consequences' in MN Schmitt and J Pejic (eds), *International Law and Armed Conflict: Exploring the Faultlines – Essays in Honour of Yoram Dinstein* (Leiden, Martinus Nijhoff, 2007)

Percy, S, *Mercenaries: The History of a Norm in International Relations* (Oxford, Oxford University Press, 2007)

Percy, S, 'Regulating the Private Security Industry: A Story of Regulating the Last War' (2012) 94:887 *IRRC* 941

Perna, L, *The Formation of the Treaty Law of Non-International Armed Conflicts* (Leiden, Martinus Nijhoff, 2006)

Peters, A, *Beyond Human Rights: The Legal Status of the Individual in International Law* (Cambridge, Cambridge University Press, 2016)

Petrov, AO, *Expert Laws of War: Restating and Making Law in Expert Processes* (Cheltenham, Elgar, 2020)

Phillimore, GG, 'Some Suggestions for a Draft Code for the Treatment of Prisoners of War' (1920) 6 *Transactions of the Grotius Society* 25

Pictet, JS, 'La protection juridique de la population civile en temps de guerre' (1939) 21:244 *IRRC* 268

Pictet, JS, (ed), *The Geneva Conventions of 12 August 1949, Commentary IV: Geneva Convention Relative to the Protection of Civilian Persons in Time of War* (Geneva, ICRC, 1958)

Pictet, JS, (ed), *The Geneva Conventions of 12 August 1949, Commentary III: Geneva Convention Relative to the Treatment of Prisoners of War* (Geneva, ICRC, 1960)

Pictet, JS, 'The Principles of International Humanitarian Law' (1966) 6:66 *IRRC* 455

Pictet, JS, 'The XXth International Conference of the Red Cross: Results in the Legal Field' (1966) 7 *Journal of the International Commission of Jurists* 3

Pictet, JS, 'The Formation of International Humanitarian Law' (1985) 25:244 *IRRC* 3

Pillet, A, *Les Lois actuelles de la Guerre* (Paris, A Rousseau, 1898)

Price, R, *The Chemical Weapons Taboo* (Ithaca, Cornell University Press, 1997)

Price, R, 'Reversing the Gun Sights: Transnational Civil Society Targets Land Mines' (1998) 52 *International Organization* 613

Program on Humanitarian Policy and Conflict Research at Harvard University, *HPCR Manual on International Law Applicable to Air and Missile Warfare* (Cambridge, Cambridge University Press, 2013)

Provost, R, *International Human Rights and Humanitarian Law* (Cambridge, Cambridge University Press, 2002)

Pustogarov, VV, 'The Martens Clause in International Law' (1999) 1 *Journal of the History of International Law* 125

Pustogarov, VV, *Our Martens: F.F. Martens, International Lawyer and Architect of Peace* (Butler WE ed and tr, The Hague, Kluwer Law International, 2000)

Quéguiner, J-F, 'The Principle of Distinction: Beyond an Obligation of Customary International Humanitarian Law' in HM Hensel (ed), *The Legitimate Use of Military Force: The Just War Tradition and the Customary Law of Armed Conflict* (Aldershot, Ashgate, 2008)

Quindry, FE, 'Aerial Bombardment of Civilian and Military Objectives' (1931) 2 *The Journal of Air Law* 474

Reed, W, 'Laws of War: The Developing Law of Armed Conflict – Some Current Problems' (1977) 9 *Case Western Reserve Journal of International Law* 17

Reus-Smit, C, 'Human Rights and the Social Construction of Sovereignty' (2001) 27 *Review of International Studies* 519

Risley, JS, *The Law of War* (London, Innes & Co, 1897)

Roberts, A, 'The Principle of Equal Application of the Laws of War' in D Rodin and H Shue (eds), *Just and Unjust Warriors: The Moral and Legal Status of Soldiers* (Oxford, Oxford University Press, 2008)

Roberts, A, 'The Civilian in Modern War' (2009) 12 *YIHL* 13

Roberts, A, 'Foundational Myths in the Laws of War: The 1863 Lieber Code, and the 1864 Geneva Convention' (2019) 20 *Melbourne Journal of International Law* 158

Roberts, A and Guelff, R, *Documents on the Laws of War*, 3rd edn (Oxford, Oxford University Press, 2010)

Roberts, GB, 'New Rules of Waging War: The Case Against Ratification of Additional Protocol I' (1985) 26 *Virginia Journal of International Law* 109

Rodgers, WJ, 'Laws of War Concerning Aviation and Radio' (1923) 17 *AJIL* 629

Rogers, APV, 'Combatant Status' in E Wilmshurst and SC Breau (eds), *Perspectives on the ICRC Study on Customary International Humanitarian Law* (Cambridge, Cambridge University Press, 2007)

Rogers, APV, *Law on the Battlefield*, 3rd edn (Manchester, Manchester University Press, 2012)

Rolin-Jaequemyns, G, 'De la nécessité d'organiser une institution scientifique permanente pour favoriser l'étude et les progrès du droit international' (1873) 5 *Revue de Droit International et de Législation Comparée* 463

Rolin-Jaequemyns, G, 'Chronique du droit international. 1871–1874' (1875) 7 *Revue de Droit International et de Législation Comparée* 70

Rosenblad, E, 'Guerrilla Warfare and International Law' (1973) 12 *Military Law and the Law of War Review* 91

Rosenblad, E, 'Area Bombing and International Law' (1976) 15 *Military Law and the Law of War Review* 53

Royse, MW, *Aerial Bombardment and the International Regulation of Warfare* (New York, Harold Vinal, 1928)

Salmón, E, 'Who Is a Protected Civilian?' in A Clapham, P Gaeta and M Sassòli (eds), *The 1949 Geneva Conventions: A Commentary* (Oxford, Oxford University Press, 2015)

Sandholtz, W, *Prohibiting Plunder: How Norms Change* (Oxford, Oxford University Press, 2007)

Sandoz, Y, Swinarski, C and Zimmermann, B (eds), *Commentary on the Additional Protocols of 8 June 1977 to the Geneva Conventions of 12 August 1949* (Geneva, Martinus Nijhoff, 1987)

Sassòli, M, '"Unlawful Combatants": The Law and Whether it Needs to be Revised' (2003) 97 *Proceedings of the Annual Meeting (American Society of International Law)* 196

Sassòli, M, 'The Status of Persons Held in Guantánamo under International Humanitarian Law' (2004) 2 *JICJ* 96

Sassòli, M, *International Humanitarian Law: Rules, Controversies, and Solutions to Problems Arising in Warfare* (Cheltenham, Elgar, 2019)

Sassòli, M, Bouvier, AA and Quintin, A, *How Does Law Protect in War? Cases, Documents and Teaching Materials on Contemporary Practice in International Humanitarian Law, Volume I*, 3rd edn (Geneva, ICRC, 2011)

Scheipers, S, *Unlawful Combatants: A Genealogy of the Irregular Fighter* (Oxford, Oxford University Press, 2015)

Schindler, D, 'L'évolution du droit de la guerre des Conventions de la Haye aux Protocoles Additionnels aux Conventions de Genève' (1982) 21 *Military Law and the Law of War Review* 23

Schindler, D, 'International Humanitarian Law: Its Remarkable Development and Persistent Violations' (2003) 5 *Journal of the History of International Law* 165

Schindler, D and Toman, J (eds), *The Laws of Armed Conflict: A Collection of Conventions, Resolutions, and Other Documents*, 4th edn (Leiden, Martinus Nijhoff, 2004)
Schmitt, MN, 'The Principle of Discrimination in 21st Century Warfare' (1999) 2 *Yale Human Rights & Development Law Journal* 143
Schmitt, MN, '21st Century Conflict: Can the Law Survive' (2007) 8 *Melbourne Journal of International Law* 443
Schmitt, MN, 'Deconstruction of Direct Participation in Hostilities: The Constitutive Elements' (2010) 42 *New York University Journal of International Law & Politics* 697
Schmitt, MN (ed), *Tallinn Manual on the International Law Applicable to Cyber Warfare* (Cambridge, Cambridge University Press, 2013)
Schmitt, MN, Garraway, CHB and Dinstein Y (eds), *The Manual on the Law of Non-International Armed Conflict – With Commentary* (Sanremo, IIHL, 2006)
Scott, JB, 'The Work of the Second Hague Peace Conference' (1908) 2 *AJIL* 1
Simpson, G, 'Paris 1793 and 1871: *Levée en masse* As Event' in F Johns, RJ Joyce and S Pahuja (eds), *Events: The Force of International Law* (Abingdon, Routledge, 2011)
Siordet, F, 'Les Conventions de Genève et la guerre civile' (1950) 32:374 *IRRC* 104
Sivakumaran, S, 'Re-envisaging the International Law of Internal Armed Conflict' (2011) 22 *EJIL* 219
Sivakumaran, S, *The Law of Non-International Armed Conflict* (Oxford, Oxford University Press, 2012)
Sivakumaran, S, 'Beyond States and Non-State Actors: The Role of State-Empowered Entities in the Making and Shaping of International Law' (2017) 55 *Columbia Journal of Transnational Law* 343
Sivakumaran, S, 'Making and Shaping the Law of Armed Conflict' (2018) 71 *Current Legal Problems* 119
Solis, GD, *The Law of Armed Conflict: International Humanitarian Law in War*, 3rd edn (Cambridge, Cambridge University Press, 2022)
Sossai, M, 'Status of Private Military and Security Company Personnel in the Law of International Armed Conflict' in F Francioni and N Ronzitti (eds), *War by Contract: Human Rights, Humanitarian Law, and Private Contractors* (Oxford, Oxford University Press, 2011)
Spaight, JM, *War Rights on Land* (London, Macmillan and Co, 1911)
Spaight, JM, 'Air Bombardment' (1923–24) 4 *BYIL* 21
Spaight, JM, 'Non-Combatants and Air Attack' (1938) 9 *Air Law Review* 372
Stern, OM, *Gender, Conflict and International Humanitarian Law: A Critique of the 'Principle of Distinction'* (London, Routledge, 2018)
Suter, KD, 'An Enquiry into the Meaning of the Phrase "Human Rights in Armed Conflicts"' (1976) 15 *Military Law and the Law of War Review* 393
Suter, KD, *An International Law of Guerrilla Warfare – The Global Politics of Law-Making* (London, Frances Pinter, 1984)
Sutton, R, *The Humanitarian Civilian: How the Idea of Distinction Circulates Within and Beyond International Humanitarian Law* (Oxford, Oxford University Press, 2021)
Tannenwald, N, 'Assessing the Effects and Effectiveness of the Geneva Conventions' in M Evangelista and N Tannenwald (eds), *Do the Geneva Conventions Matter?* (Oxford, Oxford University Press, 2017)
Traven, D, *Law and Sentiment in International Politics: Ethics, Emotions, and the Evolution of the Laws of War* (Cambridge, Cambridge University Press, 2021)
Turns, D, 'Cyber Warfare and the Notion of Direct Participation in Hostilities' (2012) 17 *Journal of Conflict & Security Law* 279
Venzke, I, 'Legal Contestation about "Enemy Combatants": On the Exercise of Power in Legal Interpretation' (2009) 5 *Journal of International Law and International Relations* 155
Veuthey, M, *Guérilla et Droit Humanitaire* (Geneva, ICRC, 1983)
Wallace, D and Reeves, SR, 'The Law of Armed Conflict's "Wicked" Problem: *Levée en Masse* in Cyber Warfare' (2013) 89 *International Law Studies* 646

Watkin, K, '21st Century Conflict and International Humanitarian Law: Status Quo or Change?' in MN Schmitt and J Pejic (eds), *International Law and Armed Conflict: Exploring the Faultlines – Essays in Honour of Yoram Dinstein* (Leiden, Martinus Nijhoff, 2007)

Watkin, K, 'Opportunity Lost: Organized Armed Groups and the ICRC "Direct Participation in Hostilities" Interpretive Guidance' (2010) 42 *New York University Journal of International Law & Politics* 641

Watts, S, 'Present and Future Conceptions of the Status of Government Forces in Non-International Armed Conflict' (2012) 88 *International Law Studies* 145

Watts, S, 'Who Is A Prisoner of War?' in A Clapham, P Gaeta and M Sassòli (eds), *The 1949 Geneva Conventions: A Commentary* (Oxford, Oxford University Press, 2015)

Wenger, A and Mason, SJA, 'The Civilianization of Armed Conflict: Trends and Implications' (2008) 90:872 *IRRC* 835

Werner, WG, 'The Law at Hand: Paratext in Manuals on International Humanitarian Law' in H Krieger and J Püschmann (eds), *Law-Making and Legitimacy in International Humanitarian Law* (Cheltenham, Elgar, 2021)

Wheaton, H, *Elements of International Law*, 8th edn (RH Dana ed, Boston, Little, Brown, and Company, 1866)

White, ND, 'The Privatisation of Military and Security Functions and Human Rights: Comments on the UN Working Group's Draft Convention' (2011) 11 *Human Rights Law Review* 133

Whyte, J, 'The "Dangerous Concept of the Just War": Decolonization, Wars of National Liberation, and the Additional Protocols to the Geneva Conventions' (2018) 9 *Humanity* 313

Wilke C, and Doutaghi, H, 'Legal Technologies: Conceptualizing the Legacy of the 1923 *Hague Rules of Aerial Warfare*' (2024) 37 *LJIL* 88

Wippman, D and Evangelista, M (eds), *New Wars, New Laws? Applying Laws of War in 21st Century Conflicts* (Leiden, Brill, 2005)

Witt, JF, *Lincoln's Code – The Laws of War in American History* (New York, Free Press, 2012)

Wrange, P, 'Introduction: Historicizing International Humanitarian Law' in M Deland, M Klamberg and P Wrange (eds), *International Humanitarian Law and Justice: Historical and Sociological Perspectives* (Abingdon, Routledge, 2019)

Wylie, N, 'Muddied Waters: The Influence of the First Hague Conference on the Evolution of the Geneva Conventions of 1864 and 1906' in M Abbenhuis, CE Barber and AR Higgins (eds), *War, Peace and International Order? The Legacies of the Hague Conferences of 1899 and 1907* (Abingdon, Routledge, 2017)

Wylie, N and Cameron, L, 'The Impact of World War I on the Law Governing the Treatment of Prisoners of War and the Making of a Humanitarian Subject' (2018) 29 *EJIL* 1327

Wylie, N and Landefeld, S, 'Prisoners of War, Civilians and the Post-World-War I Development of International Humanitarian Law' in I Rachamimov and R Kowner (eds), *Out of Line, Out of Place: A Global and Local History of World War I Internments* (Ithaca, Cornell University Press, 2022)

Index

www.ingramcontent.com/pod-product-compliance
Ingram Content Group UK Ltd.
Pitfield, Milton Keynes, MK11 3LW, UK
UKHW020243290926
15470UKWH00002B/709

9 781509 968220